Courtesy Of

21st Century
WEALTH

Susan,
Wishing you health,
and happiness in 21st Century!
Bill Scott
July 29, 2004

The Esperti Peterson Institute Contributory Series

Eileen R. Sacco, Managing Editor

Generations: Planning Your Legacy
Legacy: Plan, Protect, and Preserve Your Estate
21st Century Wealth: Essential Financial Planning Principles
Ways and Means: Maximize the Value of Your Retirement Savings
Wealth Enhancement and Preservation, 2d ed.

21st Century *WEALTH*

ESSENTIAL FINANCIAL PLANNING PRINCIPLES

Practical Answers
from America's Expert
Financial Advisors

— A Special Edition —

Robert A. Esperti   Renno L. Peterson

QP

ISBN 0-9674714-0-0
Library of Congress Control Number: 00-132058

Managing editor: Eileen Sacco
Project manager: Christy Allbee
Project assistant: Marcia Gresty
Senior technical editor: Richard W. Gumm, J.D., LL.M.
Marketing Services: Lydia Monchak
Jacket design: Richard Adelson, china60@aol.com
Composition, design, & editing services: C+S Gottfried, www.lookoutnow.com/dtp
Printed and bound in Canada by Quebecor Printing

An Esperti Peterson Institute Book
by Quantum Press LLC
Quantum Alliance[3] Companies
410 17th Street, Suite 1260
Denver, CO 80202

Contents

Preface

The face of financial services has changed dramatically over the last three decades, and there is no evidence that the rate of change is slowing down. If anything, the changes are increasing in frequency and magnitude. The way financial advice and products are sold and delivered will likely change more within the next 5 years than in any other period of our lifetimes. Financial planning is not a luxury, as it might have been in the past, but is now a necessity.

As recently as 25 years ago, financial planners were as rare as pearls in an oyster bed. There was not a great need for financial planning. The majority of people worked for stable corporations that offered financial security, including generous pensions and other benefits. Most Americans, except for the very wealthy, did not invest in stocks and bonds. Those who did invest did so without a great deal of advice and fanfare, and the options were fairly limited. Financial advice was not seen as particularly valuable or necessary because a person's well-being and retirement were in the hands of his or her employer.

Back then, Social Security was viewed as the ultimate safety net, even for those who made a very good living. Little attention was paid to the issues of early retirement, longevity, and the need to have enough money to live the good life into a person's eighties, nineties, and beyond.

As for estate planning, most people were content with a simple will to plan for death. While there were proponents of formalized estate planning, many people did not see the need; the transfer of wealth was not foremost on their minds. The people with the "real" money got a fancy will or living trust with some tax planning, but even then the planning was limited in scope. It did not, for the most part, encompass a great deal of complexity or thought. Estate planning was viewed as death planning, and death planning meant taking as little time, effort, and money as possible to make sure assets passed to loved ones.

But times change. And change they did, except faster than almost everyone anticipated. Many factors contributed to the vast changes in the social and economic fabric of society. People began to understand that they would live longer and that living longer involved having the resources and staying power to live well. The national debt became a huge issue that threatened Social Security, Medicare, and other programs for the elderly. Tax laws took a toll on retirement plans and benefits; companies began downsizing and "downbenefiting." There was less of a pie to share, and fewer people were allowed to share it.

Tax laws also grew exponentially in complexity and scope, while the stock market exploded. Many more people graduated into the "wealthy" category as the economy flourished. In response to the growth in wealth, the financial services industry developed a seemingly infinite amount of new products, services, and planning ideas from sector mutual funds to "costless collars" to derivatives to global currency-hedging transactions. The already complex financial world took a giant step toward more complexity, leaving behind a bewildered public that had to seek advice from those who specialized in financial products and services.

The concept of what "advice" constituted was also expanded. At one time, financial advice meant getting in early on a hot stock. Now, financial advice encompasses a myriad of disciplines, including asset allocation, cash-flow analysis, present-dollar pro formas, qualified retirement plan options, wealth transfer strategies, and more. Financial planning bridges tax law, elder law, estate planning, investments, accounting, actuarial science, life insurance, and psychology. No longer can one profession, or one professional, meet the needs of most people who have more than simple financial affairs.

The new wealth and subsequent demand for financial expertise drew in new competitors who recognized that there were huge profits to be made in managing and "controlling" other people's money. Estate planning was once the exclusive domain of lawyers. No more.

Accountants, financial advisors, and life insurance agents now offer estate planning services as part of their financial planning process. Investment advice, once relegated to registered representatives of the large brokerage houses, is now given by lawyers, accountants, independent financial advisors, and life insurance agents. These professionals can also offer money management services and life insurance services. Today, at least in some jurisdictions, lawyers and accountants can receive a fee for putting assets under management and earn commissions on the sale of life insurance.

In today's financial marketplace, it is very unclear whom one turns to for financial and estate planning advice. Does one have to hire a professional in every area of planning and then hope they all coordinate what they do? Is one-stop shopping available? If so, who offers it, and, more importantly, who is competent to offer it?

These questions may well be answered in the first few years of the new millennium. For now, the informed purchaser of financial products and services will rule. Those who do not take the time to educate themselves, even on a basic level, will be vulnerable to the hucksters and charlatans of the world. Worse yet, they may put themselves in the hands of well-meaning but incompetent advisors who will, at best, not offer any help and, at worst, cause financial and family disaster.

The purpose of *21st Century Wealth* is to educate the consumer as to fundamental financial and estate planning principles. The book is designed as a primer for those who are not totally familiar with the many dimensions of financial and estate planning.

21st Century Wealth is the product of a national research project that involved the planning knowledge, ideas, and expertise of the most talented estate, financial, retirement, investment, insurance, and charitable planning advisors in the United States. It is not an annotated reference book intended to cover everything about financial planning in the tiniest detail. All of our contributing authors were challenged with a single goal: to provide readers with the best possible answers to the questions they are most frequently asked by their clients. Because of the book's question-and-answer format, even the beginning investor or planner will be able to make sense out of the sometimes numbing confusion that seems to envelop financial and estate planning.

This book offers insights into the issues that are important for proper planning. For many of us, just knowing which questions to ask a competent advisor will greatly help us to become involved in the planning process. Armed with the information in this book, you will be able to enter into financial planning with more confidence.

The consistency of the questions provided by the contributors reinforced our belief that most families and individuals have similar concerns regardless of differences in their cultures, economics, and geographic locations. This consistency has been the highlight of every Institute contributory book project.

The responses of our contributing authors reflected their differing professional views, feelings, and emotions with regard to virtually every financial planning issue. As editors, we have attempted to blend these differences into an overall perspective that will provide readers with the best overview and understanding possible. At times, we have included similar questions with differing responses in order to present a variety of good approaches and allow readers to decide which one they would be most comfortable with.

Readers will find a subtle repetitiveness in the text. Rather than referring readers back and forth among several sections or chapters of the book, we have attempted, whenever possible, to include some of the same information in different sections. Our goal was to ensure that readers can turn to virtually any section and find complete information. If you read *21st Century Wealth* from cover to cover, you will doubtless encounter repetition. If you skip around, reading specific sections, you'll have all the background information necessary to understand each topic.

21st Century Wealth has four parts. Part One is about investment planning. It contains two chapters, the first of which presents a survey of investment fundamentals. The second chapter explains investment strategies that are the foundation of proper investing. In these two chapters, our contributing authors have simply and effectively taken the mystery out of the underlying principles of investing. With this information, any investor can intelligently and effectively communicate with almost any financial advisor or other professional.

Part Two covers the broad areas of estate planning and tax planning. It is divided into three chapters. Chapter 3 is devoted to defining the basic nature of estate planning: what it is and some of its basic planning strategies, many of which are often overlooked in proper planning. Chapter 4 explains the gift, estate, and income taxes associated with planning, both during a person's lifetime and after his or her death. It is must reading for anyone who is interested in or is participating in the planning process. This chapter includes some of the strategies that are commonly used to reduce these taxes.

Chapter 5 builds on the earlier material and offers some of the advanced strategies that are available when more sophisticated planning is called for. It addresses estate reduction planning and explains some of the acronyms that professionals use but clients sometimes find confusing: GRATs and GRUTs, FLPs, and CRATs and CRUTs. The chapter also includes some fascinating questions and answers about advanced planning techniques such as intentional grantor trusts, foundations, and gift annuities.

Life, disability, and long-term-care insurance are the topics of Part Three, although the emphasis is on life insurance. In our experience, life insurance goes hand in glove with financial planning and is a little-understood tool that can have a substantial impact on an overall financial plan. Chapter 6 explains the different types of life insurance and how they are priced. How life insurance is used in financial planning is the topic of Chapter 7. Disability insurance and long-term-care insurance, two very relevant areas of insurance that should always be considered as part of retirement planning, are covered in Chapter 8.

Part Four combines two very important issues: planning for retirement and saving for higher education. Retirement planning can be incredibly confusing. Setting retirement goals, choosing the right way to accumulate funds, deciding when and how to take money out of the plans, and determining the best way to invest are all huge issues with numerous ramifications. Chapters 9, 10, and 11 give basic, solid information that touches on all of these issues and more. Our contributing authors have taken complex material and reduced it to an understandable set of questions and answers that will help even the most unsophisticated investor.

A great concern of parents and grandparents is putting aside money for educating their young. With the escalating cost of higher education and the renewed interest in private schools for younger children, funding for educational purposes is on the minds of many people. Chapter 12 presents an overview of the issues and strategies used to ensure educational opportunities for family members.

We have included five appendixes. Appendix A contains a special set of questions and answers from the contributors on how to work with a financial planning professional. Recognizing that it is difficult to know what various professional designations and accreditations mean, we have provided in Appendix B an explanation of the major designations and a listing of the agencies that govern and regulate financial planning professionals. The professionals who contributed to *21st Century Wealth* were selected for participation in this project through a stringent application process that is fully described in Appendix C. Alphabetical and geographical lists of all the contributors to this book are presented in Appendixes D and E.

21st Century Wealth contains the most current information available on tax, estate, financial, and retirement planning. Many statistics relevant to this topic are indexed for inflation, however, and not yet available for 2000 and beyond. For this reason, our contributing authors have had to use 1999 figures in some of their explanations. In all cases, the theories and strategies behind the figures are completely up to date and incorporate the latest legislation affecting tax, estate, financial, and retirement planning.

As with all general reference works, readers should be careful not to treat the information in *21st Century Wealth* as a recommendation for any particular course of action in individual circumstances. No other concept came through to us more clearly as editors than the diversity of successful strategies available to individuals, as well as the damage that can result from inappropriately implementing the wrong strategy. We specifically recommend that in planning for your financial well-being, you seek advice from competent professionals in each relevant discipline.

21st Century Wealth is a collaborative effort of a number of expert financial planners. We hope that the wisdom collected in this book helps you, the reader, attain a better understanding of financial planning as we embark on the new millennium.

We are proud of the efforts of our contributing authors in bringing you such practical information and strategies for effectively implementing financial planning.

We especially wish to thank William V. Scott III for his contributions to *21st Century Wealth* and are honored to dedicate this special edition to him.

Robert A. Esperti
Renno L. Peterson
January 2000

Introduction

William V. Scott III

> *It is not the critic who counts; not the man who points out how the strong man stumbled or where the doer of deeds could have done better. The credit belongs to the man who is actually in the arena; whose face is marred with dust and sweat and blood; who strives valiantly; who errs and comes short again . . . who knows the great enthusiasms, the great devotions, and spends himself in a worthy cause; who at best knows in the end the triumph of high achievement; and who, at the worst, if he fails, at least fails while daring greatly, so that his place shall never be with those cold and timid souls who know neither victory nor defeat.*
>
> —Theodore Roosevelt

It is "the person in the arena" for whom my coauthors and I wrote *21st Century Wealth:* those who work overtime to ensure private schooling for their children; the young, two-career couples who still have the energy to help with homework and attend soccer games after a long day; the technical geniuses who write software late into the night to ensure their stock options stay in the money; the retirees who balance their Social Security and investments so as to not run out of money in case of extended medical care; those who give that extra bit of themselves to make today a better day and the future a better place for the next generation; the executives in the boardrooms; the teachers in the classrooms; the journeymen and the apprentices; and the small-business owners and their faithful employees. Whatever your lot in life, you have executed your tasks and conducted your affairs with commendable character and anticipation that your life's work may ensure financial security for yourself, your children, their children, and then theirs.

It is with great pride that I accepted the invitation to contribute to this honorable work, *21st Century Wealth.* To collaborate with my colleagues in the creation of a book that can enhance the quality of life for those who apply its words of wisdom is perhaps my legacy.

The economic environment today is certainly volatile, and we will continue to confront financial obstacles and challenges that appear greater than ever before. Our economic cycles, tax law changes, government reforms in Social Security and Medicare, and market fluctuations should not be surprising. Investment scandals, failing institutions, and political embarrassments will continue to surface as well. I remain absolutely optimistic, however, for I believe that the United States is on the threshold of a period of prosperity that will make the days of John D. Rockefeller and J. P. Morgan seem almost commonplace, especially for those who remain resolute and decisive.

It is my sincere desire that through my contribution to *21st Century Wealth,* you will enjoy a greater level of financial security during your life. Your life's work and experiences should also be preserved and passed on to countless generations to come with hope and prayers that this world will always continue to be a better place to live.

My fortune in life began in a less-than-affluent atmosphere with both parents working to make ends meet. I learned at an early age the value of financial security by first experiencing financial uncertainty. I worked my way through college and raised my own family while in military service. Although serving our great country is a career that I am proud of, and I received many rewards, awards for missions of success, and honors for battles of victory while doing so, the financial rewards were less than my family deserved. This financial struggle brought my family closer together and instilled in me a renewed passion to be involved in the world of finance. I suppose my heart has always been on Wall Street.

My fascination with finance began when I was a young man reading about the likes of Andrew Carnegie and Cornelius Vanderbilt. My financial goals led me down a path of success, first as a real estate agent, then as a mortgage banker, next as a tax preparer, and then as a stockbroker. As my professional career progressed, I evolved into an estate planner and small-business consultant.

Looking back, I can say that the formula to success is really quite simple: a large portion of hard work, consistent measures of good judgment, and generous sprinklings of knowledge along the way.

I have not yet found a cure for procrastination or a method for controlling "Lady Luck" or a prescription for fostering ambition; however, I can and will share the wisdom I have learned. Your financial destiny is yours to control. It is up to you, the person in the arena, to learn the principles involved and apply them in your financial affairs.

As you begin your journey into *21st Century Wealth,* I want to commend you for your efforts and wish you well. May your stocks soar and your dividends be many.

Acknowledgements

In closing, I must express my love and sincere appreciation to my wife and best friend of 10 years, Jill. Without her love, patience, and insightful guidance, I would still be searching for "truth North."

I would also like to thank my son, Jason, for keeping me motivated. As he completes his degree in law, he has unknowingly raised the standard for all my endeavors.

Finally, I want to acknowledge my partner in the arena, Ken Stern. It was with his encouragement that I agreed to take on this worthy project. He has inspired me to accomplish more in my life than I would have ever thought possible.

William V. Scott III is president and CEO of Strategic Planning Solutions (SPS), Inc. Headquartered in San Diego, SPS provides advisory services to high-net-worth individuals and closely held corporations. SPS has developed a unique approach to financial planning by creating a team of accountants, attorneys, and money managers. The mission: to provide cutting-edge financial research, advice, and management; expert wealth transfer and asset protection techniques; and effective tax planning solutions to all SPS clients.

Mr. Scott acquired his leadership and organizational skills while serving as a U.S. Navy diver. He currently serves on the boards of several corporations, hosts a syndicated weekly radio talk show, and is often quoted and published in several magazines and newsletters.

Bill earned the designations of Registered Principal with the National Association of Securities Dealers (NASD) and Registered Financial Consultant with the International Association of Registered Financial Consultants (IARFC), and he is the managing partner of Asset Planning Solutions, Inc.

He and his wife, Jill, have been married for 10 years and reside in north San Diego County. They enjoy scuba diving, collecting financial artifacts, and traveling overseas.

PART ONE
Investing

The investment world has its own jargon and technical terms. For those who are involved in investing, the language of investments is no barrier to understanding. However, many other people, even some who invest on a regular basis, get lost in the sometimes confusing variety of investment terminology. It is no surprise that a number of our contributing authors found that their clients ask questions about fundamental investment concepts.

In our experience, many people work very hard to build substantial net worth without a great deal of knowledge about investing and investments. These people spend their time and energy making money in a variety of businesses and professions. Far less worried about investing than about accumulating, they either do not invest or leave the investing in the hands of professionals whom they may or may not know well. There comes a time, generally when clients begin thinking about retirement, educating their growing children, or some other expensive event, that they take an interest in investing. They realize that they may have to live on their asset base for the rest of their lives. It is then that they face the reality of the investment world. At this time both spouses get involved in the financial process. Yet in many marriages one spouse has been in charge of the family finances. While this spouse may have some financial sophistication, it is likely that the other spouse does not. A learning process is critical so that each spouse can understand the family finances and what they mean for the future of all family members.

Chapter 1 introduces many important concepts that transcend the traditional view of financial planning. In fact, understanding these concepts is critical for purposes of estate and wealth strategies planning, retirement planning, and planning for children and grandchildren. The chapter is an important primer for beginning investors and even veteran investors who have trouble keeping investment terms straight. It begins with an explanation of basic investment terms and then explores some complex concepts, including modern portfolio theory. More importantly, it sets the stage for Chapter 2, in which the concepts presented in Chapter 1 are applied to investment strategies.

We highly recommend that every reader take the time to explore Chapter 1. If you are a novice, the chapter will be highly educational. If you have some knowledge of the investment field, it will provide an excellent review. And if you have a great deal of expertise, it will offer insight into how other experts are explaining and defining fundamental investment concepts.

Understanding theory is one thing; applying it effectively in the real world is quite another. It is in the application of investment theory that our contributing authors excel. They have provided a number of questions and answers on how investing should take place and how the different investment vehicles and techniques actually apply to clients. Savvy investors understand that investing is much like constructing a building. The more time and thought—planning—that is put in at the beginning, the better the end product will be. Both construction and investing are processes requiring foresight, knowledge, expertise, and patience. The end product of each is wholly dependent on the preparation in the beginning.

Chapter 2 focuses on the nuts and bolts of investing. It begins with the actual process that serious investors should go through to determine the investment strategies they ultimately must implement in order to meet their investment goals. To continue our metaphor, the owner of a building must begin with a vision of the end product and hire an architect to design and draw up the plan that will achieve the owner's vision. In investing, the end product is the investor's goals and objectives. Once the goals and objectives are understood, it is the job of the investor's advisors to design the plan necessary to reach those objectives.

The financial advisor is the architect. Once he or she completes the architectural drawings, the financial advisor becomes the structural engineer and the contractor. The investor supervises each stage, continually giving the financial advisor feedback and more information. The investor should be as much a part of the process as is the owner of a building. The outcome of each phase of the process is dependent upon the collaboration between the investor (owner) and the financial advisor (architect/engineer/builder).

The difference in the two processes, however, is profound in one respect: A building is eventually constructed, and the architect and contractor move on. A financial plan is never finished; it is always a work in process. People change, families change, lifestyles change, economic conditions change, and goals and objectives change. The overall plan must be flexible enough to assimilate a steady stream of "change orders." This element of investment planning is made loud and clear in the questions and answers that follow.

Chapter 2 takes you on a journey through the investment process, describing and explaining many important investment strategies and vehicles and how they apply to different investors. The information in this chapter will be rewarding for anyone who is interested in or involved in the investment world.

chapter 1

Fundamental Investment Concepts

ASSET CLASSES

What is an asset class?

An *asset class* is a grouping of investments that share a similar risk and return profile, that is, investments that tend to pay at the same rate or have the same characteristics or whose prices move in tandem. Different asset classes tend to move up and down in price at different times. By combining different asset classes within the same investment portfolio, you can reduce the overall risk as the price volatility is smoothed out within the portfolio.

What are the major asset classes?

There are four major asset classes:

- *Cash equivalents:* savings accounts, certificates of deposit, short-term Treasury bills, short-term bonds, money market accounts
- *Fixed-income investments:* government bonds, municipal bonds, corporate bonds, high-yield bonds, foreign bonds
- *Equity investments:* U.S. large-capitalization stocks, U.S. medium-capitalization (midcapitalization) stocks, U.S. small-capitalization stocks, international stocks
- *Tangibles:* real estate, precious metals, commodities, collectibles

Why aren't IRAs and retirement plans listed in any of these classes?

Although people frequently refer to "investing in an IRA" or "investing in a retirement plan," IRAs and retirement plans are *not* investments. IRAs and employer-sponsored retirement plans are savings vehicles established by Congress. You use the funds within these plans to purchase investments listed in the asset classes above.

What are cash equivalents?

Cash equivalents are highly liquid investments that can be turned into immediate cash. Generally, cash equivalents do not have much volatility; their value does not fluctuate because of market conditions or other factors. They are short-term investments used to preserve principal and do not offer high yields.

What are fixed-income investments?

Fixed-income investments are investments that have a fixed payment schedule. These investments are loans. The investor lends money in expectation of both specific interest payments at predetermined times and principal repayment at some fixed date. The investor accepts an IOU from the borrower, often without collateral. The promise is as good as the promisor. Fixed-income investments include government, municipal, and corporate bonds; long-term certificates of deposit; Treasury notes and bonds; and mortgages.

What are equity investments?

Equity investments are ownership interests in an asset. For example, when you own stock in a particular company, you are a part-owner of that company and are entitled to all the benefits that entails, such as voting rights and long-term ownership. With an equity investment, there is no promise that you will receive any payment from the investment at any particular time.

I hear about "large-cap stocks," "midcap stocks," and "small-cap stocks." What are the differences among these stocks?

Large-capitalization ("large-cap") stocks are stocks of companies that have a large market capitalization, usually over $5 billion. Medium-capitalization ("midcap") stocks are those of companies with a market capitalization that is usually between $1 and $5 billion. Small-capitalization ("small-cap") stocks are from companies with a market capitalization of under $1 billion.

Market capitalization is determined by multiplying the number of outstanding shares that investors own by the current share price.

INVESTMENT VEHICLES

Stocks

Common stock

What are common stocks?

Common stocks are ownership shares in a corporation. They are initially issued and sold by the corporation and then traded among the investors through the various security exchanges. Holders of common stock participate in the profits of the company through dividend distributions and higher stock prices as the company grows. Since the undistributed portion of company profits is reinvested back into the company, enabling the company to enhance sales and profits even further, the stock's price can rise. Common stocks offer no guarantees, but over time they have produced better returns than cash and fixed-income investments.

When corporations sell shares, they give up control to investors whose primary concern is profits and dividends. Owning common stock gives stockholders the right to vote on important company issues and policies. In return for selling stock shares to outside investors, the corporation receives investment money to build or expand its business.

In buying stocks, investors face the risk that the individual company will not do well or that stock prices will weaken in general. It is possible for investors to lose their entire investment. Holders of common stock cannot lose more than their investments in the shares they hold because they are not responsible for corporate debts or liabilities.

What are some of the characteristics of common stock?

Common stock has three main characteristics:

1. Stockholders receive dividends on a pro rata basis. For example, the owner of 10 percent of a company's common shares is entitled to 10 percent of all declared dividends. However, the company is under no obligation to declare a dividend. There are some stocks

(such as Microsoft) that have never paid dividends because the firm reinvests all of its earnings back into the company.

2. Common shareholders vote on the election of corporate board members and on other proposals of special interest.
3. Common shareholders are *residual owners* of the company, which means that their interest is subordinate to those with whom the corporation has contractual obligations: creditors and bondholders. In cases where the corporation is liquidated and its are assets distributed, common shareholders stand at the end of the line.

Preferred stock

What is preferred stock?

Preferred stock is an investment that has characteristics of a bond but in reality is a stock. Holders of preferred stock have more security than do holders of common stock, and they come right behind bondholders in terms of claims on company assets in the event of bankruptcy or liquidation.

Preferred stock pays a specific dividend amount, and the dividend is not subject to changes by the board of directors However, if the preferred stock has a "participating" feature, the dividend may be increased in the future under certain conditions. Preferred stock dividends can be partially paid or not paid at all. However, many preferred dividends are *cumulative:* if a preferred dividend is not fully paid, there will be no dividends paid to common shareholders until all skipped preferred dividends are paid.

Because of the consistent amount of the preferred dividend, the cumulative feature of dividends, and the seniority over common shareholders' claims on assets upon liquidation, in many instances preferred stocks behave more like bonds than like stock in the marketplace. Preferred stock, like bonds, does not carry the right to vote for members of the company's board of directors.

If a corporation has common stock holders, preferred stock holders, and bondholders, how is each paid during bad times and good times?

In Figure 1-1, you can see how each of these investors fares during a company's profitable years and not-so-profitable years. Most notably, preferred stock holders and bondholders are paid even when profits are down. It is the holders of common stock who suffer the risks of varying profits in a company.

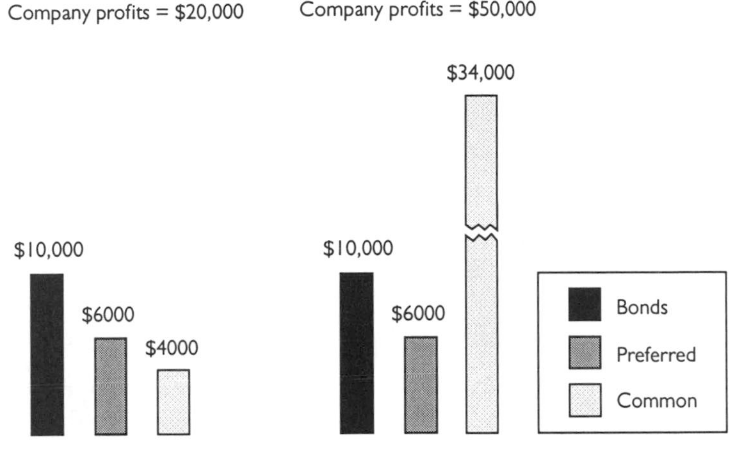

Figure 1-1 Payments to stockholders and bondholders.

Stock options

What is an option?

An *option* is a contract between two investors in which one investor agrees to purchase or sell a certain stock at a certain price within a certain period of time. The purchaser of the option contract agrees to pay the seller of the contract a premium for the opportunity to buy or sell the stock under the terms specified.

What is the difference between a call option and a put option?

The difference between a call option and a put option is that a *call* is the right to buy a security, whereas a *put* is the right to sell one. Generally a person purchasing a call believes that the price of the underlying stock will go up, while the seller believes that the price will go down.

A call option contract provides that the buyer of the contract may purchase a certain stock at a specified price, or *strike price,* within a given period of time from a seller. The seller is required to sell to the buyer the designated stock at the stipulated price if called to do so before the option's expiration date. After the expiration date, the contract is void. The seller of the contract receives a premium for agreeing to make the contract.

A put option contract is the reverse of a call option contract. The buyer of the put contract may sell a particular stock at a specified price within a given period of time. The seller is required to purchase from the buyer of the option the particular stock at the specified price if called to do so before the option's expiration. After expiration, the contract is void. The seller of the contract receives a premium for agreeing to make the contract.

Almost all option contracts are traded on organized option exchanges. The *Wall Street Journal, Barrons, Investors Business Daily,* and the finance sections of large city newspapers, such as the *New York Times* or the *Chicago Tribune,* quote option prices on a regular basis.

Why are puts and calls used?

By purchasing put and call contracts, an investor has the opportunity to control a block of stock at a much lower cost than would be the case with an outright purchase of the stock.

Suppose Mr. Jones believes that the price of the American Widget Company will rise in the future. He can buy call options for the number of shares he might want to eventually own by paying a much smaller amount than it would cost to purchase the actual shares of stock outright. If the share price goes up to a point where he finds it desirable to take advantage of his right to buy, he may do so. If the price does not go up, or perhaps declines, he can allow his call option to expire and he loses only the amount that he paid for the option. A put operates in the same manner as a call, but it grants the option holder the right to sell his or her stock rather than to buy.

Although options may appear to be a much cheaper way to purchase shares of stock than purchasing them outright, keep in mind that you have to guess right on the timing because of the expiration period of the contract.

How is the price of an option decided?

Options, both calls and puts, are traded on organized exchanges, so supply and demand play a role in determining their prices. Three factors play important roles in option pricing: intrinsic value, time premium, and volatility.

There are "in-the-money" options, "at-the-money" options, and "out-of-the-money" options. Intrinsic value greatly affects the pricing of in-the-money options. *Intrinsic value* is the value of the option (put or call) as it relates to the current value of the stock. For example, a call option with a $50 strike price when the stock is actually selling at $52 has an intrinsic value of $2 because the actual stock price is $2 above the strike price. The call option is $2 in the money.

TABLE 1-1 Intrinsic Value of Call and Put Options

	In the money	At the money	Out of the money
Call option: XYZ Company			
Stock price (XYZ)	$52	$50	$48
Strike price	– 50	– 50	– 50
Intrinsic value	$ 2	$ 0	$ 0
Put option: ABC Company			
Strike price	$50	$50	$50
Stock price (ABC)	– 48	– 50	– 52
Intrinsic value	$ 2	$ 0	$ 0

The reverse is true with an in-the-money put option. If a put option has a $50 strike price when the stock is selling for $48, the put option has an intrinsic value of $2 in the money. With the put, the buyer has the right to sell the stock at the $50 strike price, $2 above the stock's price of $48.

Table 1-1 shows examples of the intrinsic value of call and put options that are in the money, at the money, and out of the money.

Time premium is the amount of the option price attributed to the time left on the option contract until expiration. The longer the time until expiration, the more valuable, and expensive, the time premium. An option with 1 week remaining will not have much time premium in its price; an option with 3 months remaining will have a larger portion of its price attributed to the time factor remaining.

Volatility also plays a role in option pricing. Some stocks are more volatile than others; that is, their prices go up and down much more frequently and to a much greater degree. Thus, stocks with greater price volatility tend to have higher option prices than do stocks whose prices tend to be very stable, since the volatility increases the chance that the strike price will be reached.

What is a covered call?

A *covered call* is an option strategy in which the investor owns shares of a particular stock and "writes" (sells) a covered call option on those shares. The investor is covered because, as owner of the shares, he or she can "deliver" (sell) them at the strike price if called to do so by the option holder. The investor receives a premium from the option buyer in payment for entering into the contract. Generally the investor hopes the price of the stock will not go up too much so that he or she can keep the premium and not have to deliver the stock to the call option buyer.

A covered call option strategy can be executed in the money, at the money, or out of the money, each of which can accomplish different results. An in-the-money covered call will provide downside protection in case the price of the stock falls but minimal upside opportunity. Writing an out-of-the-money covered call will provide upside opportunity when the price of the stock rises but minimal downside protection if the stock falls in price.

Miscellaneous stock terms

What are value and growth stocks?

Value stocks typically have a below-average stock price or price-earnings (P/E) ratio relative to the market. They are often found in "distressed" industries, and this, in part, accounts for their attractive valuations. Value stocks typically pay above-average dividends and have below-average dividend growth. Examples of value stocks depend on the market and economy at any given point in time. Today's "beat-up" companies could very well be tomorrow's growth companies, and vice versa.

In comparison, *growth stocks* usually have an above-average stock price or P/E ratio relative to the market. However, growth stocks also have above-average profitability and earnings growth rates that make them attractive to investors. In addition, they often have no- or low-dividend yields, as management of growth companies usually chooses to reinvest earnings in lieu of distributing them to shareholders. Growth stocks today include the stocks of Microsoft, Intel, and America Online.

What are blue-chip stocks?

The phrase "blue chips" comes from the game of poker, in which the blue chips are the most valuable. When used in the context of the stock market, *blue chip* refers to the stocks of tried-and-tested companies that are the cornerstones of U.S. industry.

What is buying on margin?

In the simplest of terms, *buying on margin* allows investors to borrow some of the money they need to buy securities. Investors who do not want to finance securities purchases on their own can leverage their purchases by buying on margin. This involves setting up a margin account with a broker, signing a margin agreement, and maintaining a minimum balance. In this way, investors can purchase more shares of stock than they could pay for in cash.

The Federal Reserve Board's Regulation T limits the leveraged portion of any purchase to 50 percent of the value of the purchase price, so investors must have enough cash to purchase at least 50 percent of the securities. Investors who buy on margin make interest payments on the loan but do not have to make principal payments until they sell the stock itself. The basic objective is to have the price of the stock go up at a faster rate than the amount of interest being paid. People who are interested in buying on margin should keep in mind that leverage cuts both ways: the value of the investment decreases faster if the stock declines in value.

What is a stock split?

If a company decides that the price of its stock has risen to a point that could discourage new investors, it can announce a *stock split*—an arrangement that increases the number of shares and decreases the value of each. Most common is the two-for-one stock split, where the stock price is cut in half and stockholders now hold double the number of their shares. The total, immediate value has not changed, but psychologically the reduced price of a single share is perceived as a better value, which, it is hoped, will boost demand and cause the price to increase.

What is meant by the term "day trader"?

A *day trader* is an investor who conducts many trades each day in search of profits, which may be as little as half a point (or dollar) per share traded. Improvements in technology—especially the Internet—and the growing number of discount brokers are among the factors that have contributed to the rise in day trading by enabling "ordinary" people to engage in heavy trading at little cost.

Day trading can be very risky, especially in volatile markets where stock prices rise and fall dramatically in a matter of minutes. Lately, many day traders have focused on Internet and technology stocks, an area where daily price ranges of 5 or more points are not uncommon. The day traders' constant buying and selling is believed to have added to those stocks' volatility.

Many traders also use margins in their accounts, and this has the effect of magnifying any losses they may incur.

Day trading can be used with stocks but not with mutual funds, because mutual funds are priced only once each day.

The stock market

I've heard that baby boomers are having a dramatic impact on the U.S. stock market. Why?

Consumer spending drives stock markets. When people purchase goods and services, jobs are created, factories produce more goods, and the stocks increase in value. This is basic economics. With that in mind, let's take a look at the baby boomers and how they have affected our economy and will continue to do so for the next 10 years or so.

The baby-boom generation encompasses the people born between 1946 and 1964. This was the period of the largest number of births in U.S. history. Today, these adults are reaching their peak earning and spending years. Some economists and market analysts believe that the baby boomers have not only not stopped driving the stock market to all-time highs but have just started.

Between 1996 and 2006, every single minute seven more baby boomers will have turned 50, which, according to the Department of Labor, is the age at which a baby boomer's spending hits its high point. More people today are spending more money than ever before in history.

According to some economists, higher spending, saving, and investing habits and a continued productivity revolution may drive the Dow Jones Industrial Average upward to over 40,000 by the year 2009 or 2010.

What are market cycles?

Market cycles are periodic upswings and downswings in the stock market. These ups and downs cannot be predicted accurately, but they often can be explained logically, most of the time in hindsight.

The stock market goes up when there are more investors who want to purchase stocks than there are sellers who want to sell stocks. The stock market goes down when there are more sellers than there are buyers—classic supply and demand. In general, the stock market is a reflection of public thinking with regard to the economy, and it is a forward-looking indicator. It is widely accepted that the stock market looks forward 6 to 9 months.

Changes in market direction do not always mirror the state of the economy. The crash of 1987 occurred in a period of economic growth; the market rose during the early 1990s in the face of a recession. But most of the time the strength of the market is related to economic and political forces.

Factors that tend to have a positive effect on the stock market include an expanding money supply, tax cuts, low interest rates, political stability, and high employment. Factors that tend to have a negative effect on the stock market include a contracting money supply, higher taxes, higher interest rates offering more attractive returns in a less risky environment, political turmoil, and international conflicts.

What is a "bull" market?

When the stock market is in a general upward trend over a period of time, it is termed a *bull market.* Normally, such a trend lasts over a period of several months or more.

What is a "bear" market?

This is the opposite of a bull market. In a *bear market,* the stock market is moving steadily downward over a period of months or years. Bear markets are usually shorter and tend to be more dramatic.

What is market timing?

Market timing is an approach to investing that involves speculating on movements in the broad equity (stock) market. According to this strategy, an individual would increase his or her exposure to the stock market when the outlook is for the market to go up. Alternatively, when the stock market is expected to underperform or go down, the same person would sell his or her stocks and buy some other investment. Market timing assumes that there are methods of predicting when the stock market is about to rise or fall.

Measuring investment returns

How is investment return measured? What is the difference between yield and total return?

Yield is the dividend and interest income per share paid to a shareholder of an investment over a specified period of time. Yield is expressed as a percentage of the current offering price of the investment.

In order to understand total return, you must first understand its components, capital appreciation and income. Capital appreciation is the increase in the price of an asset. Consider a share of stock with a price of $20 at the end of 1998, which rose to $25 by the end of 1999. This $5 increase represents a capital appreciation of 25 percent.

In the case of stocks, the income return is derived from dividends. In our example the annual dividend is $1, representing an income return of 5 percent. *Total return* is defined as capital appreciation plus income. Thus the total return in our example is 30 percent.

It is important to note that while income returns are always a positive amount or zero, capital appreciation can be negative if the price of an asset falls below the purchase price. The total return would be negative if the capital depreciation is greater than the income return.

What is a dividend? How is the dividend determined?

A *dividend* is a distribution of a portion of the company's profits. The company's board of directors determines the dividend. The board will analyze the previous quarter's and year's sales, operating profits, and net income and will decide what the dividend distribution will be this quarter. The board typically meets quarterly and decides (by vote) what each quarter's dividend distribution will be. The board generally attempts to declare a dividend distribution that will not need to be reduced in the future if company profits begin to decline.

What is a company's dividend payout ratio? How is it computed? Is it important?

A company's *dividend payout ratio* is the portion of the company's earnings that is, and is expected to be, distributed as dividends. It is calculated by dividing the dividend per share by the earnings per share. For ABC Company, which distributes $1 in dividends and earns $5 per share, the dividend payout ratio is 20 percent:

$$\text{Payout ratio} = \frac{\text{dividends per share}}{\text{earnings per share}} = \frac{\$1.00}{\$5.00} = .20 \text{ or } 20\%$$

The payout ratio is important because if a company's earnings per share have consistently increased at a given rate and the dividend payout has been stable, investors can expect a given increase in dividends each year. If the dividend payout ratio has been increasing, investors may anticipate even higher dividend distributions in the future.

What is a dividend yield? How is it computed?

The *dividend yield* is the percentage return (yield) of the dividend as a function of the stock's price. It is calculated by dividing the dividend by the price of the stock. For ABC Company, which has a price per share of $50 and pays dividends of $1.50 per share, the dividend yield is 3 percent:

$$\text{Dividend yield} = \frac{\text{dividends per share}}{\text{earnings per share}} = \frac{\$1.50}{\$5.00} = .03 \text{ or } 3\%$$

What are average return and compound return?

Average return represents typical performance over a single period; *compound return* measures change in wealth over more than one period.

What is compound interest?

Compound interest is interest computed on principal plus accrued interest. Albert Einstein called it the "eighth wonder of the world." Those who have been investing for the last 21.6 years and receiving returns in excess of 10 percent have seen their portfolios double almost three times.

Compounding is dependent on two factors: time and the underlying interest rate. The longer the time period, the longer the investment is growing. The higher the interest rate, the faster the investment grows. Table 1-2 shows the results of compounding on an annual investment of just $2000.

Another aspect of compounding is that the earlier you deposit your money into savings during any given year, the greater the results. For example, if you deposit $2000 every January 1 for 10 years at 10 percent interest, you will have $35,062 at the end of the 10 years. If you deposit $2000 at the end of each year for the same 10 years, you will have $31,875—$3187 less. This is why advisors tell you to make your retirement plan contributions at the beginning of the year. The secret of compounding is the reinvestment of the interest back into the principal. This can cause an investment to experience exponential growth.

How long will it take for my money to double?

The *Rule of 72* is a good tool for estimating how quickly your money will double. Under the Rule of 72, you divide the number 72 by your investment's rate of return. The result is the number of years it will take for your money to double. For example, if your investment is earning

TABLE 1-2 Compounding on $2000 Annual Investment*

Years of investment	Total contributed	Will grow to	Growth	Percent increase
5	$10,000	$ 11,951	$ 1,951	20
10	20,000	27,943	7,943	40
15	30,000	49,345	19,345	64
20	40,000	77,985	37,985	95
25	50,000	116,313	66,313	133
30	60,000	167,603	107,603	179
35	70,000	236,242	166,242	237
40	80,000	328,095	248,095	310

*Growth of a fund to which $2000 is added at the beginning of each year. Calculation assumes that there is a 6% rate of return after taxes and that the earnings are reinvested.

8 percent, it will take 9 years for your investment to double (72 ÷ 8 = 9 years). If you think you'll earn 15 percent, it will take 4.8 years (72 ÷ 15) to double your money.

To estimate how many years it will take for your money to triple in value, you can use the *Rule of 116*. For example, at a 10 percent rate of return, it will take only 11.6 years to triple the value of your investment.

What is a P/E ratio, and how is it calculated? Is it important?

A *P/E (price-earnings) ratio* is a measure used to determine the current value of companies. It is calculated by dividing a company's stock price by its earnings per share. Suppose XYZ Company has a price per share of $100 and earnings per share of $4. The P/E ratio indicates that the market value of XYZ's stock is $25:

$$\text{P/E ratio} = \frac{\text{price per share}}{\text{earnings per share}} = \frac{\$100}{\$4} = 25$$

P/E ratios are used to compare a company's market value to the values of other companies in the same industry (its peers), the values of companies in other industries, or the value of the market in general. With these comparisons, investors can determine whether companies or industry groups are undervalued, fairly valued, or overvalued relative to their peers, industry, other industries, or the general market. Companies expected to provide returns to investors greater than those for the market in general often have P/E ratios higher than the market P/E ratio.

For example, XYZ Company's P/E ratio is 25. If other companies in its industry had P/Es in excess of 30 and the general market had a P/E of 30, XYZ Company may be undervalued. The other companies in its industry would seem to be fairly valued when compared to each other and to the general market.

Bonds

What are bonds?

A *bond* is a loan from an investor to an institution. The investor lends money to the institution (which now has incurred debt) in exchange for an interest payment over a period of years. At the end of the loan period (maturity), the institution pays the final interest payment and the original amount of the loan to the investor.

One of the major appeals of bonds is that they pay a set rate of interest on a regular basis. Another is that the issuer agrees to pay back the loan on time. Every bond has a fixed maturity date on which the bond expires and the loan must be paid back in full at par value. The interest a bond pays is set when the bond is issued. The rate is competitive at the time of issue in that the bond pays interest comparable to what investors can earn elsewhere. As a result, the rate of interest on a new bond is usually similar to current interest rates, although it will differ depending on the quality of the issuer.

Who issues bonds?

Many different entities issue bonds. The largest issuers of bonds are the U.S. government and its agencies, corporations, railroads, public utilities, municipalities, school districts, and foreign governments. When a company or government agency needs to raise cash, it can borrow the money from the public by "floating an issue."

Are there fundamental differences between bonds issued by corporations and those issued by federal, state, or local governments?

The primary difference between corporate bonds and government bonds is measured in terms of financial strength (credit rating): the larger the institution (and its power to make good on its promises to you), the greater the likelihood that you will receive your interest payments and return of principal on time.

For bonds, the federal government is the standard of safety. All other bonds are rated by rating services on the basis of the financial strength of the institution issuing the bond. Examples of rating services are Standard and Poor's and Moody's Investors Service. Though they cannot guarantee that an institution (corporate or governmental) will make all payments on time and ultimately return your principal, rating services do give the investor a way to measure the probability of this occurring.

How do bonds "come to market"?

There are two markets for bonds: the primary market and the secondary market. The *primary market* is composed of new issues coming to market (issued) for the first time. These issues are syndicated either by competitive bid or by negotiated underwriting through investment banking firms.

All previously issued and currently outstanding bonds are traded in the *secondary market.* In the secondary market, investors buy and sell bonds through a number of exchanges such as the New York Stock Exchange.

How are bonds issued?

A bond can be issued in several different forms. If a bond is *registered,* a certificate is issued in the name of the investor. *Bearer* bonds are bonds issued without investor names; those in possession of the bonds are presumed to be the rightful owners. When bonds are held in *book-entry* form, the investors' names are included on a list of owners and they receive a confirmation of ownership but no actual certificate.

How are bonds priced?

A $1000 bond has a *par amount* (also called *face amount* or *maturity value*) of $1000. Corporate bonds are usually traded in $1000 units.

Bonds are quoted in the secondary market as a percentage of their maturity value, so when a bond is trading at par, its price is 100 (100 cents on the dollar, which is what it will pay on the maturity date). If the price of the bond is less than par, say, 99, it is trading at a *discount.* In this example, it is trading at a 1 percent discount to its maturity value (100). Bonds are likely to trade at a discount if interest rates have increased or the quality of the bonds has decreased since they were originally issued. If the price of the bond is more than par, say, 101, it is trading at a *premium.* In this example, it is trading at a 1 percent premium to its maturity value (100). As the price of a bond goes up, its yield to maturity goes down, and as the price goes down, the bond's yield to maturity goes up.

What is a zero coupon bond?

Zero coupon bonds ("zeroes") are bonds that are issued at substantial discount from their face value and pay no interest. They are redeemed at face (par) value at maturity. For example, a bond which matures for $1000 in 10 years, priced to yield 7.2 percent per year, will cost the buyer $500. No interest will be received during the 10 years, and the full $1000 will be paid at the end of 10 years.

Zeroes are more volatile than bonds that pay interest. Because they pay no interest, movements in interest rates affect their prices dramatically. Issuers of zeroes have use of the money without making interest payments—a very attractive feature to them.

One drawback to investing in zeroes is that the investor has to declare the accrued interest in each year's taxes unless the bonds are municipal zeroes. Thus the investor is paying income tax on income he or she has not yet received (hence, it is known as a "phantom tax"). On the other hand, when the investor receives all the proceeds at maturity, no additional taxes will be due.

What are the different types of corporate bonds?

There are four primary types of corporate bonds:

- *Commercial paper* is an unsecured loan that is typically paid back in 30 to 90 days.
- *Convertible bonds* are bonds that can be "converted" into stock (an attractive feature if the investor expects the underlying stock to increase in value).
- *Debentures* are bonds secured only by the faith and credit of the corporation issuing them.
- *Mortgage bonds* are loans secured by specific assets, such as equipment or real property.

Why are some bonds worth more than other bonds?

Three main factors cause one bond to be worth more than another: (1) the quality of the bond, (2) its interest rate, and (3) the length of time remaining until maturity.

The *quality* of all U.S. government bonds is the same because they are all backed by the federal government. Bonds issued by different corporations are not the same. General Electric and ABC High Risk Company do not have similar quality bonds. Sometimes bonds issued by the same company are not of the same quality. For example, a bond with a first mortgage on company assets should, and usually does, have better-quality features than a debenture of the same company.

Interest rates and bond prices have an inverse relationship. In general, as interest rates rise, prices of previously issued bonds fall. Since the interest paid by a bond is constant, as interest rates rise, investors can receive higher interest returns elsewhere; as a result, they will pay less for a bond paying a lower interest rate. As interest rates fall, bond prices will subsequently rise. To maintain a market for outstanding bonds, the market adjusts prices upward through premiums or downward through discounts to reflect current market demands.

Maturity dates affect bond prices. Long maturity dates with high interest rates are valued higher than long maturity dates with lower interest rates. For example, assume that there are three equally rated bonds with 20 years remaining until maturity. Bond A has a 7 percent coupon rate; bond B, a 6 percent coupon rate. In order for bond B to have the same yield to maturity—or rate of return required by marketplace demand—as bond A, the price for bond B will have to be lower than bond A's price. Bond C has an 8 percent coupon rate. For it to have the same yield to maturity as bond A, its price will have to be adjusted higher than bond A's price.

After the price adjustments, all three bonds have the same yield to maturity. Bond A trades at par (100), bond B trades at a discount (below 100), and bond C trades at a premium (above 100).

What is a callable bond?

A *callable bond* is a bond that has a special feature allowing the issuer to "call in," or redeem, the bond earlier than the maturity date. Sometimes the call price is at a premium; other times it is at par. The call price is never below par. The call dates and prices are always documented in the bond indenture. A call date would likely be exercised if the interest rates drop after the bonds were originally issued.

Government bonds

What type of bonds does the U.S. government issue?

The U.S. government issues Treasury bills, notes, bonds, and Treasury inflation-protection securities. All these government obligations are unconditionally guaranteed for payment by the U.S. government and are direct obligations of the government. Because the full faith and credit of the federal government backs these bonds, they are considered the highest-quality bonds in the world.

Other bonds are available through agencies of the U.S. government. Though not carrying the full faith and credit of the federal government, these bonds nonetheless have some form of guarantee or sponsorship or are issued under congressional authority. Examples are investments issued by the Government National Mortgage Association (GNMA, or "Ginnie Mae") or the Federal National Mortgage Association (FNMA, or "Fannie Mae").

What, if any, are the differences among U.S. Treasury bills, notes, bonds, and inflation-protected securities?

Treasury bills are short-term payment obligations of the government that have maturities of 13, 26, or 52 weeks. Treasury bills are sold at a discount (you purchase them for less than face value), and the interest is not taxable until the bill is sold or matures.

Treasury notes have a fixed interest rate that is paid every 6 months, with maturities ranging from 1 to 10 years. Like Treasury notes, *Treasury bonds* have a fixed interest rate that pays every 6 months, but the maturities of Treasury bonds are long-term obligations of the government that extend beyond 10 years.

Treasury inflation-protection securities are bonds designed to keep up with inflation. To do this, the bond pays interest every 6 months on the basis of a formula that calculates and preserves the purchasing power of the investor. At the end of the payment schedule (at maturity), the investor receives the greater of the original face value of the bond or an inflation-adjusted principal based on the consumer price index.

What's the difference between a marketable U.S. government bond and a nonmarketable U.S. government bond?

Marketable U.S. government bonds are investments that can be bought or sold on an exchange. Nonmarketable U.S. government bonds are investments that can be traded only between the bondholder and the federal government, not on any exchange or between investors.

Are there investments available through the federal government that have little or no market risk?

The federal government issues many types of marketable and nonmarketable bonds. Savings bonds have no risk (your investment does not change in value), while other investments issued by the federal government or its agencies have *market* risk. Market risk is the possibility that, should the bondholder decide to sell the bond before its maturity, the holder might not get all his or her money back if interest rates rose after the original purchase date.

Savings bonds are not marketable; they are not traded (bought and sold) on any exchange. Savings bonds are available in three versions: Series EE, Series I, and Series HH bonds.

A *Series EE* bond is purchased at half its face value and pays interest every 6 months. Over time, the value of the bond will equal its face value. The interest earnings are tax-deferred until they are cashed in.

A *Series I* bond is purchased at full face value. Because it is a Treasury inflation-protection security, it earns both a fixed interest rate and an adjustable interest rate that can change every 6 months. The combination of the fixed and adjustable interest rates is designed to keep up with inflation as measured by the consumer price index.

Those who own EE or I bonds can choose to pay taxes each year on the earnings or defer taxation until the bonds are cashed. Additionally, both EE and I bonds can earn interest for up to 30 years.

Series HH bonds earn a fixed interest rate every 6 months for 10 years, after which the interest rate can change. The earnings are taxable each year, and the bond matures in 20 years. HH bonds cannot be purchased for cash but can be obtained by trading in EE bonds or older (no-longer-issued) E or H bonds at a Federal Reserve Bank.

Municipal bonds

What are municipal bonds?

Municipal bonds are the issues of states, counties, cities, and other political subdivisions, such as school districts.

Are there different types of municipal bonds?

Municipal bonds typically trade in multiples of $5000 and are usually either general-obligation or revenue bonds. The full taxing power of the government or its agency backs a *general-obligation bond.* The interest and principal payments are generated from taxes collected by the municipality issuing the bond. Examples of general-obligation bonds are bonds for school or prison renovation. *Revenue bonds,* on the other hand, support projects of the issuing agency and generate interest and principal payments from revenues collected from those projects. Examples of revenue bonds are those that support highways or bridges, water and sewer districts, or public transportation.

There are some other municipal bonds that fall into special categories. A *private-activity bond* benefits the government (or its agency) and private enterprise. Since this type of municipal bond serves mixed purposes, the income may or may not be taxed at the federal or state level. An example of a private-activity bond is a collaborative effort between a city government and the owner of a baseball team to construct a stadium.

Insured municipal bonds carry insurance issued by a private organization to guard against the risk of default. The cost of the insurance is expressed as a lower interest rate on the bond; therefore, the income received by the investor will be typically lower than that from an uninsured municipal bond. As with institutions, the credit rating of private insurers is available to the public and published by various rating services such as Standard and Poor's and Moody's Investors Service.

Isn't municipal bond interest exempt from income taxes?

To encourage investors to buy municipal bonds, Congress exempts most municipal bond interest from federal income taxes. In addition, if you live in the same state as the municipality that issued the bond, the income is exempt from state income taxes as well. On the other hand, if you purchase a bond issued by a municipality located outside your home state, the income is usually subject to state income taxes.

Other types of bonds

What is a collateral mortgage obligation?

Collateral mortgage obligations (CMOs) are derivative securities created from federal government–supported mortgage bonds, such as Ginnie Maes. The government bonds are placed in a trust. Participation in this trust is then sold to the investing public in the form of a CMO.

When a CMO is created, it is subdivided into classes called *tranches*. The principal repayments received by the CMO are paid by the CMO to the first tranche until it has been entirely retired. Once the first tranche has been completely paid off, mortgage principal repayments are paid to holders of the CMO in the second tranche, and so on, until all tranches have been repaid.

Since the actual timing of principal repayments is not known with certainty, there is the risk that payments will not be timely. Lower interest rates will speed up payments as homeowners refinance, paying off their previous mortgages. The contrary is also true: higher interest rates tend to slow down principal repayments.

What is a derivative security?

The word "derivative" comes from the word "derive"; therefore, a *derivative security* is one that is derived from another investment. Derivative investments are not direct investments of any corporation, agency, or government, and there are some derivatives with no certificates for the investors. There are both fixed-income and equity derivatives. For example, CMOs are forms of equity derivatives and are based on the value of the government bonds placed in the CMO trust. Derivatives afford leverage and, when used properly, can enhance returns and be useful in hedging portfolios. Because there are numerous types of derivatives, each with different investment features and characteristics, it would be wise for investors to seek professional guidance before investing in derivatives.

What are junk bonds?

Junk bonds are high-yield bonds of companies that have below-investment-grade bond ratings. These bonds usually are rated Ba, BB, or lower. High-yield, or junk, bonds pay more interest (sometimes substantially more) to compensate for the greater risk of default.

What are convertible bonds?

Convertible bonds, issued by companies, can be converted to shares of the companies' common stock at a fixed price within a certain time frame, usually at the maturity of the bond.

Laddered maturities

What are laddered maturities?

Laddering is designed to lower inflation and interest-rate risk. It generally applies to fixed-income investments such as bonds. When you ladder, you choose bonds with different maturity dates and split your investments more or less equally among these bonds. For example, a bond ladder for a person with $50,000 to invest in bonds might be structured as follows:

$10,000 maturing in 1 year
$10,000 maturing in 3 years
$10,000 maturing in 5 years
$10,000 maturing in 7 years
$10,000 maturing in 10 years

As each bond becomes due, you buy a new one. If interest rates have dropped, only that part of the total bond portfolio has to be reinvested at the lower rates. By the time the next bond matures, interest rates could have risen.

Laddering is a way to keep your fixed-income investments fluid and protected against inflation (because you have bonds maturing at regular intervals) while protecting yourself against having to invest all your money if interest rates are low. Laddered bonds can also be used as a regular source of income. As each bond comes due, you can put the money into more liquid investments. By planning these cash infusions, you can avoid having to sell other investments that would continue to produce income or appreciate, such as long-term bonds, stocks, or mutual funds.

Mutual Funds

What are mutual funds?

A *mutual fund* is an investment company that pools money from shareholders and invests in a diversified portfolio of securities. An investor in a mutual fund is a shareholder who buys shares of the fund. Each share represents a proportionate ownership in all the fund's underlying securities.

Is a mutual fund like a stock or bond?

A mutual fund is neither a stock nor a bond. It is a method of buying stocks and bonds. Money from many investors is pooled together and placed in the hands of professional fund managers who buy and sell various stocks or bonds, depending on the investment objectives, for the benefit of the combined investors.

How do mutual funds work?

A mutual fund is owned by its shareholders. A management company runs the mutual fund's day-to-day operations. This company usually serves as the fund's investment advisor. As the investment advisor, the management company has a staff of professional portfolio managers who make the portfolio investment selections. These managers are guided by objectives outlined in the fund's prospectus. On the basis of extensive research and analysis, they decide what to buy and when to buy it. With a mutual fund, investors can access a level of professional management and diversification difficult to attain on their own.

The management company charges an investment management fee that can be from .15 to 2 percent but is typically .5 to .9 percent of the total value of the fund's assets.

How did mutual funds evolve?

Mutual funds evolved at the turn of the twentieth century. They were originally trusts established by bankers and other financial intermediaries as a way of providing affordable professional money management to small investors. The first fund as we know it today was formed in 1924 by the Massachusetts Investors Trust, which gave its shareholders the right to redeem their shares at net asset value. This fund is still active today.

What features characterize a mutual fund?

Ease of purchase means investing can be as easy as calling a mutual fund company and investing directly with it through the mail. Buying through a stockbroker, financial planner, or insurance representative offers the advantage of having a professional analyze your needs and objectives, understand your risk tolerance, and recommend appropriate funds.

Investments can often be as little as $100 to get started. Accessibility to your money, or *liquidity,* is an important feature of investing in mutual funds. By law, mutual funds must stand ready to liquidate or redeem any or all shares upon notice, at their daily net asset value (NAV). Unlike a stock, which can be traded during the day and whose market price reflects price at the moment of sale, a mutual fund will reflect the price at the next close of business for all redemptions that day.

Automatic reinvestment of distributions might not seem like a significant feature, but it contributes greatly to compounding returns and can create the discipline of systematic investing (dollar cost averaging). The fund provides record keeping and administrative services that help you track the performance of your portfolio as well as the taxes.

How is my mutual fund investment taxed?

Mutual funds do not pay income taxes as long as 95 percent of the fund's income is distributed to its shareholders, who subsequently pay income taxes on those distributions. Gains from your mutual fund can be taxed in three ways: as dividends, capital gain, or realized capital appreciation.

A mutual fund holds shares in several different companies. As these companies distribute dividends, the dividends must be distributed to the shareholders of the mutual fund. These dividends are included in the taxable income of the mutual fund's shareholders.

Shareholders will have to recognize gain (or loss) if the portfolio manager decides to sell a block of stock. For example, if a portfolio manager purchased a large block of General Motors stock at $10 a share and each share increased to $40, the manager may decide to sell. The $30-per-share gain must be distributed to the shareholders in the form of short-term or long-term capital gain. Short-term capital gain is any gain taken within 12 months and taxed at ordinary tax rates. Long-term capital gain is any gain taken after holding an investment for at least 12 months and taxed at the capital gain rate, which cannot exceed 20 percent under federal tax rates.

The third type of taxable gain for shares in a mutual fund is capital appreciation. The timing of this gain is determined by the shareholder. For example, assume a shareholder invested $10,000 in a mutual fund and it grew to $20,000. If the shareholder sold the investment in the fund, the difference between the purchase price (increased by dividend and capital gain distributions previously taxed to the shareholder) and the selling price is the taxable gain. The amount of time the shares were held determines whether the gain is short-term or long-term capital gain.

It is possible for a shareholder to owe taxes on dividends and capital gains realized in the fund even while the fund's net asset value (NAV) decreased below the price the shareholder originally paid for the investment in the fund. For example, suppose you purchased shares in XYZ Fund in June at $10 per share. Between June and November, the fund realized capital gains of $.10 per share and dividends of $.05 per share. As of December 31, the value of XYZ Fund dropped to $8 per share. Hence, you experienced a 20 percent decrease in the market value of your investment in XYZ Fund but still had to pay taxes on the dividends and capital gains realized in the fund during the year.

Since there are a variety of stocks and bonds available, are there a variety of mutual funds available?

Yes. Mutual funds represent the entire spectrum of investment categories. Examples include mutual funds that invest only in U.S. Treasuries, technology companies, banks, or precious metals, to name just a few. Other mutual funds are designed to meet a certain investment objective such as a mix of income and growth or income alone. Some mutual funds invest entirely overseas; others may concentrate their investments in one foreign country; still others may be restricted to the United States.

Mutual funds can be conservative, aggressive, or in between. They can be small, medium, or large in size and can be managed by one or two people or a committee. As you can see, mutual funds come in a variety of categories, and this explains in part their popularity among investors.

Focus funds

What are focus funds?

Focus, or *core, funds* have become very popular of late because the manager of the fund limits the number of stocks in the portfolio to a core of fifty or less. An example of a focus fund is one that includes only large-cap stocks such as the S&P 500 (largest 500 U.S. stocks) but confines the investments to the top one or two stock picks of the twelve sectors.

In recent years, this strategy has given substantially higher returns to investors, but it also creates additional risk. Fully diversified mutual funds typically have 150 or more securities, thereby providing diversification and less volatility. Because of the concentration of stocks in focus funds, only investors willing to take the increased risk should buy them.

Sector funds

What are sector mutual funds?

A *sector mutual fund* is a focus-type fund that limits its stock selection to a specific industry. The industries are regional banks, health care, computers, technology, the Internet, financial services, energy, and electronics, among others. This strategy can provide higher returns to investors but is more speculative and volatile due to the lack of diversification among numerous sectors.

Index funds

What are index funds?

Index funds are designed to produce the same returns that investors would get if they owned all the stocks of a particular index. It is cost-prohibitive to own all the stocks of an index, unless, of course, the investor is a large institution. Thus private investors turn to index funds. There are many indexes; some of the better-known are listed here:

Dow Jones Industrial	Russell Top 200 Growth
Dow Jones Transportation	Russell Top 200 Value
Russell 1000 Growth	Standard & Poor's 100
Russell 1000 Value	Standard & Poor's 500
Russell 2000 Growth	Standard & Poor's Midcap 400
Russell 2000 Value	Standard & Poor's Smallcap 600
Russell 3000	Wilshire REIT (real estate)

Indexes are popular because the performances of the major stock and bond indexes often surpass the returns of mutual funds or managed money. In addition, they often have lower annual investment management costs. Index funds are considered "passive investing" because there is no active management (i.e., stock picking) involved; the fund manager simply purchases the stocks that make up the index the fund is supposed to track.

What accounts for the success of index funds?

Index funds, especially S&P 500 funds, have been very popular in recent years. The Vanguard Index 500, for example, grew from $7 billion invested to $70 billion invested between 1995 and 1999. A major reason behind the increase undoubtedly was the fund's performance, which averaged a 24 percent annual compound rate of return over that period of time, reflecting the strong bull market in large-cap U.S. stocks.

The reasons for the strong performance of S&P index funds are somewhat controversial. Some argue that the performance of index funds is attributable mostly to the low internal expenses that result from a lack of active management. Others maintain that the market for large-cap U.S. stocks has become too efficient for portfolio managers to find the kind of underpriced securities they need to buy if they are to outperform the market as a whole. Still others believe that strong performance has become a self-fulfilling phenomenon: because so many investors have chosen to index at least a portion of their portfolios, stocks that are part of the index *ipso facto* perform well because of high demand.

How is the S&P 500 index weighted?

The most common misconception about the S&P 500 index funds is that they are investments in 500 equally weighted stocks, thus achieving the ultimate market diversification. In reality, S&P 500 index funds are capitalization-weighted portfolios of 500 stocks. The more the price of an S&P 500 stock appreciates, the more weight it has in the indexed portfolio. Therefore, the risk of the index funds fluctuates with the portfolio weighting of the S&P 500 index.

Open- and closed-end funds

What are the differences between open-end and closed-end mutual funds?

The basic difference between closed-end and open-end mutual funds is the way the shares are distributed; otherwise, they are quite similar. However, this difference can lead to profound differences in mutual fund performance.

An *open-end mutual fund* issues new shares for new investors. The mutual fund also directly redeems the shares of a selling shareholder. The number of dollars inside the open-end mutual fund can grow and shrink depending upon the fund's popularity with investors. Generally the mutual funds we see or hear advertised are open-end funds.

Closed-end funds raise money for the mutual fund in much the same way that companies raise money through stock offerings. They issue a fixed number of shares at a certain price. After the shares are issued, anyone wanting to purchase them must do so from someone else who owns shares. The company will not issue new shares. Conversely, when someone wants to sell shares, he or she must find a buyer; the company does not redeem shares. Like stockholders, closed-end shareholders find buyers and sellers through an exchange such as the NYSE.

The number of dollars managed in the closed-end fund fluctuates only by performance of investments, not through the addition or subtraction of shareholder assets. These funds will often sell at a discount or a premium.

How is the price of an open-end fund determined?

Purchase and sales prices of open-end funds are based specifically on the net asset value (NAV). Therefore, the funds never sell at a premium or discount. The value of the shares increases and decreases according to the investments' performances.

The NAV is the total value of all investments and cash in the mutual fund divided by the number of shares outstanding. Thus, if a mutual fund has a total value of $10 million and has 1 million shares issued, the NAV is $10 per share.

Is the NAV used in determining the value of closed-end funds?

It seems logical that the price of a share of a closed-end fund should be its NAV, and in fact NAV is used as a reference point for closed-end fund values. However, closed-end funds can trade above their NAV (trading at a *premium price*), or they can trade below their NAV (trading at a *discount price*).

The presence of a premium or a discount often indicates the popularity of the investment. When a particular sector is popular with investors, we may see closed-end funds invest in that sector to trade at a premium to NAV. Most closed-end funds trade at a discount to their NAV.

What costs and fees are associated with buying a mutual fund?

Generally there are two costs associated with buying mutual funds: initial commissions and/or transaction fees, and the annual internal cost of operating the fund. Some funds are considered *load funds,* in which a portion of your initial investment is used to pay the stockbroker or financial advisor for his or her services in helping you select the fund. The "load" can be deducted up front on an annual basis or in arrears when you sell the funds. There are also *no-load funds,* which do not pay commissions.

All mutual funds, both load and no-load, have annual operating expenses that are deducted from the earnings on their investments. These fees are typically described as the fund's *annual expense ratio.* Not included in a fund's expense ratio or in its prospectus are the fund's transaction costs of buying and selling securities. To obtain this information, you must order a special report from the fund.

Load and no-load funds

What are no-load mutual funds?

A mutual fund that can be bought or sold without front-end sales charges, back-end sales charges, or higher-than-normal ongoing sales charges is considered a *no-load mutual fund.* In essence, the investor purchases the mutual fund at its NAV. Since no charges or "loads" are withheld from the initial investment in a no-load fund, 100 percent of the investor's money is immediately invested.

No-load mutual funds do have distribution costs, such as those associated with administration, advertising, brochures, and direct mail, and sometimes sales or commission charges, but these costs are absorbed in the fund's *expense ratio.* A no-load fund's expense ratio is the combined annual cost of its doing business. Some funds have an additional 12b-1 fee to help cover these items and to provide a form of compensation to brokerage firms that offer the funds to investors on a nontransaction basis.

What are load funds?

Load mutual funds charge sales expenses on the front end when you purchase the mutual fund stock or on the back end when you sell the stock. They also have expense ratios that may be more or less expensive than those of no-load funds. Load mutual funds come in different pricing structures.

What are A-share mutual funds?

With A shares, the securities professional who sells the fund is paid a commission, on the front end, on the amount the client initially invests. The typical commission ranges from a low of 0 percent on investments of $1 million or more to a high of 5.75 percent on smaller investments. On larger investments, the broker or investment professional is paid a finder's fee at no cost to the client.

When a commission is paid, that amount is deducted from the investor's original investment. There is usually no additional charge to sell a front-end load fund.

What are B-share mutual funds?

Class B shares have a *contingent deferred sales charge (CDSC),* or back-end load, instead of an initial sales charge.

The advisor or broker receives a 4 to 5 percent commission that is paid up front by the mutual fund company. To recover the commission it pays, the mutual fund company will impose a *surrender,* or *redemption, charge* when the investor liquidates the investment. The redemption charges gradually decline over the first several years of the investment. Once the mutual fund recovers the commission it paid to the sales professional, the Class B share will often convert to a Class A share, which usually has lower management fees. In addition, B shares typically have a 12b-1 annual charge (generally 1 percent) that enables the fund to recoup the up-front sales charge.

With some mutual funds, a shareholder can systematically withdraw up to 12 percent of the investment's value from the B-share fund without any charge.

What are Class C shares?

Class C mutual fund shares have either a minimal front-end or back-end sales charge (typically 1 percent) or no front-end or back-end charge. Instead of paying a front-end commission to the broker or advisor, the mutual fund company pays an annual commission of around 1 percent from the annual management fees it charges the investors.

Is there a difference in performance between A, B, and C shares?

A mutual fund company may offer separate funds with the same name, same objectives, and same manager that differ only by how the load is paid. For instance, there may be an XYZ Fund A, XYZ Fund B, and XYZ Fund C. The difference in their returns is solely attributable to the expenses deducted from the funds.

What are Y-share, or institutional-class, mutual funds?

A number of mutual funds limit their availability to large institutional investors, such as pension funds, or to high-net-worth individuals through registered investment advisors. Since they do not have to deal with the public, their internal costs are generally lower than those of an equivalent "retail" mutual fund, and they pass this cost savings along to the investors.

A Y-share mutual fund is distinguished by the high minimum deposit required upon original purchase. The amount usually starts at $1 million and can go as high as $5 million per investor. Y-share funds are referred to as *institutional funds* because larger institutions, such as financial advisory firms, pension and profit-sharing plans, and other large investors, can better afford the minimum required investment.

There are no front-end or back-end charges on these funds. Their expense ratios range from .20 to .70 percent.

Investors who do not have enough funds to meet the minimums required for Y shares can invest in them through their brokerage firm or registered investment advisory firm. These firms purchase Y-share funds as part of a managed mutual fund account for which they charge a management fee of about 1 percent.

In some cases, institutional funds may be available through discount brokers. Discount brokers typically require that the fund increase its expenses by .25 percent. This increase is then paid to the discount brokerage firm to allow the investor to buy it with no transaction costs.

Mutual fund expenses

What do mutual funds charge for managing my money?

Mutual funds charge a management fee and an administration fee. The management fee is typically .5 to 1 percent and is paid to the management firm for making the buy and sell decisions for the securities in the fund. The administration fee is related to the costs for annual reports, prospectuses, accounting audits and reports, and so on. This fee ranges from .1 to .15 percent.

Some funds, whether load or no-load, charge additional fees called *12b-1 fees* to pay for marketing and advertising expenses or, more commonly, for compensating sales professionals and advisory firms. By law 12b-1 fees cannot exceed .75 percent of the fund's average net assets per year; they are typically closer to .25 percent.

The total of all three fees is the *expense ratio,* which on average for all funds will run about 1.35 to 1.5 percent on an annualized basis.

The commissions for trading the securities within the fund are not reported in the expense ratio and can add an additional .1 to 1 percent to the total expense. These fees are calculated and deducted from the mutual fund daily.

Do all share classes (A, B, and C) charge the same expenses?

Normally, internal expenses are different for each class of shares. Because of differing expenses, even if everything else is equal among the funds, they will have different results. Generally, but not always, A shares have the lowest internal expenses, followed by B shares, and then C shares. B shares tend to be .7 percent higher in fees than corresponding A shares, and C shares tend to be 1 percent higher in fees than corresponding A shares.

Why are fees for index funds lower than those for other funds?

An index fund is an unmanaged portfolio of stocks. Since there is no active management or research, the expense ratio will range from .18 to .75 percent.

Hedge funds

What is a hedge fund?

A *hedge fund* is a professionally managed portfolio that invests in publicly traded securities or financial derivatives. Usually structured as a U.S. private partnership, a hedge fund is limited by the SEC to ninety-nine investors, at least sixty-five of whom must be "accredited," that is, have a net worth of at least $1 million or an annual income of $250,000. In most cases the general partner of the fund receives a fixed management fee plus a percentage (i.e., 20 percent) of all profits over a certain threshold.

Hedge funds are also known for employing exotic portfolio management techniques. Hedging activities of a fund may take the form of shorting stocks or utilizing put options and other derivatives such as financial futures and currency contracts. Many tend to hedge against downturns in the markets being traded. In addition, hedge funds may employ large amounts of financial leverage. For all these reasons, they are generally appropriate only for aggressive and sophisticated investors.

Annuities

What is an annuity?

An *annuity* is a contract between an investor and an insurance or investment company in which the investor makes a lump-sum investment or a series of investments in exchange for a stream of income in the future. Annuities can be set up to provide a guaranteed income for life.

What are the primary types of annuities?

The two primary types of annuities are immediate annuities and tax-deferred annuities. An *immediate annuity* is one in which an initial investment is made and annuity payments start immediately at a fixed interest rate over a period of years, for the life of the annuity owner, or for the life of the owner and another person (joint and survivor annuity), usually the owner's spouse. With immediate annuities, the owner cannot take out the investment as a lump sum, and once the annuitization method of distribution has been chosen, it cannot be changed.

Tax-deferred annuities allow income earned on investments to accumulate free from tax. Taxes on the earnings are paid when they are taken out, not as they are earned. In a deferred annuity, the owner retains control over how the annuity is invested and how and when the annuity proceeds are paid out.

Because of the tax-benefits and increased control, tax-deferred annuities are much more popular than immediate annuities. Within the tax-deferred type of annuity, annuities are further classified as fixed, variable, or indexed, according to the underlying investment structure of the annuity.

Can you tell me a little bit more about tax-deferred annuities?

Tax-deferred annuities allow individuals to accumulate after-tax dollars in accounts that grow tax-deferred until withdrawn. Because the growth of the annuity is not taxed, each year allows for greater potential growth than would be possible if taxes had to be paid on the income each year.

There is no maximum limit on deposits. Withdrawals made before age 59½ may be subject to a 10 percent federal penalty in addition to any income taxes due on the earnings. However, unlike the case with an IRA, you are not required to start making withdrawals at the age of 70½. You can continue compounding the growth for your lifetime. In addition, when you do take out distributions, you are not required to "annuitize" the annuity (i.e., take distributions over your life expectancy). You can take systematic distributions, such as $50,000 per year, that are not tied to your life expectancy, take random distributions as and when you need them, or take the distribution in a lump sum. Most people elect to take systematic distributions or a lump sum.

Beneficiary provisions allow tax-deferred annuities to be transferred at death directly to named beneficiaries.

Can you explain how a fixed annuity works?

With a *fixed annuity,* the investment company guarantees the principal against loss and guarantees a specific rate of return per year or per time period. Earnings accumulate on a tax-deferred basis until withdrawn. Fixed annuities usually pay slightly higher rates than do Treasury bills or CDs.

The interest rate with most fixed annuities will change on a year-to-year basis but is usually guaranteed not to go below a specific rate, such as 3 or 4 percent. Some fixed annuities lock in a fixed rate of return for a 3-, 4-, 5-, or 6-year time span.

What is a variable annuity?

A *variable annuity* has most of the features of a fixed annuity with one major difference: The investor chooses the investments within the annuity, which can be a combination of fixed and variable investments.

While the rate of return on a fixed annuity is guaranteed by the insurance, or investment, company, the rate of return on a variable annuity is based on the success of the investments chosen by the investor. The investor has the right to place money into various subaccounts such as stocks, bonds, balanced portfolios, growth, growth and income, and sector areas (e.g., international, health, financial services, banking, gold, energy, technology). The investor can split the total investment inside the annuity to diversify and balance the risk. Variable annuities are riskier than fixed annuities because there is no guaranteed rate of return. Most variable annuities offer a guarantee of the original investment *only* if the investor dies before taking distributions.

As with the fixed annuity, the investor does not pay taxes on the income or growth until he or she withdraws it.

Can you explain indexed annuities?

Indexed annuities are a cross between fixed annuities and variable annuities. In addition to offering guaranteed principal and usually a small 2 or 3 percent rate of return as a floor, they also offer the investor the ability to participate in the upside potential of an index such as the popular S&P 500.

The investor receives a specific guaranteed rate of return on his or her investment over a short time period, ranging from 1 to 5 years, although it can be longer. If the S&P 500 index is higher at the end of this time period than it was when the annuity began, the investor will receive a certain percentage (60 to 90 percent) of the gain. If the S&P 500 index is lower than it was when the investment started, the investor loses nothing—the indexed annuity guarantees there can be no loss or participation in the downside of the index.

There are numerous types of indexed annuities, but the two most prevalent are point-to-point and year-to-year annuities. A *point-to-point indexed annuity* has the S&P 500 index pricing start on the day of purchase and continue to the termination of the plan. Fluctuations in the S&P 500 index that occur between those two points have no bearing on the rate of return. The return is based only on a comparison between the start date and the termination date.

In a *year-to-year indexed annuity,* the pricing is fixed at the end of each year. The investor receives the value of the greatest upside movement of the S&P 500 index during any 1-year period within the time span of the program. The investor also receives the guaranteed interest rate. There is no loss of principal if the S&P 500 index goes down at any time or throughout the time period the investor has the indexed annuity.

Are there any penalties involved with annuities?

There are generally surrender penalties for cashing out of an annuity early, because of expenses and sales charges that have been incurred by the issuing institution. Therefore, it is important that you remain invested in an annuity between 5 and 7 years to avoid the back-end surrender penalties. An individual wanting to make an investment and then exit at the end of the first, second, or third year is usually not a good candidate for an annuity. However, most companies allow a certain amount to be withdrawn from annuities, usually 10 percent annually, without penalty.

Generally, some part of the payments from an annuity taken before the investor reaches the age of 59½ are subject to a 10 percent penalty tax in addition to the income taxes.

Annuities can be excellent investments, but they are not appropriate for everyone. They should be thoroughly explained by an investor's financial advisors and thoroughly understood by the investor.

INVESTMENT RESEARCH AND RATING SERVICES

Where do I get information on stocks?

The financial section of your local newspaper will include such information as a stock's 52-week high and low prices, dividends, yield, price-earnings ratio, high and low prices for the day, and closing price. You can do research on your own at the library if it subscribes to *Value Line, Standard & Poor's Stock Guides,* or *The Daily Graph,* which are all excellent resources. If you wish to use the Internet, you can find information on stocks at www.dowjones.com, www.money.com, and www.morningstar.com.

Every publicly traded company has some sort of shareholder service department you can call to request that information be mailed to you.

Many companies now have web sites on the Internet that you can visit to obtain or request information.

For more detailed information, you can ask your financial advisor or broker to do some research for you.

What are investment rating agencies for individual stocks?

Investors generally want to know the risks of an investment before buying, and investment rating agencies help to provide this service. The best known are Moody's, Standard and Poor's, A. M. Best, and Duff and Phelps. These agencies carefully investigate the financial condition of a company. They look at outstanding debt, revenue and profit growth, and the state of the general economy, as well as how well other companies in the same industry are doing. Their primary concern is to alert investors to particular risks affecting a company. Whenever you are studying any investment, it is important to remember that previous results do not guarantee future returns.

What are investment rating services for mutual funds?

There are several rating services that are considered the leaders in the United States. Lipper Analytical and Morningstar rate and rank the mutual funds available in the marketplace. They discuss, in great detail, previous results, charges, fees and costs, the history of the company, the portfolio manager and its management makeup, the risk involved, and the goals of the firm. Their data are based on previous results and future projections.

Although rating services are an important source of information for an investor, they should not be the only decision-making tool used in choosing a mutual fund.

How heavily should I rely on a rating system that evaluates stocks or mutual funds?

The most important consideration in using any rating system is that you should understand how the system works. Investors must remember that ratings typically are based on a security's past performance and that past performance is not an indicator of future performance. Further, rating systems can differ dramatically from each other, with one service ranking an investment highly while another rates it poorly.

Even the rating services themselves caution investors not to become overly reliant on their ratings. This is especially true for "star ratings," "honor rolls," and ratings that have single-word characterizations such as "buy," "sell," or "timely." These general statements are usually intended as quick summaries for evaluating a security rather than as the sole criterion for making informed decisions.

I am trying to figure out which mutual funds to buy and am looking at all the reports available. When I read the magazines, it seems that every fund is rated number one. How can this be?

Mutual funds are rated in many ways and over different time periods. You should look at the history of a fund for a long period of time and at its ratings by several rating companies. When comparing funds, make sure the funds are truly comparable. For example, a growth and income fund must be compared to another growth and income fund, not to a capital fund.

How do bond ratings work? And who rates bonds?

Bonds are rated as to quality by bond rating firms, such as Standard and Poor's, Moody's Investors Service, Duff and Phelps, Weiss, and A. M. Best. Table 1-3 lists the ratings used by Moody's and Standard and Poor's (S&P), the two most generally accepted rating firms.

TABLE 1-3 Bond Ratings

S&P*	Moody's*	
	Investment-grade bonds	
AAA	Aaa	Highest quality
AA	Aa	Very high quality
A	A	Good quality
BBB	Baa	Lower quality
	Lower-grade (or "junk") bonds	
BB	Ba	Speculative aspects
B	B	Very risky
CCC	Caa	Having problems
CC	Ca	In serious jeopardy
C	C	Interest stopped
D	C	Defaulted

*We have added the descriptions to give you an idea of how the services describe their ratings, but each rating service has its own opinion of each ranking.

Naturally, the Aaa/AAA-rated bonds are the highest quality. Bonds rated Baa/BBB and above are generally considered investment-grade. Bonds that have significant speculative features are usually in the lowest-rated category. It should be noted that some bonds are unrated because the bond issuers choose not to go through the expense of having their bonds rated.

MANAGED ACCOUNTS

What is a managed brokerage account?

Financial advisory and brokerage firms provide *managed accounts* for clients who want to have a stock or bond account managed on a discretionary basis. With a managed account, you delegate the responsibility for selecting investments to the financial advisor or stockbroker. The professional advisor assists you in establishing an investment policy statement and then will search through hundreds of investments to match your objectives. Stocks, bonds, mutual funds, certificates of deposit, and any other traditional brokerage product can be purchased in the account.

Many private management firms do not accept accounts under $10 million. However, there are also many financial advisory and brokerage firms that have arrangements for accounts to be established for a minimum investment of $250,000.

What are the fees for managed accounts?

A managed account is simply a traditional brokerage account, except that the investor does not pay commissions. A management fee, typically 2 percent for smaller accounts but as low as .5 percent for larger accounts (i.e., over $3 million), is charged by the financial advisor or broker on the value of the account. All transaction costs and money manager, custodian, and advisors' fees are inclusive in one fee.

My financial advisor recommends that I set up an account with a brokerage firm that will hold all my mutual funds and other investments and will manage them for an annual fee. Is this a managed account?

Yes.

TAXATION OF INVESTMENTS

What are tax-advantaged investments?

Investments such as Treasury bonds, bills, and notes, whose interest is subject only to federal income tax, have slight tax advantages. Investments in some real estate, equipment leases, and energy programs provide income tax advantages due to pass-through of depreciation, depletion, and tax-deductible expenses. Tax-deferred annuities, discussed earlier, also fall into the category of tax-advantaged investments.

What are tax-exempt investments?

Tax-exempt investments are investments that generate income that is exempt from federal taxes. Municipal bonds are the most common tax-exempt investments. Municipal bonds issued by your state of residence are also not subject to state income taxes.

Generally, the yield of tax-exempt investments is lower than that of corporate bonds. However, since the income is tax-free, the lower yield of tax-exempt investments for investors with high income is typically greater than the after-tax yield of equivalent taxable investments.

What is tax-efficient investing?

With today's sophisticated computer programs, money managers and financial advisors can now manage individual stock portfolios in a way that takes into account the actual tax situation and the tax implication of every trade for a particular investor. Traditionally, investors and money managers have looked for any losses that could be realized at the end of each year to reduce the investor's tax burden. *Tax-efficient investing* now takes this to a higher level of refinement: Before any trades are done, the computer model makes sure that the after-tax benefit of the trade is positive for the client. This is done by reducing the anticipated benefit of buying a "better" security by the tax cost of selling the "not-so-good" security and then only making the trade if it make sense on an after-tax basis.

Many experts, when attempting to manage a portfolio for tax efficiency, use three strategies:

1. They tend to buy and hold investments, because no tax liability is realized until a sale on an appreciated asset occurs.
2. They maximize the use of capital losses. This strategy requires that the portfolio be monitored for losing positions that can be sold to

capture the capital losses. These losses can then be used to offset any capital gains, thus reducing or eliminating taxes.

3. They hold no-dividend- or low-dividend-paying stocks. Since dividends are taxable as ordinary income, it is more tax-efficient to derive portfolio returns from long-term capital gains than from dividends.

To understand the effect of taxes on investments, consider an investment of $1 doubled every year for 20 years. Without taxes, this investment results in $1,048,576. But if the earnings on that investment are taxed at 35 percent every year, the results are only $22,370.66. Although this is an exaggerated example, it is estimated that the average mutual fund investor loses 3 percent of his or her total return to income taxes. Thus, a $100,000 portfolio that will grow to $964,629 at a 12 percent return over 20 years will grow to only $560,441 if the return is reduced to 9 percent as a result of taxes.

What are tax-deferred investments?

Tax-deferred investments are investments that are structured to defer income and capital gain taxes to some time in the future. If you own an annuity or cash-value life insurance, you own a tax-deferred investment. If you own an IRA or are a participant in an employer-sponsored retirement plan, your investments within the plan are tax-deferred. Your taxes are deferred until you begin taking distributions, which will then be treated as ordinary income for tax purposes.

What is taxable investing?

Any gain, including ordinary or capital, from an investment that is not tax-free, tax-deferred, tax-advantaged, or tax-favored in any way is going to be subject to taxes. The earnings from taxable investments are reported on your 1040 form as taxable income. To find out how much taxable income you have, simply review your most recent tax return.

In a securities transaction, what does "wash sale" mean?

When you sell stock for a loss and then reinvest in substantially identical securities within a 30-day period, the transaction is termed a *wash sale.* A wash sale occurs even when you buy the second block of securities before the sale of the original shares. The wash-sale rule prevents investors from capturing a loss for tax purposes only and then reacquiring the stock.

MODERN PORTFOLIO THEORY

What is modern portfolio theory?

Modern portfolio theory is a basis on which all investors can start constructing an investment portfolio. It uses investment analysis, portfolio design, and performance evaluation to quantitatively express the relationship between risk and investment return. This theory focuses attention on the overall composition of an investor's portfolio rather than the traditional method of analyzing and evaluating the individual components of the portfolio.

Modern portfolio theory is the culmination of years of investment research done by Harry M. Markowitz and others. Markowitz was the first to be credited with compiling and then applying this statistical research to a model that would help construct and evaluate individual investors' investment portfolios. Markowitz found that there is an interaction among the various segments of the market. He discovered that while the different segments of the market move to extremes over short periods, over time returns are remarkably consistent across all segments. For example, over short periods the U.S. large-cap stocks may provide higher returns than small-cap stocks, but over time the returns for both will be consistent.

Markowitz also developed, as part of modern portfolio theory, what is now known as the *efficient frontier.* This theory is grounded on the assumptions that the individual investor is risk-averse and that a diversified portfolio can be constructed that provides maximum utility for an individual investor. So, instead of evaluating each stock or bond in your portfolio, modern portfolio theory would measure your risk tolerance and design a portfolio of various asset classes that can provide an overall return in line with your level of risk tolerance. In theory, this is what every rational investor would prefer to have from his or her portfolio: the highest return relative to the level of risk the investor accepts.

Markowitz later shared in the Nobel Prize for economics as a result of this research and model.

What is the foundation of modern portfolio theory?

The theory has its foundation on four basic premises:

1. *Investors are inherently risk-averse.* Investors are not willing to accept risk except where the level of returns generated will fairly compensate for that risk.

2. *The financial markets are basically efficient.* The nature of efficient markets is such that all participants have the same information regarding the markets in general, and specific issues in particular, at the same time, although they may come to opposite conclusions as to an appropriate price for individual securities.
3. *The focus of attention should shift from individual securities analysis to consideration of portfolios as a whole.* The latter should be based on explicit risk-reward parameters.
4. *Portfolio returns should be optimized relative to portfolio risk.* In other words, for any level of risk that one is willing to accept, there is a rate of return that should be achieved.

What is the efficient frontier?

One of the key assumptions in modern portfolio theory is that all investors are rational. In other words, investors are assumed to expect the optimal return for the risk they accept. Thus a portfolio is considered to be inefficient if it receives less return than the risk it assumes (as measured by standard deviation). Conversely, a portfolio is considered efficient if the return that is realized is commensurate with the risk that is accepted. Such a portfolio is said to be on the *efficient frontier.*

Can you give me an example of this theory?

A good example is shown in Figure 1-2. All portfolios that are on the curved line are said to be efficient. They obtain the highest possible return for the risk they assume. Those that are below the curved line are considered inefficient. They incur more risk relative to the potential return. The portfolios above the curve are said to be nonexistent because a portfolio with high expected return and low risk (as measured by standard deviation) does not exist.

You will note that a portfolio invested entirely in the S&P 500 is off the efficient frontier. On a historical basis, there is a combination of investments that, for the same level of risk, would offer a higher potential rate of return or, for the same anticipated rate of return, would involve less risk.

How do I know if my portfolio is efficient?

Plotting your current portfolio on the efficient frontier is the best way to review and understand whether it is optimal and you are gaining the most utility. Asset classes such as stocks, bonds, real estate, international securities, and the subclasses of each have different risk and return

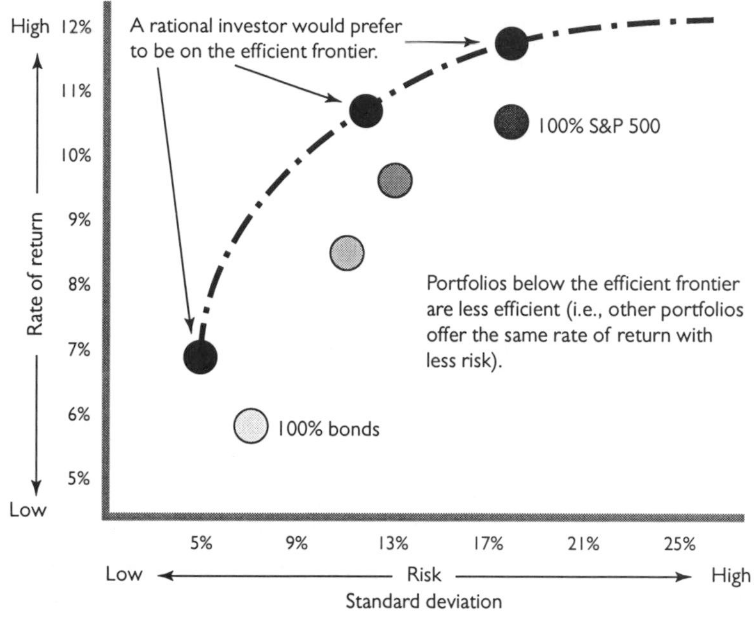

Figure 1-2 Efficient frontier.

profiles. Proper allocation across many asset classes is usually essential to obtain the most efficiency and utility from your investment portfolio. Further, it is important to understand your ability to accept risk: Do you know what the potential for loss is for your current portfolio on an annual basis? If not, how can you know if you're comfortable with it? These are some of the questions you need to ask yourself in order to make your investment portfolio efficient. A portfolio that is in tune with your personal values and financial goals will tend to enable you to sleep better at night.

How do you measure the risk of a portfolio?

The *risk of a portfolio* can be defined as the extent to which the portfolio's returns fluctuate over a given time period. This fluctuation is its *standard deviation.* The higher a portfolio's standard deviation (volatility), the higher its variability of return.

Standard deviation measures the fluctuation in an investment or portfolio both plus and minus around a mean, or average, reference point. By using standard deviation, we can measure expected volatility in an investment portfolio. We begin with the portfolio's mean (average) annual return. The larger the standard deviation number, the more dramatic the possible swings in investment return. Higher volatility is usually associated with higher risk.

Picture a child playing with a yo-yo. Standard deviation measures the length of the yo-yo string and defines the upper and lower limits to which the yo-yo may travel. So if you want a portfolio that is likely to fluctuate only small amounts, you want a smaller standard deviation number (a shorter string on the yo-yo). The optimal picture would be the child playing with the yo-yo while riding up an escalator!

What is Sharpe's ratio?

An asset's (or a portfolio's) standard deviation can be used in a ratio to evaluate different investment strategies and investment vehicles. This ratio is called *Sharpe's ratio,* after William Sharpe, the Stanford University finance professor who developed it. Sharpe's ratio is computed by dividing the asset's mean return, minus a risk-free return (such as a T-bill or bank CD), by the asset's standard deviation. The higher the Sharpe's ratio, the better the trade-off between reward and total risk incurred.

What is meant by "beta coefficient"?

The *beta coefficient* is used to measure how volatile a security is compared to the overall market. The S&P 500 is the usual benchmark, with a beta of 1. If the beta is greater than 1, the price is more volatile than the market; if the beta is less than 1, the price fluctuates less than the market. Generally speaking, the greater the beta, the greater the risk.

For instance, if your investment has a beta of 1.5 and the market is down 10 percent, your investment is probably down 15 percent. Conversely, if the market is up 10 percent, your investment could be up 15 percent.

ASSET ALLOCATION

What is asset allocation?

Asset allocation is the process of identifying and selecting asset classes and determining the proportions of each for a specific investment portfolio. It involves the way in which you weight diverse investments in your portfolio in order to try to meet a specific objective. For example, if your goal is to pursue growth and you're willing to take on market

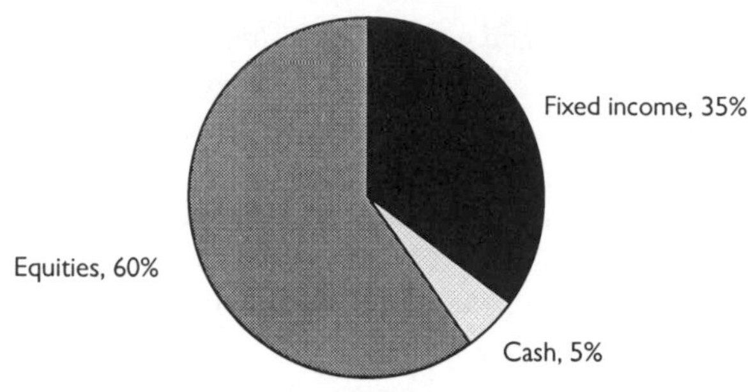

Figure 1-3 Asset allocation.

risk to do so, you may decide to place 35 percent of your assets in fixed-income investments and 60 percent in equity investments, as shown in Figure 1-3.

The asset classes you choose, and how you weight your investment in each, will normally depend on your investment time frame and how it correlates with the risks and rewards of each asset class.

Why is asset allocation so important?

A major landmark in the debate over how money should be managed occurred in 1986 with a study conducted by Brinson, Hood, and Beebower. The study sought to explain the differences among the performance of portfolios on the basis of three criteria:

1. *Asset allocation policy:* What combination of investments among various asset classes should you have within your portfolio?
2. *Security selection:* Which securities should you buy, and which should you sell?
3. *Market timing:* When should you buy, and when should you sell?

The Brinson study concluded that, on average, 93.6 percent of the variance between total returns was attributed to criterion 1—how the assets were allocated. Security selection and market timing, surprisingly, counted for very little of the variance. Brinson's findings, confirmed in a follow-up study done in 1991, have formed the basis for the practice of asset allocation in dealing with investments.

Does asset allocation reduce risk and volatility?

History has shown that different asset classes behave differently at various stages of the economic cycle, in various interest-rate climates, and in relation to each other. Asset allocation is a function of the relationships of each asset class to each other asset class and the proportionality of those assets in the portfolio. In other words, investors should search for assets that tend to have negative relationships to each other and should include assets that go up in value as the value of other assets declines. The number of assets in the portfolio is less important than the relationship among them.

Investors reduce their risk by spreading their dollars across a variety of asset classes to protect against poor performance by any single class. Allocating among several asset classes increases the chance that if the return of one investment is falling, the return of another in the portfolio will be rising (although there are no guarantees).

By combining various asset classes, an optimal portfolio can be achieved that provides returns that are somewhat predictable, and possibly greater, over an extended period of time with less volatility than would occur with only one asset class.

What does the process of asset allocation involve?

While sophisticated statistical analysis and historical performance are used to model future returns at various levels of probability, asset allocation can be simplified to a four-step process:

1. Determine your investment objectives, taking into account your risk tolerance, time horizon, tax status, and need for liquidity.
2. On the basis of your objectives, select asset classes that may help you reach those objectives. Remember that the selection of asset classes can be the greatest single determinant of future performance.
3. Determine the appropriate allocation balance among the classes (or the "weight" of each asset class in your portfolio).
4. Rebalance (reallocate) your portfolio on a regular basis. This is a natural way of buying low and selling high.

ASSET DIVERSIFICATION

What is diversification in a portfolio?

Diversification is the process of investing in several different types of assets within an asset class, such as several different mutual funds and securities. An example of a diversified portfolio is shown in Figure 1-4.

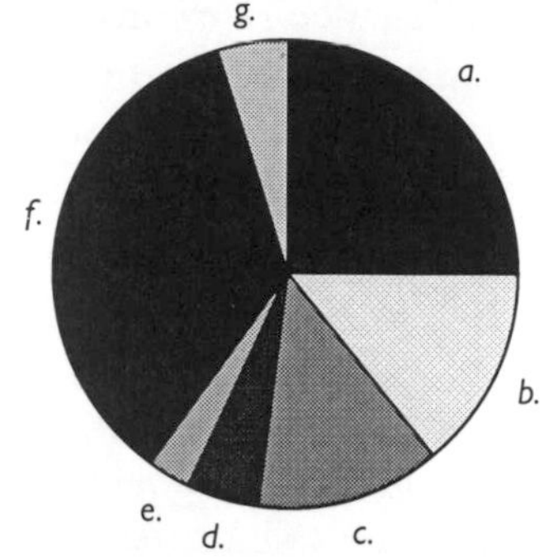

Figure 1-4 Asset diversification: equity class.

How does asset allocation differ from asset diversification?

Asset allocation refers to the selection of, and percentage of dollars allocated to, the *various asset classes* (fixed-income, equity, etc.) within an investment portfolio, as shown in Figure 1-3.

Diversification involves having several different investments within a *particular asset class.* In Figure 1-4, where we diversified among various types of stock and mutual fund investments within the equity class, we invested in only one type of bond. Had we diversified within the fixed-income asset class, we would have invested in bonds of several issuers or in a mutual fund that holds several different bond issues.

Does diversification decrease risk?

The basic purpose of diversification is to reduce your risk of loss. It is primarily a defensive type of investment policy. When you diversify your investments among more than one security, you help reduce what is known as *single-security risk,* or the risk that your investment will fluctuate widely in value with the price of one holding. For example, if you invested in two mutual funds that are both invested in large-cap stocks, both funds would tend to zig and zag at the same time. Ideally, you would want one fund to zig when the other zags to smooth out the investment performance.

A well-diversified portfolio may be capable of weathering varying economic cycles and improving the trade-off between risk of loss and expected return. Of course, diversification cannot eliminate the risk of investment losses.

Why are correlation coefficients important in diversification?

Correlation coefficients simply tell you how closely related one asset is to another asset. It is possible for the majority of your assets to correlate positively. Positive correlation generally means less diversification and more risk. That is why diversifying among several different investments within the asset classes makes sense.

International assets, for instance, usually do not correlate with U.S.-based assets over time. They have a degree of negative correlation in relation to similar assets in the United States. Individuals can actually lower the risk inherent in their portfolios by investing a portion of their assets overseas.

By understanding the correlation of each asset in your portfolio, you gain the potential to diversify risk to a much greater extent.

ASSET REBALANCING

What is asset rebalancing?

Asset rebalancing is the periodic exchange of one asset class for another to keep a portfolio's investment allocation in line with the target percentages set for each asset class. Rebalancing might be needed when one asset class outperforms or underperforms another and thus changes the desired percentage for each asset class in the portfolio.

Rebalancing a portfolio is important for two reasons. First, the portfolio remains compatible with the investor's time horizon and level of risk tolerance. Second, by selling assets that are commanding a premium and buying assets that are selling at a discount, the investor is systematically buying low and selling high.

Can you give me an example of portfolio rebalancing?

Let's assume the portfolio shown in Figure 1-3 is valued at $100,000. Our investor's asset allocation policy calls for 60 percent equity investments, 35 percent fixed-income investments, and 5 percent cash. This equates to an allocation of $60,000 in stocks, $35,000 in bonds, and $5000 in cash. Suppose that over a period of time, stocks rise 50 percent in value; bonds, 20 percent in value; and cash, 5 percent in value. The portfolio now has 65 percent allocated to equity investments, 30 percent to fixed-income investments, and 4 percent to cash (see Table 1-4).

TABLE 1-4 Effect of Investment Gains on Asset Allocation

Asset class	Beginning balance	Investment gain	Ending balance
Equity	$ 60,000 (60%)	$30,000	$ 90,000 (65%)
Fixed-income	35,000 (35%)	7,000	42,000 (30%)
Cash	5,000 (5%)	250	5,250 (4%)
Total	$100,000	$37,250	$137,250

With 65 percent of the assets invested in equity instead of the target 60 percent, the portfolio is said to be out of balance from its targeted asset allocation. In practical terms, this increase in stock holdings has raised the portfolio's risk level from that which is acceptable to the investor. The investor can rebalance the portfolio back to target by selling stocks to buy bonds; by directing new savings to bonds; or by directing future cash flows (e.g., interest, dividends, or future investments) to bonds.

Is there a computer program for rebalancing one's portfolio?

Computer programs are commonly used to rebalance portfolios. Figure 1-5 is an example of a computer-generated rebalancing report.

How does rebalancing a portfolio equate to buying low and selling high?

Let's assume that, on the basis of your risk-to-reward profile, your portfolio was originally designed with 60 percent stocks and 40 percent bonds. At the end of 1 year, stocks have outperformed bonds such that your portfolio is now 75 percent stocks and 25 percent bonds. As part of the rebalancing process, enough stock must be sold to bring the portfolio back into balance at 60/40. In other words, the high performing stocks must be sold and the lower performing bonds must be bought. Essentially, this is selling when stocks are high and buying when bonds are low. Naturally, the opposite would be done if stock prices had plummeted.

How often should I rebalance my portfolio?

A rule of thumb for rebalancing is to do so at least annually but no more than quarterly. Typically, professional advisors will set fluctuation

ASSET ALLOCATION REBALANCING for John and Jane Gardner				
Investment	**Initial Allocation**	**Current Account Value**	**Current Allocation**	**Required Account Rebalancing**
Aggressive Growth	*12.00%*		*11.6%*	
1 Fund "A"	3.00%	$29,164	2.57%	$4,856
2 Fund "B"	3.00%	$30,776	2.71%	$3,244
3 Fund "C"	3.00%	$35,844	3.16%	($1,824)
4 Fund "D"	3.00%	$35,749	3.15%	($1,729)
5			0.00%	$0
Growth	*36.00%*		*36.84%*	
6 Fund "E"	12.00%	$132,604	11.69%	$3,477
7 Fund "F"	12.00%	$138,371	12.20%	($2,290)
8 Fund "G"	12.00%	$146,813	12.95%	($10,732)
9			0.00%	$0
10			0.00%	$0
Income	*33.50%*		*33.90%*	
11 Fund "H"	15.00%	$175,331	15.46%	($5,229)
12 Fund "I"	15.00%	$175,093	15.44%	($4,991)
13 Fund "J"	3.50%	$34,004	3.00%	$5,686
14			0.00%	$0
15			0.00%	$0
Safety of Principal	*18.50%*		*17.66%*	
16 Fund "K"	15.00%	$186,145	16.41%	($16,043)
17 Money Market	3.50%	$14,118	1.24%	$25,572
18			0.00%	$0
19			0.00%	$0
20			0.00%	$0
Totals	100.00%	**$1,134,012**	100.00%	(0%)

Figure 1-5 Typical rebalancing report.

tolerances for clients. For example, on a quarterly basis, an asset class might be allowed to deviate from the target by as much as plus or minus 10 percent; on an annual basis, a tighter plus or minus 5 percent. Also, a portfolio should be rebalanced when there is a change in the investor's lifestyle. For example, as you approach retirement age, your risk propensity might be lower, requiring a restatement of the investment policy and a rebalancing of the portfolio to reflect these changes.

chapter 2

Investment Planning

THE INVESTMENT PLANNING PROCESS

What is investment planning?

Investment planning is a process that helps you systematically build and implement a sound investment plan. It has seven levels and is often depicted as a pyramid (see Figure 2-1).

1. *Objectives:* In establishing objectives, you define why you are investing and where you want your investment plan to lead.
2. *Risk tolerance:* At this level, you define your defensive posturing to protect your plan from the uncontrollable risks that investing creates. Your financial advisor will work with you to identify your tolerance to all the risks involved in investing.
3. *Buying policy:* You must develop a dominant buying policy. This policy will drive and direct the type of investments that you or your advisors buy into and sell out of your portfolio.
4. *Asset allocation policy:* Your asset allocation policy is developed in conjunction with your buying policy. It determines the categories of assets in which you will invest to meet your investment goals while staying within your risk tolerance.
5. *Management policy:* Your management policy outlines the expectations you have about, and the interaction you expect to have with,

Figure 2-1 Investment planning pyramid.

the professionals who are acting on your behalf throughout the investment process.

6. *Taxation:* It is prudent to include a taxation level of control within your plan. This level requires that you and your advisors address the obvious tax ramifications and effects that your investment earnings can have on your overall financial situation. The impact of taxation can be controlled and minimized with proper design of your portfolio and comprehensive asset management.
7. *Asset selection:* At the final level of your investment pyramid, you select the assets that will constitute your investment portfolio. Although many investors begin the planning process by selecting the assets they would like to purchase, this is often misguided. In reality, the selection of the securities that will compile a portfolio is not the foundation but the capstone of a well-designed and -implemented investment plan.

What is the key to a successful investment program?

Investing without objectives can be very difficult, haphazard, and dangerous. The key to a successful investment program is to develop (1) your financial goals and objectives, then (2) the overall financial plan to achieve those goals with economic security, and then (3) an investment plan within the context of your financial plan.

Having concrete financial goals is the foundation for planning your financial future. Your investment plan is the implementation of buying and investing strategies that will help fulfill your financial plan. Rather than thinking about financial planning as a one-time activity, think of it as a process or a series of steps that will lead to the attainment of your financial goals.

An investment program may encompass different investment vehicles, each with its own risk and reward characteristics. Successful investment plans employ various strategies designed to either increase the rate of return on the investment or reduce its risk. Self-assessment and the use of a monitoring system that incorporates periodic evaluation in light of changing market conditions complete the process.

Why is an investment strategy important?

Every serious endeavor should begin with a strategy or plan aimed at getting you to your chosen goal. A *strategy* focuses our attention and energies on those actions that systematically move us closer to our financial objectives, and it helps us tune out the many distractions that dissipate that attention and energy.

Strategy is critical in warfare, in business management, and, yes, in investment planning. The investor who lacks a strategy reacts with undifferentiated attention to every unanticipated event; before long, he or she is going everywhere, but not anywhere in particular.

What are the elements of an investment strategy?

An investment strategy is dependent upon three key elements:

1. An identifiable goal
2. A method to attain that goal
3. The competencies and resources to sustain the strategy

The investment strategy must operate within the framework of the client's investment policy (discussed later in this chapter) and must always be its servant.

What is the monitoring step?

The financial advisor monitors the performance of investments, changes in the tax law, and the general economic environment and keeps the client posted through periodic meetings. These meetings should be two-way exchanges of information: the investment professional reports facts and insights relative to the client's investment program; at the same time, the investment professional attempts to determine if any material changes have taken place in the client's financial situation, investment outlook, or attitude toward risk. This dialog, in effect, provides the feedback loop to the initial steps of the investment management process.

Financial Profile and Investment Personality

How do I most effectively work with my financial advisor to set my investment goals?

Your financial advisor must be thoroughly acquainted with your personality, your health, and your family situation, including your dependents, any special needs, the income that is needed from the portfolio, income from outside sources, and your marginal income tax rate.

Your investment constraints should be addressed. These may include industries or companies in which you do not want to invest, such as tobacco or liquor; liquidity and the need for it now and in the future; and legal constraints, such as the legal form of the investing entity (is it a trust, an irrevocable trust, a charitable trust?). Your time horizon must be discussed, not only in terms of your age or life expectancy but also in terms of the legal entity.

Typical investment objectives include financial independence, retirement, college education funding, purchase of a new car or home, improved lifestyle, and tax reduction.

You and your advisor should collaborate to put in writing the factors that make up your entire financial picture. From this information gathering come the factors that are important to you, such as your objectives, your return expectations, your risk preferences, and the real and perceived level of your wealth.

What data does my financial advisor need?

Table 2-1 summarizes the data desired by your advisor.

Gathering data from the client face-to-face not only fulfills the advisor's requirement for obtaining relevant information but also serves as an important interpersonal function between client and advisor.

What is a person's investment personality?

Two important forces affect how most of us live: actual income and the income needed to maintain our normal lifestyle. Each individual responds to these forces in unique ways, and the manner of the responses is associated with what we describe as the person's *investment personality.* This is a combination of personality characteristics that determine how

TABLE 2-1 Client Data for Financial Advisors

Family and dependent data	Important time horizons
Names, addresses, and telephone numbers	Anticipated educational, gift, or other financial requirements
Assets, liabilities, and net worth	Client and family health status
Income data	Interest and hobbies
Insurance coverages	Risk tolerance
Employee financial benefits, including stock options	Occupation and future employment expectations
Personal and, if appropriate, company tax returns	Investment experience, holdings, and outlook
Anticipated changes in lifestyle	Estate planning
Retirement planning data	Financial goals
Client-owned business information	

Source: Adapted from College for Financial Planning, *CFP Financial Planning Process and Insurance* (1994).

an individual deals with money and its investment. The investment community typically defines investment personality in terms of the investor's tolerance to risk.

What is the significance of risk tolerance in investment planning?

Risk tolerance, also referred to as *risk propensity,* is the maximum level of overall risk or volatility an investor can withstand before it becomes mentally and emotionally painful. It plays a major role in investment planning. The total risk of the portfolio should not exceed the comfort level of the investor.

What are some types of investment risk?

Investment risk means different things to different investors. Some of the more common types of risk are:

- *Market risk:* the rise and fall of securities markets
- *Interest-rate risk:* the rise and fall of interest rates
- *Inflation risk:* changes in the real value of assets and investment returns
- *Reinvestment risk:* the reinvestment of future cash flows

- *Credit risk:* the default risk of the underlying companies
- *Currency risk:* changes in the rate of foreign exchange relative to the U.S. dollar
- *Common factor risk:* risks inherent in securities of similar character, such as large-cap stocks, low-P/E stocks, and international stocks

What questions must I answer to determine my investment personality?

While the following questions do not exhaust all the possibilities, they certainly show the primary issues:

- To what extent are you willing and able to take risk? If you are risk-averse, you are fearful of losing what you have acquired in the past. If you are a bold investor, you are more fearful of losing an opportunity for sizable gain in the future.
- How patient are you? Do you think in terms of decades, years, months, or weeks? Are you sufficiently patient to allow time to become an ally?
- To what extent do you actually plan personal and financial business?
- Are you guarded or open with personal financial information?
- Are you a contrarian (one who buys investments that are out of favor and sells popular investments) or a follower?

Only after you answer these questions can you and your financial advisor develop a meaningful dialog.

Investment Policy Statement

Once my financial advisor and I have determined my investment personality, what then?

Your investment personality leads to the *investment policy statement (IPS),* in which your investment planning objectives are translated into a portfolio strategy. The IPS states the fundamental goals and objectives regarding how you want to invest your funds and states how those goals and objectives will be achieved.

The major reasons for developing an IPS are to foster clear communication between you and your investment advisor and to enable you and your advisor to protect the portfolio from ad hoc revisions to your long-term goals should short-term conditions become distressing and cause you to start second-guessing your policy.

What specific issues should be addressed in my IPS?

At a minimum your IPS should provide for:

- *Investment objectives,* including your rate-of-return objectives, risk tolerance, time horizon or investment holding period, income needs, and economic assumptions.
- *Asset allocation plan,* including primarily asset class preferences and the total percentage of the portfolio that can be allocated to a given asset class. Asset classes will include large cap, small cap, international, bonds, and cash, but these classes can be expanded to include more or to be more specific.
- *Guidelines for choice of assets,* allowing you to specifically exclude a type of stock or a specific stock from the portfolio.
- *Process for selecting funds and/or fund managers,* including the minimum requirements for being included for consideration.
- *Investment expectations,* outlining rate-of-return expectations within the context of factors such as inflation, taxes, power of compounding, risk-return trade-off, and diversification.
- *Review procedures:* establishing how performance will be reported, what benchmarks will be used for measurement, and the frequency of meetings.

In what ways does an IPS address risk?

An IPS must state asset allocation targets, boundaries, and diversification limits, as well as which types and what amounts of risk are appropriate for the client. The investment advisor's responsibility is then to maximize returns within the limits of risk set by the investment policy statement.

We will never know the future. The IPS addresses this fact by defining the parameters of risk taking that satisfy the client's needs and risk tolerances while providing the investment advisor with a road map for implementing investment strategy. The more an investment advisor matches an understanding of a client's specific requirements with an understanding of the capital markets, the greater the service to the client. No other single task of a financial advisor adds more value.

How should a financial advisor present investment recommendations?

Within the scope of the IPS, the investment professional must recommend a course of action to the client. At least one course of action should be recommended for each goal of the client.

The advisor should be careful not to overwhelm the client with multiple problems and solutions because, in the end, the client makes the final investment decisions. The investment professional's role is to use his or her superior knowledge of investment products to make recommendations and then implement decisions made by the client.

Could you give me an example of an IPS?

Figure 2-2 shows a sample investment policy statement for Donald and Emily Smith by their financial advisor, Ima Planner, after she determined Don and Emily's financial situation, goals, and other relevant criteria. Keep in mind, however, that investment policy statements may differ in format and approach from one advisor to another, and they will differ for each client on the basis of his or her specific goals.

INVESTMENT STRATEGIES

Overall Strategies

What are some commonly used investment strategies?

- *Buy-and-hold strategy:* This is the benchmark strategy. It is a passive investment strategy that calls for the investor to make an asset purchase and leave the asset alone over long periods of time.
- *Timing strategies:* This strategy attempts to improve market returns by strategically timing transactions to coincide with favorable pricing events taking place in the market.
- *Contrarian strategy:* In this strategy, investments that are out of favor are bought and popular investments are sold.
- *Value investing strategy:* This is a method of selecting stocks that are low-priced relative to empirical measures of earnings, sales, net current assets, and book value.
- *Growth stock investing strategy:* Here, the strategy is to find and purchase shares in corporations whose sales and profits are expanding at a faster rate than the overall economy.

What are the mistakes most commonly made by investors?

Although no single list of mistakes made by investors would ever be

INVESTMENT POLICY STATEMENT
Prepared for Donald and Emily Smith
by Ima Planner

1. Statement of Purpose

This policy statement is established to provide a clear understanding between advisor and clients regarding clients' objectives, goals, and guidelines and the assets placed under advisor's responsibility.

This statement shall:

- Give advisor an understanding of the investment direction that clients believe is most appropriate and prudent in consideration of their future financial needs.
- Establish the criteria to which advisor is expected to adhere in the active management of clients' personal assets.
- Communicate the performance standards advisor is expected to achieve.
- Serve as a review document to guide clients' ongoing determination of advisor's progress in meeting their investment objectives.

2. Investment Objectives

The primary investment objective of the assets placed under management is to provide for the growth of capital wealth.

Secondly, these assets are to be managed to maintain preservation of purchasing power on a consistent long-term basis.

The overall investment direction is to achieve capital appreciation during favorable markets and preservation of capital during poor market conditions.

3. Investment Expectations

Based on the investment objectives stated above, clients' primary long-term goal is to earn an annual total investment return of 9.0 percent. The secondary goal is to exceed by 3.0 percent on an annualized basis the rate of inflation measured by the Consumer Price Index.

These expectations are important to clients' objectives and should be achieved over any 3- to 5-year period.

If the return objective is not achieved over a particular measurement period, the shortfall should be explainable in terms of general economic and financial market conditions. A temporary shortfall will not necessarily indicate failure to achieve the long-term objectives.

- 1 -

4. Taxes

This portfolio is a nonqualified, or a fully taxable, portfolio. This means that all dividends or capitals gains received will be taxable in the year that they are incurred and subject to the applicable federal and state government tax rates.

In addition, and as clients are aware, some of the original assets were acquired years ago, and the repositioning of these assets is likely to induce a taxable event.

In combination with advisor's focus to increase the efficiency and appreciation of clients' investment portfolio, it is also advisor's intention to limit the portfolio's capital gain exposure. Therefore, the initial strategy will be to direct all dividends and capital gains paid by the individual mutual funds to cash. advisor believes this will help to give flexibility to future balancing and reallocation strategies by supplying some liquid assets for this purpose. Clearly and initially some gains may need to be taken in order to begin to align the portfolio with clients' risk profile. Unless otherwise requested by clients, for capital gain tax purposes, advisor may attempt to implement the reallocation strategy over more than one tax year.

5. Risk Tolerance

In simple terms, clients need to have investments in the stock and fixed-income securities markets and those investments *will* lose money when the markets go down—and these markets *will* go down. For example, equity markets almost always rise and fall with the business cycle.

In establishing clients' risk tolerance, advisor has considered clients' ability to withstand short-, intermediate-, and long-term volatility. Based on our discussions and clients' answers to the risk-tolerance questionnaire, advisor understands that clients can accept a moderate volatility portfolio. advisor's recommendation is to increase clients' current exposure to portfolio volatility (as measured by standard deviation) and allocate clients' current portfolio assets accordingly. Through repositioning clients' current assets into a broader group of asset classes, it is advisor's goal to align clients' investments with their risk tolerance and give clients' portfolio the potential for increased efficiency.

6. Investment Guidelines

Asset Mix

Clients request the use of a balanced investment approach to portfolio management to best meet their needs.

- 2-

Figure 2-2 Sample investment policy statement.

Specifically, clients require that their account conform to the following asset allocation guidelines:

- Clients' long-term asset allocation is 50 percent equities and 50 percent fixed income. clients believe it should be the function of the advisor to allocate assets among equity and fixed-income securities given the parameters stated below. These percentages will be based on the market value of investments.

	Allowable Range	
	Min	Max
Equity (including convertible securities)	30%	70%
Fixed Income (including cash equivalents)	30%	70%

It is clients' desire that the investments in the portfolio be prudently diversified to moderate risk, but not be so excessive to preclude attainment of optimal results.

Permissible Investments

The assets under the advisor's responsibility shall be invested in a manner that is consistent with generally accepted standards of fiduciary responsibility. The safeguards that would guide a prudent person shall be observed. All transactions undertaken on clients' behalf shall be for their sole benefit.

The following security classifications are permissible and suitable investments for the purpose of managing clients' assets:

- Equity securities: Plan assets may be invested in publicly traded common and preferred stocks, convertible preferred stocks, and convertible debentures. Investments may be chosen from the NYSE, regional exchanges, and the national over-the-counter market (NASDQ). All assets must have a readily ascertainable market value and be easily marketable.
- Debt securities are to be obligations of the U.S. government or agencies of the U.S. government, or corporate obligations rated A or higher by Standard & Poor's or a similar rating agency. Securities not meeting these requirements shall be purchased only with express permission of the clients.
- Cash reserves should be invested in interest-bearing securities, free from risk of loss and price fluctuation; they should be instantly saleable. Cash reserves shall consist of individual fixed-income securities such as certificates of deposit, commercial paper, U.S. Treasury bills, and other similar instruments with less than one year to maturity and/or money market funds.

- Other securities are permissible only with prior written approval of the clients.

Nonpermitted Investment Transactions

The advisor may not concentrate more than 10 percent of the portfolio in any security or issue other than obligations of the U.S. government or agencies of the U.S. government, or money market instruments described above. The cost basis of securities purchased will be used to determine the adherence to this policy.

7. Investment review

Portfolio Measurement Standards

Clients intend to review the performance of the assets managed by the advisor relative to their stated objectives and guidelines in the investment policy statement.

- Reports: Monthly reports shall include a complete list of assets, including the cost and current value of each security, estimated annual income or dividend yield, and security industry classifications.
- Investment advisor meetings: The advisor is expected to meet at least no less than on a quarterly basis with the clients to review the portfolio and investment results in the context of this investment policy statement along with the economic outlook, investment strategy, and other pertinent matters affecting the assets. The advisor is expected to communicate more frequently than quarterly as the advisor or we deem necessary.
- Notification: Clients require notification by the advisor within 30 days of key personnel changes, a material change in responsibilities, company ownership, or any other material change in the nature of the principal business activities of the advisor's company.

8. Review and Modification of Investment Policy Statement

Clients shall review this investment policy statement at least once a year to determine if it remains applicable in all respects.

Figure 2-2 Sample IPS, *continued.*

complete, it is possible to identify some of the more common mistakes to avoid:

1. *Thinking short term:* Investors intuitively know that they should think long term; however, most are motivated by emotion, based on short-term factors.
2. *Buying on impulse:* Investors too often shoot from the hip and have no general investment strategy in place.
3. *Moving assets too frequently:* Too often decisions are made on the basis of cocktail party conversations, articles in the financial press, or hot tips. Later, most investors regret those ill conceived decisions. Generally, adhering to a reasonable buy-and-hold strategy is often a better approach for all but the most sophisticated investors.
4. *Failing to successfully plan for taxes:* Consider an investment of $1 doubled every year for 20 years. Before taxes, the investment results in over $1 million; after the earnings are taxed every year at 35 percent, it yields approximately $22,370. This is strong evidence of why the tax ramifications on an investment strategy should be carefully monitored.
5. *Not utilizing professional management:* Notwithstanding the rise of Internet trading and no-load mutual funds, most investors lack the knowledge, time, and experience necessary to achieve optimal long-term investment results. It is not unusual for many people to become too emotionally involved with their investments, a situation that may result in poor decision making.
6. *Buying yesterday's winners:* It is a common tendency among investors to want to own stocks and mutual funds that have recently posted high returns. In many cases, investors find that they are disappointed by the returns they subsequently earn. Simply put, past performance is often a poor guide to making investment decisions.
7. *Not using asset allocation:* Most investors invest everything in one asset class. If the market in that class should fall, their entire portfolio return can be negatively affected.

John Bogle, founder of Vanguard Funds, stated that "successful investing involves doing just a few things right and avoiding serious mistakes."

My financial advisor projects rates of return at no more than 12 percent and mostly at 8 to 10 percent. Since the stock market has grown more than 20 percent every year for the last 4 years, why does he not use higher projections?

Since no one can predict the future with certainty, financial planners often rely on historical data in forecasting returns for planning purposes. Because equity market returns have been unusually high in recent years, many planners are uncomfortable using those returns for estimating the future. Most subscribe to the adage that because markets "regress to the mean" over time, future returns may be substantially lower than what the recent past would suggest. Furthermore, since the future is inherently unknowable, most clients would prefer to base their financial planning on a more conservative scenario rather than on optimistic forecasts that overstate the future.

I've seen ads guaranteeing 20 to 30 percent returns annually. Is that realistic?

If someone tells you he or she can guarantee earnings of 20 to 30 percent per year on your investments, be very careful—in fact, walk the other way. Odds are the person is misleading you. If an investment opportunity sounds too good to be true, it probably is. Although human nature tends to push us toward trying to get rich quick, that approach is usually a recipe for investment disaster. Patience and experienced advisors greatly increase your chances of investment success.

Is the Internet a good resource for investment information?

The Internet can be a very powerful resource. There are currently more than 40 million people using the Internet, with projections estimating 500 million users within the next few years. The Internet has helped democratize the investment process by providing widespread access to even the most specialized information, thus leveling the playing field for individual investors.

Since the technology is still in its infancy, the Internet has its own set of growing pains. Because its ultimate potential is still unknown, many of its dangers are only beginning to surface. This ultimately creates a dilemma for the regulatory agencies that protect investors. Agencies such as the NASD and SEC will aggressively pursue securities fraud or stock manipulation, but it would be an impossible logistical task to monitor every investment-related posting on thousands of chat rooms, bulletin boards, news groups, and home pages.

The Internet, like any other investment tool, must be used wisely. While most individuals have honest intentions and use the Internet as a legitimate investment tool, some may seek to distribute information and advice in order to manipulate prices or take advantage of unsuspecting investors. The general rule should be to never make an investment decision solely on sthe basis of what you read on-line. Even if motives are honest, there are no guarantees that the information is accurate or the advice is sound.

The real-time nature of the Internet, combined with its growing base of users, makes it a prime target for stock touting and bashing. Be leery of the gossip and unsubstantiated rumors that often infest these on-line sites. There is no substitute for your own detailed research via a variety of media sources. Any information you find on the Internet should be double-checked and verified. Furthermore, it is always a good idea to check with a brokerage firm, an accountant, or a trusted business advisor to get a second or third opinion about an investment.

Can you offer some tips on using the Internet wisely for investment information?

Here are six tips to help you be a smart Internet user:

1. *Be your own watchdog.* The Internet is vast, and resources are unlimited. Regulators can't keep an eye on every corner and crevice.
2. *Question all advice.* If you don't know the source of information or the motive behind the source, as is often the case on the Internet, challenge the validity of the information.
3. *Measure twice and cut once.* Never make an investment decision solely based upon what you read on the Internet. Always consult other resources.
4. *Do your own homework.* Although the Internet opens up access to a variety of new information sources, there is no substitute for your own detailed research.
5. *Use good judgment; better yet, use common sense.* Every investment has risks. As the saying goes, "If something seems too good to be true, then chances are, it probably is." This may be just a cliche, but it's right on the money.
6. *Call on the experts.* If you suspect something is shady, trust your instincts. Notify the regulators before you act.

How can I protect myself from an investment scam or a fraudulent investment?

The following tip-offs can alert you to investment frauds or scams:

1. High-pressure sales tactics
2. The need for immediate action ("Act now or you'll lose the investment.")
3. Promises that sound too good to be true
4. The promise of risk-free investments (No investment is totally risk-free.)
5. No written information or inaccurate information
6. Requests for your credit card or checking account number over the phone
7. An offer to pick up your money at your house, sometimes utilizing couriers
8. An offer of a free gift or trip

These are some of the basic warning signals, but the list is not inclusive. The best protection is to use common sense and always to research the idea thoroughly, using more than one source, before making a decision.

Cash Management Strategies

How do I begin to save for investing?

Creating wealth is largely a result of forming good habits and understanding that only assets create wealth. The simple truth is that if you form good habits and deal with your financial needs rather than purchasing unneeded luxuries, you will build wealth.

Wealth building is a matter of being aware of your income and expenses. Start by determining your monthly income and expenses. Are you saving each month, or does your "out-go" exceed your income? Assuming you can save, start saving at least 10 percent of your before-tax income. This will help you create an emergency fund.

Once your emergency account is funded, the next dollars should be directed at building your wealth on the basis of your personal financial goals.

Should I have a safety reserve? If so, how much should it be?

Yes, it is important to set up and maintain a safety reserve, which is essentially cash on hand for emergencies or unforeseen circumstances. The amount that should be set aside is based entirely on one's personal situation. A rule of thumb is to have 3 to 6 months' living expenses available in cash.

Do I really need that much money in my safety reserve?

Having an emergency or reserve account of 3 to 5 months' expenses is a rule of thumb, but it may not be appropriate for everyone. The exact amount that is necessary for you may be different because of your income level, job certainty, health insurance coverage, and short- and long-term disability benefits through your current employer.

Let's assume that job security is not an issue and you have adequate short-and long-term disability coverage at work. Let's further assume that you earn $100,000 and, after savings and taxes, your net cash flow to your family is $75,000. So 3 to 6 months' living expenses will be between $18,750 to $37,500. This is a very large sum to keep in cash.

Another way of establishing a safety reserve is to have short-term, medium-term, and long-term investments. Consider the last time you had an emergency that required you to come up with $5000, $10,000, or even $15,000. Typically, most emergencies involve less than $2000. For any expenses over that amount, you usually have 3 to 7 working days before the money is actually required. In that case, any dollars that you have invested for the short term can be used, and medium-term investments can be turned into cash. For the most part, accessibility to funds is more important than how much you have in a cash reserve.

What other emergency funding strategies might I use?

Occasionally, even with the best-thought-out plans, temporary difficulties arise that require additional cash immediately. One of the best sources of emergency funds is a *home equity line of credit.* This type of loan offers several advantages. A homeowner can often get a line of credit equal to 70 or 80 percent of the home's market value. In addition, any interest paid on the loan may be tax-deductible, assuming the homeowner itemizes deductions. A home equity line of credit does not necessarily come without its costs. One must ensure that the closing costs, interest rates, and terms of the loan are reasonable. It pays to shop around to find the best terms for your particular need.

Another source of cash is the *accumulated cash value of a life insurance policy.* Loans from life insurance policies issued before June 20, 1988, are completely tax-free, and those issued after that date are tax-free provided the contract is not a modified endowment contract (MEC). Another source of funds is a *loan from a company retirement plan,* such as a 401(k) plan, where allowed, although this does have drawbacks.

Should I prepay my mortgage or invest in the market instead?

This decision is an intensely personal one, and one that only you, not your advisor, can make. However, there are two fundamental questions you need to ask yourself: Do you think the return on your investments will exceed the money you could save by paying down the mortgage, and is that return worth the risk?

One option is to refinance your mortgage at a lower rate than that of your current mortgage and use the savings to invest in the market.

Before making your decision, you may wish to seek the advice of a qualified investment advisor who can help you determine what the risks and rewards are.

Should I use the equity I have in my home to invest in the market?

This is an extremely aggressive investment philosophy. If, like most Americans, you want to be debt-free when you retire, refinancing your home will affect that goal.

It is easy to create a scenario in which you refinanced and invested the money in an index fund averaging 30 percent a year from 1995 to 1998. But consider the results if you had refinanced at the end of 1991. The market had been up 31 percent the year before, but for the next 3 years it averaged only 6.6 percent a year. If the interest rate on your mortgage was higher than 6.6 percent during that period, the strategy would not have worked. And what if the investments you purchased with the funds lost money at the same time?

If you're even thinking of refinancing your home to invest in the market, consider these points first:

- Don't create a larger mortgage payment than you can afford from your existing cash flow.
- "Dead" equity isn't really so dead. You don't have to worry about losing part of it if it stays in your home.

I'd like to have a larger cash reserve but also want to earn a better rate of return. What would you suggest?

You may want to "ladder" your cash reserve. First, determine how much you would like to keep as a cash reserve. Then determine how much of the reserve you would like to keep in a very liquid position. Invest that amount in a money market account or a savings account. The balance of your cash reserve should be divided equally into four CDs with maturities of 6, 12, 18, and 24 months. The longer the maturity date of a CD, the higher the interest rate paid.

By keeping part of your cash reserve very liquid and laddering the remainder, you have actually created two separate cash reserves that help maximize your rate of return. If an emergency arises, the first dollars spent will come from the money market or savings account. Thereafter, a CD will mature every 6 months, allowing you to have a constant flow of cash if you need extra money.

If you do not need the money when a CD matures, you can simply renew the CD for a longer time. For example, when a 6-month certificate is due, you would renew it not for 6 months but for 24 months, since the 12-month certificate is now due in 6 months, the 18-month in 12 months, and the 24-month in 18 months. You would continue this cycle for as long as you want to keep a cash reserve.

Market Risk Reduction Strategies

How do I manage the risks in my investment portfolio?

While there are many responses to this question, here are three solid strategies that should keep you in mental control when markets overheat—as they inevitably will:

1. *Focus on your long-term goal.* If your goal is 10 years or more in the future, you are in a good position to downplay the market fluctuations. Look back at the history of markets: short-term ups and downs, but always going up over time.
2. *Understand and accept your asset allocation.* Be sure the mix of your investments matches your risk tolerance and savings goals. If it doesn't, do not overreact; shift gradually to a more conservative mix. If your asset allocation still matches your goals, stay put. Time will be your best friend.
3. *Diversify.* A properly diversified portfolio is your best defense against stock market risk.

I'd like to continue investing in the stock market, but I'm concerned about the volatility. Any suggestions?

Market fluctuations can make almost any investor nervous. But getting out of stocks when the market takes a downturn is not the answer. Don't let short-term volatility drive your long-term investment planning. Your best defense against a fluctuating market is a well-diversified portfolio and a disciplined program of periodic investments.

Spreading your investments among stocks, bonds, and cash in a strategic asset allocation that takes into account your time frame, risk tolerance, need for investment income, and long-term goals can help your portfolio produce more consistent returns, regardless of whether the stock market is up or down. When the stock market is not performing well, your returns from bond and cash investments can help supplement your stock returns.

Making regular, systematic investments in a stock or stock mutual fund is a strategy known as *dollar cost averaging.* With this strategy, you invest a fixed amount monthly or quarterly whether the market is up or down. When the market is up, your money buys fewer shares; when it is down, your money buys more shares. Over the long term, the average price you pay per share will be lower than the average price of the stock during the same period. Of course, dollar cost averaging does not ensure a profit and does not protect against loss in declining markets.

Financial experts can't predict the financial markets, and wise investors don't try. They take a structured, disciplined approach to investing that recognizes that market declines will inevitably occur.

What is the Dow theory?

Technical analysis attempts to predict future stock prices by analyzing past stock prices. It does not consider the fundamentals of a stock, such as ratio analysis, growth estimates, and other factors.

There are several technical approaches to the selection of securities. Perhaps the oldest of these is the *Dow theory,* which indicates the general direction of the market. Since security prices move together, many financial professionals believe that the direction of the market is the most significant factor in the buy-or-sell decision. According to the Dow theory, the stock market tends to move continuously in a main trend until a definite reversal occurs. The theory emphasizes critical high and low points, which, if exceeded, signal major bull or bear moves. The problem with this theory, as with many others, is that it does not work all the time. The Dow theory has been the subject of many debates in terms of its validity.

What is Barron's confidence index?

Like the Dow theory, *Barron's confidence index* is a technical analysis approach that identifies investors' confidence in the level and direction of security prices. It is based on the belief that the price difference between quality bonds and bonds of less quality will forecast future price movements. The index measures the sentiment of investors toward risk. When the yield differential is small, that is, the yields on high-quality bonds are close to those on lower-quality bonds, the ratio (index) increases, showing investor confidence. This confidence is a signal that security prices will tend to rise. Conversely, when the spread is great and the ratio (index) decreases, this is indicative that security prices will fall. Although Barron's confidence index may indicate a tendency, or trend, it, along with all other indicators, is not a totally reliable source of future stock prices.

How do trading volume and insider transactions relate to market movement?

Technical analysts place emphasis on the volume of trading and deviations from normal volume for a specific stock. A price increase on a small volume of trading does not have as much influence as one that is accompanied by heavy trading. If a price decline were to occur with heavy trading, this would indicate that many investors were attempting to sell the stock—a signal that the stock is out of favor with a broad spectrum of investors. Volume indicates the breadth of the change in either supply or demand of the stock and is a much better indicator than price alone.

Insiders, such as officers, directors, and very large shareholders, cannot legally use inside information for personal gain. However, they are allowed to buy or sell stock about which they have access to privileged information, provided the transaction is reported in advance to the SEC. Many technical analysts feel that inside transactions offer a snapshot of future earnings potential and, therefore, are a good indicator of future stock price movements.

Dollar cost averaging

Will using dollar cost averaging help reduce market risk?

The benefits of systematic investing are many. Investing dollars every month creates a great habit. You save first and then spend what's left, and this enables you to accumulate funds for the future (retirement, college educational expenses, etc.).

Since the stock market fluctuates, it is difficult to decide on exactly the best time to invest. With dollar cost averaging, you invest a small amount every month, and therefore you buy the shares at a number of different prices—some months higher, some months lower. This makes the *average* cost of the investment more likely to be lower over time than it would be if you bought all the shares at one time, perhaps at the market high.

This approach is typically more conservative, especially in a fluctuating market. You don't have to worry about "timing" the market cycles, since you will be buying at regular intervals covering many market cycles. It's a great way to get involved with the purchase of securities and a tremendous way to build assets.

How does dollar cost averaging work?

Dollar cost averaging is a time-tested strategy that can make market fluctuations work for you. It requires the discipline of systematically investing equal sums of money at regular intervals, regardless of the price of the shares. By doing this, you are able to buy more shares of an investment when the price is low and fewer shares when the price is high, thereby avoiding the common mistake of buying high and selling low. The result is that the average cost of your shares will be less than the average price, whether the market is going up or going down.

Dollar cost averaging is an investment tool that is not appropriate for short-term investments, and it cannot guarantee a profit or prevent a loss. It does, however, provide a disciplined investment program that minimizes the need for market timing and helps alleviate the effects of a fluctuating market.

Can you give me an example of dollar cost averaging?

Mr. Jones has $500,000 to invest in various mutual funds. If he puts the entire $500,000 into the market at one time, and the next day the market drops by 20 percent, he will incur a 20 percent loss. Conversely, if the market increases 20 percent the next day, he has a 20 percent gain.

If he wishes to take a more conservative approach, Jones can invest the $500,000 over a period of several months or longer. Thus, if the market has a sharp rise or fall early on, only part of his funds are exposed.

Let's say Jones decides to dollar-cost-average over a 10-month period; that is, he will invest $50,000 each month for the 10 months. If, during that time, share values decline, he will get more shares for the same $50,000. If share values increase, he will buy fewer shares. As share values fluctuate during the dollar-cost-averaging period, he will buy varying numbers of shares, thereby getting an average price for his investment.

If the market is in an upward cycle, putting the money to work all at once would be the better choice. If a downward cycle prevails, waiting to invest the entire sum is better. Dollar cost averaging is a compromise, since it is virtually impossible to know what will occur in the future.

Does dollar cost averaging always produce a profit?

No. Dollar cost averaging works in both up and down markets, but there is no guarantee that the overall strategy will produce a profit. For example, if the average cost for your stock mutual fund is $10 per share and the share price is currently $11, your profit is $1 for every share you own. If the current price is $9, your investment loss is $1 for every share you own. Dollar cost averaging is a way to potentially reduce the overall cost you pay for a single share of an investment. In a rising market you will make money (but not as much as those who purchased at a lower average cost than you do), and in a falling market you will lose money (but not as much as those who purchased at a higher average cost than you do). This strategy tends to work well in times of market uncertainty or with solid investments that nevertheless move up and down over time.

Allocation

Why should I allocate among different asset classes? Why not just put all my money in the highest-return asset?

By combining asset classes that respond differently to economic conditions, you can smooth overall portfolio volatility. Analysis of the past performance of many assets, such as stocks, bonds, and cash, makes it clear that certain assets have higher risk and/or returns than others. Even conservative investors might have portions of each asset class in their portfolios.

Asset classes react differently to various economic and market scenarios. Consequently, by combining asset classes that exhibit dissimilar reactions to the same events and conditions at any given period, you are better able to insulate your portfolio from movements in just one asset class. This is called *asset allocation.*

Throughout the past 70 years, stocks and bonds did not go up and down at the same time, nor did they change with the same magnitude of volatility. By including various asset classes in your portfolio, you decrease the risk that your portfolio will be undermined by a given market scenario. Regardless of the economic environment you are in, the asset class that is performing well will help offset the asset class that is not performing as well. This reduction of risk is a benefit of allocation.

Market timing

Why not just wait for the market to go down before buying and then sell after the market goes back up?

Investors who attempt to time the market run the risk of missing periods of exceptional returns. For example, the value of $1 invested at year-end 1925 grew to $1113.92 by year-end 1995. However, the same dollar invested over the 70-year time frame would have grown to only $10.16 if it missed the 35 best months of return. This is slightly below the Treasury-bill investment, which grew to $12.87. As you can see, the investor who left $1 in large stocks for the entire 70-year time frame earned $1103.76 more than an investor who unsuccessfully tried to time the market. Clearly, the magnitude of the opportunity loss you could incur when attempting to time the market is meaningful.

Why not just time the market instead of using asset allocation?

Market timing, in one form or another, is today widely practiced among both professional fund managers and amateur investors. Nonetheless, there is good reason to be skeptical of it. No one has been able to develop a verifiable long-term track record of consistently timing when to move into and out of the market. The overwhelming consensus among researchers who have investigated this topic appears to be that it is statistically difficult to distinguish market timing from random luck.

The next time the stock market goes down, should I pull my money out until the market is doing better?

Avoid timing the market. The market will fluctuate on a daily basis, but historically the general trend has been for the stock market to rise over time. Though history may not repeat itself, it does give us a pretty good starting point for making investment decisions. If you have a long-term investment horizon, you should stay invested for a minimum of 5 years or more, even during a down market. The reason for this patience is that no one knows when the market will turn around, and it can do so very quickly.

On July 17, 1998, the Dow Jones Industrial Average hit an all-time high of 9337. Through August and September of that year, the market slid nearly 2000 points. On October 8, that trend began to reverse, and from then through November 23, the market increased to another all-time high, 9374. Investors who sold when the market dropped may have taken a loss and may not have been invested to take advantage of the market increase.

Let's look at another example, based on data from Ibbotson Associates: Between 1982 and 1987, the market averaged a 26.3 percent compound rate of return over 1276 trading days. If, through trying to time the market, you missed just 10 of the biggest "up" days, your average compound rate of return dropped to 18.3 percent. If you missed the 20 biggest up days, it dropped to 13.1 percent—less than half the rate of return you would have earned had you stayed invested for the full 1276 days.

If you have a long-term investment horizon, you should stay fully invested even through downward trends.

Income-Producing Strategies

As a retiree, what are the main investment strategies I can use to live off my retirement assets?

A retiree must choose between two income strategies, capital preservation and capital utilization. Followers of the *capital preservation strategy* live from the income produced by their assets, without touching the principal. This strategy ensures that the investor will not outlive his or her income. A very large asset pool, however, is required to follow this strategy.

In contrast, adherents of the *capital utilization strategy* tap both income and principal for retirement expenses. With this strategy, you must make a good estimate of your life span; otherwise, you risk outliving your investments. This approach can work with a smaller asset pool, but investment performance may affect its success.

I've heard that owning growth investments during my working years and then converting to bonds during my retirement years is the best strategy. What do you think?

For many retirees, the biggest concern is outliving their investments. So combining a portfolio of income with continuing growth is important. Many retirees neglect stocks and stock mutual funds when thinking about ways to draw income from their investments. It is possible, and recommended, to structure a retirement portfolio to produce a specified amount of needed income (but not more) each month. Income that is not needed results in additional, unnecessary income taxes.

Consider your personal income tax situation when structuring your retirement portfolio. Look to dividend-producing stocks (with growth) and a blend of bonds, either corporate or tax-free. Structure your portfolio so that it receives adequate income and can grow several percentage points over inflation. Have annual reviews to determine where your portfolio and needs stand.

Is selling a small portion of my mutual fund each month a good way to provide for income?

Yes, but you have to be careful. All mutual funds are not created equal. Funds that have a high dividend and low volatility work best for a selling program.

The funds you choose to sell should provide consistent management. Avoid selling funds whose managers change the funds' objectives from year to year. Growth funds and index funds do not work in monthly income draft situations because of their volatility. Selling stock funds over a sustained bear market will likely endanger your principal.

Also, be sure to switch all dividends and capital gains within your mutual fund to being paid out rather than reinvested. Since you will owe taxes on these distributions, you can better control your tax situation by then selling additional fund shares as needed to meet your income requirements.

How can I get money out of my mutual funds on a regular basis?

If you are looking for income, you can take money out of your mutual funds by using the systematic withdrawal feature that all mutual funds have. You can choose to have withdrawals at virtually any time period, including monthly, quarterly, semiannually, or annually. If you choose a monthly withdrawal, you can specify a percentage of your investment, a constant dollar amount, or one of many other options available. Check with your fund for the available options and with your advisor for the best choice for your circumstances.

My dividends are declining. Since I am retired and dividends are crucial for me, is there anything I can do about this?

It used to be that anyone wanting regular retirement income owned at least some dividend-paying stock. High-dividend payers were utility companies, banks, and blue-chip companies such as IBM. But dividend-paying stocks, particularly those paying high dividends, are getting difficult to find.

Several factors have caused the decline in dividends. As stock market prices have boomed, corporations have responded by using the earnings they would have paid as dividends to repurchase their stock or to reinvest it in the company so that their stock prices remain high. The dividend yield of the S&P 500 today has shrunk to a dismal 1.7 percent. In comparison, in the 1960s and 1970s the average dividend yield was between 4.5 and 5 percent, and in the 1980s, it was around 3.9 percent.

Low inflation and interest rates, such as we are currently experiencing, also keep yields down.

The biggest factor in dividend decline is the growing disparity between regular income taxes and capital gain taxes. With ordinary income tax rates twice as high as capital gain rates for some taxpayers, stockholders want growth with its attendant capital gain taxes, not dividends with their attendant income taxes. In addition, stockholders don't pay taxes on the growth until they sell their stock, unlike the case with taxes due on traditional dividends.

Growth is so much in demand that even some high-yielding utility stocks have cut, or even eliminated, dividends. According to S&P statistics, the average payout ratio for utilities, which is the portion of earnings paid out as dividends, has dropped to a near record low of 35 percent, as opposed to the average payout since 1945 of 52 percent.

Yet, for retired investors or those approaching retirement, there are still solid companies that pay decent dividends. Even if yields are not as high as they might have been in the past, high-dividend-paying stocks tend to weather market declines better because the dividends become more desirable. Some mutual funds pay out reasonable yields by specializing in dividend-paying stocks or stocks with rising dividends.

There is nothing wrong with earning a greater portion of your total return from stock price appreciation. For example, you might prefer to own a 6 percent interest-bearing investment to provide your needed income rather than an investment growing at 10 percent and paying a 1 percent dividend. To substitute for dividends, you can periodically sell shares of appreciating stock for income, which will be taxed at the lower capital gain rates.

Are there other options for replacing my dividends?

You should consider the use of low-risk buffers to protect against the risk of market decline or lower dividends, especially a simultaneous decline in stocks and bonds. You can periodically take a gain from the sale of a stock or bond and reinvest it in low-risk vehicles, such as money market mutual funds, certificates of deposit, or fixed-income annuities. In this way, you will be somewhat protected against future market downturns. Another alternative is to have a portion of your portfolio invested in bonds or similar fixed-income investments. The biggest risk here is that if you become too heavily weighted in fixed-income options, your portfolio may not keep up with inflation.

How can I get monthly income from a semiannual-paying bond?

There are three ways. One is to buy bonds with alternating, or laddered, pay dates, that is, bonds that pay their interest December and June, January and July, February and August, and so on. Your broker or other financial advisor can help you design a laddered bond portfolio.

A second method is to buy monthly paying bonds such as mortgage-related, fixed-income investments, which include Government National Mortgage Association (GNMA) bonds, Federal Home Loan Mortgage Corporation (FHLMC) bonds, and collateralized mortgage obligations of the Federal National Mortgage Association (FNMA).

Alternatively, you can save the semiannual interest payments in an interest-bearing money market account, budget wisely, and use it to live on until the next pay date.

If I need income, how can I still get the growth I need to fight inflation?

There are several ways of not taking all the hay out of the barn. One is to buy convertible bonds issued by strong growth corporations. The interest rates of convertible bonds are greater than the corporation's common stock dividend rate. In addition, as the convertible bond owner, you can convert your bond to common stock after the stock reaches a higher price, called the *conversion premium.* Convertible bonds can be sold on the open market, so they are a liquid investment.

Another alternative is to invest in convertible preferred stock. Such stocks are similar to convertible bonds except preferred stock pays dividends rather than interest. Convertible preferred stock is salable on the open market and can be converted to common stock.

Investment Vehicle Strategies

Stocks

Common stock

What are some advantages of investing in common stocks?

Common stocks have outperformed all other financial instruments by a large margin. Ibbotson Associates, a reputable source of market statistics and information, has calculated that an investment in large-cap stocks would have grown at a compound rate of 11.2 percent during the years 1926 through 1998. Stocks have also been a remarkably reliable hedge against inflation. Naturally, the total return performance of common stocks depends on the time period over which it is measured.

What are the investment risks with common stocks?

Volatility of share prices is a measure of risk for common stocks and is the reason so many conservative investors tilt their portfolios away from heavy stock positions, even though, over time, common stocks have been the investor's best friend. Price fluctuations in the short term are the real concern of conservative investors, and these fluctuations can be substantial. As previously mentioned, one way to help reduce this risk is to allocate among various asset classes.

What are some specific sources of common stock risk?

Here are a few of the more important market and business risks that underlie share price volatility:

- *A downturn in economic growth:* When growth declines, so do investor expectations of future corporate earnings. Gloomy investors react to economic downturns by reducing the amount they will pay for a dollar of earnings (P/E ratio).
- *High interest rates:* In recent years, rising interest rates have almost always preceded falling share prices.
- *Loss of product or service competitiveness:* Witness the declining fortunes of IBM, DEC, Sears, and General Motors in the early 1990s.
- *Failures of management:* When management fails to innovate, lead, control operations, or exercise leadership in other areas, the company's stock suffers.
- *Government actions:* These include deep defense cuts, mandated changes in accounting rules, and legislation on emissions, minimum wages, import restrictions, and so on.

What factors affect stock prices?

"Supply and demand" is the textbook answer, because investors determine prices through their willingness to buy or sell a particular stock issue. The stock exchanges are simply forums that publicly reflect the appraised value of securities at a given time. The New York Stock Exchange trading floor used to live by the slogan "where thousands vote every day," which indicates how prices are determined.

There are many factors that affect stock prices. The price of a stock relative to its earning potential (P/E ratio) is a good measurement of value. Positive "surprise" earnings, that is, earnings that are greater than expected for a company, will often create a "buy" signal in the market for that stock. A corporation whose assets are continually increasing in size, showing a trend of solid growth, will generally show a favorable price move.

Interestingly enough, a stock split does not change the bottom line for a company, but it might create an emotional buy signal for the public, who believe they can now buy more shares at a lower price. Since companies that announce and implement stock splits often show signs of growth, some companies may use the split itself as a sign of growth.

Political and social events can also play an important role in stock market direction, as can the overall business outlook for a particular industry or company.

How do I know when to sell a stock?

One way is to establish price targets. Decide in advance the target high and low (stop-loss) prices at which you would sell the stock. Always analyze whether the stock still matches the goals and objectives you had when you bought it. Then ask yourself if you would buy the same stock today.

Your stock portfolio is like a garden. Keep it healthy and productive by pulling the weeds, fertilizing the plants, and diversifying the crop!

Can I have too many stocks in my portfolio?

As discussed in Chapter 1 under "Asset Allocation," investors should search for assets that tend to have *negative* relationships to each other—assets that go up in value as the value of other assets declines. The number of assets in the portfolio is less important than the relationship of the assets to each other. If you own a multitude of individual stocks, your portfolio may move in lockstep with the overall market. Once you have thirteen or more stocks, you are likely approaching the point of diminishing returns. By focusing your holdings on fewer, carefully selected stocks, along with assets in other classes that will balance the market ups and downs, you may have a better chance that your portfolio will outperform the market over time.

While it is generally conceded that concentrating in stocks increases risk, the reward can also be greater. If you don't mind increasing your risk, concentrating in stocks may be a viable option for you.

Should I own both value and growth stocks in my portfolio?

The differences between value stocks and growth stocks are important for investors to understand because, historically, the stock market has moved in cycles—sometimes favoring value-oriented stocks (usually during economic downturns), other times favoring growth-oriented stocks (usually during economic expansion). An investor who is over-invested in one of these types will inevitably underperform the broad equity market when that type is out of favor. For this reason, a well-diversified portfolio should include both value and growth stocks.

Preferred stock

Should I invest in preferred stocks?

Let's look at preferred stocks to see if they meet your investment goals and objectives. Preferred stocks provide the following benefits to individual investors:

- They pay a stable and level dividend, usually quarterly, which will provide income on a regular schedule.
- In most cases, the preferred dividend is higher than the company's common dividend and sometimes is more than its bond payments.
- The cumulative dividend feature of preferred stock provides good stability, consistency, and dependability.
- Preferred stock has a higher claim on the company's assets upon bankruptcy or liquidation than does common stock.

For these reasons, preferred stock is usually considered a more conservative investment than the same company's common stock, and it will probably be less volatile in the marketplace. If your investment goals include having regular income, you should consider investing in preferred stock.

Bonds

What are the benefits of bonds?

Many investors believe that stocks are the only asset class that can produce significant returns. Throughout the past 70 years, however, bonds have had less volatile returns than stocks and have occasionally outperformed them. Some of the benefits of bond investing are:

- *Diversification:* Economic events that tend to decrease stock prices often increase bond prices. Thus a diversified portfolio will exhibit much more stability during times of financial crisis than will either stocks or bonds held alone.
- *Lower risk:* Bonds typically have less volatility than common stocks. Thus investors can reduce risk by placing a larger percentage of their capital in bonds.
- *Horizon matching:* Different investors have different investment time horizons. Since bonds are available with maturities ranging from 1 day to 30 years, investors can match their particular cash or liquidity needs with the effective maturity dates of their bonds.
- *Income generation:* Bondholders receive income at fixed intervals that can be used to offset cash obligations or to increase portfolio liquidity. Since bonds are easily traded on the secondary market, bondholders can usually sell bonds for cash to meet liquidity needs.
- *Possible tax exemption:* With some bonds, investors earn income that is exempt from taxation. Municipal bonds are usually exempt from federal taxes, and U.S. government bonds are usually exempt from state taxes.

What are some of the investment risks of bonds and other debt instruments?

Every investment has an element of risk, and bonds are no exception. Some of the investment risks of bonds include:

- *Default risk:* A debt instrument is a promise to repay, but economic circumstances can jeopardize that promise. Default can take the form of late or missed interest payments or outright failure to pay interest or the principal on maturity.
- *Inflation risk:* Some income-oriented investors tied up their nest eggs in long-term government bonds paying 6.5 percent in 1976. Over the next few years, the cost of living skyrocketed on the heels of inflation, cutting the purchasing power of bondholders. This is a perennial risk with long-term fixed-income investments.
- *Interest-rate risk:* The same investors who found their purchasing power decimated by high inflation were also negatively affected in another way by the high interest rates: the market value of their bonds dropped because new bonds of the same quality and matur-

ity were issued in 1979–1980 with 15 percent yields. The investors holding the old 6.5 percent bonds had to either continue to receive the low interest rate or sell their bonds at substantial losses (discounts).

- *Currency risk:* In recent years, many investors have sought the higher yields that are often found in non-U.S. capital markets. American holders of non-U.S. debt securities are subject to all the ordinary investment risks of bonds as well as the risk that the currency in which the debt is held will lose value relative to the U.S. dollar.
- *Timing (call, reinvestment) risk:* Some bonds have a feature that allows the issuer to call the bond from the holder at a predetermined price. Such calls usually occur in a declining-interest-rate environment because the issuer can sell new bonds that pay less interest; thus the investor must give up a higher interest rate in exchange for lower rates.

Is it wise to invest in bonds when interest rates are low?

Investors concerned about this issue should distinguish between the absolute and relative level of interest rates. Clearly, as the absolute level of interest rates fell in recent years, cash flows generated by fixed-income investments also declined, making such investments appear increasingly unattractive. However, relative to inflation, which has also decreased, the real rate of return that bonds offer (i.e., the nominal yield minus inflation) is now higher than it was in many periods when the absolute level of interest rates was significantly higher.

To guard against erosion in principal value, investors should pay close attention to the maturities of the bonds they own, especially during periods when rates have the potential to increase. A strong mathematical relationship exists between the length of a bond's maturity and the bond's sensitivity to movements in interest rates. Generally speaking, the longer a bond's maturity, the more susceptible it will be to price erosion should interest rates tick upward. Figure 2-3 demonstrates the relationship between interest rates and bond prices. Given today's lower-interest-rate environment, a number of advisors are suggesting that investors limit the length of maturity on their bonds to between 2 and 10 years (i.e., intermediate-term bonds).

Should I consider investing in a callable bond?

Sure. Although callable bonds can be retired early by the issuer, the investor is often compensated for this uncertainty with a higher yield while he or she holds the bond. Many corporate and municipal bonds are callable, but only a few U.S. government bonds are.

Should I include high-yield (junk) bonds in my investment program?

Maybe. The high-yield (junk) bond market has had attractive investment performance over longer time periods (3, 5, and 10 years). However, since junk bonds have higher risk than quality bonds, include them in your investment program only if the higher risk is within your level of tolerance. Several junk bonds have defaulted in the past, and some will default in the future as well. In 1990 the default ratio was 10 percent, and the junk bond market lost 6.4 percent. On the other hand, the high-yield bond market recovered in 1991 and was up 43.75 percent at the close of the year. Between 1994 and 1999, the default ratio on high-yield bonds rose from 1 to 6 percent.

To minimize default risk, make absolutely certain that your high-yield bond portfolio is adequately diversified. Invest in bonds from different companies in different industries and sectors of the economy. Consider investing in high-yield bond mutual funds. This is an excellent way to participate in the junk bond market.

I'm 75. Am I too old to buy a 20-year bond?

Not if your objective is income; buying a bond for income does not mean you have to outlive it. Having laddered maturities of bonds will give you a higher average income. Short-term bonds usually have the lowest yields; long-term bonds, the highest. A blend of maturities generates a higher average yield.

Government bonds

If U.S. Treasury bonds are guaranteed, what makes my portfolio of bonds fluctuate?

Bond investors should understand that there is an inverse relationship between bond prices and their yields. Although the bond market is less volatile than the stock market, bonds do fluctuate in price.

If interest rates fall, bond prices rise, and vice versa. Suppose an investor purchases a 20-year, $1000 bond with a yield of 8 percent and interest payable annually at year-end. One year later, interest rates rise to 10 percent. Any person in the market for a bond can now buy that same bond with a yield of 10 percent. If the first investor tried to sell

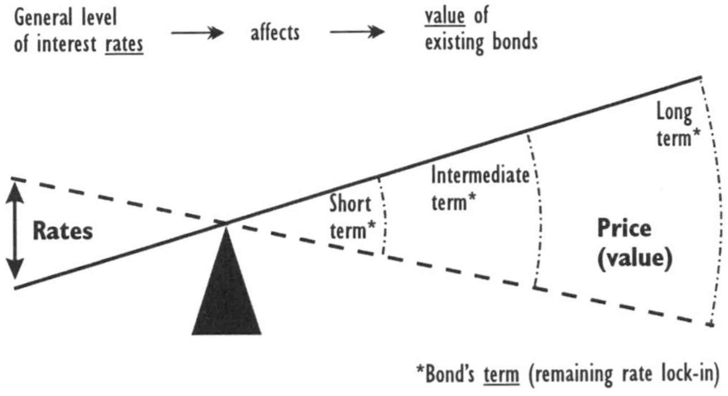

Figure 2-3 The longer the term of a bond, the greater the effect of interest rates—up or down.

his or her 8 percent bond, no one would buy it at face value. In order to find a buyer, the bondholder would need to discount the price of that bond enough to compensate the buyer for the lower interest rate. This results in a capital loss for the bondholder. He or she may also experience a loss of total return, depending on whether the interest payments received exceeded the capital loss. The opposite would happen if interest rates went down. The longer the maturity of the bond, the greater the effect on the price of the bond.

The original holder of the bond may choose to hold it until maturity. In the case of U.S. Treasury bonds, the government guarantees the return of 100 percent of the face value (or $1000) to the owner of the bond.

If the federal government is the standard of safety for bond investors, why would anyone want to invest money in bonds issued by other institutions?

Bonds issued by other institutions typically pay a higher interest rate or have special tax advantages compared with bonds issued by the federal government or its agencies.

Interest from certain federal bonds is exempt from state tax. Interest from bonds issued by governments or authorities at the local, county, or state level is almost always exempt from federal income tax; if the bondholder resides in the jurisdiction where the bond was issued, the interest is exempt from state and local income tax as well. The latter type of bond is called a *municipal bond,* an investment that can be an attractive alternative to taxable bonds or even stocks. For instance, if a prospective bondholder is in a 35 percent combined state and federal tax bracket, the after-tax return on a taxable bond paying 7 percent would be 4.5 percent. On the other hand, a 5 percent tax-free municipal bond would be the equivalent of a 7.69 percent taxable bond. This is one of the main reasons why municipal bonds can be more attractive than corporate bonds.

The safety of U.S. government bonds and the special tax treatment of municipal bonds are compelling reasons to include them in an investment portfolio. Where do corporate bonds fit in, and why are they part of virtually every diversified portfolio?

Because corporations have to compete with the safety and tax advantages of many government bonds, corporate bonds often provide a higher interest rate to attract investors. The higher rate is usually the reason that corporate bonds are included in most portfolios.

Corporations must also compete against each other for investor dollars, so interest rates can vary considerably. For instance, a financially sound but small corporation may be forced to offer a higher interest rate in order to attract investors; a medium-size company on shaky financial ground may have to offer even higher interest rates. Like the federal government, larger corporations can offer lower interest rates on their bonds because investors have more assurance that the debt obligations (interest payments) and return of principal will be paid on time.

Most corporate bonds are rated by rating agencies, so investors can select bonds that match their income objectives and risk tolerance.

In addition to having generally higher interest rates, some corporate bonds include a sinking fund, call provision, or put feature. With a *sinking fund,* the corporation is obligated to make systematic payments into a special account to ensure that the interest and principal payments are paid on time. During times of high interest rates, corporations may issue a bond with a *call provision* that allows the corporation to retire its debt early by redeeming (cashing in) the bond at face value or at a higher price than the investor originally invested. A *put feature* forces a corporation to redeem a bond at the discretion of the investor.

Municipal bonds

Are municipal bonds safe?

Generally, they are. As a matter of fact, municipal bonds that are general obligations of municipalities (state, county, and city governments) are considered second in quality only to U.S. government bonds. There are, however, many risky municipal bonds of fair or poor quality, but they are usually apparent by their lower-quality ratings.

Investors who choose to invest only in insured bonds can feel assured that no defaults will occur in their bond portfolios. Most insured municipal bonds are rated AAA on the basis of the insurance company's credit quality.

What are the advantages of investing in municipal bonds?

Here are nine reasons for considering municipal bonds:

1. *Tax exemption:* The most important feature of municipal bonds is that their interest payments are exempt from federal taxes, as well as from state taxes if you live in the state where the bond was issued.
2. *Safety:* As a class, municipal bonds are second only to U.S. government bonds in terms of safety and security.
3. *Collateral:* The Federal Reserve Board determines the extent to which securities can be used as collateral. Since it places no restrictions on the collateral value of municipal bonds, owners of these bonds are able to borrow a very high percentage of the value of their investments.
4. *Fixed income:* Municipal bonds provide a steady income from interest paid semiannually.
5. *New issues:* There is a steady stream of new municipal bond issues by local and state governments because of the need for additional public facilities to keep pace with the expanding population.
6. *Capital appreciation:* Discounted bonds offer an opportunity for appreciation in addition to current tax-exempt income.
7. *Diversification:* Investors have the opportunity to purchase a variety of municipal bonds across the country.
8. *Flexibility:* An investor in municipal bonds can choose any desired maturity date from 1 to 30 years, or longer, in order to ladder the maturity dates and reduce risk.
9. *Marketability:* In most cases, the market for municipal bonds is one of the broadest over-the-counter markets, providing investors with the opportunity to sell their bonds with relative ease.

I am retired and in a high state and federal income tax bracket. I want my investments to provide a safe income, but I remember

the "WOOPS" and Orange County defaults. What can I do to protect myself?

The tax-free municipal bonds you refer to were investment-grade bonds that failed to provide the safety implied by their ratings.

There are two ways to protect against default on municipal bonds. The first way is to purchase bonds that are "escrowed to maturity," affectionately referred to as *ETMs.* As usual, the issuing municipality backs these bonds, but it also collateralizes them with U.S. government securities, held in escrow by a third party. If the municipality defaults on the bond, the U.S. Treasury obligations are redeemed to pay the bondholders.

Often a municipality will issue bonds, receive a rating as to creditworthiness, and at a later date convert them to ETMs. Such action automatically elevates the bonds to AAA status. However, since municipalities usually do not want to pay the rating agencies to reevaluate/rerate the underlying bond, these ETMs will continue to carry their earlier, often lower, rating. This sometimes leads to pricing inefficiencies whereby an investor can receive an AAA bond at a lower, A-rated price.

The second supersafe way to buy municipal bonds without having to worry about default is to buy prerefunded bonds, referred to as *pre-re's.* Basically, these are just like ETMs in that they are collateralized. In addition, pricing inefficiencies for these bonds are created because of the bonds' stated maturities. For example, one of these bonds may have a stated maturity of 2010 but a pre-re of 2002. Thus the bond will pay the principal in 2002 even though the stated maturity is 8 years later. The investor wins by buying a bond that will pay back the principal in the short term but is priced (lower) like a long-term bond. (This, of course, assumes a normal yield curve, where longer-term yields are higher than short-term yields.)

How can I be sure of a fair price when I buy a municipal bond?

It pays to shop around. Use the services of an independent bond broker or try to buy the same bond from competing brokerage firms. Unlike the pricing of stocks, bond pricing can be very inefficient, so working with a trusted advisor can save thousands of dollars.

My broker is offering to sell me a municipal bond that he says I can buy without paying a commission. Is this possible?

The simple answer is, "Yes, but probably no." When a brokerage firm underwrites a municipal bond issue (i.e., agrees to sell a large offering to the public), the commission paid by the municipality to the brokerage firm is built into the price you pay. You are not charged a direct commission, but it is likely that you are paying a commission indirectly.

Mutual funds

Why should I invest in mutual funds?

Mutual funds are convenient and efficient investment vehicles that offer diversification, professional management, and an easy way to invest because of low initial investments and accessibility to your money.

Most investors starting out cannot afford to buy significant shares of individual securities. By pooling their money with thousands of other investors in a mutual fund, they have the opportunity to own a portion of a significantly larger portfolio.

Managing investments requires a commitment of time, resources, and expertise that most individuals either do not have or do not want to devote to that purpose. One of the most difficult tasks an investor faces is deciding which securities to buy and which ones to sell. In a mutual fund, the portfolio manager makes those decisions on your behalf, drawing on a wealth of resource information.

Mutual funds have other advantages as well. They:

- Allow fractional share purchases
- Provide liquidity (easy access to money)
- Offer simple reinvestment options
- Provide easily obtainable information about the fund
- Offer a choice of funds to meet personal goals
- Allow people to build investments through automatic deposit (dollar cost averaging)

What is the main disadvantage of owning mutual funds?

The main disadvantage of owning a mutual fund is the cost of management. The good news is that this cost is usually offset by better performance or lower transaction costs than an individual would incur. Certainly, the nominal management fee for mutual fund ownership compares very favorably with the fees charged by investment advisors for smaller accounts.

What are the risks of investing in mutual funds?

Mutual funds are investments in financial securities that have fluctuating values and, therefore, pose a risk to investors purchasing shares. There are no guarantees; a fund's value will rise and fall according to market conditions associated with the underlying assets. Even the most conservative assets, such as U.S. government agency obligations, will fluctuate in value as interest rates change.

My impression is that mutual funds are high-risk investments. Is this correct?

Mutual funds come in a wide range of types, from very conservative to ultra-high risk. Most mutual fund families offer a number of different types of funds that often include money market, bond, balanced, international, growth, and aggressive growth. Ideally, you and your investment advisor should diversify among several fund categories that collectively match your risk tolerance, time horizon, and investment objectives.

What are the advantages of mutual funds over individual stocks?

Mutual funds have the following advantages over individual securities:

1. Performance figures are readily available for analysis.
2. Fund managers can usually negotiate lower transaction costs than individual investors can.
3. Funds are already diversified.
4. Purchase and redemption can be made easily for a nominal fee.
5. Mutual funds have professional, experienced management.
6. The risk-reward ratio of a specific fund can be determined quickly and accurately.

Can you explain more about the advantages and disadvantages of mutual funds versus individual stocks?

When we hear about specific stocks rising 50, 100, and 200 percent in a year, it is very tempting to seek out and purchase those stocks. There is greater upside potential with picking the best-performing stocks than with picking mutual funds.

With a mutual fund, you are hiring professional managers whose time is devoted to learning everything possible about the stocks in their portfolio and those they are considering adding to it. They know the management, their suppliers, their customers, their competitors, the industry, the economic environment for the industry, and other factors that affect the success of the company. They have access to information as it develops and the ability to obtain answers to their questions. In addition, with a mutual fund, you have the advantage of diversification among the stocks of numerous companies, which provides an extra margin of safety in the event that the manager picks a poor performer.

With individual stocks, it is up to you to acquire the relevant information from various sources, which may or may not be accurate, and then assimilate it all in order to make a sound decision. The likelihood of your being able to have the depth of knowledge that a professional portfolio manager has is uncertain at best.

If you have sufficient time to devote to the task, access to accurate and timely information, and the skills required to evaluate your positions, individual stocks might be a good choice for you. However, you should have sufficient capital to invest so that you can have a well-diversified and properly allocated portfolio. Consider, too, the costs of buying and selling stocks. Also, with initial public offerings (IPOs), institutional investors that are major customers of the underwriter are likely to be offered the best opportunities before retail investors.

Offsetting the disadvantages of individual stocks are the management fees associated with mutual funds. Another disadvantage of mutual funds is the investor's inability to control the tax consequences of gains and losses within the fund. This is most important when investors are investing with non-IRA funds.

You must decide if you have the aptitude, temperament, time, skills, access, and capital to formulate your portfolio with individual stocks. If you are missing any one of those characteristics, you might find that mutual funds offer a better investment opportunity to achieve your objectives.

If mutual funds are diversified, how many funds do I need to own?

The answer depends on the type of funds. If you buy ten funds moving in lockstep within the same asset class, you are not diversified and you might as well have bought one fund.

When investing in a mutual fund, is it important to understand the composition of the fund's returns?

Yes. The after-tax returns achieved by taxpayers investing outside qualified retirement plans are influenced not only by the level of a fund's returns before taxes are paid but also by the composition of the fund's returns. The *composition of returns* is the breakdown between income distributions, capital gain distributions, and price appreciation derived from unrealized gains.

I bought my large-cap mutual fund in mid-July 1998. The fund reported a gain of 25 percent in 1998, but I lost 5 percent. Why do I now have 5 percent less than what I invested?

Investors need to be aware that there may be a substantial difference between returns earned at the fund level and those they realize personally. Sometimes differences may occur solely because of timing. For example, if the fund reached its high point for the year in July, when you bought it, and it did not increase or it decreased in value over the balance of the year, you would not earn a profit during the year even though the fund reported substantial gains. On the other hand, if you sold at the fund's high, conceivably you could have earned a higher annualized return for the year than that reported by the fund.

Load and no-load funds

Why should I ever buy a load fund when I can get a no-load?

If you are an investor who is inclined to do the research of selecting a fund and monitoring a fund's performance on an ongoing basis for its continuing appropriateness, perhaps a no-load fund is right for you. However, without the help of a registered investment advisor to whom you pay a fee, "no load" means "no help." The value associated with the fund selection may warrant the additional expense. Perhaps "help fund" versus "no-help fund" is a better representation.

There is a myth that no-load funds are less costly to invest in than load funds. In some cases, this might be true. However, a number of no-load funds charge other fees, such as sales fees on redemption and 12b-1 fees. In addition, it is important to examine all costs when comparing mutual funds. Investment management fees, broker commissions to trade securities within the funds, and administrative expenses can significantly vary by more than 1 percent of the fund's assets each year.

When purchasing a load fund, which class of shares is best?

Choosing from Class A shares, B shares, or C shares should be a decision you make with your financial consultant. Generally speaking, A shares work best for investors with long-term (over 10-year) needs; B shares, for those with midrange (5- to 10-year) needs; and C shares, for those with short-term (3- to 5-year) needs. C shares can also serve long-term investors if there is a desire to periodically redesign the portfolio or change mutual fund companies without incurring up-front sales charges or contingent deferred sales charges (CDSCs).

Each mutual fund class has a different *expense ratio,* so the question of which share class is better also depends on the impact of the expense ratio paid along the way. In addition, most A shares have "breakpoints," whereby you usually qualify for a discount on your load once you invest a certain dollar amount. Thus, if you invest at least the specified sum in a family of mutual funds, you may be able to reduce your expenses.

Open- and closed-end funds

What are the advantages of closed-end funds?

Closed-end funds offer several advantages to investors. The manager of a closed-end fund is able to manage the fund assets on the basis of his or her skilled perception of the market, without the concerns of capital inflow and outflow caused by share purchases and redemptions. Thus, when stock prices decline, the manager can use cash on hand to buy new investments, instead of meeting shareholder redemptions.

Furthermore, the buyer can select a a closed-end fund that is currently selling at a discount to the net asset value (NAV). For a bond mutual fund, the discount in purchase price means a higher dividend yield. Another advantage is that new money does not enter a closed-end bond fund, causing the manager to buy newer, lower-yielding bonds if interest rates have declined.

What are the risks of investing in closed-end funds?

Investing in closed-end funds involves the same risks as investing in open-end funds but has the additional risk of the potential discount to the NAV. Although you may be able to buy a closed-end fund at a discount to its NAV, there is no guarantee that you can sell it at its NAV, nor is there any guarantee that the discount will not grow by the time you decide to sell.

What are the commission costs of buying a closed-end fund?

A closed-end fund does not charge a sales load. Because closed-end mutual funds trade on an exchange, similar to stocks, the buyer pays a sales commission instead of a sales load. The sales commission can vary from firm to firm, with the lowest being that of the discount firms, which charge just a few dollars to execute the trade, regardless of the amount invested.

Index funds

What are the advantages of indexing?

Indexing, or *passive investing,* involves buying an investment product that contains the entire basket of stocks that make up an index or asset class. Proponents of indexing see the following advantages of using this investment strategy:

1. Indexing results in increased diversification and avoids fund manager risk.
2. Indexing results in lower implementation costs since the purchase is executed with mutual or pooled funds whose administrative and transaction costs are shared among all investors.
3. Passive investing offers certainty in matching the risk-reward profile and performance measurement standards established in an investor's investment policy statement.
4. Given the lack of active management in indexed funds, there is less turnover and thus they tend to be more tax-efficient.

What are the disadvantages of passive investing?

Some of the perceived disadvantages of passive investing are the following:

1. Indexing requires an efficient market, whereas active management seeks to exploit possible inefficiencies in the market.
2. The same technology that has made the development of indexing possible has also made it possible to discover inefficiencies in the market that make indexing an imperfect science.
3. Indexing can be interpreted to mean only the S&P 500 index. This can expose a portfolio to large-cap bias in the S&P 500, resulting in higher risk and less diversification.
4. Some active fund managers will begin to build cash reserves when securities become, in their opinion, overpriced. If a correction occurs, the cash portion will cushion the portfolio from the losses that would have occurred had the portfolio been fully invested. An indexed portfolio does not offer this feature.
5. An index fund will always vary from the actual index performance because of execution costs, cash awaiting investments or raised to

meet redemptions, and management fees. This is referred to as the *tracking error* of the fund.

Are S&P index funds the ultimate in tax-efficient investing?

It is a popular belief that indexing is the ultimate buy-and-hold strategy. Consequently, investors sometimes believe that they will not incur any tax liability until their shares are redeemed. The fact of the matter is that shareholders in S&P index funds can incur a tax liability before redemption. For instance, fund management may have to liquidate assets in order to meet demands for share redemption. In addition, the S&P 500 index funds experience turnover because of weighting and listing changes, both of which can trigger tax consequences. Overall, however, index funds tend to be more tax-efficient than actively managed funds.

Should I concentrate my investments in index funds?

This question has been debated for years, especially the last few years, in which S&P 500 index funds have outperformed many managed mutual funds.

In a bull market such as the one the United States experienced in the late 1990s, index funds have done well because the fund must buy the stocks in the index irrespective of a company's future prospects. This mandate creates a snowball effect: the more a stock goes up in value, the more stock the fund has to buy; the more money that is attracted to index funds, the higher the prices of the stocks in the index rise, so even more money is drawn in; and so forth.

In the opinion of some financial advisors, the opposite can also be true, thereby inflating the values of the stocks in the index on the upside and undervaluing them on the downside. Even the S&P 500 index is heavily weighted toward the small percentage of the 500 companies that are the largest. Thus, a substantial portion of the investor's money is actually going into very few stocks.

According to a recent article in *Forbes* magazine, the S&P 500 index has slightly underperformed the median of all actively managed large-cap stock funds on a rolling 5-year period since 1981. For the same period, the index actually has been trailing the median of all actively managed small-cap stock funds. In fact, data has revealed that the performance of the S&P 500 index has never exceeded the top quartiles of either group. Moreover, the study indicated that the actively managed funds tend to do better than the index during down markets.

Index funds can be an easy way to invest. Fund management fees are low because there is no active management deciding upon stocks to buy and to sell and no research is required. In addition, index funds tend to be more tax-efficient since they buy and hold the stocks in the index.

Stock funds

What are the advantages and disadvantages of investing in stock funds?

The advantages of investing in stock funds are:

1. Historically higher overall return than bonds or other options
2. More growth potential than debt instruments
3. Higher total return during economic growth

The disadvantages of investing in stock funds are:

1. Greater risk than fixed-income funds
2. More price volatility than fixed-income funds
3. In case of corporate insolvency, payments to shareholders made after payments to bondholders.

Should I buy a stock mutual fund or individual stocks?

In deciding whether to invest in a stock mutual fund or individual stocks, you should weigh the general advantages and disadvantages of each. In addition, you should consider the following specific issues.

DIVERSIFICATION You must determine if you can create proper diversification by selecting individual stocks. The old adage, "Don't put all your eggs in one basket," applies to investing in stocks. By diversifying, you can reduce risk. Generally, you should invest in many different companies to achieve proper diversification, but you may not find it possible to do this as an individual investor. A stock mutual fund is a simple, cost-effective method of diversification.

LIQUIDITY AND CONTROL Individual stocks, if they are traded actively on an exchange, qualify as liquid investments. Also, with individual stocks you control buy and sell decisions, and this allows you to better manage your portfolio, especially if you need tax efficiency.

Stock mutual funds are generally very liquid—most investors find that their liquidity is greater than that of individual stocks. Yet you have no control over which individual stocks are bought and sold or the timing of these sales. However, the record keeping in a mutual fund is simpler than that required for individual stocks, so a stock mutual fund offers a great measure of convenience.

EXPENSES When comparing the expenses for buying and selling individual stocks with the expenses of a stock mutual fund, be sure you consider all expenses: commissions (buying and selling), marketing fees, tax liabilities, and any internal 12b-1 fees.

One option to keep in mind is using the services of a private money manager. Although this arrangement is similar to mutual funds, since a professional decides what and when to buy and sell, you hold the individual shares of stock in your account and you may improve tax efficiency because you control the shares.

If some mutual funds are performing marginally better than mine, should I be concerned?

Many times, within a particular period, the performance of mutual funds varies. To make an informed comparison of funds, it is important to determine *why* one fund is doing better than another. Let's assume a fund has always been an average performer and nothing major has changed with the internal mechanics of the portfolio. That is, it has the same investment objective, the same portfolio manager, and the same expenses. If that fund then has an outstanding year or quarter, you can pretty much base its good performance on luck.

When comparing funds in the same category, such as growth, value, or income, you should look for consistency. Find out how the funds have performed year after year. If possible, stay with funds that are in the top 20 percent each and every year within the same asset class.

If you are comparing rates of return, the difference in the rates from a marginal performer and an above-average performer may not seem significant, but over the long term it has a large impact. For example, $10,000 invested for 20 years at a 10 percent annual rate of return results in a value of $67,275 but at a 10.5 percent annual rate of return results in approximately $73,662. The $6387 difference is a 9 percent increase in the amount of money that you have ($6387 ÷ $67,275 = 9%). As you can see, over time, even a small difference in rate of return can turn into significantly large dollars.

Bond funds

Is it better to own individual bonds or a bond mutual fund?

In choosing an appropriate strategy for investing in bonds, you should consider the following four issues.

DIVERSIFICATION By diversifying, you reduce risk. You have to purchase the bonds of a number of individual companies to achieve proper diversification. Purchasing many bonds can be expensive, however, since bonds usually require a minimum investment of $10,000. Thus, a portfolio of twenty bonds requires a $200,000 investment.

A bond mutual fund by its nature is diversified. While some bond funds require a minimum investment, it is likely that you can find one that meets your budget. By investing in a bond mutual fund, you can reduce the amount of your investment and at the same time achieve diversity.

LIQUIDITY Bond mutual funds are generally very liquid, since they redeem fund shares for cash and are traded on major exchanges. Individual bonds are liquid only if they are actively traded on a recognized exchange.

EXPENSES When you invest in individual bonds, there are commissions on buying and selling. Generally, because of the amount of money being invested by an individual, commissions on purchasing individual bonds can be much higher than the expenses for purchasing shares in a bond mutual fund. However, in comparing expenses, it is important to consider all expenses, including commissions (buying and selling), marketing fees, and any 12b-1 fees.

PREDICTABILITY OF INCOME A portfolio of individual bonds can give you a much more predictable income stream and better predictability of liquidity than can a bond mutual fund. When an individual bond matures, the holder is assured of the principal regardless of market conditions. This is not the case with mutual funds. In a mutual fund, there is no maturity date. Shares may be sold at a share price that on any given day could be higher or lower than the original purchase price.

Choosing and purchasing the fund

With over 11,000 mutual funds to choose from, how do I select the most suitable funds for my portfolio?

When deciding which mutual fund to invest in, you should look at the following criteria:

1. The mutual fund type (stock, bond, futures, money market, balanced, indexed, sector, etc.)
2. The mutual fund's objective (aggressive growth, moderate growth, income, safety)
3. The current rate of return
4. The average total return in the last 3 to 5 years
5. The corresponding index and/or benchmark returns over the same periods
6. Load fees (sales and redemption charges)
7. Annual operating expenses (management fees, advertising costs, and marketing costs, expressed as a percentage of average net assets)
8. The level of risk (high, medium, low)

These criteria are helpful in comparing mutual funds to ensure proper diversification. It is important that you do not concentrate more money in a specific asset class (e.g., too many mutual funds) than is necessary to reach your goals.

Is it possible to invest in mutual funds that are aligned with social or ethical values?

In the early 1950s, the Roman Catholic Church removed tobacco and alcohol stocks from its investment portfolios. This began what is referred to today as *socially responsible investing (SRI),* a philosophy of investing that has attracted tens of billions of dollars. SRI mutual funds embrace various causes such as environmentalism, pro-labor, anti-nuclear energy, and the ethical treatment of animals. Investors can direct investment dollars to mutual funds that embrace the investors' philosophies or eliminate or mitigate exposure to certain industries. Many of these funds also have very respectable track records.

Should I buy the "hot fund" of the year?

Every mutual fund needs to be evaluated over a period of time, so look at the 1-, 3-, 5-, and 10-year averages. Managers of "hot" mutual funds do not tend to stick around very long. Once they have a good track record, they usually move on to positions with the biggest bonuses. So it is important to find out how long the manager has been with a fund and the fund's history.

Should mutual funds be purchased directly from the fund family or through a brokerage account?

Buying your fund at the fund company can avoid transaction costs, but doing so has some limitations. If you purchase your mutual fund shares through a brokerage account, you can receive a consolidated statement of all your mutual funds, stocks, and other securities.

If you want to sell your mutual fund and move to another fund company, the brokerage account makes it very simple to sell and buy. If you are in a mutual fund directly, you must request a sale, the company transfers the cash to you, and you send it to the new fund company.

Even though in some cases the costs may be higher with the brokerage account, most investors see brokerage accounts as the better choice.

Why is it important to stay within the same family of funds if I decide to change my investments?

Staying within the same family of funds is important if you paid a sales charge or if you will be subject to a deferred back-end sales charge when you sell out of the family. This is because you can switch among the funds in a family without being subject to a new sales charge.

I'd like to be able to switch my fund to cash at a moment's notice without having to call my broker. Can that be done?

Yes; just about every mutual fund has a toll-free number. If you signed up for telephone switching, you can change your investments over the phone without having to call your broker or investment advisor.

Selling the fund

When should I sell a mutual fund?

Any of the following situations might indicate that it is time to sell:

- *Your investment objective changes and no longer matches the objective of the mutual fund.*
- *The portfolio manager is not living up to the expectations expressed in the fund's prospectus.* If the portfolio manager is consistently underperforming for several quarters, you should seriously consider liquidating the account. One or two bad quarters should not be the reason for liquidating, as a manager cannot be right all the time.
- *The fund gets too large to be able to take meaningful positions in individual stock issues.* For some individuals, this might be the time to move to a smaller, more nimble fund. There are exceptions, of course: Vanguard and Fidelity funds have formidably managed ac-

counts in excess of $1 billion. Bond mutual funds are also an exception, because the larger a bond fund, the lower the expense ratio should be. In addition, the more bonds a fund holds, the less chance there is that the fund will be hurt if some of its bond issuers default.

Unit investment trusts

I like the idea of owning a specified list of stocks or bonds, but purchasing the entire list requires more money than I want to invest. A mutual fund seems to be the closest answer, but I don't care for the frequent buying and selling that goes on in the typical fund. Is there an alternative that will meet my investment needs?

A *unit investment trust (UIT)* is a hybrid investment that has the attributes of mutual funds *and* individual securities (stocks and/or bonds). A UIT is a named list of stocks or bonds that will not change during the course of the investment. In most cases your money will be evenly distributed among the listed securities, the management fees will be low or nonexistent, and sales charges will be about the same as or less than the charges for an A-share load mutual fund.

UITs are usually sold through financial advisors or intermediaries, are liquid, and emphasize a buy-and-hold strategy. They are used by investment professionals to complement mutual funds, replace certain categories of mutual fund–heavy portfolios, or meet stock or bond requirements not available through individual securities or mutual funds.

International investments

Should part of my portfolio be invested in international stocks or mutual funds?

For most investors, the answer to this question is yes. When added to a portfolio of domestic investments, foreign securities actually reduce the risk of the overall portfolio. Stock and bond markets throughout the world rarely move up and down at the same time. The correlation is actually random, and this helps lower the risk and volatility of the overall portfolio.

Because foreign securities make up over 50 percent of the total world stock market, investors have a variety of options available in purchasing international stocks. These options include the purchase of foreign stocks and bonds listed on foreign exchanges, the purchase of American depository receipts (ADRs) listed on U.S. exchanges, the purchase of stock in multinational companies, and the purchase of international or global open- and closed-end mutual funds.

U.S. residents who invest overseas must weigh additional considerations that affect potential return. Political risk, foreign taxation, and the fluctuation of the U.S. dollar relative to each foreign currency are risks not inherent in the U.S. markets. Due to the risks and uncertainties associated with international investing, using mutual funds or private money managers is generally the preferred way to invest overseas.

Given the increased interconnection among countries' economies, can an investor truly diversify by adding non-U.S. securities to a portfolio?

Historically, adding foreign securities to a U.S. portfolio increased returns while reducing risk. Higher returns in large part reflect the low or imperfect correlation of returns among the world's capital markets. More recently, however, as the world's economies have become more interconnected, many of the major world markets have tended to move in a more synchronized fashion, especially during times of extreme volatility. Examples of such volatility that had major effects on U.S. markets are the devaluation of the Russian ruble and the major currency problems in Thailand and Indonesia.

Nevertheless, mutual funds that invest in foreign countries should continue to be part of an investor's portfolio. For most average investors, investing in mutual funds that are not limited to investing in a particular country or region is often the better course of action because the fund managers have the freedom to reallocate capital in response to changes in global economic conditions.

What percentage of my total portfolio should be invested in the international category?

Although the rule of thumb that many people use is to allocate 10 to 30 percent of the total portfolio to international assets, the percentage that you should invest in international securities depends on your investment plan. In the long-term, adding foreign investments to your portfolio reduces overall volatility.

How do I purchase stocks of foreign corporations?

Many international companies are now listing their stocks on U.S.

exchanges using American depository receipts (ADRs). Investing through a domestic exchange is an excellent way to invest internationally because foreign companies are then required to follow U.S. accounting rules.

Another method is to invest in mutual funds that invest internationally.

What is the best type of international fund to purchase for my account?

Many investors prefer to be in funds that allow the fund managers the greatest flexibility to purchase securities in the regions they wish, such as Asia, the Pacific Rim, Latin America, Europe, North America, or any combination.

Typically, the name of the fund indicates the region in which the fund manager can invest. A global fund includes all regions (including the United States); an international fund includes all but the United States; and a Europe or Asia fund is limited to just Europe or Asia. If an investor wants to leave the regional decisions to the fund manager, a global fund is appropriate. If an investor wants to exclude stocks in the United States, an international fund is the proper investment vehicle.

What is the European Union, and what is its significance for investors?

The *European Union (EU)* is a group of fifteen countries that joined together in 1999 to form a common economic area. The EU includes Denmark, Greece, Sweden, Britain, Austria, Belgium, France, Italy, Portugal, Finland, Germany, Luxembourg, the Netherlands, Ireland, and Spain.

The purpose of the EU is to facilitate the movement of people, goods, services, and capital through the adoption of a common set of institutional structures. Members of the EU will gradually move toward a common currency (the euro), centralized monetary policy (implemented through a European Central Bank), and standards for managing domestic fiscal policy. In addition, banking and capital markets will be governed under a common set of regulations.

Many commentators believe that investors will look more favorably on Europe because of the EU. First, there is the matter of the EU's sheer size. Taken as a whole, the EU constitutes a significant economic entity. In addition, there is the expectation that significant investment opportunities will be found as a result of the many cross-border corporate consolidations, the labor mobility, and the corporate expansions that are likely to occur.

Skeptics point out, however, that such benefits may prove elusive and that the EU may not in the end prove to be viable due to irreconcilable cultural, economic, and political differences of the member countries. Nonetheless, most would agree that the EU is at least off to a good start and that the initial convergence of the participating countries has gone far better than expected.

Hedge funds

Aren't all hedge funds high-risk investments?

The popular misconception is that all hedge funds are high-risk or volatile and that they all use global macro strategies and place large directional bets on stocks, currencies, bonds, commodities, and gold, while using a high degree of leverage. In reality, less than 5 percent of hedge funds are global macro funds. Most hedge funds use derivatives only for hedging or don't use derivatives at all, and many use no leverage.

I've heard that only big pension funds can invest in hedge funds. Is that true, or can an individual invest in a hedge fund?

Many endowments and pension funds allocate assets to hedge funds, as do many sophisticated investors who have lived through and understand the consequences of major stock market corrections. Hedge funds typically have very high minimum investments, usually around $1 million per unit, although there have been some hedge funds recently with lower minimums of approximately $100,000 per unit. In addition, the investor has to prove that he or she is a sophisticated/accredited investor as defined by the SEC accredited-investor rule (net worth of $1 million or annual income of $250,000).

How is a hedge fund structured?

Hedge funds are usually structured as limited partnerships. Investors buy units of the partnership. The manager of the fund can be the general partner (but not always), and the investors are the limited partners.

What are the advantages of a hedge fund over a mutual fund?

Hedge funds are extremely flexible in their investment options because they use financial instruments generally beyond the reach of mutual funds. SEC regulations and disclosure requirements largely prevent mutual funds from using short selling, leverage, concentrated investments, and derivatives. The flexibility of hedge funds gives them the ability to better manage investment risk. Unlike many mutual fund managers, hedge fund managers are usually heavily invested in their own fund and share the rewards as well as the risk with the investors.

How are hedge fund managers paid?

Hedge fund managers receive incentive compensation only when returns are positive. In contrast, mutual fund managers get paid on the volume of assets managed, regardless of performance.

What are the fees and commissions that I would have to pay in a hedge fund?

Since hedge funds are in limited partnership form, the fees and commissions vary from fund to fund. You need to carefully read the prospectus before purchasing a unit in a hedge fund.

Are investments in hedge funds liquid? Can I get my money out if I need to?

Investments in hedge funds can be somewhat illiquid, depending on the hedge fund. Some funds allow monthly liquidation, some allow it quarterly, and some have certain lockup provisions that prohibit liquidation in the first year. Liquidation rights are discussed in detail in the prospectus of the fund.

Annuities

What are some advantages of annuities?

Tax advantages and the need for baby boomers to save more efficiently for retirement are the main reasons the sales of annuity products have skyrocketed. Qualified plans have a ceiling for contributions, built-in "reverse discrimination" because of coverage requirements, and complex red tape. Many individuals, retirees, and employers have turned to tax-deferred annuities to supplement their retirement savings and to lower their annual exposure to taxable interest and investment gain. Listed below are some of the advantages of annuities:

1. Unless an annuity is owned by a for-profit corporation or other entity, all income and growth is tax-deferred until it is withdrawn.
2. By reallocating taxable investments to deferred annuity investments, it is possible for an individual to lower taxable income each year and thus the taxes he or she pays. A retiree with a large amount of taxable interest income can reallocate assets to annuities and potentially reduce or eliminate the tax liability he or she pays on Social Security benefits. Why? Because a person with lower taxable income pays less tax on Social Security benefits.
3. When distributions are made, taxable interest or gain comes out on a pro rata basis.
4. The beneficiary designation on the annuity allows the proceeds or death benefit to be paid directly to the designated beneficiary without having to go through probate.
5. On the death of the annuity owner, the owner's spouse, if he or she is the beneficiary, can roll the annuity contract over into his or her own name and the tax deferral will be retained. All other beneficiaries must elect to annuitize the benefit within 1 year of the owner's date of death or to take the total amount in one distribution or in a series of even or uneven distributions within 5 years from the date of death of the deceased.
6. The owner of the annuity can choose between guaranteed investment accounts or the many types of variable subaccounts. The subaccounts include, but are not limited to, stock, bond, balanced, specialty, and international investments. The insurer behind the annuity offers professional management of the subaccounts. The owner can transfer between these accounts at will without incurring a taxable event.
7. About two-thirds of the states offer at least some creditor protection for annuities.

What are some disadvantages of annuities?

Some disadvantages of annuities are:

1. Compared with other investment vehicles, none of the taxable income or growth from an annuity is taxed at the favorable capital gain rate.
2. Annuities have higher administration costs compared with other investment vehicles, as well as mortality and expense charges, that

can offset the performance of the subaccounts considerably, especially in down markets.

3. All taxable distributions taken before the age of 59½ are subject to a 10 percent tax penalty, unless the taxpayer has some qualifying event, such as disability or death.
4. At the death of the annuity owner, all the profit is subject to ordinary-income tax in the beneficiaries' hands, since there is no stepped-up cost basis as there is with stock or mutual funds. (Step-up in basis is discussed in detail in Chapter 4.)

In October 1997, Price Waterhouse, LLP, performed a study for the National Association for Variable Annuities. The study concluded that for long-term investors, variable annuities continue to remain attractive investments even though there is the potential for better capital gain tax treatment with mutual funds.

How do I get money out of my annuity?

If you are over 59½, you have several choices for taking distributions from annuities, regardless of the kind or type of annuity:

1. *Lump sum*
2. *Random withdrawals,* whereby you withdraw as much money as you want when you want.
3. *Annuitization:*
   a. The *straight-life,* or *life-with-no-refund,* option provides you with periodic payments for your life. Upon your death, all payments cease and no death benefits will be paid to your beneficiary.
   b. The *installment refund,* or *life-refund,* option provides you with periodic payments for life, but if the full purchase price of your annuity has not been returned to you before your death, the balance is paid to your beneficiary.
   c. *Life and term certain* provides you with periodic payments for life. It is a combination of *installment-refund* and *term-certain* options with regard to your beneficiaries. If you die within a fixed number of years after you begin taking payments, your beneficiary will receive the payments until the end of that period. If you die after the fixed period ends, your beneficiary will receive nothing.

  d. *Joint life* provides payments until your death or that of another individual (usually a spouse), whichever occurs *first.*
  e. *Joint life and survivorship* provides payments until your death or that of another individual (usually a spouse), whichever occurs *last.*

4. *Systematic (term certain),* which provides you with periodic payments for a set period of time. If you live beyond that period of time, the payments to you stop. If you die before the payout period ends, your beneficiary receives the payments for the balance of the period.

My annuity is tax-deferred like my retirement plan and IRA, so am I also required to take minimum distributions after age 70½ from the annuity?

No. There is no mandatory withdrawal rule imposed at 70½.

Fixed and variable annuities

How is the interest rate on a fixed annuity determined?

The interest rate on a fixed annuity is initially set out in the annuity contract; the issuing institution determines the rate.

Many fixed annuities have a variable fixed rate; that is, the rate will change on a year-to-year basis. It is usually guaranteed not to go below a specific rate, such as 3 or 4 percent. Fixed annuities usually pay slightly higher rates than Treasury bills or CDs at the time of purchase. Some fixed annuities give a fixed rate of return for a 3-, 4-, 5-, or 6-year time span, but most change their rates on an annual basis.

Fixed annuities are attractive to conservative investors who desire a guarantee of return of principal and a guaranteed minimum interest rate.

Why invest in variable annuities?

Retirement is generally the reason most people cite for investing in variable annuities, because accumulating assets to generate income during the retirement years is their objective. To provide for an adequate income stream, one must think long term and plan a strategy accordingly. The tax-deferred nature of the variable annuity is attractive.

Common sense dictates that avoiding needless risk has merit. Common sense also tells us that extending our willingness to assume some risk can reap commensurate reward. When viewing the risk of running out of money toward the end of our lives, opting for greater growth potential may make sense. Further, the many choices of variable subaccounts and qualified managers can provide enough diversity to implement a proper risk-reward investment strategy.

In summary, a long-term strategy of investing in variable annuities may make saving for retirement more effective.

What is the guaranteed death benefit of a variable annuity?

With many variable annuities there is a death benefit guarantee on each contract anniversary which ensures that the account value will never drop below the level it is at on that date. For example, the contract owner deposits $100,000 into the account, and by the fifth annual anniversary the account has grown to $160,000. In the subsequent year the owner dies, but during that year the stock market has gone down, so the account is worth $140,000 when the owner dies. How much would the beneficiary receive? Most people would say $140,000. However, the guaranteed death benefit locked in the $160,000 on the last contract anniversary, so the beneficiary will receive $160,000. This provision can vary depending on your contract, so please review the specific details carefully.

I've heard that variable annuities cost more than pure mutual funds. Are they worth it?

It all depends. Variable annuities are typically .4 to .65 percent more expensive than a comparable mutual fund portfolio. The additional costs, known as *mortality and expense charges,* pay for guaranteed death benefits and the expenses and profits of the insurance company. Sometimes, the costs associated with the underlying subaccounts are less within the variable annuity than they might be with a comparable mutual fund, making the total added cost less than it might appear from simply reading the prospectus.

The added costs may be offset by the tax savings that annuities provide. Understanding and evaluating the economics of a variable annuity requires knowing your current tax bracket, as well as making assumptions as to its likely level in the future. In addition, you must decide the length of time the funds will remain in the variable annuity or mutual fund, both during the period in which they will be growing as well as the time frame during which you will take money out. Given this information, most variable-annuity companies will provide you with hypothetical comparisons of the performance of the annuity and that of mutual funds.

Whether you should own mutual funds or variable annuities, or a combination of the two, depends upon your individual circumstances. A thoughtful evaluation should be performed before you make a decision.

Should I invest in a variable annuity or a fixed annuity?

Your objectives determine whether you need a fixed or variable annuity. The company issuing the fixed annuity guarantees a fixed rate of return. There is no market volatility as there is with the variable annuity.

The primary advantage of a variable annuity is being able to invest on a tax-advantaged basis through the annuity's subaccounts. Although, historically, variable annuities have substantially outperformed fixed annuities over time, fixed annuities still have their place for the conservative fixed-income investor whose priority is a guaranteed rate of return. If you require a higher return than that offered by fixed annuities and are willing to take the additional risk, a variable annuity is an ideal choice.

Annuity exchanges

If I'm disappointed with the performance of my existing annuity, can I replace it with a more competitive annuity?

Yes. It is common to replace one annuity with another. However, such an exchange should be done only after a careful comparison of the advantages and disadvantages.

If you decide to make the exchange, be sure that the transfer is done directly between the existing annuity company and the new annuity company. By meeting this requirement, among others, you comply with Section 1035 of the Internal Revenue Code, which allows the tax-free exchange of one annuity for another. Without the protection of Section 1035, income taxes would be due on the accumulated gain in your existing annuity.

By using the "1035 transfer" method, can I consolidate several annuities into one new annuity account?

It depends. Many annuity companies will not permit you to consolidate several annuities and protect your transferred tax deferral. Others will. Make sure you are working with a financial advisor who thoroughly understands annuities, including tax and product issues, because you may trigger a taxable event if you do not consolidate the annuities properly.

I have an old fixed annuity. Can it be changed to a variable annuity?

Yes it can, under the Section 1035 tax-free exchange privilege. You must complete and submit the application for the variable annuity along with the transfer paperwork for your existing fixed-annuity contract. The variable-annuity company will then establish your new annuity contract and request transfer of the funds from your fixed-annuity company.

Real estate

What do I need to know about investing in real estate?

Direct investments in real estate can be financially rewarding if you understand the risks, take the time to educate yourself, and plan properly. To have a successful real estate investment, you may be required to wear several hats, including those of investment analyst, leasing agent, property manager, mortgage loan analyst, turnaround specialist, and so on. So, before taking any steps to invest, educate yourself or hire professionals who can help you, or both.

What are the most important ingredients for a successful real estate investment?

The two most important ingredients for a successful real estate investment, especially residential or commercial rental real estate, are location and management. Historically, well-located, properly managed real estate has done well. A good location is measured by demand, while good management is a function of obtaining and keeping good tenants while maintaining competitive rents and minimizing expenses.

How do I find a good real estate investment?

The first step is to know what to look for. For example, when looking for residential rental property, look for an area where people want to live, such as near schools, shopping, and transportation. Make sure the properties you look at are in compliance with zoning laws and are mechanically and structurally sound.

Once you have located one or more prospective properties, analyze the financials for each one. To obtain the most accurate financial numbers, get a copy of the part of the seller's tax return that pertains to the property. It will have the property's income and expenses. You should then prepare a second income and expense form to include your adjustments, such as a reasonable vacancy factor, probable increases in property taxes (due to the sale), potential debt service (mortgage payments), and any other adjustments you think are reasonable.

Use your reconstructed 1-year analysis as a basis for projecting various future cash flows and the potential future sale price. These numbers should all be adjusted for taxes (including the savings from depreciation) to get to the bottom line. The final numbers will help you determine your overall rate of return, which is often referred to as the *internal rate of return (IRR).*

Don't forget to include a management fee when calculating your cash flows. Any good financial calculator can help you compute the IRR, which is the best way for you to compare different types of investments.

You can achieve success in all your real estate investments by making a careful analysis of the location, the structural soundness, the management requirements, and the return as projected by your IRR calculations.

Can I invest in real estate without all that effort?

Investing in real estate investment trusts (REITs) or limited partnerships typically demands far less involvement than direct real estate purchases. Even so, investors who choose these investments should thoroughly research their risks and potential returns.

Managed Account Strategies

What are the advantages of investing through a managed account?

A managed account has a number of advantages. First, there is no incentive for the broker to "churn" the account to generate commissions, since there are none. Second, the financial advisor or broker is paid to continue a high level of service and to be actively involved in guiding you toward the attainment of your goals. Your success and the professional's success are tied together.

STRATEGIES FOR REDUCING TAXES

How can I minimize my income taxes?

To reduce income taxes, you should position your investments in four different bundles, as follows:

1. Some investments should be made on an after-tax basis in such vehicles as mutual funds, bonds, real estate, cash, and CDs. The principal in these investments has already been taxed, but the interest, dividends, and capital gains will be taxed in the year that they are realized. This pot of money can provide liquidity if you need it.
2. Invest your before-tax dollars in vehicles that will grow tax-deferred. Examples are 401(k) plans, traditional IRAs, SEP plans, qualified pension and profit-sharing plans, 403(b) tax-sheltered annuities, and Section 457 plans. As you contribute money to these retirement plans, you typically take a tax deduction in the year you make the contributions. If you take distributions after age 59½, they are taxed as ordinary income. If you take distributions before age 59½, they are not only taxed as ordinary income but may also be subject to a 10 percent penalty, although there are many exceptions to this penalty.
3. You should consider investing some after-tax dollars in tax-deferred annuities, tax-efficient funds or portfolios, or individual growth stocks for holding long term. Contributions are not tax-deductible, but most of the growth that is generated grows tax-deferred until sold.
4. You should invest after-tax dollars in vehicles that provide tax-free returns. Examples are municipal bonds, some limited partnerships, Roth IRAs, and cash-value life insurance. Although you do not get a tax deduction when investing in these vehicles, the income and distributions may be tax-exempt or tax-free. In the case of municipal bonds, the income received is exempt from income taxation by the federal government and, in some cases, is free from state and local income tax. It should be noted that any realized capital gains on municipal bonds are fully taxable. Some limited partnerships can actually eliminate your taxes through tax credits.

By investing in all four bundles, you will be in a position to help control how much tax you will pay on your investments and when you will pay it. You may be able to have a cash flow that is substantially greater than your taxable income.

Municipal Bonds

Are municipal bonds and tax-free municipal bond funds always totally free of taxes?

The simple answer is no. Realized capital gains on the sale of a municipal bond are taxable. Capital gains (or losses) can occur as bond values move in the opposite direction of interest rates. The interest *directly* received or reinvested is free from federal taxes and from state taxes on bonds issued by the state in which the investor resides. Let's assume you purchase an individual municipal bond or a municipal bond mutual fund for $10,000. Falling interest rates cause the bond's value to rise to $11,000, and you sell the investment. You will have a taxable capital gain of $1000, which will be either a short-term or long-term gain, depending on how long you held the bond investment.

For retirees who pay tax on their Social Security benefits, tax-free interest can *indirectly* lead to an increased tax bill. This is because all tax-free earnings are added into the formula for determining how much Social Security is actually taxed. So even though the tax-free interest is not directly taxed, it increases the amount on which the tax is calculated, subsequently causing more of your Social Security benefits to be taxed.

How can I compare the tax benefit of a municipal bond with a comparable taxable bond?

To know whether you should invest in tax-free bonds or taxable bonds, you need to compute the *taxable equivalent yield (TEY)* of a tax-free bond. The formula is as follows:

$$\text{Taxable equivalent yield} = \frac{\text{tax free yield}}{1 - \text{your federal income tax rate}}$$

Using this formula, let's assume you are thinking about investing in a tax-free bond that pays 5 percent and your effective federal income tax rate is 31 percent:

$$\text{TEY} = \frac{.05}{1 - .31} = 7.24\% \text{ taxable equivalent}$$

To meet or beat the after-tax yield of this municipal bond, you would have to buy a taxable bond that pays at least 7.24 percent.

Mutual Funds

Do any mutual funds manage their portfolios for tax efficiency?

Believe it or not, managing a growth mutual fund with sensitivity to taxable capital gains was not a common practice until recently. Now, a number of mutual fund families have one or more funds that place a high priority on minimizing taxable capital gains and income taxes. This is partly done by the portfolio managers keeping the turnover of portfolio holdings to a minimum.

Should I buy mutual fund shares just before a dividend date?

When a mutual fund declares a dividend, no incremental benefit accrues to the shareholder. All that has occurred is that the fund has paid out cash, thereby reducing the value of each share by the exact amount that was paid out. Thus, if the net asset value was $30 per share the day before the dividend, and a $1-per-share dividend is then paid, the fund value becomes $29 per share as the dividend is paid, assuming, of course, that there was no gain or loss in share value due to market conditions.

If the shareholder reinvests the dividend, the shareholder's fund will have the same value the day before and the day after the dividend due to the additional shares or partial shares the shareholder bought with the $1-per-share dividend. If the shares are held in a taxable account, income tax will be due on the dividend, even though no cash value was received. Thus, it is generally recommended that you not buy mutual fund shares shortly before the dividend is about to be paid.

Why do I have to pay capital gain tax on my mutual fund when I didn't sell it?

When an investor purchases shares in a mutual fund for a taxable account, she or he is buying a portfolio of individual stocks or bonds. These stocks and bonds will be purchased and sold at various times throughout the year. Therefore, the mutual fund will have what is known as an *imbedded gain* (or *imbedded loss*).

Assume the fund manager purchased a stock 4 years ago and it doubled in value. The manager then sells the stock in the year that you invest in the mutual fund. A capital gain distribution will be made to you (mutual funds are required to distribute capital gains earned throughout the year) even though you did not participate in any of the appreciation of that stock over the previous 4 years.

Some investors are shocked to discover that in a year when their mutual may have earned only 5 percent, they have to recognize a 10 percent capital gain. The seemingly unfair requirement that investors pay taxes on money they didn't receive is somewhat mitigated by the fact that the capital gain distributions do become part of their cost basis. A higher cost basis reduces their tax liability if they ultimately liquidate their shares for a gain.

When you purchase a fund for a taxable account, find out how much imbedded gain there is within the fund. Imbedded gains are reported by many of the mutual fund research publications.

I have all my dividends reinvested in my mutual fund, so why do I have to pay taxes on money that I never received?

Dividends are taxable in the year they are paid. Whether you actually take the money or request that it be reinvested in additional shares of the fund doesn't matter. Because you have the right to take the money if you so desire, your decision to reinvest the dividend is essentially the same as taking the money and then writing a check to invest it into the fund. The reinvestment mechanism is merely for your convenience.

My accountant told me that I need to keep all the confirmations showing my purchases, sales, and reinvestments in my mutual fund so that when I sell it I can determine my gains and losses. I paid taxes on the income already, so why are the confirmations important?

Your confirmations contain important information that affects the cost basis in your mutual fund as well as the holding period. Your cost basis determines the amount of gain or loss that you will report on your income tax return when you sell your mutual fund shares. Your holding period determines what part of your gain or loss is short-term or long-term. You should keep accurate records of each purchase, sale, and reinvestment so that your accountant can properly calculate capital gains and losses when you close out a fund.

How can I minimize the taxes on my losing mutual fund?

Because of the way mutual funds are structured, the price of a fund's shares may drop, giving you an unrealized loss, but the fund may still create taxable income in the form of a distribution. This income is not a problem if the fund is inside a tax-favored account, such as a qualified retirement plan, variable annuity, or individual retirement account. No taxes are due on any fund distributions because you will pay taxes when you eventually withdraw from the tax-favored account.

If you hold a fund outside a tax-favored account, you may want to consider some tax-loss selling of funds before the end of the current tax year. In *tax-loss selling,* you sell some of your losing investments to offset gains on other investments. If your losses exceed your gains, you can still use up to another $3000 in losses to offset ordinary income. Anything above the $3000 in excess losses can be used to offset other capital losses and be carried over into future years to offset gains.

Assuming you want to sell one or more losing mutual funds, there are some important points to keep in mind:

1. Get an estimate from the fund of its year-end distribution; this may have an impact on your decision of whether to sell or hold.
2. Calculate your adjusted cost basis in the fund (original investment plus reinvested dividends and capital gains) to make sure the fund really is a loser for you. Even if the fund is down for the year, it still may be well above your adjusted cost basis.
3. A rule of thumb to consider is to sell funds that are doing worse than their peers. Your fund may be down, but if it is not down as much as comparable funds, you may want to keep it.
4. You can sell a losing fund and buy it back later to avoid upsetting your portfolio mix. Do not buy it back within 30 days, or the transaction will be considered a "wash sale," in which case you cannot take the loss. As an alternative, sell the fund and use the proceeds to purchase a similar fund, but be careful that the new fund is not *too* similar to the old. If it is (e.g., selling one index fund and buying a similar index fund), the transaction might be deemed a wash sale.

If I liquidate one mutual fund containing accumulated capital gains and transfer to another within the same "family of funds," will this trigger any taxes?

It does not matter that the transfer is done within the same mutual fund family. According to the Internal Revenue Code, the transaction is a sale followed by a purchase. Hence, it will trigger taxes to the extent that there are accumulated capital gains at the time of sale. The only time such a transaction does not trigger taxes is when the funds are held in a tax-advantaged vehicle, such as an IRA, qualified retirement plan, life insurance, or deferred annuity.

My municipal bond fund had taxable capital gains this year, but I thought such funds were tax-free. What happened?

Interest paid from municipal bonds is tax-free, even if the bonds are held in a mutual fund. Mutual fund bond managers sell and buy bonds on a daily basis, sometimes creating capital gains. Capital gains generated from municipal bonds held in a mutual fund are subject to taxation. As a shareholder in the fund, you must pay capital gain tax on your portion of the gain.

Rebalancing Assets

What are the tax consequences of rebalancing my portfolio?

If your portfolio is held in a tax-qualified account (pension, traditional IRA, 401(k), 403(b), etc.), there are no income taxes generated by rebalancing. However, if your account is a personal investment portfolio, the sale of an asset will generate either a capital gain or a capital loss. In this situation, care must be given to the tax consequences of rebalancing.

Annuities

Do annuities have any negative tax and financial aspects?

There are some negative tax and financial aspects of annuities that need to be considered in the decision-making process. The accumulation portion of an annuity that is in excess of the total contributions made to the annuity is always taxed as ordinary income rather than capital gain income when a distribution takes place.

In a traditional stock mutual fund, much of the return is taxed as a capital gain. In a variable annuity, however, withdrawals attributed to stock investments are taxed as ordinary income.

The tax differences between a variable annuity and a comparable mutual fund can be substantial: the maximum federal long-term capital gain tax is 20 percent, while the maximum ordinary-income tax rate is 39.6 percent.

This difference in income tax rates tends to be a nonissue with fixed annuities, where the income earned on a comparable investment such as a bond or CD is taxed on a current basis at the same ordinary-income tax level.

Yes, but doesn't the ability to continue to defer the taxes eventually offset a potentially higher tax rate in later years?

In theory yes, but there are professionals who take a contrary view. There is no question that the tax-deferral benefit of variable annuities has a great attraction. This tax advantage is one reason that annuities have had such a phenomenal growth in sales over the years. In fact, the math some advisors use shows that the variable annuity appears to be a better investment than a comparable mutual fund. However, some analyses tend to show that other investments, even if not tax-advantaged, may have superior results.

Because of the expenses of many variable annuities, it can take 12 to 14 years for an annuity to outperform a comparable mutual fund. Thereafter, the annuity may show superior results because of its tax-deferred nature. But if an investor chooses a fund manager who is dedicated to tax efficiency or invests in an index fund whose turnover ratios tend to be lower than those of an actively managed fund, an in-depth analysis may show that a comparable mutual fund would have a greater overall net after-tax return, in both the short and the long terms.

Of course, it is important that an investment be considered on the basis of the investor's objectives, only one of which may be tax deferral. And it is important to work with financial advisors who monitor your investments carefully to ensure that the account is managed in a tax-efficient manner.

When I take withdrawals from my fixed and variable annuities, how am I taxed?

Both fixed and variable annuities give you three withdrawal options—lump sum, random, and systematic—and each option is taxed differently:

- *Lump sum:* You take the entire amount at one time and pay taxes on all earnings and gains in the year you receive them.
- *Random withdrawal:* The accumulated taxable portion, or earnings and capital gains, comes out first, and all taxes are due on the amounts when received. This is known as the "last-in, first-out"

(LIFO) method. "Last in" are the investment earnings, which are considered first out and taxed at ordinary-income tax rates.

- *Systematic withdrawal and annuitization:* Each individual payment is considered part return of principal and part accumulated growth. The ratio is the same as that of the total annuity account. In other words, if the total annuity value is $100,000, of which 75 percent is tax-deferred growth and 25 percent is principal, each payment distributed will be considered 25 percent nontaxable return of principal and 75 percent taxable ordinary income.

PART TWO

Estate and Tax Planning

Estate planning continues to be listed as one of the most important elements of financial planning. The huge increases in wealth that the United States has experienced have created exponential growth in the number of millionaires and even billionaires. In spite of this great wealth, it is apparent from the questions and answers we received from our contributing authors that there remains a great deal of confusion among the public about all aspects of estate planning.

Most of the questions that clients of our contributing authors are asking deal with the most fundamental issues of estate planning. One would think that the more sophisticated issues in estate planning would get most of the attention, but just the opposite was true in the research presented by our contributing authors. Their clients have a great interest in understanding the basic techniques of planning, including the real, people problems of planning. They want to understand the planning process itself and how this process can be used to help facilitate effective planning. These topics are covered in the questions and answers in Chapter 3.

The questions and answers in Chapter 4 address the essential tax issues of estate planning. They cover often misunderstood concepts, from how the new unified credit is being phased in to the ramifications of annual gifts. Generation skipping and the avoidance of the terrible penalty tax are the subjects of many questions, reflecting a vital concern about leaving property to grandchildren and other generations.

Finally, Chapter 5 offers an overview of the most current, sophisticated, and proven techniques being used by many families who face federal estate tax. This chapter will give you a perspective on what planning strategies are available to you and a basic understanding of how they affect estate and generation-skipping issues.

Estate planning continues to be a very important and sensitive issue for most people. You will find that the estate and tax planning chapters of *21st Century Wealth* are an excellent primer for preparing yourself for the estate planning process.

chapter 3

Fundamental Estate Planning Concepts

MOTIVATION FOR ESTATE PLANNING

What is estate planning?

Traditional *estate planning* is the process of preparing for the orderly and efficient transfer of assets at death. It usually involves preparing wills or fully funded revocable living trusts and often encompasses life insurance planning through irrevocable life insurance trusts.

Estate planning is also *living planning.* If you have minor children, estate planning is planning for the support of yourself, your spouse, and your children should you become disabled. Your planning should include funds for school, day care, medical expenses, and college and graduate school, as well as the regular budgetary expenses of running your household.

In addition, estate planning includes retirement planning, gift and income tax planning, and creditor protection planning.

When should I begin planning the disposition of my estate?

Once you begin to accumulate wealth or purchase life insurance policies, you should initiate the process. There are infinite planning options available to you when you are in your thirties or forties that significantly *narrow* as you get older because the tax cost of transferring assets to others becomes more prohibitive and techniques such as programs of gift giving in order to mitigate the effects of estate taxes become less effective. Too many people begin planning when it is too late. *Do not procrastinate!* For any one of a number of reasons—such as fear of attorneys, fear of death, fear of professional fees, and superstition or apathy—many savvy individuals who have accumulated substantial wealth do not have estate planning documents and do not consider the implications this omission will have upon their families.

Nobody likes to contemplate his or her mortality or to think that death is imminent; many of us will live to our life expectancies, but others of us won't. No one knows the future, so it is an imperative, both theoretically and practically, that we plan as if there were no tomorrows. Ultimately your spouse, children, and other family members and loved ones will be the ones who will benefit from your planning. Procrastination of your estate planning opportunities only favors the IRS, so plan now while you are healthy and alert.

Which bodies of law govern the estate planning process?

The Internal Revenue Code and its regulations set the rules for federal estate and gift taxes, income tax, and generation-skipping tax. The federal courts adjudicate these rules when there is a difference of opinion between the taxpayer and the IRS.

Each state has its own statutes with regard to inheritance, estate, and gift taxes, as well as wills, trusts, general and limited partnerships, and so on. Its courts interpret these statutes with case law whenever there are disagreements as to what they say.

Do I really need to plan my estate? Won't the laws of intestacy distribute my assets to my wife or family members?

Many individuals rationalize not planning by believing that their wealth will "automatically" pass to loved ones anyway or that "going through court administration is not a big deal," or that "when you're dead, who cares."

When you don't plan your estate, your state will do so for you. The "laws of *intestacy*"—dying without a will or a will substitute such as a revocable living trust—are the state's way of writing your estate plan for you. Each state has it's own way of distributing its citizens' wealth, but, in general, each jurisdiction gives a major share to the surviving spouse and the balance to the surviving children. The usual ratio between the respective spouse's and children's shares is generally 50/50, but it can vary depending upon factors such as second marriages.

Without your own estate plan, your family will be subject to unnecessary probate and administration costs, as well as estate taxes if you have a taxable estate. And, worse yet, your assets may not pass to the individuals whom you love the most, namely, your spouse, children, and grandchildren; in the amounts you want them to have; and at the times you would like your loved ones to receive them, especially if they are too young, too inexperienced, or just incapable of managing their inheritance. You can easily solve these problems with basic estate planning.

I had my estate planning documents prepared several years ago. Do I need to have them reviewed periodically?

If you are like most people, your personal and financial situation today is nothing like it was when your children were in diapers or were still in college. Or your financial situation today is nothing like it was before you retired and received your employer's retirement plan distribution. It is just wishful thinking to believe that once a will or trust is drafted, it rarely, if ever, has to be revised. Estate planning is *lifetime planning,* and it is always evolving as your life changes, whether through births, deaths, divorce and remarriage, changes in your finances, and so on. It is a dynamic process that seeks to capture the dynamics of your situation as it currently exists. In addition, the laws periodically change.

Planning one's estate is like trying to hit a moving target. As you age, the target moves. As such, wills or trusts, and all other estate planning techniques, must be reviewed regularly—at least every 1 to 5 years—in order to be certain that they are still on target.

What is the greatest enemy of the estate planning process?

The greatest enemy of estate planning has to be procrastination. Incredibly, it is our nature to feel that we are immortal and will always have the proper amount of time to do our estate planning. This thinking ignores the many lifetime benefits of estate and financial planning. Each of us must ask ourselves: "If I do not plan, whom will it hurt the most?" "How much will it cost if I don't plan?" And, "How much do I really care about my loved ones and their financial security?"

Why don't more people plan their estates?

Professionals often hear such comments as "What do I care how much money my kids get after I am dead; nobody ever left me anything." Or,

"Whatever they receive will be more than I did." Many professionals believe that such statements camouflage one of the main reasons why more people do not estate-plan: because they are more frightened about running out of money while they are alive than they are of their heirs' paying estate taxes after their deaths. They are fearful and insecure about the amount of their resources, and this fear does not generally have much to do with the actual resources at hand. It is felt just as strongly by people with estates of many millions of dollars as it is by people with modest estates. Also, many people do not realize the very real problems of probate and estate tax that may seriously affect their families until they have personally experienced them after the deaths of their parents or close family members.

Even though some people can minimize the importance of reducing estate taxes, it is difficult to minimize the impact of 55 percent maximum federal estate tax brackets and 82 percent maximum brackets when estate taxes are combined with generation-skipping taxes. We've seen affluent taxpayers spend hours with their CPAs or tax attorneys trying to save every last dollar in income tax and yet ignore the much larger impact of federal estate tax.

Assuming that what you're saying about the fear of running out of money is correct, how can people get over this fear?

The surest way to alleviate fear is to replace it with the certitude of education. People who have a fear of estate planning can overcome that fear by reading as much estate and financial planning material as they can, by seeking out the best professional advisors, and by listening and learning from those advisors.

Are the tax benefits of estate planning really worth it?

With proper planning, it is possible to get most families down to a near-zero estate tax level. This may equate to saving thousands or even hundreds of thousands of dollars.

In general, what do I have to do to "zero-out" my estate tax?

For many families, proper use of basic estate planning tools such as the revocable living trust is sufficient to zero-out the estate tax. For families with large estates, more sophisticated strategies may be necessary.

In order to reduce estate taxes, families and individuals must first be willing to give up *ownership* of a portion of their accumulated wealth.

Notice, we say "ownership," not "control." The federal government taxes what you own; it does not, generally, tax what you control.

Wealthy clients who have taken the time to educate themselves in planning strategies begin to get comfortable with the fact that they can still control their assets even though they do not have technical legal title to them. However, how much, and in what mix, they should divest themselves of ownership presents a daunting planning challenge, one that is usually met successfully through the assistance of competent estate and financial planning advisors who will use sophisticated computer programs to test the cost-benefit ratios of various estate planning strategies and interpret the results.

These industry software programs allow professionals and their clients to make informed decisions by utilizing their own particular criteria regarding which assets should be transferred, and in what amounts, to various estate planning vehicles designed to reduce, if not altogether avoid, egregious gift and estate taxes. The variables in these software studies should include at a minimum the yield on all assets from the date of the plan until life expectancies, sources of retirement income and projected benefits, and, most importantly, conservative estimates on the family's need for funds to support an ongoing lifestyle consistent with the family's history and projected needs, all of which should be indexed for inflation.

Once it is determined that there is enough in the way of liquid assets to maintain a family's lifestyle, clients and their advisors can explore the alternatives for minimizing estate and gift taxes. Since the clients are deeply involved in the creation of the analysis, advisors can help them determine their *comfort zone* with each alternative—a process similar to determining risk tolerance for investing. In the end, the best plan is not the one that produces the best numbers but, rather, the one with which the individual or family is most comfortable.

When should my children be brought into the estate planning process?

It is not unusual for people to feel uncomfortable about discussing their estate planning matters with their children. Long before a family crisis, it may make sense to provide your children with an overview of your estate plan and your intentions with regard to their inheritance. Laying out everything in a pleasant, businesslike setting will go a long way in resolving any differences that may come up after you are gone.

GOALS OF PROPER ESTATE PLANNING

What are the basic estate planning goals?

Estate planning should achieve four major goals:

1. Avoid probate.
2. Give what you have to whom you want the way you want and when you want.
3. Control your assets while you're alive and when you are disabled.
4. Save every tax dollar, professional fee, and court cost possible.

Keep in mind that these are the major goals for most people. You will undoubtedly have a great many additional objectives that will be unique to your own situation.

Avoid Probate

What is probate?

Probate is a legal process conducted in the probate court to effect the transfer of ownership of assets from a deceased person to the deceased person's heirs. The term "probate" actually refers to the proving of the validity of a will. A will is not valid until proved so in court. Once the validity of the will is proved, the probate court administers the will under its jurisdiction.

In addition to this death probate, there is also *living probate,* conducted when a person becomes incapacitated. So a more complete definition of probate is that it is the process in which a court takes control of your assets if you are no longer able to manage them yourself, either because of death or because of mental disabilities.

Probate costs vary greatly among the states; nonetheless, probate is time-consuming and potentially expensive. For these reasons, avoiding probate should certainly be incorporated into the goals of an estate plan.

If I have a will, don't I avoid probate?

Many people mistakenly think that by having a will they are avoiding probate. However, just the opposite is true. A will guarantees probate because the purpose of probate is to prove the validity of a will.

What is so bad about probate?

There are numerous reasons why it is best to avoid probate, and this is true even in states like Florida or Nevada, where the probate process is considered to be less complex and relatively simple:

- *Expense:* The costs associated with probating your estate, including attorney fees, probate costs, appraisals, and so on, generally range from 3 to 8 percent, depending upon the state in which you live. In some states, such as California, this percentage is applied against the gross value of your assets before subtracting mortgages or other liabilities.
- *Delay:* Probate takes time—and in many states can easily take a year or more before settlement—and heirs can suffer financial hardship during this needless waiting period.
- *Complexity:* If you have property, such as real estate, in more than one state, your heirs will likely face separate probate proceedings in each state where the property is located. These multiple probates, called *ancillary administrations,* can significantly add to the cost and time delay of settling an estate.
- *Public:* The probate process is totally public. Some companies make it a practice to have salespeople and other employees read probate proceedings in order to ascertain financial information about the inheriting individuals and families; thus, families may be needlessly exposed to "fortune hunters." This public court process also makes it easier for unwanted third parties such as ex-spouses, in-laws, and creditors to contest the estate.

What are the basic methods used by financial professionals to help their clients avoid probate?

To reduce the risk of probate, the most widely used technique is the *revocable living trust.* Any assets held in this trust are not in any way subject to the probate process. In other words, they are protected from probate. Although there are limitations to any trust arrangement, if the client's objective is to avoid the cost, delays, and publicity inherent in the probate process, a revocable living trust is often the technique financial professionals recommend to their clients.

Another interesting way to avoid probate is through *joint tenancy,* in which property is titled jointly with rights of survivorship between spouses. Jointly titled property can be a viable will substitute. But, once again, the client's objectives and goals have to be considered because the disadvantages of owning property jointly, including its adverse estate tax consequences on the second death, generally far outweigh its advantage of avoiding the probate process. Other probate-avoidance techniques used in some circumstances by professionals are *pay-on-death (POD) accounts* and *beneficiary designations.* Utilization of these techniques has to be assessed on an individual basis, and anyone considering these options should definitely consult with a financial professional or attorney before implementing them. Ultimately, joint tenancy, POD accounts, and beneficiary designations are effective only in a small percentage of nontaxable estates that do not have any "family complications" such as second marriages or "his," "her," and "our" children.

What does a will do?

A will allows a decedent to direct the flow of assets at the time of his or her death. Without a will or a will substitute, one is said to have died *intestate.* As a result, the state of the decedent's domicile will determine the distribution of assets in accordance with that state's intestacy law.

A will is revocable during life, inoperative until death, and applicable to the situation that exists at death. A will does not avoid probate; rather, it directs the probate court as to the decedent's wishes. A will does not control property that is held in joint tenancy with rights of survivorship; such property passes to the surviving joint tenant outside of the will. Life insurance, annuities, IRAs, and qualified plans pass by beneficiary designation outside of the will unless they name the decedent's *estate* as the beneficiary. Parents with minor children use their wills to nominate guardians in the event that the children are left orphaned.

Wills can create *testamentary,* or postdeath, trusts, or they can direct that specific assets be distributed ("poured over") to preexisting living trusts at the deaths of their makers. Wills cannot, however, take care of their makers in the event that the makers become disabled.

How do we choose between a will and a living trust?

The choice of a will-centered estate plan or a living trust–centered estate plan should be determined by your goals but usually is determined by a comparison of the key advantages and disadvantages of each type.

A will:

- Can be easily contested
- Guarantees probate and the attendant expenses, time delays, and publicity, as well as potential ancillary probates
- Can provide instructions only for the care of the maker's spouse and/or the maker's family after the maker's death; it cannot provide

for the care of the maker and his or her family during the maker's disability or incompetence

A properly drafted, fully funded living trust:

- Avoids both living and death probates
- Is private and not a matter of public record
- Is a legal contract that can cross state lines and control the maker's property in multiple states
- Takes care of the maker and the maker's family in case of disability.
- Provides for the care of the maker's spouse and/or the maker's family after the maker's death

An experienced attorney, CPA, or financial professional can assist you in additional comparisons specifically pertinent to your situation.

Revocable living trusts

What is a living trust?

A *living trust* is a legal document that an estate planning lawyer drafts. It resembles a will in that it provides your directions for the management and distribution of your assets upon your death. Unlike a will, however, a living trust also contains your instructions for the management of your assets in the event of your disability.

You are the maker of the trust agreement, and you are a *life beneficiary* of the trust (a person who enjoys the use of the properties of the trust) or you and your spouse are life beneficiaries of the trust. You must name a *trustee* (manager) of your trust; if you like, you can name yourself as your own trustee.

You transfer, or retitle, your assets from your name to the trustee of your trust—a process commonly referred to as *funding* the trust. This means that you, as trustee of your own trust, maintain full control over the property in the trust while you are alive, file your tax returns as you always do, and can buy, sell, or give away property in the trust. You can amend or alter the terms of the trust or revoke them in their entirety any time you wish.

By transferring your assets to your trust, you maintain control of the assets during your life but have removed those assets from the probate process after your death. Upon your death, the trust may terminate or may continue for the benefit of your family, depending upon your instructions.

Most often the trust includes instructions specifying that upon your death or upon the death of the surviving spouse your children or other loved ones will become the *remainder beneficiaries,* the persons who enjoy the remaining property of the trust.

Usually you name a bank, trust company, relative, or friend to be your *successor,* or *backup, trustee* should you die or become unable to serve as the trustee. Regardless of who you choose, your trustee is legally obligated to manage your trust property as you instruct in the document, and must do so under the strictest of fiduciary standards.

How does a revocable living trust avoid probate?

Because your property is in the name of your trust, and your trust—unlike you—cannot become incapacitated, it does not have to go through a living probate process. Because your property is already titled in the name of and owned by your trust at your death, there is no need for the probate court to effectuate transfer of ownership from you, as the deceased, to your heirs. The trust merely continues on according to the instructions that determine its operation. It is specifically designed to function without bureaucratic red tape when its maker becomes disabled or dies.

How important is it to have a revocable living trust if I become disabled?

A major reason for having a revocable living trust, and one that many experts consider more important than avoiding probate, relates to your potential for becoming incapacitated. You are four to six times more likely to become incapacitated than you are to die in the next year, according to insurance industry morbidity statistics. Therefore, it is important for you to plan for the possibility of your or your spouse's disability so that the two of you can be cared for in the manner you desire during a period of incapacitation.

Without a living trust that provides for your care during any disability, your loved ones will have to take you through the legal process of a living probate, or *conservatorship,* with the help of lawyers and the probate judge. Even though your spouse or adult children would most likely be appointed by the court to manage your affairs, they would have to report annually to it and would be subject to all the legal costs and red tape of the court system. This court process may last much longer than a death probate—it continues for as long as you are disabled.

A revocable living trust allows you to choose, in detail, how you want your affairs handled and lets you set the priorities that you wish followed. Furthermore, your successor trustees will be able to manage your affairs beginning the moment you are incapacitated without the intervention of any court or government agency, which would cause delay in continuing your financial affairs.

The entire conservatorship process is cumbersome and needlessly bureaucratic and can easily be avoided with a living trust plan.

I want to control how my family receives my wealth. Can a living trust help with that?

Although wills can contain instructions for distributing assets to heirs, wills may be subject to continued court involvement. On the other hand, revocable living trusts can also contain instructions for distributing assets to heirs, and trusts avoid probate court. Because of these benefits, as well as others inherent in such trusts, the revocable living trust is recommended over the will in most situations.

A revocable living trust provides flexibility, enabling you to control how and when your assets will be distributed to loved ones or charity after your death. You may, for example, pass assets with "strings attached."

One of our clients had a son who was a follower of a rock group. He would follow the band from concert to concert and sell t-shirts to make enough money to eat and travel. His parents were worried about his irresponsible lifestyle and propensity for spending money. So in their trust they arranged for the son to have $1 of their estate for every dollar he legitimately earned. In doing this, our clients found a unique way of providing their son with some incentive, and perhaps motivation, to live a bit more responsibly.

Many practitioners believe that clients should never leave anything of any consequence to their loved ones outright, or "free of trust." They believe that everything should be left in trust for the heirs' benefit in order to protect the heirs in a way they cannot do for themselves. If you chose to follow this philosophy, you could, for example, specify in your trust that each of your children is to serve as his or her own trustee along with cotrustees for his or her lifetime and that the trust provide for your children's needs as they arise. In this way, you have allowed each child to manage his or her own funds in the way he or she desires; yet, by retaining everything in trust, you have to some degree protected each child's assets from the claims of creditors, which could easily arise from a failed business venture, an overzealous litigant (e.g., as a result of an auto accident), or even an ex-spouse in a divorce.

By leaving assets in trust, you may be concerned that you will be overcontrolling your children after your death. But you can provide as much latitude to your children as you like: your attorney drafts the terms of the trust in accordance with your wishes. Thus, the terms can be as restrictive or as nonrestrictive as you choose, on the basis of your knowledge of each child's situation.

With a living trust, can I be sure that my children will leave what I left to them to their own children or to their brothers and sisters if they don't have children?

Yes. You can include instructions to this effect in your revocable living trust or in a will. The terms can specify your exact wishes as to what will happen upon the death of a beneficiary.

Whether you allow your children to leave their respective trusts to anyone they desire at their deaths or whether you restrict their ability to do so is your decision. In most families, it boils down to this question: "Should we give our children the right to leave remaining trust assets that we gave them in the first place to anyone they wish—including their spouses, who might remarry and disinherit our grandchildren; or should we restrict that right by allowing them to leave those assets *only* to our descendants—their brothers and sisters or our grandchildren?"

What are the disadvantages of a trust?

Some people see expense and funding as drawbacks to trusts.

EXPENSE One objection to a revocable living trust is that it is more expensive than a will. True enough. Wills have been priced very low for years by attorneys who count on reaping the probate fees in years to come. Executors of wills do not have to retain the attorneys who drafted the wills as the probate attorneys, but most do.

A living trust–centered plan is only *initially* more expensive than a will. The cost of a will and its after-death probate administration almost always exceeds, by a large amount, the cost of a funded living trust and its private after-death administration.

FUNDING Some people find it annoying to have to change ownership of their property to their living trusts. It can be time-consuming to have to determine what they own, how they own it, and how to fund each of the assets properly to the trust. But this process has to be done only once and, with the help of professsional advisors, can be easily accomplished. If people think it is annoying for them while they are alive and well, think of what a problem it will be for their loved ones if they become disabled or die.

The choice is this: People can either "probate" their own estates themselves while they are alive or pay the courts and lawyers to do it for them after they are no longer around to answer questions such as, "Where is the deed to the house?"

Most people who have gone through the funding process, one asset at a time, report that they feel a great sense of relief and peace of mind knowing that they finally have their records in order.

If I have a living trust, do I still need a will?

Yes. A living trust document can be a very powerful estate planning tool, but a comprehensive estate plan should also include a *pour-over will*—a last will and testament. Under the law, you can name guardians for your minor children only in a will, and a new will makes clear that the trust now governs your estate plan.

A pour-over will also serves as a safety net. Once you create a trust, you must always remember to transfer your assets into the trust. If any of your assets are not in the trust at the time of your death, the pour-over provision in the will instructs your personal representative, or executor, to place them in the trust so that they can be managed and distributed according to your trust instructions.

Any assets controlled by the pour-over will may have to go through probate. You should periodically review your trust-centered estate plan to ensure that all your assets are titled in the name of the trust or, in some cases, that the trust has been named the beneficiary of assets such as life insurance, IRAs, and retirement plan funds.

If I have a living trust, will my family avoid paying estate taxes?

This is one of the biggest misconceptions that people have with respect to living trusts and estate planning. A properly funded living trust avoids probate when you pass away. However, probate and the federal estate tax have nothing to do with one another. In order to save federal estate taxes, your lawyer must incorporate estate tax planning provisions into your living trust.

My property is titled in the name of my trust. Is it protected from lawsuits?

No. Most living trusts are *revocable,* which means they can be revoked, amended, or canceled at the discretion of the maker. Because you control the assets in the trust as the trustee and you can revoke the trust as its maker, funds in a living trust are at the same risk in the event of a judgment against you as they would be if they were titled directly in your name. However, your trust may be designed to protect your assets from your beneficiaries' spouses and creditors after your death.

Trustees of a revocable living trust

Who should be my trustee while I'm alive?

You can act as your own trustee, thus eliminating any professional fees. Also, as your own trustee, you can retain the same control over your assets and do anything with them that you want just as you did before establishing the trust. If you prefer, you can select another individual or an institution, such as a bank or trust company, to serve as your trustee or to serve as a cotrustee with you.

Can I provide for different trustees over my trust at different times?

Yes. You can name yourself as its initial trustee, or yourself and your spouse as its initial trustees, and can name different people to serve as trustees upon any one or more of the following events: your disability; your and your spouse's disability; your death; the death of your spouse if he or she survives you; your beneficiaries' deaths, incapacity, or divorce or some other criteria.

You can name different trustees for different contingencies and remove and replace them in your trust instructions as you wish.

How should I select my trustees?

No duty known to the law is higher than the duty a trustee owes to the beneficiaries of a trust. Trustees are charged with following the trust maker's instructions to the letter. They must make sophisticated tax and legal decisions, as well as important investment decisions that maximize returns while providing timely income and principal for the distributions specified by the trust maker. It is preferable that they be intimately familiar with the family's dynamics and needs and with the specific background and needs of each of the beneficiaries.

Being a trustee can be a massive job. As a result, most professionals recommend teams of trustees, or a cotrusteeship.

Who should be my trustee after I die or become disabled?

A trustee should be someone you highly trust. Your successor trustee should be a person (or persons) or institution that you have utmost confidence in; that you know is honest, good with financial matters, and familiar with your objectives; and that will carry out the distribution and administration directions and guidelines you have established in your estate planning documentation.

In addition, you need to make sure that the person, persons, or institution will accept the responsibilities of being your trustee. You should name several alternate trustees in case your initial choices should later choose not to act.

Can I name more than one trustee?

Yes. You can name as many cotrustees as you like.

Should I choose an individual or a corporation to serve as my successor trustee?

Each has advantages and disadvantages. With a corporate trustee, a bank or trust company, you have the assurance of ongoing professional management and accountability. However, this may cost your estate more in fees, and you are not likely to have the personal, individualized care that can be provided by a friend or family member who is familiar with the beneficiaries and their particular needs.

An individual trustee may find that the responsibility of managing assets and dealing with beneficiaries is more of a burden than was anticipated when he or she accepted what was perceived as an "honor" bestowed upon him or her by you. In addition, there is significant fiduciary liability attached to the trustee's management of assets and to the trustee's decisions that impact the beneficiaries' right to income and principal. A beneficiary who feels improperly served might bring suit against the trustee, even though no wrongdoing occurred.

If you choose personal trustees, it is important that they have the time, knowledge, and skill required to both manage the investment of assets and deal with trust beneficiaries or the good judgment to seek the assistance of competent professionals. Since any individual may become unwilling or unable to serve, you should name several contingent successor trustees as well.

Can I name both individual and corporate trustees as cotrustees?

The appointment of cotrustees may be an option if the corporate trustee will agree to the arrangement (most readily do). It may also be possible to name one or more individuals as trustees and an institution as investment manager. It is important to determine what your objectives are with respect to the management of assets and their distribution to your beneficiaries before making these decisions.

What if the person I named dies or becomes incapacitated?

Your attorney may draft your documents to allow for a *contingent* successor trustee or cotrustees to take the place of a named individual who is unable or unwilling to serve as trustee.

For example, a husband and wife name each other as initial cotrustees on each other's trust and as guardian of their minor children. The couple has a car accident in which the husband is killed and the wife is incapacitated. As a result, neither is able to serve as trustee or guardian. Because their attorney drafted their trust agreements and pour-over wills properly, the couple provided for this situation by naming a successor guardian and contingent successor trustees to make the financial decisions until the wife is able to resume making the necessary financial and administrative decisions.

It is also possible that the first set of contingent successor trustees may be unable or unwilling to serve, so it is prudent to name a succession of successor trustees to ensure the proper administration of your trust instructions.

We have great trust and faith that my brother will make a great successor trustee, but he lacks financial experience. What should we do?

There are a couple of ways to handle this kind of situation. You could name another individual or a bank or trust company to serve as a cotrustee with your brother—a cotrustee who has more financial experience than your brother and to whom you could delegate, in your trust, the financial decision-making authority.

A second alternative would be to name one or more "trusted advisors" to whom your brother could turn for input and counsel as he needs it. In this instance, your brother would be the final decision-making authority, but you can include instructions within the trust document stipulating that you want him to seek counsel from these advisors regarding investments, distribution issues, guardian financial support, and so on. These advisors would step in to assist your brother just as they have undoubtedly helped you while you've been in charge. This type of planning can also relieve your brother of the anxiety of being the only decision maker and allow him to make better decisions.

Can I appoint all my children as cotrustees?

Naming cotrustees is usually good business. Naming all your children as cotrustees, however, may invoke sibling rivalry and "if you scratch my back I'll scratch yours" thinking. Also, there may be too many children to expect that they can transact business efficiently. Generally speaking, if cotrustees are needed, you may want to consider individuals other than your children.

Does every trustee have to receive a fee?

It is usually advisable to provide in the trust document for the "reasonable and customary trustee's fee as permitted by state law" or to refer to an institution's fee schedule so that the trustees will be encouraged to act and be compensated for their work. If you have appointed cotrustees, it is usual for them to divide the trustee fee on the basis of the duties each fulfills.

What do trustees charge?

Each institution has its own fee schedule, and the amount charged under that schedule will vary depending upon the extent of the services that are rendered. In general, however, a trustee's annual fee runs from .5 to 2 percent of the value of the assets being managed, depending upon the degree of management involved.

It is very common for family members and close friends who are named as cotrustees to forgo all or a major portion of the fees they would ordinarily receive. However, in certain circumstances there may be income and/or estate tax benefits to their taking the fees.

Funding a revocable living trust

What does funding a trust mean, and why is it important?

Once a revocable living trust is implemented, it needs to actually become the owner of your assets. The process of transferring ownership to the trust is called *funding* the trust. In some cases, funding also includes naming the trust as beneficiary of annuities, life insurance, IRAs, and retirement plans. Trust funding is vitally important because without it your trust is largely ineffective and you will have wasted your time and money creating it.

Think of it this way: Your trust is a brand-new automobile, and you are its proud new owner. It looks great, smells wonderful, and has every driving convenience available. But if you don't put gas in the tank, it can't function to take you anywhere. It might as well be a lawn ornament. It's the same for your trust: your property is the gas that makes it run.

We have property in more than one state. Can we put all our property into one revocable trust?

Yes, and this is one of the greatest advantages of the revocable living trust. Without a trust, not only will the property you own in the state where you are legally domiciled be subject to probate, but the property you own in another state will go through an ancillary probate in accordance with that state's laws. For example, if you own your home in Illinois and own land in Florida, your heirs will have a probate proceeding in Illinois and an ancillary probate in Florida—whether you have a valid will or not.

By funding both properties into your single living trust, you eliminate the need for both probate proceedings.

How can I obtain help with funding my living trust?

There are several resources you may want to consider when funding your living trust. The first is the attorney who drafts your estate planning documents. Usually, he or she will need to file the deed of trust for any real estate that is being placed in your trust and may fund your non-real estate assets for you or give you letters or instructions that will help you transfer those assets. However, your CPA, CFP, or financial advisor can also help with retitling non-real estate assets or with completing forms to name your trust as beneficiary. Examples of such assets are bank accounts, investment accounts, motor vehicles, and IRAs.

Considering how important it is to have your assets properly titled once your revocable living trust has been created, it would be wise to seek the assistance of all your advisors in funding your trust.

Our trust is long and filled with very personal information. Do we really have to give a copy to the bank, the brokerage house, and so on, just to fund it?

Your bank and brokerage firm need to know who has authority to act on behalf of your trust, as this information will insulate them from potential legal liabilities.

It is usually sufficient to provide these companies with a document sometimes called a *memorandum* or *affidavit* of your trust, rather than giving them the entire trust. The memorandum or affidavit usually shows the name of the trust and a list of the trustees and successor trustees. It may be accompanied by the Trustee's Powers section of your trust or an abbreviated listing of the authority you and your successor trustees have over assets that are placed into the trust.

Do we have to file a different income tax return for our trust?

Assuming your living trust is *revocable,* which means you maintain control over it and can make changes to it until your death or legal incapacity, you will not have to file a trust income tax return while you are living. You can continue to file your single, joint, or separate personal tax return using your Social Security number as usual. At your death, a separate tax return may be required for the trust. The successor trustee should seek proper professional advice on preparing this return.

Joint tenancy

Isn't joint tenancy the simplest and easiest estate plan?

Joint tenancy with the right of survivorship is probably the most common form of estate planning and, to a certain extent, the simplest and easiest form. When the first tenant dies, the jointly owned assets are, by operation of law, distributed to the other tenant; thus the assets avoid probate when the first spouse dies. But, compared with alternative forms of planning, joint tenancy may be, for many estates, the worst estate planning method of all.

For most people, the primary reason for titling assets jointly is to avoid probate. The truth, however, is that joint tenancy merely postpones probate; it does not totally avoid it. For example, Mike and Mary, husband and wife, own a home in joint tenancy. If Mike dies first, Mary will become the sole owner without the need for probate or another court action. However, when Mary subsequently dies, a probate proceeding will be necessary to transfer ownership of the home to her heirs.

Since joint tenancy delays probate, why shouldn't I use it?

There are several reasons to avoid using joint tenancy in your estate plan. You may find yourself defending against a lawsuit because you hold an asset as a joint tenant and are now being held responsible for the other tenant's actions. For example, if you were to title your automobile jointly with a child who later gets into an accident, you could be named as one of the defendants in a lawsuit relating to the accident. Or you may have an accident with the car and unnecessarily expose your child to a lawsuit because of your own negligence.

With joint tenancy you may lose control of bank accounts, stock accounts, mutual funds, annuities, and so on, as either joint owner can access or sell such assets without the permission or knowledge of the other owner. And if one owner has a problem with a creditor or lawsuit, the other owner may lose the asset through garnishment or another court action. Some jointly titled assets, such as real estate, cannot be sold without both owners' signatures, so a problem arises if one of the owners decides not to sign. The only option may be to file a lawsuit so that the court can partition the asset and then order its sale.

Joint tenancy can also result in an unintended disinheritance. For example, Dick and Barb each have a child and grandchildren from previous marriages. The most valuable asset in their estate is their "dream" lake home. Let's assume that Dick dies first. As the surviving joint tenant, Barb now owns the entire home and can leave it to her child and grandchildren when she dies, thus disinheriting Dick's child and grandchildren.

Or suppose Barb, with good intentions, creates a joint tenancy after Dick's death with her child and Dick's child, but her child predeceases her, leaving Barb and Dick's child as the joint owners. On Barb's death, Dick's child will become the sole owner, with no legal obligation to share ownership with Barb's grandchildren. Barb would have unintentionally disinherited her own grandchildren because she used joint tenancy.

There may also be gift tax implications resulting from putting your property in joint tenancy with people other than your spouse. For example, my neighbor, Louise, purchased a new home and titled it in joint tenancy with her stepdaughter. By doing so, Louise made a gift to her stepdaughter equal to 50 percent of the value of the home.

Because the amount of the gift was considerable, a substantial gift tax was the unintended result.

Joint tenancy has other drawbacks: Beneficiaries receive the assets all at once, even when they are not able to manage them; the assets may be subject to a court conservatorship if you become ill or disabled before you die; you may need the joint tenant's consent and signature to transact business; there may be more estate taxes if you are married or after your other joint tenant dies; and the assets may be immediately subject to claims of your beneficiaries' spouses and creditors after you die.

Joint tenancy with right of survivorship is not the simple estate planning device that many people believe it to be. Most advisors never recommend it. In contrast, virtually all the problems discussed above can be avoided with a properly drafted revocable living trust or many of the other estate planning tools discussed in this book.

Why is joint tenancy with right of survivorship a poor way to title my marital assets?

Most people seem to have a love affair with joint tenancy. For a husband and wife whose joint estate does not exceed their $1,350,000 combined exemption amount ($675,000 for individuals), joint tenancy may be adequate for estate tax purposes. It does not, however, help avoid probate upon the death of the surviving spouse or upon the simultaneous deaths of both spouses.

For couples having estates larger than the combined exemption amount, this type of joint tenancy can subject a family to federal estate taxes that could have been easily avoided. This is because the spouse who dies first cannot use his or her exemption amount.

If you hold property jointly with a spouse in a noncommunity property state, at your death only your 50 percent of the property receives a "step up" in basis (cost basis "stepped up" to fair market value at date of death). This means that if your spouse desires to sell the property after your death, he or she may have to pay unnecessary capital gain taxes on his or her 50 percent of the property, which did not receive the step up.

It usually makes sense to divide jointly held assets before death into separate or individually held assets or into *tenancy in common.* If you live in a community property state, you will likely want to retitle your marital assets as community property or, even easier, establish a written community property agreement (if allowed by your state statutes) in order to receive the additional advantage of the step-up-in-basis income tax benefit on 100 percent of your marital assets.

My will gives all my children equal shares in my estate, but I'd like to simplify everything for my local daughter, who will be handling things for me when I get older. Should I put her name with mine on all my accounts to make it easier for her to administer my affairs?

Jointly titled assets or assets controlled by beneficiary designations are not controlled by a will or trust. This means they are not part of the property distributed by either of those documents. Naming your daughter as a *joint owner* on your accounts could compromise your intended distribution. Your one daughter would actually end up owning title to all the assets from the joint accounts and would have no legal obligation to share them with her siblings. Even if she intends to make distributions to her siblings, the distributions would have to be made as taxable gifts.

In addition, the minute you place your daughter's name on the accounts with yours, you subject your assets to the claims of her creditors and to many of the other problems described above with respect to joint tenancy.

Beneficiary designations

How can I keep my bank accounts from being frozen at my death?

Many states no longer freeze bank accounts at death, particularly if they do not impose a state inheritance tax. Also, in many states, a *payable-on-death (POD)* registration can be used to keep a bank account out of probate. The account would be titled "James Jones, POD Baby Jones and Teen Jones." This registration provides no ownership for the children until the death of James. Then, Teen Jones and Baby Jones become the owners of the account. Since this bypasses probate, there is no need to freeze the accounts during the probate process. However, a POD account may create many of the problems associated with joint tenancy (described above), so it is preferable to title POD accounts in the name of your living trust, which can specify who is to receive them—without probate.

Wouldn't it be adequate planning to simply name my estate as the beneficiary of my life insurance?

Naming your estate as the beneficiary of your life insurance is bad planning, for several reasons:

1. Life insurance payable to a named beneficiary will not be subject to probate proceedings. But if you name your estate, your life insurance proceeds *must* go through probate and be subjected to its costs and delays.
2. Life insurance payable to a named beneficiary is not subject to the claims of your creditors. Insurance proceeds that are left to your estate will be subject to the claims of your creditors.
3. The state defines the heirs of your estate, who may or may not be the heirs you would choose. Unless you have a will or trust, the life insurance proceeds may pass to the wrong heirs. Even if the correct heirs get the proceeds, they receive a large amount of money without instructions for its intended use. In short, you may be placing assets in the wrong hands or in the right hands but in the wrong way!
4. Life insurance proceeds payable to an estate are subject to federal estate tax.

The better choice may be to name an irrevocable trust as the beneficiary so that you can avoid these traps.

Give What You Have to Whom You Want the Way You Want and When You Want

What are the primary nontax estate planning considerations?

There are a number of very important nontax considerations that every spouse, parent, and grandparent should consider. The primary ones are as follows:

- Who should inherit the assets in terms of general amounts or percentages?
- Who should inherit specific assets and personal effects?
- Should the assets be distributed outright or be left in trusts?
- If they are left in trusts, should separate trusts be established for separate beneficiaries, or should common trusts be used for classes of beneficiaries?

- Over what period of time and in what manner should each inheritance be distributed?
- What persons and/or institutions should be named as trustees or cotrustees?
- How should the trusteeship be configured?

Why is it important to decide which specific assets are to pass to each beneficiary?

Some assets cannot be divided, and others have value only in a particular beneficiary's hands. For example, should stock in a closely held business be passed equally to three children when only one of them is very active in the business and the other two have successful careers apart from the business? You may want to specify in your will or trust who is to receive the stock.

Also, many assets—such as personal effects—may be better handled by simple written instructions or lists that you can personally maintain and change. (Personal property lists are discussed in detail later in this chapter.)

To spouses

Can I leave some or all of my estate to someone other than my surviving spouse?

You may be able to leave only a portion of your estate to someone other than your spouse because virtually every state has laws which protect the rights of a surviving spouse. Typically, these laws allow a surviving spouse to make a claim against an estate for between 33⅓ and 50 percent of the estate, including a right to recover his or her entitled, or *statutory,* share from transfers intended to circumvent the laws.

What are the obstacles to creating a smoothly working, carefully coordinated estate plan in families composed of second marriages?

With second marriages, estate planning can become very complex and emotional. Often one spouse, or both spouses, has been married multiple times and has children from one or more of the previous marriages as well as the current marriage. All of these relationships must be explored to determine what provision will be made for each class of heirs. Each spouse has individual decisions to make about his or her own children and grandchildren and about how and what he or she will leave to the other spouse. There are also many issues relating to who will control the assets after one spouse dies and how the assets will be distributed after the death of the surviving spouse.

One of the most perplexing planning situations arises when a current spouse is close in age to the children of the previous marriage. The older spouse must decide if he or she will leave assets to the younger spouse to defer estate taxes until the younger one's subsequent death, thereby making the children from the previous marriage wait perhaps many years until the death of their stepparent to receive their inheritance. The older spouse must also decide if the surviving spouse will have any right to determine whom the assets will go to after his or her death.

To children

What are the practical implications of planning for the timing of trust distributions?

Minors cannot receive or hold property until they reach the age of majority (18 years of age in some states and 21 in others). Trusts are needed to hold their inheritances until they reach this age.

Most children are neither ready nor mature enough to handle large inheritances at any age, especially the "threshold" age of 18 or 21. Distributions of vast amounts of money to adult children or distributions of moderate amounts of money to very young ones can destroy, rather than build, responsible lives. Also, some children have mental, physical, or emotional handicaps that require special trusts that specifically address their needs.

Even if your children are capable of handling money, you may want their inheritance to be held in trust, with the children as trustees, to better protect them from the claims of spouses and creditors and to reduce the possible estate tax when the inheritance subsequently passes to their children.

Your trust can be drafted to allow for the distribution of your assets to your beneficiaries in exactly the manner you deem most appropriate.

Can I distribute part of my assets to my children upon my death and the remainder of my assets to them upon my wife's death?

Yes. Tax issues aside, you are generally free to distribute your property at death any way you desire, subject to the surviving spouse's rights (discussed above) and the claims of your creditors. If the distributions to your children at your death do not exceed your exemption amount ($675,000 in 2000 and 2001), no estate taxes will be due.

Do I need to treat my children equally in my estate distribution plan?

No. How you distribute your assets upon your death is a personal matter. You may choose to have your assets distributed equally among your children or in whatever proportions you deem appropriate. You may even disinherit certain children entirely. It is, of course, important that you have a qualified estate planning attorney prepare your will or trust to specifically set forth your distribution objectives and intentions.

How can I use the assets in my estate, after my death, to encourage my heirs toward worthwhile endeavors, rather than simply creating a generation without the incentive to accomplish anything?

Find a professional who will work with you to create a *family incentive trust.* This type of trust encourages virtuous and worthwhile pursuits, while perhaps discouraging undesirable behavior, through the strategic use of monetary incentives. Just what is worthwhile or undesirable is entirely up to you, as the creator of the trust, because, after all, it is your money.

A family incentive trust can be used for many circumstances. For instance, you may want to reward educational achievements, such as a high school, college, or graduate degree, or vocational accomplishments with additional funds; or you may want to provide the opportunity for a child to stay at home to raise his or her children rather than be forced into the workplace to supplement the family income. You may also want to stop trust distributions in some situations, say, because of substance abuse. The menu of virtuous incentives and their undesirable counterparts is limited only by your creativity and the number of individuals for whom you are planning.

I'm holding a mortgage on the home of one of my children. What are my options as to what will happen to it upon my death?

Your death does not extinguish your child's responsibility to pay back the mortgage unless you specify this in your will or trust. There are several ways you can handle this note:

- You can forgive the remaining balance at the time of your death and not have it included in the estate assets that are distributed, especially if you have specified which assets will be left to each of your children.
- If you want to have an equal distribution of all your assets, your planning documents can request that the balance outstanding on the note be computed into your estate and that your executor or successor trustee subtract that amount from the child mortgagor's portion of the assets.
- You can make your trust or estate the payee of the mortgage and have the payments continue to be made to that entity.

You should consult a professional advisor regarding the potential income and estate tax implications of each option.

Most of my wealth consists of my interest in a small business. What questions should I consider in planning its succession?

When a person creates a business from scratch and makes it a "life's work," at some point he or she must confront the issue of business succession. The first step is to decide if the business should be sold or kept in the family. There are both retirement and estate distribution issues to consider. If a person can afford to keep the business after retirement, the question of who will manage it becomes very important.

Another consideration is who will get the business. Should it be divided equally among all the children, or should it be directed to only the children who are active in the business? Should the children working in the business get controlling ownership? Should there be a buy-and-sell agreement or first right of refusal to purchase the business? Should the children who have elected to work outside the business get stock, or should they get other assets? Is it appropriate to equalize the division, or should some other measure of fairness be used?

What can I do if the value of my business represents most of my estate?

A further planning complexity is presented when the closely held business represents the vast bulk of an estate's value and there is little or no liquidity present to pay federal estate taxes. Many times, after estate settlement costs, all that is left for the heirs is the business. In such cases the best way to preserve the business is usually through the use of properly structured life insurance to pay the estate settlement costs and taxes.

My largest and most valuable asset is a successful business, but only two of our four children are involved in it. How do I treat all our children fairly with an appropriate inheritance and avoid family conflict over the disposition of the business?

Dealing with the diverse needs and often conflicting objectives of beneficiaries is always a challenge. Doing so is more complicated when the major financial asset is not easily divisible or when there are adverse tax consequences or other factors ruling against liquidation. Assuming that you and/or your spouse is insurable and that funds are available for premiums, an appropriate amount of life insurance, properly owned and arranged, is often the best way to provide the desired inheritance for family members who are not active in the business or have financial needs that conflict with business ownership.

You should seek the advice of your estate, tax, and financial professionals to assist you in planning for a family business.

I have heard that I should formally disinherit my disabled son to protect his government benefits. Is that the only way I can do so?

If you have an adult handicapped child or some other disabled family member who is potentially eligible for or is collecting Medicaid, Social Security income, or Social Security disability benefits, you may want to disinherit this individual in your will to avoid disqualifying him or her for future government benefits. One of the requirements for Medicaid eligibility is that an individual must have less than $2000 in countable resources. The receipt of an inheritance will temporarily disqualify the individual for Medicaid benefits until the inheritance is spent down to below $2000.

Alternatively, prudent parents often leave the disabled child's share under the trusteeship of a *special-needs trust* to provide supplemental income to augment the available government benefits. State Medicaid authorities continue to attack trusts holding assets on behalf of Medicaid recipients, so you will want to work with an attorney who specializes in this area to ensure that you can provide for your son but not disqualify his government benefits.

Can you explain what a special-needs trust is and how it works?

Medicaid pays medical expenses for the poor and the disabled but has limits on the amount of assets that a recipient can own or earn during each year that benefits are paid. A *special-needs trust* keeps assets available for the benefit of a disabled beneficiary without disqualifying the beneficiary from government assistance programs. The trust must be carefully drafted so that it does not interfere with qualification for government aid. If a disabled beneficiary's interest in a trust is deemed by the government to be an available resource, it may disqualify that loved one from receiving government benefits.

To avoid jeopardizing a child's ability to receive government benefits, the trust should not mandate that monies be used for the child's basic necessities such as food, shelter, or clothing. These needs are generally covered through government programs. The trust funds should be used to supplement those programs, and the language of the trust should convey that intent.

Can a Medicaid-eligible recipient refuse his or her inheritance in order to protect continued Medicaid eligibility?

Although a qualified disclaimer will redirect the inheritance to some other person, for purposes of Medicaid eligibility, the inheritance will be treated as having been received and then transferred by the Medicaid recipient. This results in loss of benefits.

To grandchildren

My children are all doing quite well financially. Can we leave our estate to our grandchildren instead?

The decision of who will inherit your money rests with you, provided that you have properly drafted legal documents to carry out your wishes. Many grandparents prefer giving money while they are alive to their grandchildren instead of, or in addition to, making bequests at their deaths. Sharing your wealth with needy family members while you are alive can bring you, and them, great joy. It is often wise, however, to leave some of your estate to grandchildren, as this may avoid an unnecessary second estate tax when your children die and pass the estate to your grandchildren.

The only difficulty with giving or leaving your property to grandchildren is that doing so may subject it to the federal estate tax and to the gift generation-skipping tax, which is separate from the ordinary estate and gift tax. When added together, these taxes can amount to 82 percent.

You should be aware of how to properly utilize your generation-skipping tax exemption (discussed in detail in Chapter 4) if you want to give or leave property to your grandchildren.

To pets

I worry about the well-being of my pets after I am gone. Can I provide for them in my will or trust?

Emotional ties between owners and their pets can be very strong. Pets can fill relationship roles as trusted friends for many years or even as surrogate children and companions for empty nesters or widowed owners. They are usually considered part of the family, so it is natural for their owners to think about their well-being.

Owners' feelings aside, pets are not permitted to hold title to property or assets, and trusts for their benefit are considered by the law of most jurisdictions as "honorary" only.

Naming someone in your will or trust to act as your pets' caretaker may provide the requisite peace of mind. You should ask your intended guardian if he or she will assume this responsibility, and you should name one or more contingent individuals in case your first choice is unable or unwilling to honor the request.

It is not unusual for pet owners to leave to the caretakers bequests commensurate with the importance they place on the responsibility of caring for their family pets. Even though trusts that name pets as their beneficiaries are honorary only, skilled estate planning attorneys have a number of ways to ensure that, after their owners are gone, family pets will indeed be taken care of and the caretakers properly reimbursed for appropriate expenses.

Control Your Assets While You're Alive and When You Are Disabled

Durable powers of attorney

If I become incapacitated, who will make my financial decisions?

This is a very good question and one that very few people address before becoming incapacitated. If you should become incapacitated without having done prior planning for that contingency, the probate court, with all its administrative bureaucracy, will appoint a guardian over your person and a conservator over your financial affairs. These individuals or institutions may or may not be the persons or organizations whom you would choose were you able to do so; and even if they are, you will incur the expenses and delays of the judicial process.

In order to bypass this bureaucratic process, your living trust should appoint your disability trustees and should contain all your postdisability instructions for providing for you and those persons dependent upon you. In addition, in a separate document known as a *durable special power of attorney,* you should authorize one or more individuals to transfer property that is not in your trust *only* to your trust so that your disability trustees can use it to care for you during your disability under the terms of the trust.

What if I don't have a living trust?

If you do not have a trust, you can use *a durable general power of attorney* to name one or more individuals to act in your stead with regard to your property. Unlike the durable *special* power of attorney, which allows the attorney-in-fact to transfer your assets only to your trust, the durable *general* power of attorney gives your attorney-in-fact the power to act in your place to sell your assets, transact business, or do whatever he or she feels is necessary to care for you during disability.

Can you tell me more about a durable general power of attorney?

It is a written document that specifically gives authorization to others to act on behalf of its maker after he or she becomes disabled. It is very common for trust makers to name more than one person to hold such a power.

Powers of attorney almost always give the holders the ability to buy, sell, or lease assets, sue on a maker's behalf, collect from creditors, and even operate a maker's business. They also usually grant certain tax powers such as the right to sign and file income tax returns and the right to make or disclaim gifts.

What is the significance of the term "durable" in a power of attorney?

The term "durable," when coupled with "power of attorney," means only that the power is expressly intended to, and in fact does, survive the disability of the document's maker. A power of attorney that is not durable becomes invalid as soon as its maker is disabled.

What is the significance of the term "special" in a power of attorney?

The term "special" means that the power of attorney is expressly limited to a set of special instructions contained in the power that generally restrict the holder to very specific matters. Most special powers of attorney provide that the holder can only transfer assets into the maker's living trust. Thereafter, the trustees will discharge their strict fiduciary duties in following the disability instructions they were given in the trust.

Are durable general powers of attorney as good as durable special powers of attorney?

Durable special powers of attorney ensure that your assets will be subject to the control of trustees you have selected who are absolutely bound by the trust instructions you left for them. On the other hand, a durable general power of attorney does not contain instructions. It gives the holder broad powers to do whatever he or she determines is appropriate in regard to your affairs. Unfortunately, what he or she deems appropriate may be quite different from what you think appropriate in a given situation or circumstance.

Regardless of which type of power of attorney you use, once you regain your competency, you again take over your affairs either as an individual or as the trustee of your living trust.

Burial instructions

Should we write our burial instructions in our will or trust?

Although you can do so, your will or trust might not be consulted before your burial, so using either document to convey burial instructions is generally not a good idea.

Whether or not you have prepaid funerals, burial plots, or other final plans, leaving a *letter of final instructions* that details the "where," "what," and "how" can greatly help to reduce the overwhelming stress your loved ones will be under at that time and is an extremely thoughtful gift you can leave to them.

Grief and/or guilt can lead to many misinterpretations of your thoughts and set in motion actions that might be contrary to your wishes. This is why your letter of instructions is so very important.

Some attorneys accept the responsibility of safekeeping such a letter; if you decide to go this route, be sure to tell your closest loved ones whom they should contact in the event of your death. Other attorneys suggest that you keep the letter in a place your loved ones have access to and that you notify them of the location.

Living wills

What is a living will, and how is it used?

A *living will* (also referred to as a *medical directive*) is a document in which a person states whether or not life-sustaining procedures should be used to prolong his or her life. This document is given legal authority under the Natural Death Act or the right-to-die statute within each state.

With modern medical technology improving by the minute, the possibility of prolonging life can go far beyond what we've ever imagined. Yet many people are unwilling to suffer the loss of their dignity and possibly their net worth as the necessary payment for prolonging their lives when death is imminent and irreversible. In short, they want to retain the right to control decisions regarding their medical care, including the withholding or withdrawing of life-sustaining procedures. The living will laws typically contain safeguards to ensure peace of mind, such as a requirement that two physicians examine the patient and determine that recovery is no longer likely before life-sustaining treatments may be withdrawn.

A person who creates a living will can revoke that document at any time by destroying it, directing its destruction, or signing a written revocation.

What is a durable power of attorney for health care, and do I need one in addition to a living will?

The *durable power of attorney for health care* is a document, authorized by the laws of most states, that allows a person or persons of your choosing to make your medical decisions for you if you cannot. It covers decisions on issues that may arise before you are terminally ill—such as operations, transfusions, nursing care, various treatments, and tube feeding.

You should probably have a durable power of attorney for health care in addition to a living will (although in some states the two may be combined into one document). It is important that you periodically review your living will and power of attorney for health care to be sure they still comply with your state's law.

Personal property lists

Should we leave instructions on how we want our personal property distributed?

Yes, you should write a *memorandum of tangible personal property* to control the manner in which you want your possessions distributed.

Can I leave keepsakes to people I care about who are not receiving any other distributions from my estate?

Of course. Grandchildren, other relatives, or friends who may not be receiving or expecting any type of financial inheritance upon your passing might treasure a personal keepsake by which to remember you. Your personal representatives or trustees who are entrusted with distributing your personal effects will have a much simpler task if you make a clear, definitive list of who should receive which items.

However, if there is a specific item of unusual value, particularly one that people might fight over, it is advisable to make a "specific bequest" of that item in your will or trust agreement.

Are there any formalities to preparing a personal property list?

Your will or living trust must contain a reference to the list. The list (often called a *memorandum of tangible personal property*) should describe the items clearly, and you should sign and date the list. Some states may require that the list be notarized or signed by witnesses, but you do not have to follow the strict signing formalities that wills and codicils require in order to be legally binding.

Can I update this list, and if so, how often should I update it?

You should review and update your list as frequently as necessary, but at least once a year. Pick an annual event—start of spring training, New Year's Day—and use it as a reminder to review your list. It is best to pick an event other than a birthday or wedding anniversary, as later in life these dates can be emotionally trying if you are left on your own.

I know I should complete my personal property list, but the task seems a bit overwhelming. How do I start?

Initially, set aside any concerns about matching people with items and simply begin an inventory of your physical possessions. Completing this inventory is just a matter of writing things down as you come across them. Don't worry about valuing or categorizing them yet. As you do the inventory, don't forget to note any items you may own that you do not keep at home: artwork; jewelry; coins; items at the office, out on loan, or held in a safe deposit box; and so on.

Once your inventory is in order, you are ready to categorize the items either by value or by type of possession (jewelry, furniture, etc.). Start with the first item on the list and think about which of your loved ones would truly enjoy or appreciate it the most. Some people ask their loved ones to pick out something they want.

Next to each item, write down the person's name; repeat this process for each possession on your list. Don't worry if you come across items you can't match up with someone who'd really want to receive them, because you may think of someone later or these items can be divided among your named beneficiaries according to your instructions in your will or trust.

How do I leave my possessions if I don't have a separate list?

Most people leave them in either of two ways:

1. They give their children and/or grandchildren the right to make the distribution decisions on the basis of agreement among them. If they cannot agree, the personal representative or trustee has the authority to distribute or sell the assets and divide the proceeds equally.
2. They instruct their personal representative or trustee to distribute the personal property in the same manner as the remainder of the estate.

Estate Planning Documents

What is a document locator form?

This often-neglected document organizes your estate and helps your beneficiaries account for all your assets. It lists your assets; who holds title to them (most likely your trust); where the assets are located; where the evidences of title, such as property deeds, are located; and the location of safe deposit keys, passbook savings accounts, and insurance policies.

You would be surprised how many millions of dollars are never claimed from banks and insurance companies every year because heirs are unaware of the existence of bank accounts or insurance policies. The document locator form can save your trustee and family a lot of needless time and aggravation and help ensure that your plan is carried out quickly and efficiently.

chapter 4

Estate Tax and After-Death Income Tax Planning

Is it worth knowing about and planning for estate taxes since, from what I've heard, Congress is considering eliminating them?

It seems that change and rumors of change are always with us, especially in regard to Congress and taxes. Therefore, it is imperative to adopt an appropriate philosophy for dealing with possible or proposed estate tax change or repeal.

In the real world, the repeal of estate taxes is unlikely, but continuous change is probable. This is why estate planning is a process, not an event.

If the current taxing approach were to face major overhaul, we quite likely would see estate tax shifted to income tax items and possibly the loss of the stepped-up basis in inherited assets, which could affect a much larger percentage of the population than the existing estate tax does. In short, plan using the rules now in place, and remain flexible enough to monitor and adjust your plans.

I'm single and my total estate is less than $675,000. Why should I worry about federal estate tax?

This type of thinking has cost many families huge amounts of unnecessary taxes. Whether you are single or married, the fact that your current estate value is under the applicable exclusion amount in 2000 and 2001 does not mean that you will avoid federal estate taxes in the future. Estate taxes are levied against the value of your assets at the date of your death.

Between now and then, the value of your assets may increase significantly as the result of several factors: inflation, prudent investing, income that you don't consume (e.g., interest in CDs and other bank accounts that you continually roll over), income compounding inside of annuities and IRAs, and mutual funds that you don't withdraw.

Even if your estate increases only 7 percent a year, it will outpace the scheduled increases in the applicable exclusion amount. In roughly 10 years it will double in value, and in 20 years it will be about four times the value it is today! It is future values such as these that will determine—at the date of your death—whether or not your estate is subject to federal estate tax.

My spouse and I have never been wealthy. How can we have an estate tax problem?

"Wealth" is defined many different ways. Most people would not consider the face value—death benefits—of their life insurance as an entry on their financial statements. However, the federal estate tax law specifically taxes the proceeds of life insurance that is owned at death. If you or your husband own life insurance—even if it is term insurance—that will pay a large amount of money when either of you dies, you may have a significant estate tax problem. When life insurance proceeds are added to the fair market value of your home, retirement plan assets, and other assets, the $1,350,000 threshold is reached rapidly.

FUNDAMENTAL TAX CONCEPTS

The Unified Estate and Gift Tax System

What is the federal estate tax?

The *federal estate tax* is a tax levied against the value of all property owned by a decedent at the time of his or her death. Any assets owned or controlled by the decedent at the time of death are included in his or her estate for federal estate tax purposes.

What is the gift tax?

The *gift tax* is a tax levied against the value of property given away during life. In essence, it is levied against the value of anything you give away before you die.

What, then, is the unified estate and gift tax system?

The federal estate and gift tax is a tax assessed on the transfer of assets for less than full and adequate consideration. The *unified* nature of the system reflects the fact that federal estate and gift tax is imposed on all property transferred in a taxable manner regardless of whether the transfer takes place during the donor's lifetime or after his or her death.

The tax is imposed at one set of rates and is also assessed progressively—that is, each taxable event builds upon previous taxable events. The cumulative, or progressive, nature of the tax ensures that the highest marginal rate on the latest taxable transfer will be applied. Thus transfers move the donor up the progressive rate structure as they occur. For this reason, current gifts are added to previous gifts to determine the tax bracket applicable to such gifts. Also, lifetime gifts made after 1976 are added to the gross estate of the decedent to determine the applicable estate tax bracket for testamentary transfers.

What does "cumulative" mean?

If a taxpayer makes taxable gifts, the value of those gifts is added to his or her estate at death. Thus the federal estate tax that will be paid is in a higher bracket.

For example, suppose Susan made taxable gifts of $100,000 and gave her daughter a home worth $300,000. Susan dies in 2000 with an estate of $400,000, which she leaves to her son. Susan's estate tax will be based on transfers of $800,000 ($400,000 during life and $400,000 at death). Her estate will pay the federal estate tax at the $800,000 bracket, reduced by available deductions and credits.

What are the federal estate and gift tax rates?

The rates are shown in Table 4-1. They are applied to the net estate, or the cumulative transfers.

TABLE 4-1 Federal Estate Tax Rates

If value of taxable estate is			
Over	**But not over**	**The tax is**	**Of the amount over**
–	$ 10,000	18% of amount	–
$ 10,001	20,000	$1,800 + 20%	$10,000
20,001	40,000	$3,800 + 22%	$20,000
40,001	60,000	$8,200 + 24%	$40,000
60,001	80,000	$13,000 + 26%	$60,000
80,001	100,000	$18,200 + 28%	$80,000
100,001	150,000	$23,800 + 30%	$100,000
150,001	250,000	$38,800 + 32%	$150,000
250,001	500,000	$70,800 + 34%	$250,000
500,001	750,000	$155,800 + 37%	$500,000
750,001	1,000,000	$248,300 + 39%	$750,000
1,000,001	1,250,000	$345,800 + 41%	$1,000,000
1,250,001	1,500,000	$448,300 + 43%	$1,250,000
1,500,001	2,000,000	$555,800 + 45%	$1,500,000
2,000,001	2,500,000	$780,800 + 49%	$2,000,000
2,500,001	3,000,000	$1,025,800 + 53%	$2,500,000
3,000,000*		$1,290,800 + 55%	$3,000,000

*For estates between $10,000,000 and $17,184,000, the benefit of the graduated rates is phased out, resulting in an additional 5 percent tax on the estate.

How does the government determine the value of my estate?

The government starts with your *gross estate,* which includes:

- The value of all property owned by you at your death: personal effects such as jewelry, books, and furniture; automobiles; real estate; stocks, bonds, and bank accounts; notes and mortgages payable to you

- Proceeds of life insurance owned by you or payable to your estate as beneficiary
- IRAs, annuities, and retirement plan funds
- Amount of gift tax paid on gifts made within 3 years of death
- Gifts with a retained life interest
- Value of all property held in your living trust
- Value of the unlimited right to transfer property held in trust (general powers of appointment)
- Fifty percent of the value of community property (for residents of community property states or those with community property acquired in such states) and of joint tenancy property owned only by spouses. (Other joint tenancy assets may be 100 percent includable unless the other joint tenant can show that he or she contributed funds toward the purchase of the property.)

The following items are then deducted from your gross estate to determine your *net estate,* to which the federal estate tax will be applied:

- Funeral costs
- Expenses of administering your estate
- Creditor claims/indebtedness
- Property taxes and final income tax
- Charitable bequests
- Qualifying bequests to surviving spouse

The Generation-Skipping Transfer Tax

What is the generation-skipping transfer tax?

The goal of the federal estate and gift tax system is to tax wealth at each generation as it passes from one to the next. Historically, wealthy individuals sought to avoid the federal estate tax in two ways:

1. They (first generation) distributed their assets directly to their grandchildren (third generation) either during their lifetimes or upon their deaths in order to pay the federal estate or gift tax just once instead of twice.
2. They created trusts that provided income to their children with the principal, or remainder, going to their grandchildren and subsequent generations, thus avoiding taxation in the children's estates

even though the children had the benefit of the income from their parents' money.

In either case, the government did not get the opportunity to tax the property at the second generation (the taxpayer's children) because the property "skipped" over the second generation.

Congress believed this type of planning was "abusive" and instituted the generation-skipping tax to tax the "skip" just as if the property went directly to the second generation. Today, the Internal Revenue Code imposes a *generation-skipping transfer (GST) tax* on gifts of property that bypass a generation. The tax is a flat 55 percent, and it is imposed in addition to the normal estate and gift taxes. This creates an egregious tax situation: If the federal estate tax and generation-skipping tax are added together, they can amount to an 82 percent tax!

COMMON TAX REDUCTION STRATEGIES

What are the basic federal estate and gift tax strategies?

Basic federal estate and gift tax planning involves using the following five tax strategies:

- *Spousal giving:* Each married person receives an *unlimited marital deduction* that allows the person to transfer to his or her spouse, during life or at death, any amount of assets free of federal estate and gift tax. Thus the value of the donor's, or deceased spouse's, gross estate is reduced by the value of the property passing to the donee, or surviving spouse. (There is an exception to this rule for non-U.S.-citizen spouses.)
- *Applicable exclusion amount giving:* Every estate receives a *unified credit* of $220,550 (in 2000 and 2001) against the taxes owed on the estate of a decedent. This $220,550 credit is the equivalent of exempting, or excluding, $675,000 from estate tax. Thus, each taxpayer has a $675,000 (in 2000 and 2001) exclusion or exemption to give away tax-free during life or at death. This *applicable exclusion amount* can be given to as many or as few individuals as the taxpayer chooses during life or at death. The amount is scheduled to increase gradually to $1 million by 2006.

- *Annual exclusion giving:* Each taxpayer can give away $10,000 (in 2000, indexed annually for inflation) every year to as many or as few individuals as he or she wishes. There is no limit on the total number of individuals or years.
- *Generation-skipping transfer tax planning:* Each individual is allowed to pass a total of $1,030,000 (indexed annually for inflation) to descendants more than one generation removed without incurring GST tax.
- *Charitable giving:* There is no federal estate or gift tax on property or cash given directly to qualified charities.

Federal Estate Tax

The unlimited marital deduction and the marital trust

U.S.-citizen spouses

Can I leave all my property to my spouse without having to pay estate taxes?

The Internal Revenue Code currently allows a person to transfer all of his or her estate to a surviving spouse federal estate tax–free. This is commonly referred to as the *unlimited marital deduction.* You can take advantage of the unlimited marital deduction by leaving your property outright and free of trust to your spouse or by leaving it in trust for your spouse.

How do I leave it in trust for my spouse?

You create a *marital trust* exclusively for the benefit of your spouse.

I've heard that a marital trust doesn't save tax but only defers it. Is this true?

The unlimited marital deduction does saves tax on the first spouse's death, but the property remaining in the marital trust at the surviving spouse's death is included in his or her estate for estate tax purposes.

Can my marital trust have other beneficiaries during my spouse's lifetime?

No. If it does, it will not qualify for the unlimited marital deduction, so its assets will be fully taxed for federal estate tax purposes.

How do I create a marital trust?

You can create a marital trust in your will, which would be called a *testamentary marital trust,* or you can create it as a subtrust under the terms of your living trust.

What must my spouse receive from the marital trust in order to qualify for the unlimited marital deduction?

To qualify for the tax-free treatment of the marital deduction, your spouse must be a U.S. citizen and the trust must provide that she or he receive:

- All the trust income for life without any qualification on that right
- The right to require that the trust assets be invested in income-producing property

Can my spouse receive more than just the marital trust income?

The only requirements are those listed above for the minimum rights that you must give your spouse in a marital trust. Beyond those, the range of generosity you can build into your marital trust is almost unlimited.

You can give your spouse the right to take all the trust assets—income and principal—at any time he or she wants them, as well as the right to use those assets in any way he or she desires. You can also stop as short of those unlimited invasion rights as you choose. For example, you may give your spouse the right to access principal only if there is a medical or financial need not met by other available assets.

Can I specify where some of the trust assets are to go on my husband's death if I die first?

You can specify where all the trust assets go on your husband's death. The marital deduction law does not require that a spouse be given any right to take principal from the trust or to have the power to direct where the principal goes on his or her death.

Alternatively, you can give your spouse, through a general power of appointment, the right to give the trust property to anyone he wants or, through a limited power of appointment, the right to give it to a limited group of people, such as your descendants, in any way he wants.

Are you saying I can not only provide for the financial security of my husband during his life but also make sure that my children receive the remainder of the trust after his death?

Yes. You can provide that your assets be transferred into a *qualified terminable interest property (QTIP)* marital trust. Your husband will receive all the income and, if you wish, as much of the principal as he needs. You would further provide that the balance of the trust go directly to or stay in trust for your children after his death.

The use of a QTIP trust will also defer the assessment of a federal estate tax until the death of your spouse. This is an especially attractive option for individuals who are in a second marriage and wish to ensure that their hard-earned assets will ultimately end up in the hands of their own descendants.

What is a QTIP trust?

"QTIP" is an acronym for "qualified terminable interest property." A *QTIP trust* is an estate planning tool that allows you to obtain an estate tax marital deduction while providing your surviving spouse with full income from and limited rights to the principal in the marital trust.

Although QTIP trusts are popular, they are not appropriate for every estate. Some people prefer QTIP trusts over other marital deduction devices because a QTIP trust provides the surviving spouse with income during his or her life but can restrict that spouse's ability to get to the trust principal. Many people do not want to restrict that right when planning for a spouse.

How does a QTIP trust work?

You can provide that your property be transferred to a marital trust for the benefit of your spouse (assuming your spouse survives you). There will not be any estate tax on property transferred into the QTIP trust at the first spouse's death. While your spouse is still alive, the trustee of the QTIP trust must distribute at least annually the income from the trust to your spouse. Your spouse may also have limited access to the trust principal during his or her lifetime under the standards you set forth in your trust instructions.

When your spouse dies, the property that is left in the QTIP will be included in your spouse's estate for purposes of calculating his or her estate taxes. Then, after the estate taxes are paid, the remaining trust property is distributed to whomever you named as the remainder beneficiaries in your trust agreement.

If I remarry, can I use the marital deduction again?

As long as your spouse is a U.S. citizen, you can use the marital deduction again.

Noncitizen spouses

What if my husband is not a U.S. citizen? Does that change how much of my estate I can pass to him tax-free?

Until a decade ago, noncitizen spouses could receive property tax-free from their citizen spouses through the marital deduction and then move back to their native countries to escape federal estate and gift taxes in the United States.

Congress became concerned that such property would be out of reach of the IRS and entirely escape federal gift and estate taxes, so it changed the law to restrict the tax-free nature of inheritances received by surviving noncitizen spouses.

Can I leave any of my property to my noncitizen spouse without immediately paying federal estate tax?

Yes, but the only way you can do so is by leaving the property for your spouse's benefit in a *qualified domestic trust (QDOT).* If a QDOT meets the following requirements, it will qualify for tax-free federal estate tax treatment:

- The qualifying property must be left in the trust, and the income must be paid at least annually to the surviving spouse for his or her life.
- At least one trustee must be either a U.S. citizen or U.S. trust company.
- No principal distributions can be made unless the U.S. trustee withholds tax on those distributions.
- The trust must contain some sort of security arrangement to ensure payment of federal estate tax on the surviving spouse's death.

Note that principal distributions might be made without tax being withheld if they qualify as hardship distributions.

What does "hardship" mean?

A *hardship* is an immediate and substantial financial need relating to the health, maintenance, education, or support of the spouse or of any person the spouse is legally obligated to support. Distributions that do not qualify for the hardship exception are subject to federal estate tax.

Can I qualify for the marital deduction when making gifts to my noncitizen spouse?

Lifetime gifts to noncitizen spouses are subject to restrictions. While there is no limit on the amount of money that a husband and wife who are citizens can receive tax-free from each other during their lifetimes, the maximum gift amount to a noncitizen spouse is $103,000 each year (indexed annually for inflation). If gifts exceed this amount, federal gift tax will be due on the excess amount.

The applicable exclusion amount and the family trust

What is the unified credit?

The *unified credit* is a credit against federal estate and gift taxes.

What is the applicable exclusion amount?

The federal government allows a person to transfer a certain amount of property federal estate tax–free. This tax allowance, which is actually granted in terms of a credit against taxes due, is called the *applicable exclusion amount (AEA).* The AEA used to be called the *exemption equivalent* or *exemption amount.* It is the amount that is not subject to federal estate tax.

What are the unified credit and applicable exclusion amounts for 2000 and 2001? Are the amounts going to change?

The amounts are shown in Table 4-2. The Taxpayer Relief Act of 1997 increases these amounts through 2006, as you can see in the table.

How does the applicable exclusion amount help me reduce or eliminate my estate tax exposure?

Let's assume that the value of your estate is $1,350,000 and that on your death in 2000 you leave the entire estate to your wife. There is

TABLE 4-2 Phase-in of the Unified Credit

Year	Unified credit	Applicable exclusion amount
2000	$220,550	$ 675,000
2001	220,550	675,000
2002	229,800	700,000
2003	229,800	700,000
2004	287,300	850,000
2005	326,300	950,000
2006 & later	345,800	1,000,000

no estate tax at your death because of the unlimited marital deduction, so your wife's estate is now $1,350,000. Upon her death (for the sake of simplicity, we'll assume she also dies in 2000 and her estate value remains the same), her taxable estate is $1,350,000. Your wife can pass on only her applicable exclusion amount of $675,000 tax-free, and your applicable exclusion amount was wasted. As a result, the amount of the tax is $270,750. With proper planning, the estate tax could have been $0.

What happens, from a federal estate tax perspective, if my wife dies first but all the assets are in my name?

When asset ownership is concentrated in the name of one spouse, just as in the example above, the other spouse's applicable exclusion amount is wasted. If your estate is $1,350,000 or more, there will be at least $270,750 of unnecessary federal estate tax on the death of the surviving spouse. (The result may be different if you live in a community property state.)

What happens if we own all our property in joint tenancy?

The same unfortunate result can occur if a married couple own all their property in joint tenancy. When one spouse dies, all the property automatically passes to the surviving spouse by operation of law, leaving no assets to utilize the first spouse's exclusion amount. Thus the applicable exclusion amount of the first spouse to die is wasted.

Isn't there a way for both of us to take advantage of our applicable exclusion amounts and maybe save even more in taxes?

Yes. With proper planning, each spouse can use his or her $675,000 amount to reduce federal estate tax on death. Estate planners create *family trusts,* sometimes referred to as *credit shelter, B,* or *bypass* trusts, within wills or living trusts to hold the $675,000 applicable exclusion amount of the first spouse to die. As a result, $675,000 is sheltered from tax not only at that spouse's death but at the surviving spouse's subsequent death because that amount is not included in that spouse's estate. When the second spouse dies, his or her applicable exclusion amount can be applied against entirely different assets. By planning this way, up to $1,350,000 (2 × $675,000 in 2000 and 2001) can be sheltered from federal estate tax.

To take maximum advantage of the applicable exclusion amount, both spouses must have a minimum of $675,000 in their estates and have family trust provisions in their wills or trusts. In this way, regardless of the sequence of their deaths both applicable exclusion amounts will be used to reduce the overall federal estate tax burden by a minimum of $270,750.

Can you give me an example of how this works?

Assume your estate is $1,350,000 in 2000 or 2001. You create a will or living trust that directs $675,000 into a family trust for the benefit of your husband and children and the balance of $675,000 either directly to your husband or to a marital trust for his benefit.

We'll assume for this example that you die first. The $675,000 passing to the marital trust for your husband does so federal estate tax–free because of your unlimited marital deduction. The $675,000 that you put in the family trust is not subject to tax on your death because it is sheltered by your applicable exclusion amount.

If your trust is properly drafted, upon your husband's subsequent death, *no* family trust assets—principal or appreciation—are included in his estate for federal estate tax purposes, so they pass estate tax–free to your children. Only the property remaining in the marital trust will be included in his taxable estate. Assuming your husband's taxable estate (including the value of the marital trust) is not more than the applicable exclusion amount then available, it will also pass tax-free because it is sheltered by his applicable exclusion amount. Figure 4-1 shows a diagram of this common example of family trust planning.

I'm single. Can I do this two-trust planning and get the benefit of two estate tax exclusion amounts?

No. A single person has only one applicable exclusion amount, which is shown in Table 4-2.

What are the common provisions in a family trust?

Generally, family trusts are drafted in one of two ways:

- *Exclusively for spouse:* The surviving spouse receives all the income from the family trust and the greater of $5000 or 5 percent of its principal at a minimum each year, as well as principal in the trustee's discretion for health, education, maintenance, and support.
- *Spray, or "sprinkle," family trust:* The surviving spouse, children, and grandchildren (or other designated individuals or class of individuals) receive income and principal in the trustee's discretion for their health, education, maintenance, and support. The trustee is frequently instructed to give primary consideration at all times to the needs of the surviving spouse.

At the surviving spouse's death, the balance is either retained in trust for or distributed free of trust to the remainder beneficiaries, who are usually the children or grandchildren of the couple.

With either alternative, the spouse may have a limited testamentary power to appoint the property, as he or she chooses, among your children or other descendants.

Are these the minimum or maximum rights I have to give my spouse in the family trust?

They are the maximum. If you were to grant your spouse greater rights in the family trust, the IRS might take the position that your spouse controlled the assets. Consequently, at your spouse's death, the full value of the trust property would be included in his or her estate for tax purposes—the outcome you sought to avoid by using the family trust.

Which is the best of the two family trust alternatives suggested above?

The spray, or sprinkle, trust alternative is by far the best of the two

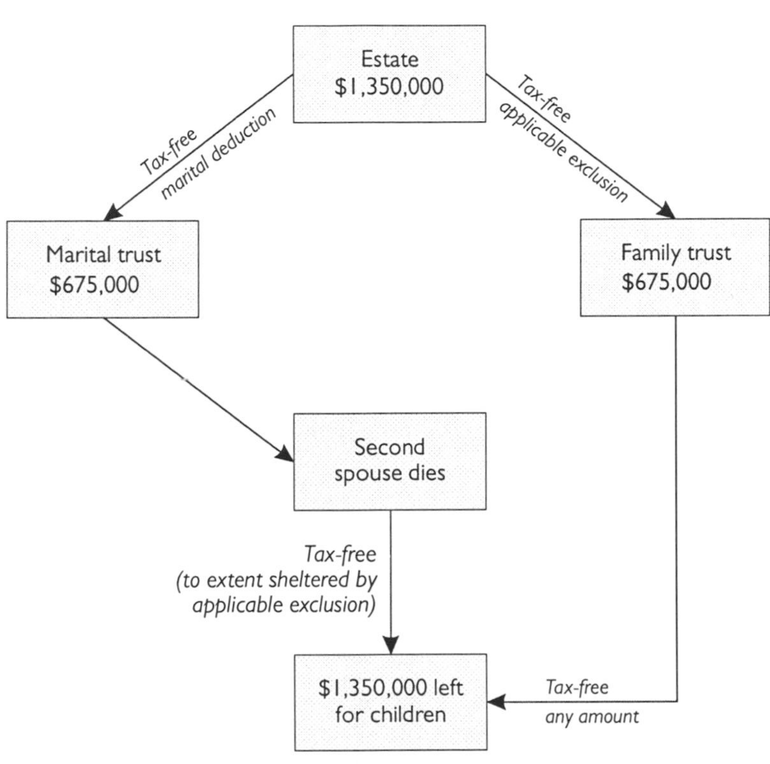

Figure 4-1 Basic two-trust plan.

when viewed from an after-death income or gift tax perspective. In the first alternative, the trustee can make distributions only to the spouse. In the spray family trust, the trustee is distributing money directly to the beneficiaries, who are quite often the children or grandchildren, so the income distributed to them will be taxed in their tax brackets rather than in the surviving spouse's higher income tax bracket.

From a gift tax perspective, the second method is also superior. Under the first method, when the surviving spouse receives distributions and gives all or a portion of the distributions to his or her children and grandchildren, the surviving spouse is deemed to have made a gift and will have to use his or her $10,000 annual exclusion to keep it free of federal gift tax. If, however, the trustee distributes principal directly to the children and grandchildren under the spray trust provisions, the amounts will not use up the surviving spouse's annual exclusion, so it can be used elsewhere in addition to the amount of the trust distributions.

Can my spouse receive any income from my family trust after my death?

As we discussed earlier, a surviving spouse can be given all the income from the trust and up to $5000 or 5 percent of the trust principal, whichever is greater, each year. Additional sums of principal that may be needed for the health, support, maintenance, or education of the spouse can also be made available in the trustee's discretion under very liberal standards.

What is the real benefit of a family trust?

The beauty of a family trust is that, as long as it is drafted and funded properly, the assets in the family trust *plus* any appreciated value will pass federal estate and gift tax–free to the beneficiaries. Thus if you fund a family trust with assets worth $675,000 and their value appreciates to $1,675,000 because of prudent investing, the increase of $1 million can be distributed totally estate and gift tax–free to the beneficiaries of the trust.

Does a family trust pay income tax?

A family trust pays income tax only on the income that is not distributed to its beneficiaries. Professionals call this *retained income.* If income is retained by the trustees, the family trust will pay tax on that income. It is generally a poor idea to retain income in the trust when it has beneficiaries who are in income tax brackets lower than the trust's tax bracket. The trust income tax brackets are very unfriendly, reaching the maximum federal 39.6 percent at just $8650 of taxable income (indexed annually for inflation). If all the beneficiaries are in the highest marginal bracket, it will not matter whether the income is retained or distributed from an income tax planning perspective.

Can my spouse be the trustee of the family trust?

Your spouse can be the sole trustee or a cotrustee of the family trust. You can give your spouse the right to remove the other cotrustee(s) at any time for any reason as long as he or she names a new cotrustee who is not related or subordinate to him or her. In this way, your spouse can pretty much control the affairs of the trust without having enough control to put the trust in his or her estate for tax purposes.

Can a family trust provide for my parents, in-laws, or siblings?

A family trust can provide for any beneficiary, even one who is not related to the will or trust maker. It is not uncommon for people to name their parents, in-laws, and needy siblings as *secondary* beneficiaries of their family trusts. Designating them as secondary beneficiaries means that their needs can be taken care of only *after* the needs of the surviving spouse, children, and grandchildren are met. In some cases, a separate portion of the family trust may be set aside for a particular nonspouse beneficiary to be sure his or her needs will be met.

The marital trust and the family trust combined

First marriages

We have three children and an estate of $1,350,000. How do we use our applicable exclusion amounts?

As previously discussed, to fully utilize two federal estate tax applicable exclusion amounts ($1,350,000 in 2000 and 2001; up to $2 million by 2006):

- Create marital and family trusts in your wills or living trust.
- Title your assets properly. If your property is held in joint tenancy or the assets are owned disproportionately, it will be impossible for you and your spouse to take advantage of both amounts.

It is important that you review the differences between the marital and family trusts. The primary purpose of a marital trust is to ensure that the needs of the surviving spouse are met and that the assets left for your spouse will qualify for the unlimited marital deduction. The primary purpose of the family trust is to provide for your spouse and other family members and use your applicable exclusion amount.

How is my property allocated between the marital and family trusts?

When a two-trust approach is used, after the first spouse's death, the family trust is normally funded first with an amount up to the applicable exclusion amount and the marital trust is normally funded with the balance of the decedent's estate. As a result, no federal estate tax is due at the first death, and the applicable exclusion amount plus its appreciation is sheltered from federal estate tax on the surviving spouse's death.

If my wife were to die first, could I create these trusts in my will or living trust at that time?

You cannot. If you do not plan properly while you are both alive, you will lose the use of the first spouse's federal estate tax applicable exclusion amount.

If I have provisions for family and marital trusts in my will or living trust, do I need to revise it as the applicable exclusion amount increases between now and the year 2006?

Generally, the answer is no. Most will and trust documents use "formula" language tied to the applicable exclusion amount available at the time of death rather than specific dollar figures. If your document contains such language, there is no need to revise it as the exclusion amount increases. Even if the term used is "exemption equivalent" or "unified credit" instead of "applicable exclusion amount," you do not need to revise the document.

However, if the wording in your will or trust document refers to a dollar amount, you should arrange to meet as soon as possible with your attorney. Also, if you intend to immediately distribute a large portion or all of the family trust to nonspouse beneficiaries (such as children of a previous marriage) upon your death, you should review your planning to be sure an appropriate amount will still pass or be available to your spouse.

Is titling of assets important in my estate preservation plan?

In order to ensure the full use of the applicable exclusion amount for each spouse, at least that amount in assets must be titled in each spouse's name or separate living trust. For example, if it is 2002 and the individual applicable exclusion amount is $700,000 when you create your wills or living trusts, you and your spouse should each have $700,000 of assets titled in your separate trusts.

Second marriages

My wife and I want to make sure that each of us is taken care of after the other's death and that the balance of each of our estates goes to our children from previous marriages. Would a QTIP trust be a good idea in our situation?

Yes. A qualified terminable interest property, or QTIP, trust can be used if you and your wife want to provide the surviving spouse with a stream of income while he or she is living and then pass the principal of each of your estates to your respective children. This arrangement guarantees that the surviving spouse will receive income for life and that the value of the property placed in the QTIP trust will escape estate tax liability until his or her subsequent death.

I'm remarried to a man quite a few years younger than I am. I want to provide for his lifetime financial security, but I do not want my children from my first marriage to have to wait until my husband's death to receive their inheritance. What are my alternatives?

Remarriages routinely create an economic conflict of interest between children from a previous marriage and a surviving spouse, particularly if there is only a small age difference between the children and the second spouse. In addition to considering a QTIP trust for your husband's income needs, you might want to consider an immediate distribution of a portion of the family trust to your children or, if that will be needed to support your husband, some immediate tax-free funds for your children, which could be generated through the use of life insurance funded in an irrevocable life insurance trust. In this way, your children would not have to wait for what may be many years until your husband's death before they can receive their share of your estate.

Administration of the trusts

What has to be done to administer the marital and family trusts after one of us dies?

A number of timely steps must be taken to administer this two-trust planning:

- *All the deceased's assets should be appraised as of the date of death.* The appraisal will determine the value of the estate and the amounts to be placed into each of the trusts. It will also assist in establishing the cost basis of the assets so that the heirs can avoid unnecessary capital gain tax if they sell appreciated assets.
- *The assets must be allocated between the trusts.* Which assets will go into each trust is a function of the total value of the estate and the value of individual assets, as well as the specific provisions of the will or trust agreement involved.
- *The allocation must be reviewed.* The surviving spouse should review with his or her accountant, estate planning attorney, and financial advisor the pros and cons of placing specific assets in one trust or the other.

How does one decide what assets to put into which trust after the death of the first spouse?

From a tax perspective, it would be better to place growth or appreciating assets, whenever possible, into the family trust, where their appreciation will pass estate tax–free on the second death. It is generally better to place income-producing assets in the marital trust. Income-producing assets generally appreciate at slower rates than do those that produce little or no income.

Do the marital and family trusts file separate income tax returns?

Each trust is a separate taxpayer and must file its own return. A family trust files a return and pays income tax on the retained income not distributed to its beneficiaries. The marital trust must distribute all its income to the spouse at least annually, so that income is taxed to the spouse. If the spouse is entitled to or receives all the income of the family trust, that income is also taxed to the spouse. When all the trust income is taxed to the spouse, the tax return for the trust is typically simple and inexpensive.

Gift Tax

Are there such things as nontaxable gifts?

Yes. Payments made on behalf of individuals for certain educational or medical expenses are not subject to gift tax. Thus they do not count against the taxpayer's annual exclusion or applicable exclusion amount.

The annual exclusion

Should I consider making gifts to my children or heirs?

The tax answer is fairly obvious: If, by making gifts, you remove property from your estate, you will save tax on the capital appreciation and income on that amount over the years between the time of the gifts and your death.

The personal reasons for making gifts are much more complex. There are a number of questions that you may pose as to whether or not to make gifts to your children, grandchildren, or others, regardless of the tax considerations. You should ask yourself: "Can I afford to make gifts?" "What if I need the money later to live on or to use for a contingency of some kind such as nursing home care?" "What will my children do with it?" "Will they save it or spend it?" "Should I put conditions on my gifts?" These questions require much soul-searching and wisdom before you decide to give away all or a portion of your estate.

Can the sale of property to another person ever be considered a gift?

Yes. When the sale price of a transferred property is less than the fair market value of the property, the difference can be considered a gift. For example, if you sold your son 100 acres of the Jones Family Farm for $100,000 and the fair market value was $300,000, the IRS would take the position that you made a gift of $200,000 to your son. This amount would be subject to federal gift tax to the extent that it exceeds your annual exclusion and applicable exclusion amounts.

Even if you do not report the gift and the IRS does not know about it, you cannot be certain that it will escape notice. This is because the IRS reserves the right to go back over the records of your entire lifetime after your death to calculate federal estate and gift taxes.

How much can I give away without paying gift tax?

In addition to giving away the applicable exclusion amount ($675,000 in 2000 and 2001), you can give away as much as $10,000 per year to each person you wish without paying any tax at all. This is known as the *annual exclusion,* and it is indexed annually for inflation. If a husband and wife combine their annual exclusions, they can transfer $20,000 to anyone they wish. This technique is called *gift splitting.* The people who receive such gifts do not have to be related to the gift giver.

In order to qualify for the annual exclusion, the gift must be a *present-interest* gift; that is, the donee (recipient) must be able to take and use the gift at the time it is made. A gift in trust is not a present-interest gift unless the terms of the trust specify that the donee can elect to take and use the entire amount of the gift within a reasonable period of time after it is made.

The gift tax amounts are now indexed to inflation, but since the amount is rounded down to the nearest $1000, it will likely not be until the year 2001—assuming a 3 percent inflation rate—that the annual exclusion reaches $11,000.

What is meant by "split gifts"?

In a *split gift,* two spouses combine their individual annual exclusions of $10,000 to make a tax-free gift of $20,000. For example, if your spouse agrees to gift-split, you could give $20,000 to each of your grandchildren even though the funds belonged entirely to you.

Are annual exclusion gifts meaningful for tax planning purposes?

Annual exclusion gifts can be an extremely valuable way of minimizing estate taxes, particularly if the assets are likely to appreciate in value. For people whose estate values will exceed the applicable exclusion amount and who are interested in moving value to the next generation, it is imperative that they make use of their annual exclusions each and every year.

For example, a husband and wife with three children can each give $10,000 to each child annually, for a total of $60,000 per year removed from their combined estate without having to use either of their applicable exclusion amounts. Not making a $10,000 annual gift is the equivalent of writing a totally unnecessary check for $5500 (assuming a 55 percent maximum estate and gift tax bracket) to the federal government in terms of future estate taxes.

More important, growth on the gifts is also removed from the couple's estate and thus escapes estate tax. For example, assume a husband and wife do not make a $20,000 gift and this asset grows at 7.2 percent net after tax. In 10 years the $20,000 will be worth $40,000, and in 20 years it will have grown to over $80,000. If this amount is included in their estate and they are in the top marginal bracket, $44,000 will have to be paid to the federal government.

The applicable exclusion amount

When and why would it be appropriate to give away as much as the applicable exclusion amount?

In any estate whose value exceeds the applicable exclusion amount ($675,000 in 2000 and 2001) or may grow to exceed the applicable exclusion amount before death, it makes sense to consider this strategy. A major reason to make such gifts is to put the future appreciation on the assets into someone else's hands. This is particularly appropriate when there is a significant estate and additional growth will only exacerbate the estate tax exposure.

It is imperative that you make sure that any assets you give to your children or other beneficiaries will not be needed by you in the future.

In other words, give away only what you can afford to give away. Your financial advisor can help you make this determination.

Should I use some or all of my applicable exclusion amount in addition to my annual exclusion?

Professionals frequently recommend that their clients use some, if not all, of their applicable exclusion amounts during life by transferring assets out of their estates. However, the drawback to this strategy is the fact that the recipient receives the given assets with the same tax basis as the donor. In other words, there is no step-up in basis as there is when assets are inherited. Gifts made during life maintain the donor's original or substituted basis. Transfers at death receive a step-up to fair market value as of the valuation date. (Step-up in basis is discussed in detail later in this chapter.)

Can I save potential estate taxes by using my entire applicable exclusion amount now?

This can be an excellent tax strategy. Assume a parent gives his or her applicable exclusion amount of $675,000 in the year 2000 to a daughter. No tax is due on the transfer. The $675,000 is removed from the parent's estate and will completely avoid estate tax upon his or her death. Further assume that the daughter has invested the money wisely and it has increased to $3 million. In effect, $2,325,000 (the increase in value) has been passed to the daughter free of all estate or gift taxes. If the parent dies after 2006, when the applicable exclusion amount reaches $1 million, there will be an additional $325,000 of applicable exclusion available to apply to other assets.

If I want to give all or part of my $675,000 applicable exclusion amount during my lifetime, do I have to give it outright?

This type of gift need not be an outright gift. It can be a gift to a trust for the current or future benefit of family members or other heirs.

Stocks and annuities

If I give my children stock that is worth less than I paid for it, can they sell it and take a capital loss?

No; this is not possible. However, they will pay capital gain tax on any increase.

Is it wise to make gifts of stock options?

This is an extremely complex area, but it provides opportunities to pass on significant wealth to others at a lower transfer tax cost. Option holders can eliminate or at least minimize gift taxes by making gifts of the options when they have a low value.

What can I do from an estate tax planning standpoint with a very large deferred annuity that I no longer need for income purposes?

The concept of *annuity maximization* examines the estate tax impact of owning an annuity at death. When this concept is properly employed, the annuity is simply used as a source for funding a lifetime giving program through systematic or random withdrawals from the annuity to fund gifts.

Generally, for persons over the age of 65, the annuitization of the annuity using a life-with-no-refund option can be very effective when the individuals use the annuity payments to purchase life insurance outside the estate (i.e., in an irrevocable life insurance trust).

Gifts to minors

How can property be given to minor children?

Lifetime transfers to minors are often made to take advantage of the $10,000-per-person annual exclusion or to position the assets so that investment returns will be taxed at lower rates.

In most states, minor children cannot hold legal title to property, so gifts to minors are generally made using one of the following vehicles:

- A custodial account in accordance with the state's Uniform Transfers to Minors Act or Uniform Gifts to Minors Act
- A minor's trust in accordance with IRC Section 2503(c)
- A properly structured irrevocable trust that gives minor beneficiaries annual withdrawal rights that are exercised by their guardians

Are there any special income tax rules that apply for gifts to minor children?

There are special rules for the taxation of children's investment income while they are under the age of 14. If such a child has investment income exceeding the indexed limit ($700 in 2000), the tax on that income—commonly referred to as the "kiddie tax"—is based on the parent's top marginal tax rate. *Investment income* is defined as any income other than earned income and may consist of interest, dividends, royalties, rents, and profits from the sale of assets.

Once children reach the age of 14, they are considered to have their own tax status but may be in brackets that are significantly lower than those of their parents.

What is the Uniform Transfers to Minors Act?

To provide an efficient means for making gifts to minors, most states enacted either the *Uniform Transfers to Minors Act (UTMA)* or the *Uniform Gifts to Minors Act (UGMA).* Any gifts made under these statutes are treated as complete for purposes of property, income, and gift tax laws.

Under UTMA or UGMA, you can easily establish a custodial account. (There is no need to consult an attorney, whose services are normally required to establish a trust.) A donor appoints a custodian to hold, invest, or spend assets for the benefit of a designated minor beneficiary. The custodian maintains control of the assets on behalf of the minor until the child reaches the age of 21 (or 18 in some states). Some states allow you to designate a UTMA custodial account to be held through age 25.

Is a gift or transfer made under UTMA irrevocable?

Yes; the gift is irrevocable. The minor's Social Security number must be used for tax-reporting purposes. The custodial property will be held and used for the benefit of the minor beneficiary until she or he reaches the age specified in the state's UGMA/UTMA, typically either 18 or 21. At that point, the remaining assets must be turned over to the beneficiary, to do with as she or he pleases. If a large amount is involved, it may be advisable to use an irrevocable trust to make gifts to a minor because the donor can specify whatever age he or she desires for the distribution to be made.

Who may serve as custodian, and what are his or her responsibilities?

The custodian may be the donor of the gift, another adult, or a trust company. However, if the person who made the gift appoints himself or herself as custodian and subsequently dies before the funds are distributed to the child, the IRS will consider the custodial property to be part of the transferor's estate for estate tax purposes. Similarly, if a parent of the child serves as custodian and dies before the funds are distributed to the child, the IRS will include the account in the parent's estate even if the parent never contributed property to the account. Therefore, if parents give money to their children under the UTMA, it may be advisable to have a third party act as custodian. If a large amount is involved, it may be preferable to use an irrevocable trust to make gifts because it can avoid this potential exposure to estate tax.

A custodian is obligated to use prudent management in dealing with the property belonging to the minor. A custodian may use the assets as he or she deems best for the use and benefit of the minor but may not use the funds for his or her own benefit, other than the possible reimbursement for reasonable expenses incurred during the performance of his or her duties.

What is the advantage of making gifts to minors via irrevocable trusts?

Making gifts to a minor via a trust enables the donor/trust maker to delay the child's receipt of the property until a prespecified age. The trustee can be given broad investment powers and, through the use of the trust, can maintain control of distributions to the minor until whatever time the donor feels is appropriate for turning over the trust assets to the child. In addition, the assets of a properly drafted irrevocable trust are not includible in the donor/trust maker's taxable estate.

Can employment of a minor in a family business be used to help the planning process?

Employing a minor in a family business can reduce the overall family tax bill by shifting income to an individual in a lower tax bracket. It can also provide the $2000 earnings that can help establish either a Roth or a traditional IRA (discussed in Chapter 10) for the minor.

There are a number of income tax advantages. The business obtains a deduction for a reasonable salary given to the child, and shifting income to the child reduces the parent's self-employment income and income tax. Any salary received by the child is considered earned income and, therefore, not subject to the kiddie tax rules for minors under age 14. As long as the owner pays the child an amount equal to or less than the standard deduction for compensation, there will be no tax on this income. Also, children under age 18 working for an unincorporated business are not subject to Social Security taxes.

If the child is making less than the standard deduction and would not be paying taxes anyway, the Roth IRA might be more suitable than a deductible IRA. However, the child may want to consider making deductible contributions to an IRA as these contributions can offset earned and unearned income. This would allow the family business to pay an additional $2000 above the standard deduction and still not pay tax. An important point to remember is that the family business must make certain that the wages are reasonable for the work performed and that the services performed are necessary to the business.

Generation-Skipping Transfer Tax

What is the generation-skipping transfer tax exemption?

Current law allows each person to distribute to generations more remote than children a total of $1,030,000 (indexed annually for inflation) in assets without the imposition of a generation-skipping transfer (GST) tax. The distributions can be made during life or at death.

How can I ensure that some of my assets will be distributed to or for the benefit of my grandchildren?

You can provide in your will or trust that all or any portion of your assets be distributed either directly to your grandchildren or to a trust for your grandchildren's benefit.

If this is an avenue of planning you wish to pursue, it is essential that you retain an attorney who understands the intricacies of the generation-skipping transfer tax, how they interrelate with other planning opportunities, and how to draft a trust document to take advantage of the maximum GST tax exemption available under the law.

Is it possible to use a large IRA or other tax-deferred retirement account to take advantage of the GST tax exemption at the IRA owner's death?

Yes. If a grandparent dies with a grandchild as IRA beneficiary, it may be possible to spread the distributions over the grandchild's life expectancy, producing a much greater ultimate inheritance because of the longer tax deferral. To avoid the imposition of the GST tax on the account, the grandparent's executor must allocate all or part of the grandparent's GST exemption to the retirement account.

PAYMENT OF TAXES

Estate Taxes

What liquidity needs will my family potentially face after my death?

Liquidity needs generally include:

- Federal estate taxes (maximum: 55 percent)
- Federal income taxes (maximum: 39.6 percent)
- State income taxes (percentage varies)
- Probate and administration costs, if living trust is not used (3 to 10 percent of gross estate)
- Payment of maturing debts
- Maintenance and welfare of family members
- Payment of specific cash bequests
- Funds to continue running family business, meet payroll and inventory costs, and recruit replacement management

How are estate taxes paid?

The payment of estate taxes is generally satisfied by:

- *Cash:* If cash is available within the estate, it can be used to pay the estate tax bill, which is due within 9 months of the person's death.
- *Sale of assets:* Assets of the estate can be sold. Unfortunately, the full value of an estate's assets may not be realized because the assets are sold in a "forced sale" to quickly raise the cash needed to pay the taxes. This may be devastating to a family because the estate tax due is based on the full market value of the asset at the date of death and not on the discounted sale price.
- *Loans:* If there are insufficient liquid assets within the estate, the heirs can borrow the needed funds from a private lender. The interest on the amount borrowed adds another burden to the estate.
- *Life insurance:* Insurance proceeds can be used to cover all liabilities.
- *Installment payments:* If the estate meets certain criteria, a portion of the tax liability may be payable in installments with interest.

How long after my death does my family have to pay my estate tax liability?

The federal estate tax return, Form 706, must be filed with the tax payment within 9 months after the decedent's death. The Internal Revenue Code imposes a penalty of 5 percent of the amount of the tax for each month of delinquency (with a maximum of 25 percent) unless the person responsible for filing the return can show that the delay is due to reasonable cause and not willful neglect. If good and sufficient cause is shown, an extension, usually limited to 6 months, can be obtained for filing the return but interest will be assessed.

Can I receive an extension of time for paying federal estate tax?

The IRS has provided very limited relief for the payment of this tax:

1. If the deceased is the owner or partner in a closely held business and his or her estate qualifies, the executor may elect to pay the taxes attributable to the business over a period of years. The maximum for this extension is 14 years; only interest payments are required in the first 4 years, while the remainder of the payments must be made in equal increments to pay off the principal over a 10-year period. This option falls under Section 6166 of the Internal Revenue Code.
2. A direct appeal can be made to the district director, who under evidence of "reasonable cause" can grant an extension of up to 10 years. Although not specifically delineated, reasonable cause could include the impossibility of the estate to pay the taxes due. This extension is generally given only under unusual circumstances and should not be relied upon as a viable option.

In both situations the IRS acts as a general creditor and will hold a lien against the assets in the estate until the taxes are paid in full.

Heirs' Income Taxes

Capital gain tax and step-up in basis

Are the appreciated values of my real estate and stock portfolio taxed as they pass to my heirs?

The values of your real estate and stock portfolio, as well as of most of the other assets in your taxable estate, receive a *step-up in basis.* This means that an asset's cost basis is stepped up (or possibly down) to the asset's fair market value at your death. Thus, there is no capital gain tax on the difference between what you paid for the assets and their values at your death. However, any increase in value after the date of death is subject to capital gain tax when your heirs sell the assets.

Can you give me an example of how this works?

If you paid $1000 for stocks that are worth $10,000 on your death, the stocks would receive a step-up in basis to $10,000 as valued on the federal estate tax return. The $9000 increase would not be subject to capital gain tax. If your trustee or an heir sells the stocks later for $11,000, the capital gain would be $1000 ($11,000 – $10,000) and the capital gain tax would be $200 (20% × $1000) plus state taxes if applicable.

Do my children get a step-up in basis on appreciated property I give them while I'm alive?

They do not. Your children will receive a *carryover* basis on appreciated property you give them. In essence, they step into your shoes as to the cost of the property. If your basis in the stock was $1000 before you gave it to them and they later sell the stock for $10,000, they will have $9000 of gain subject to the capital gain tax. Nevertheless, compared with holding the stock until your death, the gift may still make sense: it enables you to avoid the much heavier, 50 to 55 percent estate tax on the full value.

Does jointly held property receive the same step-up in basis?

If a married couple own property in joint tenancy with rights of survivorship and one of them dies, the tax result is as follows: The deceased spouse's half of the property receives a step-up in basis; the surviving spouse's half of the property retains its original cost basis. Couples who live in community property states and own property jointly receive an additional benefit (as discussed below).

Can you give an example of how step-up in basis and capital gains are figured for jointly held property?

Let's assume that a couple pays $1000 for stocks that are placed in joint tenancy. At the time of the husband's death the stocks are valued at

$10,000. Thereafter, they increase in value to $11,000 and are sold by his widow for that amount.

The widow's new basis in the stocks is $5500: $500 for her 50 percent of the original $1000 cost basis plus $5000 for the husband's 50 percent interest stepped up to the date-of-death value. When the widow sells the stock later, her new basis of $5500 is subtracted from the sale price of $11,000, resulting in a $5500 taxable gain.

How is property held by spouses as community property taxed for income tax purposes?

If spouses own community property, they receive a decided capital gain tax advantage over spouses who own property as joint tenants because the entire value of the community property receives a step-up in basis.

Let's assume that a couple pays $1000 for stocks that are owned as community property. At the time of the husband's death the stocks are valued at $10,000. Thereafter, they increase in value to $11,000 and are sold by his widow for that amount. The widow receives a 100 percent step-up in basis in the value of the stocks, to $10,000. When she later sells the stock for $11,000, the sale results in a $1000 taxable gain.

The community property states are Alaska, Idaho, Washington, California, Arizona, Nevada, New Mexico, Texas, Louisiana, and Wisconsin.

What happens if I leave my children stock, which I want them to hold on to, whose cost basis is higher than its fair market value at the time of my death?

Annual gift tax rules aside, if you bequeath this stock to your children, they will own it at its fair market value at the time of your death. Your higher cost basis, and the ability to sell the stock for a tax loss, dies with you. If you truly want your heirs to hold on to this stock, you should consider selling it, taking the tax loss yourself, and simply waiting 31 days before you repurchase the stock yourself—this will permit you to take the tax loss and establish your new cost basis in compliance with the tax code's *wash-sale rules.* Afterward, if the stock rebounds and appreciates before your children inherit it, they'll receive a step-up in basis to the value at your time of death.

Alternatively, you could sell the stock, and thus be entitled to the tax loss, and give the cash proceeds to your children so that they can purchase the stock on the open market and their basis will be at the new purchase price.

Income in respect of a decedent

I've heard that heirs sometimes have to pay income taxes on their inheritance. How can that be?

Most assets receive a step-up in basis upon the death of their owners. A few assets, however, do not get this favorable income tax treatment. Instead, all or a portion of the asset is considered *income in respect of a decedent (IRD)* and is taxed as ordinary income when received by the heir.

What is IRD property?

IRD property does not receive a step-up in basis to its fair market value at the owner's death, even though it is included in the decedent's gross estate. It consists of amounts that a decedent would have included in gross income had he or she lived to receive them. Examples of IRD property are:

- Qualified retirement plan or IRA assets other than after-tax contributions
- Deferred compensation, including any unpaid salary or bonuses
- Survivor benefits under a joint-survivor annuity
- Unpaid fees, commissions, or royalties
- Accounts receivable, including rent and accrued interest
- Uncollected payments due under an installment obligation
- Unpaid lottery winnings
- Earnings inside a deferred annuity

IRD income retains the same character (i.e., rent, royalty, etc.) as it would have had in the decedent's hands, and it is taxable upon receipt at the recipient's income tax rate.

Can you give me an example of how IRD works?

Mike had a nonqualified deferred-compensation plan with his employer. Each time he received a payment under the plan, he reported the payment as income on his tax return. At the time of his death, Mike had received only five of the fifteen annual payments under the plan.

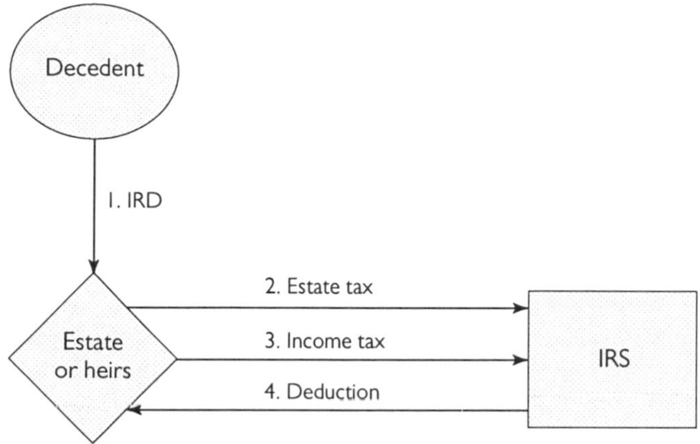

Figure 4-2 Income in respect of a decedent. (1) Heir receives income that decedent was entitled to but was not yet required to report during his or her lifetime. (2) IRD is included in the gross estate for federal estate tax purposes. (3) IRD is reported as ordinary income by the heir in the year received. (4) Heir receives a federal income tax deduction for federal estate tax attributable to IRD.

Each time his heir receives one of the remaining payments, she must report it as income.

How is income in respect of a decedent taxed?

To avoid confiscatory levels of taxation, a special income tax deduction is allowed for IRD. Even though the full amount of the IRD is taken into gross income as it is received, its recipient is allowed to deduct the portion of the federal estate taxes paid by the estate that is attributable to the IRD.

Can you give an example of how the IRD deduction works?

Joan's gross estate was valued at $3 million and included $100,000 of IRD. Her estate paid an estate tax of $1,070,250 after taking into account her unified credit. Without the $100,000 IRD in the estate, the estate tax would have been $1,017,250, a difference of $53,000. The $100,000 of IRD (if received all in one year) will be subject to ordinary income tax, but $53,000 of that amount can be deducted as it is the amount of estate tax attributable to the $100,000 IRD.

IRD taxation is illustrated in Figure 4-2.

Will my tax-deferred annuity be taxable to my heirs?

Your beneficiaries will pay income taxes on the annuity just as you would have paid them. The portion of the payments representing principal (contributions) will be distributed tax-free, and the portion representing earnings will be taxed.

chapter 5

Advanced Estate Tax Reduction Strategies

I've heard there are ways to reduce the value of my estate. What are they?

Sophisticated estate planning can involve many different techniques to reduce the value of an estate for federal estate tax purposes. Sometimes, only one primary method is used. Other times, a combination of methods is used. The direction one goes in depends, in every case, on an individual's planning goals and financial situation.

Some of the more effective estate reduction techniques are:

- Making gifts through the use of irrevocable trusts, such as qualified personal residence trusts and grantor retained income trusts
- Using installment sales between family members and trusts
- Establishing private annuities
- Making gifts of assets that have been discounted in value
- Making gifts through charitable devices such as charitable remainder trusts, charitable lead trusts, and private foundations
- Purchasing life insurance through an irrevocable life insurance trust (ILIT) to remove the proceeds from the estate, to provide liquidity for payment of estate taxes, or to replace inheritances that were given to charity. (See Chapter 7 for a detailed discussion of ILITs.)

Since most of these planning strategies require irrevocable trusts, we begin with the general concepts that pertain to all irrevocable trusts.

UNDERSTANDING IRREVOCABLE TRUSTS

What is an irrevocable trust?

An *irrevocable trust* is a trust that cannot be changed or amended by its maker after it has been signed. Irrevocable trusts are used to make gifts "with strings attached" to the trust beneficiaries.

Gifts can be made outright or in trust. Gifts in trust are subject to a set of written instructions. These instructions (the terms of the trust) are the strings attached to the gift. Donors who make gifts in trust, rather than outright, are able to control how and when the gift is enjoyed by the beneficiary.

Why are irrevocable trusts used in estate planning?

Irrevocable trusts offer significant tax planning advantages:

- In many cases, assets placed into irrevocable trusts are not included in the maker's gross estate and thus are not subject to federal estate tax.
- Transfers of assets to an irrevocable trust while the maker is alive allow the maker to reduce or avoid many of the fees and expenses incurred upon death.
- The assets held in an irrevocable trust can be used to provide income and principal to the trust's beneficiaries while minimizing federal estate and gift tax.
- The assets held in an irrevocable trust are protected from the claims of a beneficiary's spouse or creditors.
- Irrevocable trusts can include generation-skipping tax planning provisions.

If it's irrevocable, won't I lose control of the assets I put in the trust?

When you establish an irrevocable trust, you don't really give up total control. As the trust maker, you establish the ground rules in the trust document through your instructions, and you appoint the trustees to enforce those instructions.

Can I be the sole trustee of my irrevocable trust?

In most cases, it is not advisable for you to be the sole trustee. If you are, you may lose certain tax and asset protection benefits.

What do I have to give up in order to get the tax benefits of an irrevocable trust?

To keep the assets of an irrevocable trust out of your taxable estate and to keep the trust's income out of your taxable income, you must give up several things:

- You have to give up the power to revoke or amend the trust.
- In most cases you have to give up the right to receive income or principal from the trust and the right to designate—except in the trust document—to whom or in what amounts trust income or principal is to be paid.
- If you put stock of a controlled corporation (one in which you and related persons have 20 percent of the voting power) in the trust, you must give up your stock voting rights. Otherwise, the stock will be included in your estate.

What's the difference between an irrevocable trust and a revocable living trust?

The major difference is reflected in the trusts' respective names. A *revocable living trust* is like a will in that you can change or amend, cancel, or revoke it at any time for any reason. With an *irrevocable trust* you can't retain the power to revoke or change its terms. If you could, the trust property would be treated for tax purposes in the same way as property in a revocable living trust: it would be included in your taxable estate.

An irrevocable trust is nothing more than a complete and absolute gift made with "strings attached." You can place the contingencies, requests, and prohibitions you want into your irrevocable trust terms, but you cannot retain the right to change or alter it after you sign it.

Is there any way that an irrevocable trust can be changed or modified?

An irrevocable trust can be changed or modified by a court in a *reformation* proceeding if the court determines that clerical errors were made and that the change will not be injurious to any of the beneficiaries. Also, there may be limited powers given to the trustee and/or beneficiaries that permit them to effectively change the trust within certain limits.

You've said that using an irrevocable trust for making gifts removes the gift from my estate. Is there a way to qualify these gifts in trust for my annual exclusion?

To qualify gifts to a trust for the annual exclusion, the trust must contain "demand-right" language or instructions. To understand demand-right trusts, let's first review the gift tax annual exclusion. The gift tax law allows you to exclude from the gift tax computation the first $10,000 (indexed annually for inflation) that you give in any year to any person as long as the gift is a gift of a "present interest," as opposed to a "future interest." The tax law defines a *present interest* as the "unrestricted right to the use, possession, or enjoyment of property or the income from property."

For example, if you give one of your children $10,000 outright, whether in cash or by transferring assets into the child's name, and thus you have no further control over the property, you've made a gift of a present interest, which qualifies for the annual exclusion. But suppose you give the cash or assets to a conventional irrevocable trust of which your child is the only beneficiary, and the trust calls for the trustee to hold the assets during the child's lifetime and make payments from income or principal as needed for the child. In this case, you have made a gift of a *future interest,* and the transfer to the trust will not qualify for the annual exclusion unless the transfer is accompanied by demand rights.

A *demand right* is also called a *withdrawal right* or a *Crummey power* (after the court case that first permitted it for gift tax exclusion purposes). It is the right given to beneficiaries of an irrevocable trust to withdraw the contribution made to the trust up to the annual exclusion amount within a certain period of time from the date of the gift (usually 30 to 45 days). The inclusion of demand-right language in the trust document qualifies the gift as a gift of a present interest for purposes of the annual exclusion. The shortest period of time that the tax court has approved for a demand right is 15 days.

Of course, your purpose in setting up your irrevocable trust will be undermined if your beneficiary actually exercises his or her power to withdraw the demand-right amount. While the demand right gives your beneficiary the legal right to demand a withdrawal, in the usual family situation all that is required is to explain to the beneficiary that your overall estate plan, and the family's best interest, will be served by *not* exercising the demand right.

What's a Crummey trust?

A *Crummey trust* is an irrevocable trust with demand rights in it. There is nothing crummy or shabby about a demand-right trust. The name "Crummey trust" comes from a tax court case that approved the use of a demand right to make a gift to a trust eligible for the trust maker's gift tax annual exclusion.

What types of investments can an irrevocable trust own?

An irrevocable trust can own all types of assets. You can specify which assets it can own, refer to the state statute that lists those assets, or combine both approaches in your trust instructions.

Care must be taken if certain assets are owned by an irrevocable trust. For example, if the trust is to hold S corporation stock, special provisions must be added to the trust to ensure that the S corporation status will not be jeopardized.

It is always a good idea to fully discuss the uses to which an irrevocable trust will be put with your tax advisors so that the trust will be properly drafted to accommodate the assets it will hold.

REMOVING ASSETS FROM THE ESTATE

Why would we remove assets from our estate?

When you remove the value of assets from your taxable estate, along with all future appreciation on the assets, the savings in estate taxes can be substantial, possibly as much as 55 percent of the value of the assets.

Grantor Retained Interest Trusts

What is a grantor retained interest trust?

A *grantor retained interest trust* is an irrevocable trust in which the maker retains an income interest for a term of years. There are five varieties of grantor retained interest trusts:

- Qualified personal residence trust (QPRT)
- Grantor retained annuity trust (GRAT)
- Grantor retained unitrust (GRUT)
- Tangible personal property trust (tangibles GRIT)
- Grantor retained income trust (GRIT)

Qualified personal residence trusts

What is a qualified personal residence trust?

A *qualified personal residence trust (QPRT)* is a special type of irrevocable trust specifically sanctioned by the Internal Revenue Code. The maker of the QPRT transfers, or gives, a personal residence or vacation home to the QPRT. The maker reserves the right to reside in the home for a specified term of years (the *initial term*). After the initial term has expired, the home belongs to the trust beneficiaries, usually the maker's children, or the trustee continues to hold it for their benefit.

Because you are transferring a "remainder" interest in the home to the beneficiaries, the value of the home for gift tax purposes is substantially reduced from its fair market value at the time you transfer the home to the trust. When the initial term ends, assuming you outlive the term, the fair market value of your home and all future appreciation are removed from your taxable estate.

Can we continue to live in the home after the expiration of the initial term?

You can continue to live in the home by leasing it from the trust beneficiaries at its fair rental value. The home (or the proceeds from the sale of the home) becomes an investment for the beneficiaries.

How is the value of a gift to a QPRT determined?

The Internal Revenue Code outlines the basis for calculating the present value of a future gift under a QPRT. Most financial planners and attorneys have computer programs that perform the necessary calculations. The factors that influence the calculation are the current value of the home, the age of the trust maker, the current IRS actuarial tables, the initial term of the trust, and the current government-adjusted *applicable federal rate (AFR).* The AFR equals 120 percent of the federal midterm rate published monthly by the Internal Revenue Service.

Can you give me an example of how a QPRT works?

Mr. Johnson, age 65, has a home with a fair market value of $500,000. He transfers it to a QPRT and retains the right to live in the home for 10 years, with the remainder interest going to his children. Assuming an 8 percent AFR, the present gift value of the remainder interest to the children is $176,055. At the end of the trust's initial term, the value of the residence is $1 million.

By using a QPRT, Mr. Johnson reduced the size of his estate by $1 million (the fair market value of the home at the end of the initial term), continued to live in his home for 10 years, and used only $176,055 of his applicable exclusion amount in transferring ownership of the home to his children.

We own our home as joint tenants. How do we transfer it to a QPRT?

If your home is in your joint names, you can change the title to only one spouse's name (preferably the younger or healthier spouse). That spouse would then create a QPRT and transfer the home to it. Alternatively, you can each create a QPRT, with each of you transferring your interest in the home to your own QPRT.

If a house is divided into two separate interests, the makers may be entitled to a discount (often from 15 to 40 percent) on their respective shares of the home in their trusts. The discount is determined by a qualified appraisal of the property.

Many tax advisors advocate the use of two QPRTs rather than one for two reasons. The first is the additional discount that may be taken. The second is that if one spouse dies before the end of the initial trust term, only that spouse's half interest in the home is included in his or her estate. If there is a single QPRT and the maker dies, the whole home is included in his or her estate. Two QPRTs reduce risk, unless, of course, one spouse is not expected to live for the term of the QPRT.

Can you give us an example of this approach if we own our home jointly?

Assume that Mark and Joan Gardner have a $5 million estate. The Gardners, both age 60, are in good health and have four children. Their primary residence is valued at $1 million. The Gardners would like to find a tax-efficient way to transfer the value of their jointly held home and all future appreciation to their children. Their tax advisors suggest that they use a QPRT.

Mark and Joan each create a QPRT. Each one transfers his or her half interest in the residence into his or her trust, retaining a right to live in the home for 15 years, the term of the trusts. They arrange to rent the home at the end of the term, and they name themselves as trustees of their respective trusts. An appraiser determines that the value of each half interest in the home is $350,000—a 30 percent discount from fair market value.

Each QPRT contains a "reversion" provision which provides that if either spouse dies during the initial term of the trust, the decedent's interest in the residence will revert and become part of his or her estate. Thus, if one spouse does die before the end of the initial term, only half of the home reverts to his or her estate; the other half will still remain in trust for the remainder of the designated term and ultimately go to their children. If both Gardners live for at least 15 years, the residence will belong equally to their four children.

Using these factors, and assuming a 7.2 percent AFR, the Gardners make a combined taxable gift of $174,350. If the property appreciates at 4 percent annually and they live to the end of the initial trust term, the Gardners will have removed an asset worth approximately $1.8 million (value at the end of the initial term) from their estate while using only a fraction of their applicable exclusion amounts. Because the gifts are future-interest gifts, the annual gift tax exclusion cannot be used, so the Gardners will use $174,350 of their combined applicable exclusion amount ($1,350,000 for 2000 and 2001) to avoid paying gift taxes. The Gardners' QPRT strategy is diagrammed in Figure 5-1.

Through this strategy, the Gardners leverage a portion of their combined applicable exclusion amount and transfer their home to their children at a fraction of the home's actual value. And they do so without giving up the ability to continue residing there for the term of the trust and beyond.

Are there any risks or disadvantages with a QPRT?

Although a QPRT is a fantastic estate planning tool in the right situation, there are three main pitfalls with this technique.

1. *The transfer to the trust is irrevocable.* You cannot change your mind later. You will no longer own your home outright. However, while your home is in the QPRT, you have virtually all the rights of outright ownership; and after the term of the QPRT ends, you can lease it back from the new owners, your trust beneficiaries.

2. *If you die before the trust ends, the entire value of the property will be included in your estate for estate tax purposes.* From a tax-saving standpoint, nothing will have been accomplished at all. Because of this, it is often argued that this technique is a "maybe-win-big" but "nothing-to-lose" proposition. One way to minimize this problem might be to divide the ownership among several QPRTs with different term lengths.

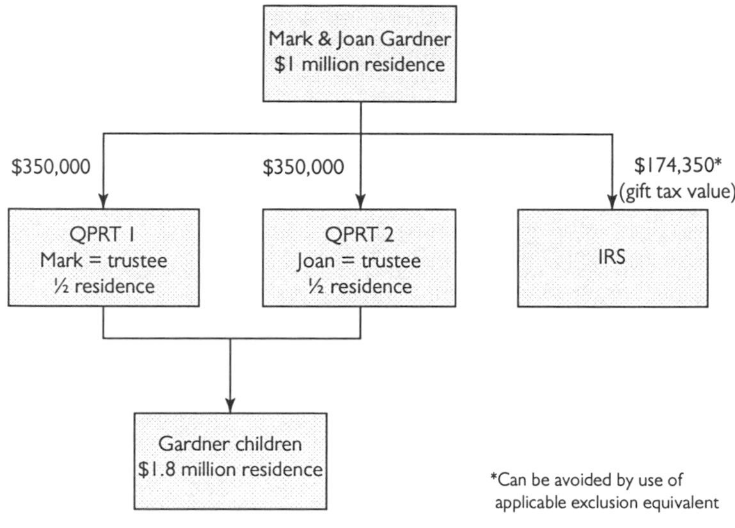

Figure 5-1 The Gardners' QPRT strategy.

If you outlive the trust, you've transferred a large asset and avoided the estate tax. The total tax savings could be in the hundreds of thousands of dollars. If you don't outlive the trust, you're no worse off than you would be if you hadn't set up the trust in the first place.

3. *The beneficiaries may have to pay capital gain taxes.* If you survive the term of the trust, your beneficiaries will have a "carryover" cost basis (your cost basis at the time of the transfer to the QPRT) because they received the property as a gift. This will result in capital gain taxes if they sell the home. Alternatively, if you retain the home and leave it at death to your beneficiaries, the property will receive a "stepped-up" basis equal to its fair market value at the date of your death. The beneficiaries could then sell the home without capital gain taxes.

The theory behind the QPRT is that estate tax savings (possibly up to 55 percent) will more than offset the capital gain taxes that your beneficiaries will have to pay as a result of the potentially low carryover basis. If the beneficiaries keep the property and it ultimately passes through their estates, the property will be entitled to a full step-up in basis for their heirs, thus eliminating the accumulated potential capital gain taxes.

What's so good about leasing my home back after the QPRT ends?

Leasing your home from your children may not sound like a good idea at first blush. However, this leaseback feature has tax advantages. By paying rent to your children, you further reduce your estate. In addition, this arrangement enables you to transfer more than the gift tax annual exclusion to your children.

Income tax is payable by the children on the rent they receive, but no gift or estate tax is due. Federal income tax is, at most, 39.6 percent, while estate tax can be as high as 55 percent. Furthermore, the children can offset the income with the deductions associated with rental real estate.

If you are concerned that your children will be unwilling to enter into a lease at the end of the trust term, you can arrange a lease with them in advance. In at least one private-letter ruling, the IRS held that as long as the rent paid under the prearranged lease is a fair market rent, the value of the home will not be included in the parents' estate.

Can we sell our home if it is in a QPRT?

A properly worded QPRT has flexibility for changing circumstances. For example, a QPRT can allow you to:

- *Sell your home and not replace it.* The proceeds of the sale will belong to the trust (and, ultimately, the beneficiaries), but you will be entitled to annuity payments during the remaining period of the trust. (See the discussion of grantor retained annuity trusts later in this chapter.) During the initial term of the trust, a sale may in some cases take advantage of the income tax exemption upon the sale of a primary residence.
- *Sell your home and replace it with another home.* If the value of the new home exceeds the value of the original home and you make up the cash difference, you are making an additional gift to the trust that may cause additional gift tax and require a calculation similar to that for the original gift. If the value of the new home is less than the value of the original home, the additional cash from the sale will create an annuity as described above.

If there is a mortgage on my house, can I transfer it to a QPRT?

If there is an outstanding mortgage on the residence, you should either pay off the mortgage or remain personally liable for the mortgage. Otherwise, the mortgage payment will be treated as an additional future-interest gift to the trust beneficiaries, thus using up more of your applicable exclusion amount or, if it is exhausted, necessitating the payment of gift tax.

Do I lose the income tax benefits of home ownership if I transfer my home to a QPRT?

If you are making mortgage payments, you can continue to deduct the mortgage interest payments just as you would if you still owned the home outright. You can also deduct the property taxes. Also, if you sell the home during the initial term, you can exclude up to $250,000 ($500,000 per couple) of gain on the sale of the property as long as it was used as a primary residence for 2 out of the 5 years preceding the sale.

Can I transfer rental properties or large amounts of land to a QPRT?

No. You may place only two residences into QPRTs. One QPRT must be for your primary residence. The other can be for a secondary residence, such as a vacation home, but the residence must not be considered an "investment property" under the applicable Internal Revenue Code provisions.

You may contribute an undivided fractional interest to a QPRT. This routinely occurs when a husband and wife own a residence or vacation home jointly. Each of them creates his or her own QPRT and transfers an undivided half interest into it.

A QPRT must include a personal residence or vacation home and only a reasonable amount of land appropriate for residential purposes. Household furnishings cannot be transferred to the trust.

Can the home in a QPRT pass to my grandchildren at the end of the term?

Beware of possible generation-skipping transfer tax if the ultimate distribution is to a grandchild. The amount of the generation-skipping gift is determined at the end of the trust term and may be greater than the GST tax exemption in effect at the time. Generally speaking, a QPRT is not ideal for generation-skipping planning.

Grantor retained annuity trust

What is the primary purpose of a grantor retained annuity trust?

Grantor retained annuity trusts (GRATs) are used primarily by people who want to transfer income-producing assets and future appreciation to their children at a discounted value for estate and gift tax purposes but would like to continue to receive cash flow from the assets for a period of time.

How does a GRAT work?

The maker of the trust transfers assets to the trust and retains an annuity interest in the assets for a period of years called the *initial term.* At the end of the initial term, the assets pass to the remainder beneficiaries. The amount of the gift to the beneficiaries is the fair market value of the property transferred to the GRAT minus the value of the maker's retained annuity interest.

An annuity interest differs from a true income interest in several respects. An *annuity interest* is a fixed amount that has to be paid at least yearly by the trust. For example, if a 10 percent, 15-year GRAT is funded with $100,000 worth of assets, the trust must pay the maker $10,000 per year for 15 years. The annuity amount must be paid even if the assets in the trust do not create income. If the income generated by the assets is insufficient to satisfy the $10,000 annual payment, the trustee of the GRAT must use principal to satisfy the annuity payments.

The value of the retained annuity interest is determined in much the same manner as the value of the retained interest in a QPRT (discussed earlier in this chapter). The regulations of the Internal Revenue Code contain valuation tables for annuity interests. The valuation of a retained annuity interest is based on the following factors:

- Value of the assets
- Amount of the annuity payment desired
- Frequency of the annuity payments (monthly, quarterly, annually)
- Timing of the payments (e.g., at the end of a calendar quarter or the beginning of the quarter)
- Number of years the payments will be made
- Age of the maker
- Current government-adjusted applicable federal rate (AFR), which is 120 percent of the federal midterm rate for the month in which the GRAT is funded

What types of assets are best suited for GRATs?

Because the annuity amount must be paid each year, a GRAT should be funded with assets that will appreciate in value and produce a cash flow. A GRAT is far less effective if the assets do not produce income and do not increase in value.

What is the primary advantage of a GRAT?

If, over the term of the GRAT, the income and appreciation of the income-producing assets in the trust are greater than the AFR interest rate factor used to value the maker's retained interest, the additional income and appreciation will accumulate for the remainder beneficiaries without additional gift taxes. This can result in significant transfer tax savings. In addition, the maker can use the annuity payments for support until reaching the age at which he or she can begin taking distributions from IRAs or other retirement plans.

What are the primary disadvantages of GRATs?

If the maker dies before the GRAT term ends, at least part of the value of the assets held in the trust is included in the trust maker's gross estate. In this situation, there may be a lost opportunity cost; that is, the maker might have been able to use another tax planning strategy that may have been less effective than the GRAT had the GRAT worked but would have been more effective had the maker not died before the GRAT's term ended.

Generally, GRATs should not be used for generation-skipping planning. As with a QPRT, the value of the gift for generation-skipping transfer tax purposes is not determined until the GRAT term ends. This means that if assets in a GRAT appreciate in value, they may exceed the generation-skipping exemption amount.

Grantor retained unitrust

What is a grantor retained unitrust?

A *grantor retained unitrust (GRUT)* is very similar to a GRAT but has two primary differences. Instead of a fixed annuity payment, the payment is a *unitrust* amount, which is a percentage of the value of the trust's assets as valued each year instead of just once. For example, if a maker funded a 15-year GRUT with $100,000 of investments with a 10 percent unitrust amount, the trust would pay the maker $10,000 in the first year. If, however, the value of the assets increased in the second year to $120,000, the trust would pay $12,000 to the maker. Conversely, if the value of the assets decreased to $90,000, the payment would be $9000.

What are the disadvantages of GRUTs?

As with a GRAT, if the maker of a GRUT dies while the trust is paying him or her, some part of the value of the assets is included in the maker's estate. Also, the assets in a GRUT must be valued each year to determine the unitrust payment, so the amount may vary up or down from year to year. In a GRAT, a valuation is generally made only once, when the trust is first funded.

GRUTs are also not as efficient in leveraging gifts as are GRATs. Because the unitrust interest in a GRUT can vary from year to year, the value of the maker's retained interest tends to be lower, making the gift of the remainder interest higher.

Since the most attractive feature of GRATs and GRUTs is discounting, practitioners generally use GRATs because of their greater discounting potential.

Tangible personal property trust

How does a tangible personal property trust work?

Most tax advisors would say this type of trust does not work at all because of its restrictions. A *tangible personal property trust* (tangibles GRIT) is a grantor retained interest trust that is funded with tangible property that cannot be depreciated. This limits usable property to artwork, antiques, or undeveloped land. Intangible property such as stocks, bonds, businesses, and the like, cannot be used.

In a tangibles GRIT, the maker creates an irrevocable trust for a term of years and reserves the right to use the assets in the trust for that term. At the end of the term, the assets pass to the trust beneficiaries. The assets do not have to be income-producing.

The restriction making tangibles GRITs impractical is the method of valuing the maker's right to use the property for the term of the trust. The valuation rules require that other comparable transactions be used to establish value. For example, if a person were to transfer a valuable painting to a trust for 10 years and retain the right to hang it in his or her home for that period of time, the value of the retained interest would be comparable to the cost a museum would be willing to pay to lease that painting for 10 years. It is difficult, if not impossible, to find a museum that would lease a painting for 10 years. Whether the asset is a painting, an antique, or undeveloped land, the maker faces the same valuation conundrum.

Grantor retained income trust

Wasn't there a popular planning technique called a GRIT?

Yes. It was such an effective estate planning tool that it was banned in large part by Congress and replaced with GRATs and GRUTs.

The old *grantor retained income trust (GRIT)*—or "statutory GRIT," as it was called—worked like this: The maker created an irrevocable trust for a term of years while retaining the income from the trust assets for that term. When the term expired, the assets passed to named beneficiaries. The regulations of the Internal Revenue Code included tables for valuing the retained income interest and the remainder interest. The value of the remainder interest was considered a gift of a future interest to the trust beneficiaries.

People manipulated GRITs by funding them with assets that did not create income but just appreciated in value. Since the gift element of the trust was calculated by assuming that the trust assets would create income, a gift windfall resulted. The maker would not have any income but would pass huge amounts of appreciation to the beneficiaries for a low gift cost. It didn't take long for Congress to close this loophole.

Are GRITs still allowed?

They are, but they have been limited considerably. The beneficiaries cannot be members of the maker's immediate family. For purposes of a GRIT, the maker's family includes the maker's spouse; any ancestors or lineal descendants of the maker or the maker's spouse; and any brothers or sisters of the maker, as well as their spouses. This definition leaves only nieces and nephews and other, more remote, relatives. Most practitioners agree that the use of these so-called *nonfamily GRITs* is restricted to individuals who are not married or who have a great deal of wealth and want to make gifts to people outside their immediate families.

In addition, the Internal Revenue Service, through regulations and rulings, requires that the assets placed in a nonfamily GRIT must indeed be income-producing.

Installment Sales

What is an installment sale?

In an *installment sale,* a buyer gives a seller a promissory note that calls for installment payments of principal and interest over a set period of time. Thus the seller does not have to recognize the full gain on the sale at the time of the sale but can spread the gain over the period during which the payments are being received. Each payment is treated as part return of the seller's original investment, or cost basis, and part gain and interest. If the property sold has been subject to excess depreciation, the recapture of that depreciation must be reported in the year of sale. However, any gain above the recapture amount may be eligible for installment treatment.

What are the advantages of an installment sale?

Since an installment sale spreads income over 2 or more tax years, the gain might be taxable in lower tax brackets. If the sale is at fair market value, the note bears a reasonable term and interest rate, and the payments are in fact made, future appreciation of the asset may be removed from the seller's estate.

Intentional Grantor Trusts

What is an intentional grantor trust?

An *intentional grantor trust (IGT)* is an irrevocable trust with special language that ensures the trust will be a grantor trust. The irrevocable trust is treated as owned by the maker (grantor) for income tax purposes. Thus, the maker must pay income taxes on any ordinary or capital gain income generated by the trust.

Why would I want to use an intentional grantor trust?

An IGT is used to remove property from the grantor's taxable estate while allowing him or her to maintain limited control over the property and use losses and deductions to offset the trust's income. As the grantor pays taxes on income generated by the trust, the grantor is also effectively giving away more of his or her estate without using his or her annual exclusion or applicable exclusion amount.

How does an IGT work?

The maker establishes an intentional grantor trust, but he or she cannot be either a beneficiary or a trustee of the trust. The maker funds the trust with a small gift. Most experts recommend that the gift equal at least 10 percent of the value of the property that is going to be sold later to the trust. The trust maker and the trustee then enter into a purchase-and-sale agreement for assets that the maker expects will appreciate substantially in the future, such as stocks or a closely held business interest. The maker then transfers the assets to the trustee and takes a promissory note from the trustee as payment. Typically, the note is a balloon note, with interest-only payments for several years. The note carries a fairly low interest rate but otherwise includes all the terms usually found in a commercial loan.

Using the income and appreciation generated by the purchased property, the trustee makes the interest payments to the maker as required under the note. When the note matures, the trustee pays the maker in full, often with the property the trustee originally bought from the trust maker. In the meantime, the property has been significantly appreciating. The appreciation, minus the interest payments to the maker, eventually passes to the trust's beneficiaries transfer tax–free. In this way, the maker has frozen the value of his or her estate by transferring to the next generation most of the appreciation and income from his or her assets.

Why is the trust intentionally made a grantor trust?

An IGT presents interesting estate and tax planning possibilities. Here are some examples:

- *Lowering the tax rate:* The highest marginal tax rate for trusts and individuals is 39.6 percent. However, a trust reaches that tax rate at $8450 of income (adjusted for inflation each year), while a married individual filing a joint return is not taxed at that rate until income reaches $283,150, as adjusted for inflation. Therefore, if the maker wants to create an irrevocable trust but avoid the 39.6 percent tax rate on trust income, an IGT may be a good idea.
- *Offsetting losses:* If the maker has net operating losses currently or from previous years, the income generated by the trust can be offset against his or her losses. Similarly, the maker may be able to use large charitable deductions to offset trust income.
- *Leveraging gifts:* Since the maker pays the income tax on trust income and capital gain, trust assets will increase and accumulate without being reduced by taxes and principal distributions can be made to beneficiaries free of income tax.
- *Avoiding tax on capital gains:* Because the maker is treated as the owner of the IGT and is, in substance, dealing with himself or herself, the maker can engage in transactions with the trust on a tax-free basis. For example, the maker may sell an appreciated asset to the trust in exchange for a promissory note. In doing so, the

maker removes the asset from his or her estate, including all future appreciation. The maker's estate will include the payments he or she received before death and the present value of any remaining payments on the note. However, the maker reports no gain on the sale and no income from the interest payments. The IGT does not receive interest deductions.

How does an attorney create an intentional grantor trust?

When creating an intentional grantor trust, an attorney adds language to the trust that allows the maker to retain certain rights over the trust and its assets that are more than merely administrative. For example, if the maker is given the power to substitute trust assets for other assets of equivalent value, the trust will be deemed a grantor trust. This power, however, is not likely to cause the trust assets to be included in the maker's estate for estate tax purposes.

Private Annuities

What is a private annuity, and does it save estate or gift taxes?

There are occasions when it may make economic and tax sense for a parent to sell all or part of his or her business or other income-producing assets to a child or children. A way to structure such a sale is through a private annuity.

With a *private annuity,* a seller, usually a parent (or parents), sells an asset to a child (or children) in exchange for the child's unsecured promise to pay an amount for life to the parent who sold the asset. If the transaction is structured properly, it can be an effective way to transfer income-producing assets from one generation to the next without gift or estate tax exposure.

The primary advantages of a private annuity are that it removes an asset's future appreciation from the seller's estate in an arm's-length transaction (that is, at market value and upon reasonable terms) and, at the same time, enables the seller to receive an income. Some of the annuity payment is considered a return of the seller's original investment and is not taxable. Upon the seller's death, the annuity ends. None of its value or the value of the original assets sold is included in the seller's estate.

Are there any disadvantages in using a private annuity?

There could be. A private annuity is a gamble. If the seller lives longer than his or her life expectancy, the cost of the transaction can be very expensive for the children. Also, the seller's estate may not be substantially reduced if the seller does not spend the money received via the annuity payments.

Private annuities work best when the seller is not expected to live for his or her life expectancy. The Internal Revenue Service requires, however, that the seller have at least a 50 percent chance of living for 18 months after the annuity agreement is entered into. For an unhealthy seller, a doctor's certification that the seller will more likely than not live for 18 months is a necessity.

It is also important that the annuity be structured so that the value of the annuity is the same as the value of the assets purchased. If they are not equal in value, the Internal Revenue Service may claim that a gift has been made.

How is a private annuity different from a note or mortgage?

A promissory note is usually secured by the asset being sold. The payments on a note are generally calculated using a principal amount, a fixed number of payments, and a market interest rate.

Private annuity payments are calculated using the purchase price of the assets, the seller's life expectancy, the number of payments required, and a government-imposed interest rate.

What is the difference between a private annuity and a commercial annuity?

A *commercial annuity* is issued by a life insurance company. A *private annuity* typically involves only family members; as the name suggests, it is a private transaction. Both a commercial annuity and a private annuity use the annuitant's (seller's) life expectancy in calculating the payments to the annuitant. However, at the death of the annuitant, the life insurance company keeps the money that he or she tendered in exchange for a lifetime income. With a private annuity, the family members (usually the children) keep any remaining property at the death of the annuitant.

What types of assets work best for a private annuity?

Assets that produce income, such as bonds, dividend-paying stocks, or real estate, or assets that appreciate in value, such as growth stocks or options, are appropriate to use in a private annuity transaction. Also, interests in small businesses, if the businesses are paying dividends, are candidates for private annuity transactions.

What types of assets cannot be used in a private annuity?

Hedge funds are inappropriate for private annuities because of their high potential tax liabilities. IRAs and qualified retirement plans cannot be sold via a private annuity without losing their tax-exempt status. And encumbered real estate may cause income tax problems.

Is a private annuity a secured obligation?

No. A private annuity cannot be secured by the underlying property.

Who bears the risk of making the annuity payments?

The buyer is responsible for making the annuity payments to the annuitant/seller. In a typical private annuity, the children bear the investment risk in ensuring that there are adequate earnings to make the annuity payments to the seller, their parent or parents. Furthermore, the Internal Revenue Service has ruled that the buyers must have "adequate" assets in addition to the assets transferred through the private annuity. If they do not, the IRS will attack the transaction as not having "economic substance."

What are the income tax ramifications of a private annuity for the seller?

Each annuity payment is divided into three components: recovery of basis, capital gain, and ordinary income.

- *Recovery of basis:* the return of the seller's original principal or capital investment.
- *Capital gain:* the excess of the present value of the annuity less the adjusted basis of the property.
- *Annuity amount:* ordinary income. It is similar to the interest on an installment note, but it is not interest per se.

Once determined, these three elements apply to each annuity payment made. However, once the seller recovers his or her entire basis, the entire capital portion of the payment (recovery of basis and capital gain) is taxed as a gain; the remainder is still taxed as ordinary income.

Can you give me an example of how a private annuity is income-taxed?

Assume that Jenny, who is 65 years of age, sells a commercial building worth $500,000 to her two children in return for a private annuity. The adjusted basis in the building and land is $200,000. The annuity represents an unsecured promise to pay Jenny $59,887 a year for the rest of her life. Assuming an 8 percent IRS interest rate for valuing the annuity and a life expectancy for Jenny of 20 years, the payment is broken down into three parts: (1) The principal component of each payment is $10,256, (2) the capital gain is $15,385, and (3) ordinary income is $34,246.

How is the buyer taxed?

For tax purposes, the buyer, known technically as the *transferee,* is treated like a purchaser of the annuity property, except that amounts paid in excess of the purchase price are not deductible. In effect, the transferee is paying after-tax dollars. This is the "price paid" in order to be able to cancel the obligation on the death of the seller.

During the seller/annuitant's lifetime, the buyer/transferee's basis in the property is the present value of the annuity promise, as of the date of the agreement. This is the basis that the buyer/transferee will use in calculating depreciation and determining gain or loss if the asset is sold or exchanged.

If the buyer actually makes payments in excess of the present-value amount, the basis is increased to reflect these additional payments.

For determining a loss on a sale or exchange, the basis is the total of payments actually made minus any allowable depreciation. The present value of any annuity payment not yet made is disregarded, but any additional annuity payments made after such a loss are simply treated as further losses.

If the sale price exceeds the payments made to date but is less than the present value of the promised annuity, the sale may not result in a gain or loss. Subsequent payments may cause the transferee to recognize a loss if the total of the actual annuity payments exceeds the sales price.

The transferee's basis after the death of the annuitant is the total of all payments he or she has made (minus any depreciation deductions allowable with respect to the annuity property).

What issues does the IRS look at when examining a private annuity?

Here are some of the issues the Internal Revenue Service will bring up when it examines a private annuity transaction:

- Does the seller/annuitant have at lease a 50-50 chance of living 18 months?
- Does the income from the annuity differ significantly from the income produced by the property that was transferred?
- Does the annuity agreement impose liability on the buyer/transferee and specify that the payments are to be made without regard to income generated by the property transferred?
- Is there a promissory note? (An annuity does not have a note.)
- Has the seller/transferor relinquished complete ownership over the property?
- Does the individual or trust that is paying the annuity have assets or income in addition to the property transferred as part of the private annuity transaction?

Can an intentional grantor trust be used with a private annuity?

Yes. An IGT is an excellent vehicle to use in conjunction with a private annuity. Typically, parents who want to sell an income-producing asset first establish an IGT. They then make a gift to the IGT equivalent to 10 percent of the value of the assets to be purchased. The gift will be taxable, but it gives the IGT economic substance, which the Internal Revenue Service requires.

The IGT and the parents would then enter into a private annuity agreement, based on the fair market value of the property. Because an IGT is a grantor trust, any trust income is taxed to the sellers, not to the trust or its beneficiaries. The annuity payments are received tax-free by the sellers because of the grantor trust rules.

Family Limited Partnerships

What is a family limited partnership, and how can be it be used?

Family limited partnerships (FLPs) are partnerships created among family members. They are one of the methods used by parents to minimize estate taxes, by transferring out of their estate assets that will appreciate, while maintaining total and complete control of those assets. A family limited partnership can be used with investment assets.

A traditional purpose of FLPs has been to apportion investment income among children in lower income tax brackets, thereby increasing the family's total spendable income. However, the FLP has recently come into vogue for use in long-range estate planning to remove the fair market value of assets from a parent's or grandparent's estate. Significant discounts to the fair market value may also be achieved with FLPs due to minority and liquidity discounts, which can allow for larger nontaxable gifts.

An FLP may also offer some protection against the claims of ex-spouses and creditors of the limited partners of the FLP.

How does a family limited partnership work?

Mary and Tom Jones own investment real estate and marketable securities with a value of $10 million in the year 2000. If they were to retain the assets until their deaths in 2020 and the value grew at 7 percent, the assets would be worth $40 million, which would be subject to estate tax.

On the other hand, Mary and Tom can create an FLP and transfer the assets to it. Mary and Tom are the general partners of the FLP; thus they maintain full control and management authority over the assets and receive a management fee for their services. In the year 2000, they give 20 percent of the FLP ($2 million) in the form of limited partnership interests to their children.

Are there any discounts available with an FLP?

Continuing with the above example, the discounts that Mary and Tom may be able to achieve are:

- *Lack-of-control discount:* Since a limited partner in an FLP has little control over the partnership, such an interest is worth less than its proportionate share of the total asset value. For example, assets worth $10 million if sold in their entirety to a buyer who could control them will be worth much less to someone buying only a limited partner interest, which grants the buyer little power to control.
- *Lack of marketability discount:* An interest in a family limited partnership that has no public market is rarely salable for its proportionate share of the total value. It would sell for much less, if it sells at all.

Thus, with the discounts, possibly as much as 30 percent or even more of the 20 percent interest in the assets, assets that might otherwise be worth $2 million might be valued at $1.4 million for gift tax purposes. As a result of creating the FLP and using the discounts, Mary and Tom made a gift of $1.4 million that can be offset by their combined applicable exclusion amount at the time of death, while removing from their estate $2 million plus future appreciation on that proportionate interest. It is important that professional valuation specialists be used to value the discounts; otherwise, the IRS may impose taxes and penalties.

In addition to the initial gift, additional gifts can be made over subsequent years to remove even more of the estate tax value from the estate.

Should I use a corporate general partner for my family limited partnership, or can I serve personally as the general partner?

A corporate general partner would be another layer of liability planning and thus is often recommended by planning specialists as the general partner of an FLP.

GIVING ASSETS TO CHARITY

How can charitable giving be considered an estate planning tool?

When you leave an asset to your heirs, they may receive as little as 45 percent of its value while the IRS receives the balance in the form of estate taxes. Depending on the type of assets you own, there are ways of ensuring that your heirs receive their share while the IRS's share is diverted to your favorite charity. You could also receive an income tax deduction as well as avoid paying capital gain tax on appreciated assets.

What nontax benefits do I derive from charitable giving?

It is often said that one should not let the tax tail wag the dog. While there are tax-related benefits for charitable giving, the act of giving, even without such benefits, is, in and of itself, beneficial. People who are inclined to be generous receive the positive emotional benefits that are attributed to charitable giving. Their lives take on additional meaning and significance. In fact, physical and mental health apparently improve as a result of a giving lifestyle!

Outright Gifts to Charity

How can I be sure my donations will be put to good use?

It is important to do your homework. According to the standards developed by the Council of Better Business Bureaus, every charity must apply at least half of all its income to its particular activities. Fund-raising activities should not absorb more than 35 percent of contributions that are received by a charity. However, because of incompetence or outright fraud, many charities flaunt these guidelines.

To protect yourself, before donating to a charity, contact your local Better Business Bureau or the State Charities Registration Office in your area to make the requisite inquiries. In addition, you should obtain the following information: (1) the percentage of funds raised or donated that actually goes to the charitable causes for which the charity was organized and (2) examples of how the charity has benefited the cause over the past years.

You should also consult IRS Publication 78, which lists qualified charities, to ensure that your donation is deductible. If the charity you are considering is not listed, you must make certain that the organization holds an IRS determination letter recognizing that it is, in fact, a charity.

What happens to the deduction if my adjusted gross income can't support it in the year I make the gift?

You have a 5-year period to carry forward any excess deductions.

Can an individual make a gift to a charity on December 31 and count it in the same year for tax purposes?

For income tax purposes, the date on which a gift is *completed* determines whether the gift qualifies as a current-year income tax deduction. To determine this, the *relation-back doctrine* rules are applied. If a gift is to a charity, the taxpayer must establish three things: (1) unconditional delivery of a check by the donor, (2) timely presentation of the check by the donee, and (3) timely payment of the check upon presentation by the donor's bank. If these conditions are met, the check "relates back" to the date that it was delivered to the charitable organization.

Are there any assets that do not qualify as gifts to charities?

Contributions of your time and services do not qualify. Also, contributions of free rent or free use of office space are not allowed.

Can I make a gift of my life insurance policy?

Yes. The value of a life insurance policy for purposes of making a gift is essentially based upon the cash value of the policy and not the death benefits.

What is a charitable stock bailout?

In a *charitable stock bailout,* you transfer a certain number of closely held shares to a qualified charity. By doing so, you are eligible for an income tax deduction as well as a gift tax deduction on the transfer. The income tax deduction is usually permitted for the full fair market value of the stock if it is long-term capital gain property, but it is limited to your cost basis in the stock if held short-term. The entire value of the gift is deductible for gift tax purposes.

Obviously, the charity would prefer to have cash, rather than stock, which has little or no market. An ideal way for the charity to get cash is by selling the stock back to the closely held corporation.

If you employ this technique, you must be absolutely sure, before you make the gift, that there is no binding agreement between you and the charity for the stock to be redeemed at a particular time. If there is such an agreement, the IRS may claim that, in effect, you redeemed the stock (a taxable transaction) and donated the proceeds to charity. If done correctly, the charity will be in receipt of much desired cash, and you will receive a charitable deduction while keeping your pro rata ownership in the company.

Gifts in Trust

Can I use a trust to make gifts to charity to get better results than the standard income tax deduction?

Yes. Special irrevocable trusts called *charitable remainder trusts* and *charitable lead trusts* are commonly used to make gifts to charities.

Charitable remainder trusts

My income needs are presently being marginally satisfied from low-income, highly appreciated property. After my death I would like to give the property or its value to charity. What's the most efficient way to accomplish this?

The most efficient way to give appreciated property to a charity while retaining lifetime income is through a irrevocable *charitable remainder trust (CRT).* You can transfer appreciated property to the CRT and earmark the property or its value for eventual distribution to charity.

Upon transfer, you receive a tax deduction for a portion of the gift. At your option, the property can be sold through an independent trustee without incurring capital gain tax. At this point the proceeds would, typically, be reinvested in various securities to pay you an income stream for life or for a period of years. At your death or the end of the period of years, the trust principal will be distributed to the charity.

What, exactly, is a charitable remainder trust?

A CRT is an irrevocable trust that provides a very attractive way for taxpayers to convert appreciated assets into far more productive assets for meeting their financial goals while potentially avoiding adverse income, estate, or gift tax consequences.

You create a CRT and transfer assets into the trust. The trust, in turn, may keep the assets that you gave it or sell them and invest the proceeds in income-producing investments. The terms of the trust specify that the trustee is to pay you, the donor, a certain amount each year for a stated period or for your lifetime. The percentage of income that must be paid annually to the donor cannot be less than 5 percent of the value of the trust assets. At the end of the term or at your death, the trustee turns over the principal (also known as the *remainder interest*) to the charity you named in the trust agreement.

When you contribute assets to the trust, you take a charitable income tax deduction in the year of the gift. The value of the deduction is the original value of the gift minus the present value of the income going to you.

When the trustee of the CRT sells the assets donated to it, the trust does not pay any tax on the gain since the CRT is charitable in nature, so all the proceeds can be reinvested to produce income.

In setting up a CRT, you may name yourself as the trustee so that you can manage the investment of the funds in the trust. Alternatively, by using a professional trustee such as a bank or the charity itself, you can help ensure that the arrangement complies with the complex legal rules, which must be followed to retain the tax benefits of the CRT. The charity could be your alma mater, a museum, church, or private foundation, or any other qualified charitable institution.

Can you give me an example of how a CRT works?

Rob has publicly traded stock worth $1 million in which he has a cost basis of $200,000. This stock has a dividend yield of 2 percent, which provides Rob with an annual income before taxes of $20,000. He would like to have a higher income from this investment. If he sells the stock to reinvest, he will owe long-term capital gain tax of $160,000 [($1 million – $200,000) × 20%] plus any applicable state taxes. If he then invests the net proceeds of $840,000 (assuming no state tax) and draws out 7 percent per year, he will have an annual income of $58,800 before taxes.

If, on the other hand, Rob contributes the stock to a CRT, he receives an income tax deduction in the year of the gift. Then the CRT can sell the stock without incurring capital gain taxation. Rob can now draw an annual income of 7 percent of $1 million, or $70,000. This is roughly 19 percent more income than he would have if he sold the stock himself.

The tax advantages of a CRT seem obvious, but can the trust income benefit my spouse as well as me?

The income beneficiaries of the trust can be any number or combination of persons—spouse, children, grandchildren, friend—living at the time the trust is established. However, distributing trust income over more than two lives in different generations effectively reduces or eliminates the tax deductibility of the gift. Even so, appreciated property transferred to the trust can still be sold without capital gain tax.

What are the best assets to use in a CRT?

The best assets to contribute to a CRT are highly appreciated assets in which the donor has a low cost basis, such as stock or real estate. If the owner of the asset sells it without the use of a CRT, the gain on the sale would be subject to capital gain taxes, whereas the trustee of the CRT can sell the asset without incurring capital gain taxes.

What are the benefits of a charitable remainder trust?

The main advantage of a CRT is the opportunity to avoid capital gain tax upon the sale of appreciated assets. However, a CRT can also provide a current income tax deduction that is calculated on the basis of the value of the assets contributed, the ages of the donors, and the annual income to be received by the donors during their lifetimes.

The trust does not pay income or capital gain tax on its appreciation or earnings. As a result, the portfolio can be managed and bought and sold by the donor/trustees during their lifetimes without income tax or capital gain tax consequences, thereby providing greater flexibility to investment management decision making and diversification. Distributions to the donors, however, are normally subject to income tax.

There may be some creditor protection benefits.

Last, but certainly not least, assets contributed to the trust escape federal estate tax.

Don't my heirs lose their inheritance if I use a charitable remainder trust?

On the surface, a charitable remainder trust appears to benefit you and the charity at the expense of your heirs. However, with a well-constructed estate plan this need not be the case. You can establish a *wealth replacement trust* and give it a portion of the income stream you and your spouse will receive from the CRT. The trust will use those funds to purchase a single insurance policy on the lives of both you and your spouse. The trust, not you, owns the insurance policy, so the proceeds on the policy are not included in your estate and pass tax-free to your children after you and your spouse have passed away.

By structuring your charitable and replacement gifts this way, you maximize the gift to your charity, the income for you and your spouse, and the inheritance for your children. (See Chapter 7 for a more detailed discussion of wealth replacement trusts.)

Is it possible to set up a CRT at my death?

You can include provisions in your will or living trust that create a CRT after your death. This type of trust is called a *testamentary CRT.* It can pay income to your beneficiaries for a stated time period or for their lifetimes. Afterward, the remaining assets will pass to a specified charitable organization. For example, let's say you want to provide for your father after your death. Through a testamentary CRT, you can arrange that he receive an annuity from the trust until he dies and that the remainder at his death pass to the charity you specify in the trust.

This kind of planning provides for both your father and charity, and since you are making a partial charitable donation at the time of your death, your estate receives a deduction for a portion of the trust value. (Government tables determine the size of the estate tax deduction on the basis of the value of the asset in the trust, the term of the trust, and the amount to be paid to the beneficiary).

Are there different types of CRTs?

There are several different types of CRTs:

1. Charitable remainder annuity trust (CRAT)

2. Charitable remainder unitrust (CRUT)
3. Charitable remainder unitrust with net income makeup provisions (NIMCRUT)

Charitable remainder annuity trusts

What is a charitable remainder annuity trust?

A *charitable remainder annuity trust (CRAT)* is designed to pay the beneficiary each year a fixed dollar amount or a fixed percentage of the initial value of the property transferred to the trust. The annuity amount paid must be at least 5 percent of the original principal amount but not more than 50 percent of that amount. Because the amount paid to the beneficiary is based upon the initial value of the asset, the amount remains fixed regardless of whether the value of the asset increases or decreases or whether the asset generates income. For example, if a 7 percent, 15-year CRAT is funded with a $100,000 asset, the trust must pay the maker $7000 per year for 15 years. The annuity amount must be paid even if the asset in the trust does not create income. If there is insufficient income to satisfy the $7000 annual payment, the trustee of the CRAT must use principal to satisfy the annuity payments.

Charitable remainder unitrusts

What is a charitable remainder unitrust?

A *charitable remainder unitrust (CRUT)* pays a fixed percentage, the "unitrust amount," of the CRT assets each year based on an annual determination of the value of the trust assets. This percentage must be at least 5 percent but not more than 50 percent of the original principal of the trust and must be chosen by the donor before creating the trust. Although the percentage remains fixed, the actual amount that is paid each year will vary depending on the annual value of the asset. For example, suppose a 7 percent CRUT is funded with a $100,000 asset. In the first year, the trust must pay the maker $7000. If the value of the asset in the second year is $90,000, the unitrust amount will be $6300. If the value of the asset in the third year is $120,000, the unitrust amount will be $8400. If the trust does not earn enough income in a year to pay the unitrust amount, the trustee must make up the difference with capital gains or principal.

Why would I ever use a CRAT rather than a CRUT?

If your projected need for income payments from the trust involves a fairly short number of years or a known fixed amount, the CRAT may be a better choice than the CRUT. The CRAT will provide a much larger charitable income tax deduction, and it is slightly less difficult to administer since you do not have to recompute the required payments each year. A CRAT is sometimes used by an adult child to provide a known annual payment amount for his or her elderly parents (the income beneficiaries).

Charitable remainder unitrusts with net income makeup provisions

What is a charitable remainder unitrust with net income makeup provisions?

A *charitable remainder unitrust with net income makeup provisions (NIMCRUT)* is a special variation of a CRUT. In any year that the trust does not earn sufficient income to make the required unitrust payment, it can accrue an "IOU" liability for the shortage. In any year that it earns more than the required payment, it can use the overage to make up for the shortages in previous years. Suppose we have a 7 percent CRUT funded with a $100,000 asset. In the first year, the trust earns $7000 and pays the maker $7000. Assuming the value of the asset in the second year remains $100,000, the unitrust amount to be paid is again $7000. However, the trust earns only $6000, so the makeup account accrues a liability of $1000 to be paid at a later date. In the third year, the value remains at $100,000 and the trust earns $9000. The unitrust amount for the third year will be $8000—the $7000 required unitrust amount plus the $1000 due from year 2.

We want to create a charitable plan now that will provide us with an income flow that starts in a few years, when we retire. Can we do so?

You can accomplish your goal by using a NIMCRUT which requires that only the income from the underlying investments be paid out up to the agreed percentage. The unpaid amount is accounted for within the trust records as an IOU account; it is paid out in later years from trust income that exceeds the stated annual unitrust amount. The trustee and your financial professional can work together to invest the trust assets in a way that regulates the income from zero to the full amount of the unitrust amount.

By establishing a NIMCRUT you can effectively defer income and its taxation until you are ready to receive it. This creates additional principal accumulation, which, in turn, generates even more income. As a result, this method often provides a substantial flow of income to supplement other retirement income sources.

Charitable lead trusts

I don't think life insurance and a wealth replacement trust will work for me, but I'd still like to give to charity without depriving my children of their inheritance. Is there another alternative?

You might consider a *charitable lead trust (CLT),* which is the reverse of a charitable remainder trust. With this arrangement, you give assets to the CLT, which then pays an amount to a qualified charity that you designate in the trust agreement for a specified period of time. In a *charitable lead annuity trust (CLAT),* the trust pays the charity a fixed amount each year. In a *charitable lead unitrust (CLUT),* the trust pays the charity a fixed percentage. When the period of years expires, the remaining trust assets return to you or are distributed to your heirs or to your will or living trust, which provides for your heirs.

If the beneficiary of the remainder interest is anyone other than the donor, gift taxes may be levied on the transfer. The gift tax implications of a CLT are calculated by subtracting the present value of the amounts passing to the charity from the property's fair market value. Because your heirs have no rights to the assets until the CLT terminates, you receive a substantial discount on the value of the contributed assets for federal gift tax purposes. So with a CLT, you can make regular donations to charity and ensure that the trust assets will eventually go to your children or grandchildren.

What about the estate tax when I die?

If you did not retain any interest or power over the CLT during your life, the trust will not be included in your gross estate on death.

Gift Annuities

What is a charitable gift annuity?

A *charitable gift annuity (CGA)* is a contract between a donor and a charity. The donor makes an irrevocable gift of property to a qualified charity in exchange for a the charity's promise to pay the annuitant (usually the donor) a fixed amount for his or her lifetime or for a fixed period of years.

The primary benefits of a typical CGA contract include a lifetime of income, a current income tax deduction, and avoidance of capital gain taxes.

The payments from the CGA to the annuitant can be either immediate or deferred.

What are the tax benefits of a CGA?

The tax benefits of a CGA include an income tax deduction for the value of the gift(s). The amount of the deduction will vary depending on the type of annuity (fixed period versus life) and the age of the annuitant.

A portion of each payment (typically 25 to 60 percent) received by the donor, or other beneficiary, will be considered tax-free return of principal until the assumed cost of the annuity has been fully recovered (usually at life expectancy). After this point, the remaining payments will be taxable as ordinary income.

When evaluating a CGA, you should also compare the relative benefits of a charitable remainder trust.

What type of property can be contributed to a CGA?

Contributions to a CGA can be made in cash or marketable securities.

Hard-to-value property, such as real estate or stock in a closely held or family corporation, may not be appropriate from the charity's perspective, as the charity must pay a fixed amount to the annuitant on the basis of the asset's value at the time of the gift even if the property is later sold for less. In fact, some states, such as New York, prohibit a charity from issuing a gift annuity in exchange for hard-to-value property.

A charity will generally avoid taking gifts of mortgaged property in exchange for a CGA. Such a gift could create taxable income for the donor (in the amount of the mortgage taken over by the charity) and potential tax problems for the charity.

Private Foundations

What are the benefits of establishing a private foundation?

People give money and property to charity for a number of reasons. Among the most common is the desire to help society by funding worthy causes while enjoying the income and estate tax benefits derived from charitable giving. Despite this benefit, one of the concerns a donor may have is the loss of control over money and property given to charity. To meet this concern, a donor can create a *private foundation* that will distribute donations and income to charitable causes favored by the donor.

A donor creates and funds a private foundation that is designed to achieve one or more specific charitable purposes. The donor selects a board of directors or trustees to manage the foundation. The directors or trustees can be paid reasonable compensation for their services. This provision often adds to the attractiveness of private foundations because donors can select family members to serve in this capacity.

What is the tax treatment of gifts made to a private foundation?

Gifts to a private foundation are generally deductible as follows:

- Cash contributions are deductible up to 30 percent of a donor's contribution base.
- Gifts of appreciated property are deductible up to 20 percent of a donor's contribution base.
- With a few exceptions, appreciated property contributed by a donor is deductible only up to cost basis. One major exception is gifts of publicly traded stocks, which are deductible at fair market value.
- Lifetime gifts of cash or appreciated property that exceed the applicable 20 or 30 percent limitation can be carried forward for up to 5 years.

Isn't my income tax deduction for a gift to a private foundation lower than that for a gift to a public charity?

Yes. If you make a cash contribution, the deduction for a private-foundation gift is limited to 30 percent of your contribution base but for a public-charity gift it is expanded to 50 percent of your contribution base. If you give long-term capital gain property, the deduction is limited to 20 percent for a private-foundation gift and 30 percent for a public-charity gift.

Aren't foundations only for the superwealthy?

Foundations are for the charitably inclined, regardless of income level or estate size. Whether or not a foundation fits your planning desires is something that only you and your advisors can determine. If you are considering this approach to charitable giving, you should compare the relative benefits of a community foundation, donor-advised fund, and private foundation.

What administrative requirements are necessary to properly run a private foundation?

Private foundations must publish a detailed public annual report covering investments, grants, trustee fees, and staff salaries. Additional administrative requirements include monthly accounting, annual audits, and various state and federal reports. Private foundations normally retain legal counsel to monitor regulatory changes and any activity that would adversely affect the charitable status of the foundation.

A 2 percent excise tax on investment income is a cost foundations must bear. In addition, private foundations must distribute at least 5 percent of the fair market value of their assets each year.

Donor-Advised Funds

I'm swamped by the administrative requirements of my private foundation. Is there an alternative to private foundations?

An attractive alternative to a private foundation is a *donor-advised fund (DAF).* A DAF is essentially a private foundation administered by a community foundation or a public charity. For a relatively small fee the DAF can receive charitable donations, handle all administrative requirements, and dispense fund assets to various charitable organizations for the donor. Because the DAF falls under the umbrella of a public charity, your gifts will generally qualify for a tax deduction up to 50 percent of your adjusted gross income, and gifts of appreciated property are generally tax-deductible at the full fair market value for state and federal tax purposes.

Can I control the distribution and timing of my charitable donations and still receive the maximum deduction?

You can achieve both goals through a donor-advised fund. Though small in number, there are DAFs offered through public foundations that distribute proceeds to a virtually unlimited number of qualified charities, as well as assist donors in establishing charitable projects that are not specifically addressed by any known charity.

By making gifts (cash and noncash) to a DAF, you can advise the fund trustee of your wishes regarding the sale (if applicable), distribution, and timing of the gift proceeds. Though the trustee retains ultimate fiduciary responsibility for the proceeds in the trust, a DAF can sometimes be managed by the donor's financial consultant and include such investments as stocks, bonds, or mutual funds.

Donor-advised funds provide a complete accounting of gift distributions, anonymity, and potential tax-deductible treatment of gifts up to 50 percent of the donor's adjusted gross income. Additional benefits for the donor include ease of administration, complete tax reporting, and a creative alternative to private foundations for charitable gift planning.

Real Estate Investment Trusts

Is it possible to give encumbered property to a charitable remainder trust?

Internal Revenue Service rules prevent charitable trusts from holding a donor's mortgaged assets. However, by means of a *real estate investment trust (REIT),* such property can be used to help charities. In this arrangement, a donor transfers encumbered property to a limited partnership, an operating partnership of the REIT. In exchange, the donor receives operating partnership (OP) units equivalent to the equity in the property. The REIT pays off all debt and receives OP units equivalent to the debt payoff. The donor can now give the OP units debt-free to a charitable trust, which can exchange them for stock in the REIT and receive dividends. With plans for REITs to become publicly traded in the near future, the charitable trust may elect to diversify its assets and hold other securities besides the REIT.

PART THREE

Risk Management and the Art of Insurance

Like it or not, insurance is an important element of financial planning because it is a risk management tool. Unfortunately, insurance of any kind is not necessarily the most popular topic in financial planning. In spite of the less-than-enthusiastic response the topic of insurance elicits, we have found that a basic understanding of insurance, at the least, leads to appreciation of what it can do and, at best, motivates its use in planning. Good financial planning dictates that a client's risk and risk tolerance be defined and then addressed in the most economical and appropriate manner. The purpose of Part Three is to give you an understanding of insurance principles and how they can be applied in a financial plan.

Sometimes, a little bit of history can put a subject into perspective. Insurance as we know it is a relatively recent innovation; it was a product of the early days of capitalism. Insurance was initially developed by groups of merchants who understood that life is full of risks. These merchants knew that catastrophe was waiting to happen, but they did not know how or when or to whom it would happen. Rather than each merchant's taking on the full risk, groups of merchants pooled funds to insure against the risks. Mostly, these risks involved the voyage of a sailing ship filled with goods or an overland trading expedition. The pool of money was used to help those who suffered damage or loss. By having everyone pay some premium, risk was reduced for all. The lucky ones who avoided catastrophe paid premiums for peace of mind, but the cost of the premiums was far less than the cost of a catastrophe. The unlucky ones who suffered were compensated for their losses, thus reducing the impact of the disaster.

From this modest beginning, insurance has grown into a very sophisticated business involving thousands of companies and trillions of dollars. Yet the concept of insurance has not changed. It is still a method of managing risk. But now insurance is much more sophisticated and efficient. The insurance industry offers numerous policies and services that were unheard of just 30 years ago.

Modern insurance is founded on a concept known as the *law of large numbers.* On the basis of many years of carefully compiled statistics for large numbers of people, insurance companies can predict with uncanny accuracy the percentage of people in virtually every given area who will die, who will become disabled, who will need health care, and who will face other types of disasters.

From these statistics, insurance companies develop policies to insure against risk. They determine how much money must be raised from how many people to insure against a particular event. For example, life insurance companies know that in any given year, a certain number of people in every age group will die. They determine what amount of money is necessary to put together a product that will pay all death claims, pay the expenses of the product, and give a reasonable rate of return to the company. Every life insurance product, health care product, and casualty product is designed in this manner, or at least very close to it.

Because of the competitive nature of insurance, there are many companies offering a variety of insurance policies. They are represented by agents who are charged with finding prospects for the purchase of their policies. Just as with any other commodity, the market determines the success or failure of each product and, ultimately, of the companies themselves.

Our contributing authors offered materials that were concentrated in the areas of life insurance, disability insurance, long-term-care insurance, and health insurance. Their questions and answers clearly demonstrate that their clients are concerned with understanding the various kinds of insurance policies and their applicability to specific needs.

Chapter 6 deals with the basic kinds of life insurance, term and permanent. Our contributing authors take us through a description of these two categories of life insurance and their uses. Much of the chapter relates to permanent insurance and its place in financial and estate planning. This information plays a vital role in the determination of the need for insurance, which is the topic of the second half of the chapter. Our contributing authors and their clients are vitally concerned that the decision of whether to purchase life insurance, and what kind to purchase, be an informed one.

Chapter 7 provides a complete analysis of the use of life insurance in financial planning. It offers ideas on how much insurance is needed in prudent planning and what insurance needs must be covered in a comprehensive financial plan. Suggestions are given on how insurance should be purchased and owned. The contributing authors include insights into some of the more sophisticated planning techniques, such as irrevocable life insurance planning and paying premiums using the split-dollar method. The chapter is a comprehensive survey of how life insurance is used as an effective method for creating and protecting an estate.

Finally, Chapter 8 addresses some of the most vital insurance topics that face our country today: disability, long-term care, and health. As our population ages, few topics are as timely and important as how to reduce the risks associated with the rising costs of health care. The questions and answers in Chapter 8 stress that a good financial plan must consider the costs of aging. They offer an understanding of the basic policies that are available and the ways that are used to determine if and when they are need.

Insurance is part art, part science. It depends on a myriad of factors that determine the need for insurance and its role in managing risk. A financial plan must address the risks and financial impact of failing health and the death of a family member. Part Three will help you define and develop this part of your planning.

chapter 6

Life Insurance

TYPES OF LIFE INSURANCE

There are so many different policies available today. What are the basic types of life insurance?

There are two basic types of life insurance: temporary and permanent. Each type of coverage has many variations.

Temporary coverage is better known as *term insurance.* Term insurance is designed to provide a specified coverage for a stated period of time (the term). The premium or cost for term insurance usually increases with the insured's age, as the chances of a person's dying get greater every year. Term insurance pays a death benefit but builds no equity (or cash value).

Permanent coverage is insurance that can be continued (assuming premium payments are made) for the insured's entire lifetime, regardless of age. Permanent insurance pays a death benefit and builds equity.

Table 6-1 presents an overview of the various types of insurance discussed in this chapter.

How do I find out which type of insurance is best for me?

No one type of policy is always best. The best policy is the one that fits your personal situation and risk tolerance. It is important to analyze the insurance policies of several qualified insurance companies. Whether you choose whole life, universal life, variable life, or term life is irrele-

TABLE 6-1 Types of Life Insurance

Type of policy	Key features
	Temporary insurance
Term	Simple and economical until later years. Often best for short-term needs. No cash value or tax advantages. Increasing premium but may be level for periods of up to 20 or 30 years, depending on age and health. May have a feature that allows conversion to permanent insurance without evidence of insurability.
	Permanent insurance
Whole life (also called *straight* or *ordinary life*)	Guaranteed death benefit at a guaranteed premium for the lifetime of the insured. Guaranteed cash value. Retirement income with risk. Tax deferral combined with death benefits.
Universal life	Flexible premiums. Flexible death benefits. Interest-sensitive policy, generally with some guaranteed rate of interest and guaranteed mortality charge. Insured shares the risk up to guaranteed amounts.
Indexed life or equity-indexed life (a form of universal life)	Flexible premiums. Cash value (and, in some cases, death benefit) fluctuates with the performance of an index of stocks. Can provide a hedge against inflation. Typically has a minimum rate guarantee below the guarantee rate on the insurance company's regular universal life policies. Medium level of risk.
Variable life	Flexible premiums. Death benefit and cash value fluctuate with performance of investment portfolio (stocks, bonds, etc.). Protects against inflation. Policyholder can direct funds within separate investment subaccounts. Higher level of risk and costs.

vant. Whichever policy makes the most sense in your particular situation will become evident. In some situations, you may consider using a variety of policies from various companies to give you the best diversified portfolio with the most flexibility.

Term Insurance

What types of term insurance are there?

There are three types of term insurance: annual renewable term, level term, and decreasing term. Table 6-2 describes each of these types.

TABLE 6-2 Types of Term Insurance

Type	Premium	Death benefit
Annual renewable	Typically increases every year	Stays level
Level	Stays level for 5, 10, 15, 20, or 30 years, at the end of which the premium increases (usually significantly) unless the insured has another physical exam proving that he or she is still in good health	Stays level
Decreasing	Stays level	Decreases over time

Annual renewable term is usually the least expensive term insurance in the early years but becomes more expensive as time passes. If a level death benefit is needed for a number of years and then the need for the insurance will expire, it is often less expensive to purchase level term. Decreasing term is most commonly purchased to pay off mortgages if the borrower should die while the mortgage is outstanding. Death benefits of term life insurance pass income tax–free to beneficiaries.

What are the disadvantages of term life insurance?

Most people are aware of term insurance because it offers substantial benefits at low cost, but this is usually the case only for a short period of time—generally while the insured is young and healthy. As its name suggests, term insurance is beneficial only for short-term uses. Thus, term insurance is generally not prudent for someone who wants to maintain insurance coverage for a long period of time or for the rest of his or her life, as is the case in estate planning. Well over 70 percent of all term life insurance policies terminate before a claim is paid—that is, insureds outlive the terms of their policies.

Permanent Insurance

Are there different types of permanent policies?

There are three basic types of permanent life insurance policies: whole life, universal life, and variable life.

How does permanent insurance differ from term insurance?

The premiums for term life insurance are priced on the basis of the risk of the insured's dying during the term. In annual renewable term, the premium goes up each year because the risk of dying goes up as the insured ages. Term life insurance does not have any built-in extra premium in the beginning years to offset the cost of higher premiums as the insured ages.

Permanent insurance premiums in the early years of the policy are higher than those for the equivalent amount of term insurance, but the premiums are generally designed not to increase in later years as the insured grows older. Because the actual insurance costs in the early years of a permanent insurance policy are low, the higher premiums result in an excess. The excess premiums are invested in an internal side fund to create the cash value in the policy to help cover the greater risk, and cost, of the insured's dying as he or she ages. For the most part, the excess premium that is invested and the resultant cash value (equity) differentiate permanent insurance from term insurance.

Does permanent life insurance have any tax advantages?

Yes. Permanent life insurance has some significant tax advantages:

- *Income tax–free death benefit:* The beneficiary of a life insurance policy generally receives the death proceeds free from all federal and state income tax.
- *Tax-deferred accumulation of cash:* As the cash value of the insurance increases, whether through dividends, interest, or capital gain, no income tax is assessed. If a policy is later cashed in, there may be income tax but only to the extent that the cash value is in excess of the actual premiums paid. However, if the policy remains intact until the death of the insured, all growth inside the policy is free from income tax as it is paid out in the form of a death benefit.
- *Access to cash funds on a tax-advantaged basis by borrowing or withdrawing the cash value:* It is possible to withdraw or borrow the cash value of a policy without paying any income tax on the growth. In this sense, a permanent policy is much like a tax-deferred savings account.

Whole life insurance

What are the basics of a whole life policy?

A traditional *whole life insurance policy* is permanent life insurance that provides a guaranteed premium, guaranteed death benefit, and guaranteed cash value upon timely payment of the required premiums.

How does a whole life policy build cash value?

Whole life, sometimes called *ordinary life* or *straight life,* is a traditional form of insurance policy designed to help consumers handle the high cost of insurance in later years when premiums would become prohibitively expensive because of the increasing risk of death. By averaging the insurance costs and amortizing them over the projected lifetime of the policy, whole life premiums are usually level and the death benefits are guaranteed for the life of the insured. The fixed annual premiums are based on the insured's age and health at the time the policy is issued.

As the whole life insurance premiums are paid, cash value builds up in the early years because the premiums are greater than the actual insurance costs. This excess is invested as part of the general portfolio of the insurance company. The company's portfolio is usually invested in fixed-income instruments such as bonds, mortgages, and government securities.

Dividends are paid on the policy's cash value to the extent that mortality costs (death benefits paid), expenses, and investment performance are more favorable than the assumptions used to establish the guaranteed cash values and premiums. These dividends build up with interest and can provide some flexibility if applied toward premium payments. The excess may build up to a level that allows the owner to limit the premium payment period of the policy, but this result is not guaranteed.

Whole life polices can develop significant cash values that can be accessed by the owner of the policy through surrenders or policy loans. The cash value accumulates on a tax-deferred basis at a rate based upon numerous factors, including the investment experience of the insurance company.

How is interest earned in a life insurance policy?

Interest is generally paid internally in a life insurance policy through dividends or an interest *crediting,* or *earning, rate.* In determining the interest rate, the insurance company must consider the amount it will be able to earn on its investment portfolio minus various expenses.

Most insurance companies offer a guaranteed interest crediting rate for the life of the contract. This rate currently ranges between 3 and 4 percent annually.

Unless contractually guaranteed for a stated period of time, the crediting rate is subject to change at any time. Insurance companies are not required to notify their policyholders of such changes.

Universal life insurance

What is universal life insurance?

Universal life insurance differs from whole life insurance in that universal life policies itemize the protection element, the expense element, and the cash-value element. By separating the three elements, the insurance company can build more flexibility into the policy. This flexibility allows the policy owner, within certain guidelines, to modify the death benefit or the premium in response to changing needs and circumstances. For example, a universal life policy can have a level death benefit or an increasing death benefit (i.e., initial face amount plus cash value).

Typically, the greater part of a universal life policy's cash value is invested in fixed-income investments, such as bonds, mortgages, and government securities. These investments are considered to be a part of the general assets of the issuing insurance company.

How can the death benefit vary in a universal life policy?

A universal life policy has two parts to it, its cash value and its insurance amount, which insurance companies call the "at-risk" amount. The death benefit is the sum of these two amounts.

A universal life insurance policy's death benefit comes in two forms. It can remain level or it can increase over time. To understand how these two forms work, let's first look at a *level death benefit.* As premiums are paid, part of each premium goes into the cash value and part of it goes to pay the cost of insurance. As the cash value increases, the amount of insurance protection (the at-risk amount) declines. For example, if you purchased a $100,000 policy and your cash value was $10,000, you have actually purchased $90,000 worth of insurance. If you were to die, the beneficiaries would receive the full $100,000 of insurance, but it would consist of the at-risk amount ($90,000) and the cash-value amount ($10,000).

With an *increasing-death-benefit* policy, the death benefit (the at-risk amount) stays the same even as the cash value increases. For example, if you purchased a $100,000 policy and the cash value reaches $10,000, your death benefit is $110,000, the at-risk amount plus the cash value.

I don't understand how the cash value and the premiums paid on my universal life policy work. Can you help me?

Here is how a universal policy works: When a premium is paid, most companies deduct certain administrative charges from it. The balance, called the *net premium,* is then credited to the cash value. Each month, the insurance company deducts certain amounts from the cash value to cover the mortality costs (death benefits), as well as for any riders to the policy or any supplemental benefits that are part of the policy. Also, each month, interest is credited to the cash value on the basis of the amount of cash value in the policy and the current declared interest rate, which changes periodically as determined by the insurance company.

Most universal life policies have a decreasing surrender charge, which is deducted from the cash value if the policy is surrendered. This feature allows the insurance company to recover certain expenses associated with issuance of the policy if the policyholder surrenders the policy in its early years.

What are some of the advantages and disadvantages of universal life insurance?

The flexibility that is built into universal life insurance allows people to purchase more coverage than would be possible if the same level of premium dollars were paid for whole life. There is a "cost" of this flexibility in terms of risk. In a universal life policy, the mortality charge (cost of the death benefit) and the interest paid can vary from the assumptions made in computing a "target" premium.

This issue of risk is the most misunderstood element in the purchase of insurance. If the original policy assumptions are not realized (i.e., interest rates go down or mortality charges go up because of an increased number of deaths per thousand), the policy may not perform as planned unless more or higher premiums are paid into the policy.

Universal life insurance allows the owner to vary the frequency and amount of the premiums and even to skip planned premiums as long as there is sufficient cash value to cover current charges. In addition, a universal life policy may include an increasing death benefit. Another feature of universal life is the owner's ability to make lump-sum deposits or lump-sum withdrawals from the policy, which makes it similar to a bank account.

What is indexed insurance?

Indexed insurance, more properly called *equity-indexed insurance,* is a form of universal life insurance. In equity-indexed universal life, the policy's investment earnings are tied not to the insurance company's general account portfolio but to the performance of some known and published stock index. The most commonly used index is Standard and Poor's 500 index.

The obvious appeal to the insured is the possibility of higher rates of return than fixed-interest investments normally offer because the policy owner will participate in a percentage of the upside of the index's increase. A strong advantage of an equity-indexed policy over other types of policies is that the cash value is not subject to a great deal of risk, since there is a guarantee that it will not be reduced below the original investment. In addition, there is a modest (2.5 to 3 percent) guaranteed rate of return. Because of the guarantees, equity-indexed universal life has been described by some as being the "perfect compromise": more potential for upside gains, without the same measure of downside risk as is the case with variable life insurance.

All equity-indexed plans are not identical; different companies have different versions. While all the plans have similarities, some important differences exist in option types, option durations, guarantee rates, minimum-interest provisions regarding guarantee rates and option gains, bailout provisions, and other unique features.

It is important that you review and discuss these variations with your insurance advisors before buying an equity-indexed policy, as is the case with any policy. Buying an insurance policy is like buying a car. Just because you've seen one four-door, front-wheel-drive sedan, you shouldn't conclude that you've seen them all. An honest and knowledgeable insurance advisor is an invaluable resource in choosing the right policy for your needs.

Variable life insurance

What is variable life insurance?

Variable life insurance can be structured as whole life (fixed premium) or universal life (flexible premiums). The whole life design is sometimes known as a *modified premium variable life* policy, whereas the universal design is known as a *flexible premium* or *variable universal life* policy.

Variable life is a form of insurance in which the cash values are invested in separate subaccounts, instead of in the insurance company's general account. The subaccounts are made up of a variety of pooled investments that are similar to mutual funds. With variable life, the policy owner chooses among various subaccounts offered by the insurer and thus can make investments in common stocks, bonds, and other assets that may provide higher long-term results than would an insurer's general account.

Separate subaccounts enable the policy owner to participate more directly in gains and losses realized by the markets. Thus, good performance in one of the subaccounts may make it possible to reduce premium payments, increase the death benefit, withdraw previously paid premiums, or do some combination of each.

Generally, insurance companies offer no guarantees for the cash value in a variable life policy; the investment risk falls on the shoulders of the policy owner. However, since assets in a variable insurance contract are segregated from the insurance company's general account, they are protected against any insolvency by the insurance company and are not affected by the investment performance of the company's general account. If the policy's subaccounts do well, the cash value can be much greater over a longer period of time than it would be in a traditional life insurance policy. However, if the subaccounts do poorly, they can actually have lower returns than would be the case in a traditional whole life or universal life policy. A number of variable life policies guarantee death benefits for various periods of time regardless of the underlying investment performance of the cash value.

How are premiums determined in a variable universal life policy?

The actual funding parameters for a variable universal life policy are dependent upon the face amount of insurance issued and the insured's age, sex, and health status. On the basis of this information, a target premium is determined by the insurance company. This is the amount of premium the company requires, assuming a specific stated rate of interest, to keep the policy in force to age 100 (or other specific ages, if the policy is designed to endow earlier) on an endowment (policy cash value equals the death benefit) basis.

For analogy purposes, the target premium is sometimes known as the "floor"—the amount the policy owner needs to contribute on an ongoing basis to meet the stated policy objectives based on certain assumptions of interest, mortality charges, and expenses. Once the floor is established, excess funding levels can be determined, for example, to help establish a source of supplemental retirement income. The excess funding level is sometimes known as the "ceiling." The closer the policy owner is to the ceiling, the greater the policy equity leverage. For premiums contributed in excess of the target/floor, there are no additional mortality charges, but the state premium sales tax (usually in the 2 percent range) and the policy sales load (usually in the 1.5 percent range) are levied. Thus the more premiums contributed, the greater the growth of cash value in the contract.

How does variable universal life differ from traditional universal life?

Variable universal life is similar to traditional universal life in that the policy owner can vary the life insurance protection and the premium payments. The primary difference is in the investment choices inside the policy. With traditional universal life, there is one investment alternative: a periodically adjusted rate determined by the insurance company on the basis of the performance of its general investment account. As a safety net, there is a guaranteed minimum rate of interest (e.g., 4 to 6 percent) as well as guaranteed maximum mortality charges and costs.

With variable universal life, the cash value can be invested in separate subaccounts that provide a number of investment choices. The subaccounts include very conservative money market accounts, high-grade corporate bonds, growth and income funds, large-company stock funds, and international funds. Thus the policy owner can build a portfolio appropriate for his or her particular needs and risk tolerance. Typically variable life policies do not offer guaranteed rates of return, so the cash value is dependent upon the performance of the investments in the subaccounts.

How do variable life policies compare to traditional whole life policies?

Variable life policies are generally more expensive than policies invested in general accounts because they have added administrative costs relating primarily to their separate subaccounts. The additional cost typically ranges from .25 to 1.5 percent. The potentially higher return from investments in the subaccounts can often make up for the higher costs associated with variable life.

Traditional whole life policies operate within a "black box," making it hard to determine what the real costs are. Because variable life policies are subject to federal securities laws, their pricing must be specifically and clearly broken down and identified. Traditional whole life policies do not have this requirement.

In a whole life policy, the insurance company can take as much of the spread between the guaranteed rate and the actual rate earned as its board of directors decides.

Securities laws require that there be separate disclosure of both current and guaranteed costs in each category of a variable life policy. There is no opportunity to use profits from one specific pricing category to offset excess costs incurred in another pricing category.

Moreover, with variable life, the cash values in the separate subaccounts are protected from an insurance company's insolvency. In contrast, the cash values of whole life policies are included in the general account assets of the company, so the policyholders' cash values are subject to the general creditors of an insolvent insurance company.

On the other hand, with a variable life policy, the policy owner, not the insurance company, bears the investment risk and determines the asset allocation that is appropriate for his or her situation.

Can only some life insurance agents sell variable life?

In a variable life policy, the separate subaccounts can be U.S. or foreign equity large-cap, midcap, or small-cap investments, U.S. or foreign fixed-income bond investments, money market accounts, or even a guaranteed account with the insurance company. Because of these underlying investments, variable life insurance is considered a security, much like a stock or bond, and the law requires that an agent who sells variable life must be licensed to sell securities and must be registered with the National Association of Securities Dealers (NASD). The agent must provide a prospectus with the policy illustrations so that there is complete disclosure as to pricing and investment experience. Thus only persons holding both a securities license and a life insurance license can sell variable life policies.

Second-to-die life insurance

What is second-to-die life insurance?

Second-to-die life insurance, sometimes called *survivorship* or *joint-life insurance,* insures two people but pays a death benefit only upon the death of the second one of them to die. Survivorship life insurance can be in the form of term, whole life, universal life, or variable life insurance. This type of life insurance is usually used in estate planning because it pays a death benefit after a husband and wife have died, which is often when the need to pay estate taxes arises.

What is the basic difference between second-to-die life insurance and first-to-die life insurance?

A second-to-die life insurance policy insures two people. The death benefit is payable upon the second death; there is no death benefit payable at the first death.

A *first-to-die life insurance policy* insures multiple lives. Generally the death benefit is payable when the first insured dies.

What is a major reason for purchasing a survivorship policy?

The major reason for purchasing survivorship life insurance is to provide liquidity to pay the estate taxes on the death of the surviving spouse. Since most couples utilize the unlimited marital deduction (see Chapter 4), estate taxes are not usually due until the surviving spouse dies. That is, if one spouse dies and transfers his or her property to the other spouse, there is no federal estate tax. However, upon the surviving spouse's subsequent death, estate taxes may be due if the value of that spouse's estate exceeds the applicable exclusion amount. Thus the need for second-to-die life insurance.

The proceeds from second-to-die life insurance are included in the surviving spouse's estate unless planning is implemented to avoid this result. Many times, second-to-die life insurance is owned by a married couple's adult children or by an irrevocable life insurance trust.

What are the advantages of second-to-die insurance other than having the proceeds available to pay death taxes when the surviving spouse dies?

There two other primary advantages of using second-to-die insurance:

- *Premiums are lower.* Because the insurance company normally has the use of the funds for a longer period before paying the same death benefit as that on a comparable single-life policy, it generally can charge a lower premium.
- *Uninsurable spouses can be covered.* If one spouse is uninsurable or has a high rating because of health, it is possible to insure that spouse through second-to-die life insurance because the life expectancy of two people is longer than that of even the healthy one alone. Depending on the insurable party's age and health, however, the premium may be only slightly lower for the survivorship policy than it would be on the insurable party's life alone.

Is there an age at which my spouse and I would be considered too old to economically buy second-to-die coverage?

By using actuarial tables, insurance companies are able to provide coverage on an economic basis even for persons who are quite old.

It is important to remember that the cost of insurance is dependent upon both age *and* health. For example, a couple in their early fifties may both be in poor health, and the respective rating (added premium due to health) may dictate that they not purchase the insurance coverage. In contrast, a couple in their eighties who are in good health can obtain a cost-effective insurance policy. A number of insurance carriers issue policies on individuals who are in their eighties.

I'm considering the purchase of second-to-die life insurance. What are some of the questions I should ask my insurance professional?

Before purchasing a second-to-die insurance policy, you should ask the following questions:

- *Can the insurance premiums fluctuate depending on investment performance?* If so, ask your advisor for projections of premiums and cash values based on three different rates: currently projected rates, minimum guaranteed rates, and midway between the two. This will give you an idea of the volatility of the policy.
- *Is the insurance company projecting improvement in mortality, causing the cost of the life insurance protection to go down over time?* If this is the case, is that taken into account in projecting premiums? Overly optimistic projections can underestimate the amount and/or number of premiums needed to provide the long-term insurance coverage desired.
- *Does the premium or cash value change when the first insured dies?* The insurance company's risk increases significantly when only one life is insured. Some projections are applicable only when both the insureds are alive; if that is the case, ask your advisor to compute projections assuming only one insured is alive.

Is there any rule of thumb regarding how much coverage an insurance company will approve for second-to-die life insurance to pay estate taxes?

In applying for life insurance coverage, you will have to disclose your net worth on the application. You can reasonably expect that an insurance carrier will offer coverage equivalent to 100 percent of the current estate settlement costs.

If you can show projected future growth of your estate, and depending upon your and your spouse's life expectancies, you can apply for insurance to cover the expected increase in estate settlement costs.

Modified endowment contracts (MECs)

What is a modified endowment contract?

Life insurance has a tremendous income tax advantage because the cash value of a policy can increase free from income tax. Any interest or gain that occurs inside the policy is not taxed until the policy is fully surrendered, and even then it is taxed only if the cash value exceeds the premiums paid. If it does, the policy owner can withdraw or borrow the policy's cash value (subject to certain rules) without having to pay income taxes on the gains inside the policy. In this way, a policy owner can effectively have access to funds that otherwise would be subject to income tax.

Before 1988, some insurance companies designed policies that more closely resembled an investment than life insurance. They were investments wrapped within a thin layer of life insurance that allowed a great deal of tax-free or tax-deferred accumulation without offering very much life insurance protection. These policies were eventually viewed by the Internal Revenue Service and Congress as abusive tax shelters, so *modified endowment contract (MEC)* rules were developed for policies issued after 1988 to curtail this perceived abuse. Simply put, the rules require that a minimum amount of life insurance protection exist relative to the premium investment being made in a policy.

How do the MEC rules apply to an actual policy?

Under the Internal Revenue Code, a life insurance policy issued on or after June 21, 1988, can become a modified endowment contract if it becomes too investment-oriented (i.e., the cash-value–death benefit ratio exceeds minimum testing levels). For a policy to be considered a MEC, the aggregate premiums paid into the policy during its first 7 years (known as the "7-pay testing limits") must never exceed the aggregate guideline level-premium test for the same testing period. The guideline premiums depend on the age of the insured when the policy is issued.

A policy issued before June 21, 1988, can also become a MEC if "material changes" occur to the policy. If this is the case, the policy is subject to the MEC testing rules. An example of a material change is a change in the amount of the death benefit.

What happens when a policy meets the MEC definition?

If a policy is defined as a MEC, the policy owner cannot access its cash value on a withdrawal or borrowing basis without incurring immediate taxation, at ordinary-income tax rates, on the policy gains. If the cash value in a MEC is accessed before the insured is 59½ years old, there is a 10 percent penalty on the amounts distributed as income, unless the distributions are taken for reason of disability or they are annuitized (equal payments over the life expectancy) to the policy owner.

Does it ever make sense to disregard MEC testing?

Yes. You do not need to be concerned about MEC rules if your insurance objective is to provide death proceeds to a named beneficiary at your death and you are not interested in accessing the policy cash value during your lifetime on a tax-favored basis.

You should work with your insurance professional and other advisors when considering the purchase of life insurance that may violate the MEC rules. You and all your advisors should understand the ramifications of such a choice.

FACTORS TO CONSIDER IN PURCHASING LIFE INSURANCE

In deciding which life insurance to purchase, what factors should I consider?

When choosing a life insurance policy, at a minimum you should consider the financial ratings of the company as well as the company's policy offerings.

Company solvency is extremely important because you want to be certain that the company you choose will still exist when it's time for it to pay the benefits. There are reporting services available that analyze and report on issuing companies. To be an informed purchaser, you should review the reports of these services for the company or companies you are considering. You should also find out how the issuing company treats its existing policyholders and determine the integrity of the company's illustrations.

Because life insurance policies differ enormously, policy selection is vital in purchasing life insurance. The key to policy selection is to ascertain the real risk you are insuring: What is the desired objective of the coverage? Is the need for coverage short-term or long-term? Is the risk for which insurance is needed permanent or temporary in nature? Will the policy have the death benefit that is desired when it is needed?

Finally, the cost of the policy selected must be reasonable relative to the risk undertaken for all parties involved with the contract.

How do I get all the information I need to decide which life insurance company and policy are best for me?

As you are probably well aware, there are a great many life insurance companies and an even greater number of policies. Thus, while it may be possible for a consumer to locate all the information needed for making an informed decision, it would be very hard to do so.

There is an appropriate old saying: "If you do not know your jewels, know your jeweler." You should find the best insurance professional you can. He or she will present you with all the information you need and will be able to answer all your questions concerning life insurance. Appendix A, at the end of this book, will help you locate a qualified advisor.

What factors should I consider when shopping for, and buying, term life insurance?

There are five factors to consider in the purchase of term life insurance:

1. *Match the length of the term to the need.* If the purpose of the insurance is to provide coverage for a specific period of time, the policy should have coverage at a guaranteed rate for the necessary term. For example, if you need insurance until your children finish college and if the youngest child is 5, a 20-year guaranteed level-premium policy may be appropriate. A shorter-term policy, such as a 10-year guaranteed level-premium policy, may have a very high premium beginning with the eleventh-year renewal. Since you would still need the insurance another 10 years, the premium may be prohibitive and you may not be sufficiently healthy at that time to buy a different policy.

2. *Understand nonguaranteed reentry and projected renewal rates, as opposed to guaranteed renewal rates.* Some quote services, in an effort to showcase the lowest possible rates, routinely quote *reentry rates* on their illustrations. This practice has been universally condemned as unethical and deceptive because it is so easy to mistake reentry rates as expected renewal rates. Unfortunately, policy owners are later surprised to learn that in order to qualify for reentry, they must have a new medical exam and show evidence of good health—restrictions that are explained only in the fine print. If the insured is unable to qualify for reentry, the rate required to maintain the policy may be higher than expected.

Projected renewal rates are less deceptive because they represent the insurance company's estimated renewal rate and do not require any evidence of good health. However, they are not guaranteed and the company can raise the premiums at any time.

3. *Look for the best value rather than the lowest price.* Before selecting the lowest-price policy, a savvy consumer will consider the company's financial strength and the policy's features, including the length of the guarantee period, convertibility rights, available riders, and other features. Usually, for very little extra money, it is possible to buy a policy with better features and more flexibility from a company with superior financial strength.

4. *If you are a tobacco user, find a company that will still give you reasonable rates.* Whether a person is a two-pack-a-day smoker or just enjoys an occasional cigar, most insurance companies' rates for smokers are more than double those for nontobacco users. However, some companies treat tobacco use much less harshly, and their rates can be significantly lower. The key is finding the right company.

5. *Purchase enough coverage.* Do you know any widows or widowers who have complained about receiving too *much* in life insurance benefits? How much is your life worth to your family? With today's rates, there is really no reason not to have enough coverage. Have your insurance professional match your need with your budget so that you can get as much coverage as is necessary to fulfill your need.

I'm well into my senior years. Can I get life insurance at my age?

Many older people assume that because of their age and various health problems, they are uninsurable or the cost of insurance will be too high. The truth is, many good insurance companies are willing to make attractive offers of insurance on older people, even those with health problems. There are even a few companies that will offer a contract of insurance on someone older than 90.

To find out which companies are right for you and to obtain the best offer, it is a good idea to "shop" four, five, or more companies at the same time. Most professional independent agents will do the shopping for you.

How often should I review my life insurance?

Unless there is a major event in your life—a divorce, additional children, more debt, unexpected financial success, or the like—a review once every 2 years should be adequate. If you own variable life insurance, however, you should meet with your advisor at least once a year to review the allocation of the cash value to the investments in the subaccounts.

I'm considering replacing my existing life insurance. Are there any risks in doing so?

Yes. Before replacing an existing contract, closely compare it with any new contract in terms of the following: price, guarantee periods, convertibility, financial strength of the insurance companies, and available riders, if applicable.

Be aware that a new contract entails the start of a new contestability period for material misstatements (usually lasting for the first 2 years). Also, a new contract does not cover suicide (usually for the first 2 years).

If the existing policy is a permanent (cash-value) policy, a more detailed analysis should be made to reflect the cost of any applicable surrender charges as well as the acquisition costs of the new policy.

In virtually all states, an agent taking an application for a new policy intended to replace a client's existing policy is required to file a replacement form. This form, sent to the company that isssued the original policy, gives that company notice that its policy owner is considering (and has applied for) a replacement policy. Unfortunately, most life insurance companies do very little with this notice, and the insured is rarely presented with both sides of the story. Remember, the agent presenting the replacement has a vested interest in selling you a new policy—his or her commission upon the sale. If the company being replaced does not present the other side of the story, you may be making a decision without enough information. Before you replace an existing policy, you should always clearly determine that such a decision is in your best interest.

Most importantly, do *not* cancel any existing coverage until the new policy has been approved, paid for, and delivered to you.

Can I exchange one insurance policy for another without triggering any income tax on the gain inside my existing policy?

The Internal Revenue Code, in Section 1035, provides for the tax-free exchange of life insurance policies. To qualify under this provision of the law, the new policy and the existing policy must be on the life of the same insured. For example, you cannot exchange an individual policy for a second-to-die policy.

Tax-free exchanges of life insurance are generally used when a policy with a substantial cash value is being replaced by a newer, more appropriate policy. Because of the sensitive nature of insurance replacement and the rules that must be met to effectuate a tax-free exchange, it is imperative that expert advisors be involved in the process.

What are the income tax ramifications of cashing in my old life insurance policy?

Any cash surrender value received that exceeds the cost basis of the policy is ordinary income in the year the policy is surrendered. The cost basis of the policy is the total of the gross premiums you paid, reduced by any amounts you previously received from the policy that were excludable from income. Any additional premiums that you paid for supplemental benefits, such as double indemnity or waiver of premium, are not included in the cost basis of the policy.

Your insurance company or agent should be able to help you determine the taxable amount, if any, that you must take into income if you surrender your policy.

Is there an alternative to cashing in an old life insurance policy I no longer need?

There are several alternatives:

1. Exchange it for a paid-up policy for a lesser face amount.
2. Receive, under the existing life insurance contract, an extended term insurance policy for a period of years depending on the cash value existing in your current policy.
3. Depending on the size of your policy, its structure, your age, and your health, you might be able to sell the policy to a company that purchases such policies at a discount to the death benefit. In many cases, especially if you are older or your health has changed since your policy was issued, these companies will pay you more for the policy than you will receive if you simply cash it in.

What does "paid-up" insurance mean?

When a policy is *paid up,* no further cash premium payments are projected. However, "paid up" does not mean "guaranteed paid up" unless this is specifically stated. Instead, it usually means that the cash value is sufficient, if left in the policy, to pay all insurance charges until the insured dies, on the basis of current (but not guaranteed) assumptions for interest earned, mortality costs, and expense charges. It also means that the cash value will increase annually without further cash premium payments and will ultimately equal the desired death benefit at age 100.

The Cost of Insurance

Does all life insurance cost the same?

Absolutely not. Each life insurance company prices its policies differently, on the basis of the company's:

- Investment portfolio performance
- Experience in any given area of insurance
- Projected mortality (life-expectancy) costs
- Overhead expenses
- Level of retention of policyholders
- Profit margin
- Underwriting-rating assignments

In analyzing various life insurance companies and policies, it is imperative that the analysis be based on comparable components in each of these areas, rather than simply comparing one illustration to another. Most people are quite surprised by the differences that can exist given the competitive market.

Isn't it always best to buy the lowest-price life insurance policy?

Life insurance is often a long-term agreement between the policy owner and the insurance company. Although cost should be a consideration, it should not be the only factor in choosing a policy or a company. Other important considerations are the financial strength of the insurer and the contract provisions inside the policy.

Also, as a prospective purchaser, you should consider whether you are willing to pay the least possible annual cost forever or a higher annual cost for a specified number of years. Lower annual premiums today often result in a greater overall cost over time unless death occurs early. The ability to vary the amount of premiums (within limits) to fit within cash-flow considerations is also an important item to consider.

I have a level term life insurance policy. After the initial period of guaranteed premiums, what will my insurance cost?

Each policy, if renewable, has a contractually guaranteed maximum renewal premium that can be illustrated and is shown in your policy. This amount is the most you will have to pay to renew the coverage.

Most insurance companies also illustrate the current renewal rates, which represent the *expected* future renewal rates. These rates are lower than the maximum renewal rates and are not guaranteed. They can be higher or lower than expected but never higher than the guaranteed maximum renewal premium.

There is also a process referred to as *reentering* or *reentry.* After your initial guarantee period ends, you can reapply for new coverage. If you qualify, you can begin a new period of guaranteed rates (in effect, a new policy), which will generally cost less than your current or maximum renewal rates. However, since your future good health is not guaranteed, the ability to reenter is not guaranteed. And although reentry premiums are often attractive, illustrating such rates without showing the current and maximum renewal rates, and doing so in the absence of a complete explanation (as if to imply that they are the same as renewal premiums), is universally condemned as unethical and deceptive.

If you select a short-term policy with the expectation of using the reentry feature down the road but then you fail to qualify for reentry, you will face extremely high rates thereafter. You will then have only two choices: Pay the increased cost, or lose your coverage.

I've heard that level term life insurance rates have fallen dramatically in the past few years. Why?

Today, life insurance companies obtain more and better information about prospective clients before they accept people at their lowest rates. In the past, exams and blood tests were performed for only the larger policies and older applicants. Now, virtually everyone must submit to a paramedical exam, including blood and urine tests. Life insurance companies can be more selective and therefore lower their risk. This translates into lower premiums.

In addition, advances in medical care have made it possible for people to live longer than ever before. Thus life insurance companies do not have to pay death benefits as soon. The savings have been passed on to the consumer in the form of lower rates. However, term rates may rise in the near future if insurance companies are required to increase their reserves to meet new actuarial standards.

What is the most expensive kind of life insurance?

Normally, credit life is the most expensive. *Credit life* is insurance on mortgages or loans on real estate, cars, credit cards, and other major purchases.

The Underwriting Rating

What does my underwriting rating mean?

Your *underwriting rating* is the level of risk the insurance company is willing to put on your life. The ratings used by most companies are "preferred," "standard," and "substandard." A preferred rating is the best rating available with most life insurance companies. If you are assigned this rating, you are a better-than-average risk and the insurance company's price will be adjusted accordingly—you will receive one of the lowest prices offered.

In addition to using the above three ratings, companies also use letter or number ratings, such as "A" through "N" or 1 through 14 (with A and 1 representing the least risk in these groups). These ratings mean that you are an above-average risk and, therefore, must pay a higher annual premium to obtain comparable coverage. This, of course, is to offset the financial risk to the insurance company.

Obtaining the lowest underwriting rate possible is a critical step in the company selection process. Your life insurance professional will do all he or she can to obtain the best rating possible based on your health.

What are the differences among preferred-plus, preferred, standard, and substandard rates?

Although the qualifications for *preferred* rates vary among companies, generally the insured must be in excellent overall health. There can be no participation in any hazardous activities, and there must be no history of drug or alcohol abuse.

The criteria for *preferred-plus* rates are even more stringent. The insured cannot use tobacco in any form or engage in any hazardous activities and can have no history of drug or alcohol abuse. According to actuarial tables, people who meet these criteria are likely to live the longest. Each company may have a different name for its preferred-plus rates, but these rates represent the lowest available premiums.

When comparing policies, please understand that even if you are in excellent health, there is a good chance you will not qualify for the best rates. In fact, only 5 percent of all applicants get "super-preferred" rates. Typically, about 60 percent qualify for the regular preferred rate. The rest fall into the standard category, or worse. However, the specific criteria for the rates differ widely among the various insurance companies, and it is not uncommon for an individual to be classified as "preferred" by one company and "standard" by another.

Standard rates generally apply to persons who have some minor health impairments. Examples of standard risks include persons who have cholesterol levels of over 260 or who are 50 pounds overweight.

Substandard rates apply to persons who are having more than minor health problems. Companies charge them additional premiums depending on the risk factors involved.

Options for Uninsurable Lives

I've been told that I'm uninsurable. Is it still possible for me to purchase life insurance?

Maybe. Many times the factors that one life insurance company uses to determine uninsurability are not the same factors that another uses. It is very likely that there are insurance companies willing to insure you even though you have been rated uninsurable by other companies. Even professionals are amazed by the vast differences among various carriers' underwriting decisions, especially regarding persons of older ages.

Before making an offer of insurance, an insurance company will review your medical exam and medical history. Typically, the company's assessment will range from a medical rating of "preferred" through a health grading schedule that frequently has as many as sixteen to twenty health classifications ("tables") ranging from "preferred" to "decline." It is not unusual for one company to rate a person's health differently than another does. Each company makes adjustments in the premium rates it charges on the basis of its assessment of your health.

The insurance may be relatively expensive for the coverage, or there may be contingencies in the insurance before binding coverage. If you have a definitive need for life insurance and have been rated uninsurable, continue the effort to obtain insurance until you have exhausted all probable resources.

If I'm rated uninsurable today and cannot obtain insurance on my life, can I, at some later date, become insurable?

Possibly. Many life insurance companies have instituted a waiting period for persons whom they have deemed uninsurable. After *x* number of years, if the person's health has stabilized or improved, life insurance may become an option.

As a general rule, you should seek a determination of insurability from more than one company. Continue to pursue other insurance companies and policies until you feel all possible sources have been exhausted. At that point, you should have your agent request information from each insurance company as to what you can do to increase the likelihood of obtaining life insurance in the future.

What are my options if I cannot get life insurance?

You have a number of alternatives. Two options are using a surrogate insurance plan and insuring the lives of your children.

What is a surrogate insurance plan?

If you are single and uninsurable or married but your spouse's health is no better than yours, there is an alternative called the *surrogate insurance plan.* This plan places insurance on the life of a relative, such as a brother or a sister, for the benefit of *your* children. While this is a new and unique approach, there are a handful of insurance companies that accept the logic that children have an insurable interest in a relative other than their parents.

To illustrate, suppose you and your spouse have an estimated estate tax of $5 million and are uninsurable. Your brother and his wife are willing to assist in your planning. Their average age is 65, and they are both in good health. Assume that to produce $5 million of coverage with a second-to-die policy, it would cost approximately $800,000 (single pay based on current assumptions). After having your brother and his wife approved for insurance coverage, you would transfer $800,000 to an irrevocable life insurance trust. The trustee would purchase the insurance and, upon the second to die of your brother and his wife (your children's aunt and uncle), the death proceeds of $5 million would be available for paying the taxes on your $10 million estate for the benefit of your children.

If your brother and his wife die before you, the $5 million from the policy proceeds will be in your irrevocable life insurance trust collecting interest until it is needed at your death to pay taxes. If you or you and your spouse die first, the estate taxes will have to be paid, but upon the death of your children's aunt and uncle, the $5 million will be available to replace the funds that were used for the estate taxes.

In effect, the surrogate insurance plan does the same job as regular life insurance. For persons who are not eligible for life insurance coverage, it is an excellent alternative.

My spouse and I are uninsurable. How does insuring the lives of our children work as an alternative?

If you do not have a close relative willing to participate in your life insurance planning or if insurance is not available to your relatives, you can place insurance on your children for the benefit of your grandchildren. Although your children's share of your estate will be reduced by federal estate taxes when you and your spouse die, the leverage you can achieve by insuring the lives of your children is substantial. Thus, the return to your grandchildren could be significantly more, and you can take comfort in knowing that the taxes lost upon your death will be more than made up later, for your grandchildren.

Can you give an example of how we can protect our family by insuring our children?

Sure. Assuming the same $5 million estate tax liability, if your children are in their early forties, it might take only $200,000 in a single premium to provide the entire $5 million. If you choose to pay a higher premium, you could purchase a larger policy for your grandchildren and make up for inflation. It might even be possible to create a dynasty trust that could provide benefits to many generations of your heirs.

Either way, despite the initial problem of uninsurability and the fear of losing $5 million to taxes forever, insuring your children will recover the entire tax loss and help ensure financial security for your grandchildren.

Are there any other options if I am uninsurable?

There are a number of other ways to protect your family. Here are some of the better options:

- Join a credit union that has a group member life plan. Most programs will give members a small amount of life insurance without evidence of insurability.
- When applying for loans, take advantage of the lender's credit life insurance. Almost all lending institutions offer such insurance for the amount of the loan without insurability issues.
- Check with your employer regarding its group life plan to see if there is optional group life coverage available. Many plans allow additional coverage within certain limits without medical information.
- Seek out a life insurance professional. He or she may be able to find limited coverage at a cost you can afford.

TABLE 6-3 Comprehensive Ratings of Financial Strength

Rating service	Review focus	Size of companies reviewed
A. M. Best	Surplus adequacy, profitability for past 5 years, liquidity	All U.S.-domiciled companies with 5 years' operation and minimum $2 million capital and surplus
Duff & Phelps	Management evaluation, asset quality, earnings performance	Any, at request of company
Moody's Life Insurance Credit Report	Consistent profitability, management quality, asset quality	Any, at request of company
Standard & Poor's	Liquidity, management strategy, business profile, earnings, investments, capitalization, financial flexibility	Any, at request of company

Can we purchase second-to-die life insurance even though my husband is uninsurable because of health?

Most companies will accept one uninsurable spouse in placing a second-to-die contract. If you are trying to purchase a policy for estate tax purposes, it should be fairly simple to find a company that will insure both you and your spouse. The insurance carrier will look at the health of the insurable person because the odds are that the healthy person will be the second to die.

I'm healthy, but my spouse is in poor health. Should we buy an individual policy on me or a second-to-die policy on both of us?

It would be advisable for both of you to apply for insurance. Once the respective underwriting offer is made, you can determine if it makes better economic sense to insure the healthier spouse alone or both of you on a second-to-die policy.

A key factor is the difference in your ages. If a younger spouse is in good health and the older spouse is in poor health, it can make economic sense to insure the younger spouse alone. However, each case must be looked at individually.

TABLE 6-4 Statistical Ratings of Financial Strength

Rating service	Review focus	Size of companies reviewed
Weiss Research	Capital adequacy, investment safety, profitability for past 5 years, stability of operations	U.S.-domiciled companies with $1 million capital and surplus
Standard & Poor's	Business profile, earnings, investments, capitalization	All companies with $1 million of net premiums and 5 years' operation without an S&P CPA rating

The Insurance Company's Financial Position

How are life insurance companies rated?

There are five major services that rate insurance companies for financial strength: A. M. Best, Standard and Poor's, Moody's Life Insurance Credit Report, Duff & Phelps Credit Rating Company, and Weiss Research.

In establishing a rating, each of these services considers various factors that determine the financial strength of the life insurance company and its ability to pay claims. However, each one analyzes an insurance company's strength in slightly different ways.

The first four services provide *comprehensive ratings* that are based on interviews conducted within the insurance company and on other information not publicly available. The rating services charge the carriers a subscription fee to do the comprehensive ratings. (See Table 6-3.)

Weiss Research and Standard and Poor's provide *statistical ratings* at no subscription charge to the carriers. These services use information publicly available and data from state regulators and then apply proprietary formulas to assess a company's financial strength. (See Table 6-4.)

Do the rating services rate all life insurance companies?

Not necessarily. A life insurance company must subscribe to a particular rating service in order to receive the comprehensive rating, but it does not subscribe to receive the statistical rating. Some life insurance companies subscribe to only one rating service, while others subscribe to several. The size of the insurance company may also determine whether the company is rated.

The number of services through which a life insurance company is rated is not, in and of itself, an indication that the company is superior or inferior to another insurance company. However, you may feel more secure knowing that your life insurance company is highly rated by more than one rating service company.

What ratings do these services issue?

The ratings for insurance companies follow the systems used in rating bonds. See Table 1-3 (page 42) for an overview.

Should I consider a life insurance company that doesn't maintain the highest rating with any one of the rating service companies?

Rating service companies evaluate an insurance company for your benefit. All things being equal, select a life insurance company that maintains the highest rating. However, insurance companies that do not maintain the highest rating should not necessarily be overlooked, as one of those companies may be able to provide you with insurance that otherwise might be cost-prohibitive or even provide you with insurance when other companies have classified you as uninsurable. Of course, you should be sure to select your life insurance coverage only after analyzing the financial strength and rating of each insurance company under consideration and determining which company can provide you with the finest underwriting and the most cost-beneficial coverage.

How do I compare one company to another?

The ratings services do that for you, but you should still look into a company to determine its margin for safety. Specifically, you should get answers to the following questions:

- Is the company's surplus (net worth) adequate for its obligations?
- Is the company's liquidity sufficient to meet its ongoing income needs? Liquidity includes current cash flow (operating income) as well as short-term investments and investment-grade bond holdings.
- Are the company's riskier investments of high quality and of sufficient diversification? Although the majority of a company's general assets are conservatively invested, a portion is invested in higher-risk instruments to bolster investment return. The critical benchmark is

to have a ratio of less than 150 percent of high-risk investments to adjusted surplus.

- Has the company demonstrated consistent annual earnings?
- What is the management's stability, experience, and quality? What is the company's strategic vision for its future?

By looking for answers to these questions and reviewing the company's ratings, you can achieve a satisfactory comfort level for dealing with a specific company.

Why is the surplus of a life insurance company important in the selection process?

The *surplus* is the net worth (assets minus liabilities) of an insurance company. If an insurance company experiences financial difficulties, such as a lower-than-anticipated return on its investment portfolio or higher-than-anticipated mortality claims, the surplus is the financial cushion that allows the company to weather difficult times. Both the amount of surplus and the percentage of surplus to assets should be analyzed in determining the strength of an insurance company.

How do I determine which insurance company is right for me?

There are approximately 1800 life insurance companies in North America. Working with an advisor/agent who is objective, knowledgeable, and experienced will certainly help you through the selection process.

You should try to narrow down your selection to no more than five insurance companies, all of which should be able to meet each of your objectives. Then determine which of these companies can provide you with the best policy at the lowest cost for the desired coverage.

Should I diversify my insurance portfolio by buying from more than one life insurance company?

Diversification of life insurance companies and policies depends on your net worth compared to the amount and purpose of your insurance coverage. For example, if the amount of your life insurance is small relative to your overall financial condition, one strong company may be sufficient to accommodate your objectives. On the other hand, if the amount of coverage is significant relative to your net worth, the risk should be diversified among several companies to reduce your exposure with any one entity.

The Life Insurance Proposal

What is a life insurance illustration?

A *life insurance illustration* is a projection of what may happen if every cost and assumption illustrated by the issuing company is achieved. The two major uses of illustrations are (1) showing the customer the mechanics of the policy being purchased and how the policy values or premium payments change over time (the emphasis is on how and what, rather than how much) and (2) projecting estimates of future performance and comparing the costs or performance of different policies.

Always remember that illustrations are not contractual guarantees of future performance. Do not allow an illustration to create the illusion that the insurance company knows what will happen in the future and has used that knowledge to create the illustration. Illustrations should be used only to help you better understand the workings of the policy and to help the insurance company and the agent communicate aspects of the particular policy design. Further, when similar policies are being compared, full disclosure not only is essential but is required by state insurance regulations and/or by the NASD if the policy is a variable one.

What do all those columns on a proposal actually mean? How can a layperson understand them?

Those columns are required so that consumers will not be defrauded. Any qualified life insurance professional can explain an illustration. If your agent cannot, you should find one who can.

In general, an illustration contains the following information:

- Insured's current age
- Year of the contract
- Schedule and amount of premiums
- Guaranteed cash value
- Nonguaranteed cash value
- Guaranteed and nonguaranteed death benefit
- Guaranteed costs of insurance

The guaranteed amounts will be there as long as you pay the scheduled premium, while the nonguarantees are projections of future performance, which cannot be relied upon.

In the illustration's footnotes, you will typically find a cost index for 10-year and 20-year periods. The cost index can be used as a guide to compare other policies with the illustrated policy. Pay close attention to the columns of values so that you understand what is guaranteed and what is not.

How do I compare illustrations from different companies?

The following points will help you compare the illustrations of various insurance companies with one another:

- A life insurance policy has guaranteed factors and current assumptions that are used when illustrating the policy. Some of these factors and assumptions are mortality rates, interest or crediting rates, expenses, loan rates, persistency, endowment projections, optional benefits, comparable timing assumptions, and the insured's current "insurance age." When comparing illustrations, you need to make sure that you compare each of these items.
- It is important to determine whether the mortality rates illustrated are consistent with the company's current experience. Did the company build in any mortality improvement projections? Do the mortality rates include additional expense charges? Are they based on attained age rates? Are there any decreases in mortality charges at specific target points? Are the decreases retroactive, or are they progressive from the target point forward?
- Is the interest rate credited a gross or a net rate? If the policy is a traditional (whole life or universal life) policy, do the rates illustrated exceed the interest crediting rate the company is currently earning? Are the crediting rates on a portfolio basis (aggregate investment return of the company's general invested assets) or an investment-year basis for a specific, definable investment of a block of assets? For variable contracts, do the crediting rates include the separate subaccount management fees?
- Do the projected expenses reflect the company's actual experience? Are the listed expenses adequate to meet the actual expenses of the company for this policy?
- Does the policy loan rate and loan interest crediting rate (the difference is the net loan spread) reflect a constant assumption? If there is a reduction in the net loan spread, what is it and when does it begin; that is, does the net loan spread drop from 50 to 25 basis points, and at what age does it begin to drop?
- Does the illustration include nonguaranteed persistency bonuses (extra investment crediting to policy accounts if a specific percentage of policies sold in a given time frame remain on the company books for a specified period of time)?

- Are the illustrations projecting a premium assuming endowment at age 100 or at another age? Do they assume endowment at all?
- Are option benefits illustrated (waiver of premium, etc.)?
- Are the values illustrated shown as of the beginning or the end of the policy year?
- Is the insurance age correct? Some companies use an "age-nearest-birthday" basis, while others use an "age-last-birthday" basis.

Consider obtaining a copy of the "Illustration Questionnaire," published and distributed by the American Society of Financial Service Professionals. It includes twenty-five questions to ask an insurance company to help you better understand any illustration.

Illustrations are tools to evaluate, not guarantee, policies. As the "Illustration Questionnaire" states, "It is safe to say that the sales illustrations will never accurately portray the policy's actual performance."

Should I purchase insurance solely on the basis of illustration comparisons?

Absolutely not. Insurance illustrations vary widely from one company to another. They contain too many variables to enable you to decide which life insurance is right for you simply from an illustration comparison. Make sure you fully understand the strength of the insurance company, the various policies the company offers, and the various options and riders within the insurance policy itself. Remember, options can be customized to ensure your objectives.

I have a life insurance illustration that shows that my premiums will "vanish." What does that mean?

A *vanishing-premium illustration* shows that if all underlying illustration assumptions are met, from the date of policy issuance to the death of the insured, then the premiums illustrated, together with the earnings on the policy, will at some future date be sufficient to allow the policy to continue in force with no additional premiums.

However, the term "vanishing premium" can be misleading because it might suggest to the buyer that the policy is guaranteed to be paid up at some predetermined point in time or after a certain amount of premium has been paid. Because there are a variety of assumptions built into the illustration, the failure of any one of them to occur could require premium payments beyond the illustrated vanish point.

chapter 7

Life Insurance in Financial Planning

DETERMINING THE NEED FOR LIFE INSURANCE

How do I know whether I need life insurance?

To determine if you are a candidate for life insurance, ask yourself the following questions:

- Do I have family members who rely on my income? (Consider what would happen to them if you were to die suddenly.)
- If I do die suddenly, how much of my income will my family need to replace and for how long?
- How much debt do I have that needs to be paid off in the event of my premature death?
- How much money should I set aside for my children's college education?
- What are the expected estate tax obligations and expenses at my death and my spouse's death?
- Do I have a business partner who would rather not be in business with my spouse if I died?
- Do I have expected retirement income that may better serve my spouse if I purchase life insurance rather than choosing one of the company's survivorship options?

- Do I want to create an estate for my family or equalize my estate for tax purposes?

If any of these questions are applicable to you or your family, you should seek out a life insurance professional and begin educating yourself about the need for life insurance planning. While not everyone needs life insurance, it is surprising how many people do not have enough information about life insurance to make an informed decision as to how it may be useful for them.

Why should I buy insurance now? Why not wait until I'm older?

So many times when an individual can qualify for a life insurance policy and is in excellent health, he or she does not see the need for purchasing life insurance. So the person waits, assuming that he or she can purchase the coverage when it is absolutely necessary. Evidently such individuals hope that they can delay the purchase until the day before they become disabled, become uninsurable, or die. But this is an unrealistic assumption. Wait-and-see decision making on insurance works only for a few. And even when it does, the individuals who are still in good health and can qualify for insurance at a later age pay more for their insurance.

In most cases, individuals who wait will have to pay higher premiums because they are older. Sometimes they have to pay even more because they are rated "substandard," or they cannot purchase life insurance at all because they are totally uninsurable.

What are some of the basic decisions I need to make when considering the purchase of life insurance?

As part of your planning, you and your advisors need to determine:

- How much life insurance you need
- What kind of life insurance is appropriate
- Who will own and pay for it
- How the premiums will be paid

Amount of Coverage

How much life insurance do I need?

Determining the amount of life insurance that you need is not a difficult process. The first step is to determine what income and assets your dependents would have if you were to die today. Include any personal life insurance, savings, investments, or real estate or personal property that they could sell. This will give you the total resources available at the time of your passing.

Next, determine what resources your dependents will need. You should consider the following factors:

- *Immediate liquidity needs:* These include funds for death-related administration expenses, including federal estate and state inheritance taxes; funeral expenses; and any other liabilities your dependents will need or desire to pay at your death, such as your home mortgage, car loans, or line of credit.
- *Financial objective needs:* These might include a cash reserve emergency fund and any amounts for future goals such as education, a new home, and the like.
- *Income needs:* These are found by calculating your family's annual expenditures and offsetting them with any income that may come into the household, including income from family members' employment, Social Security benefits, or survivor's pension income.

Once you decide on the financial needs of your dependents, you must determine if there is a difference between what your family has now and how much your family is going to need. This difference is the amount of additional insurance that should be purchased on your life.

Can you give me an example of how to compute the insurance needs of a family?

Of course. Let's assume that Gary wishes to find out if he needs life insurance. His financial information is as follows:

1. He earns $75,000 annually.
2. He has determined that his family can maintain their standard of living for the next 20 years on 80 percent of his current income, or $60,000 annually.
3. He assumes that his spouse will invest the insurance death benefit proceeds at approximately 7 percent interest and that inflation will average 4 percent per year.

On the basis of a present-value mathematical model, Gary will require a lump-sum death benefit from life insurance of $1,228,198 to provide his family with an annual indexed income of $60,000 for 30 years. In the first year, Gary's family take $60,000 of income from the $1,228,198. They invest the remaining $1,168,197, which will earn $81,774 at 7 percent interest. They take $62,400 of income in the second year. The remainder is once again invested, and so on, for 30 years.

Why is an inflation factor used to index income in computing the needs of my family?

Inflation is a reality that cannot and should not be ignored. In our example, the $62,400 of income in the second year has the exact same purchasing power as the $60,000 of income in the first year, assuming 4 percent inflation. Each year of income must be indexed in this manner to keep pace with inflation.

How do I determine how much life insurance I need for estate taxes?

To calculate the amount of life insurance you need to offset your inevitable estate tax bill, you need to determine what your total net worth will be when you die. This, of course, is easier said than done. If your and your spouse's estate is properly planned using the unlimited marital deduction, together you can avoid taxes on the first $1,350,000 (in 2000 and 2001; up to $2 million in 2006) and delay payment of taxes on any amount above $1.35 million until the second death. But then, watch out! Every dollar over the applicable exclusion amount is taxed at a minimum rate of 37 percent, rising to 55 percent on estates over $3 million! Worse (or better) yet, your estate, and the size of the problem, is most likely still growing.

If you are wondering whether it makes sense to use life insurance as a method of liquidating and discounting your estate tax liability, consider this: If you are healthy, you can generally do so for just pennies on the dollar.

Is there a rule of thumb for calculating the amount of insurance I need?

Take your salary or income and multiply by 15. For example, if you make $100,000 per year, you can qualify for $1.5 million of life insurance. Use this simple formula and pretend you died last night. Would $1.5 million keep your family where they would have been had you lived?

Policy Selection

What are the advantages of using cash-value life insurance?

A cash-value policy offers a permanent death benefit payable to your family as long as the policy is kept in force by premium payments. The cash-value element gives your family access to liquidity for various personal needs, such as children's education, retirement needs, or cash emergencies.

What if I have a temporary need for life insurance as well as a permanent need?

Many permanent policies allow you to have term insurance "riders." Thus, instead of buying separate term and permanent insurance policies, you can have both types of policies in one package. This saves you an annual policy fee and possibly additional expenses associated with having separate policies. For example, let's say you have a permanent need for $100,000 of coverage and a temporary insurance need for $250,000. You can purchase a $350,000 policy, of which $100,000 can be earned for the rest of your life but the $250,000 portion will run out in 20 years or can be canceled when you want.

Is whole life worth considering?

Certainly. *Whole life insurance* is appropriate if you have a permanent need for life insurance, you need the highest guarantees on the death benefit, and you do not need flexibility in the death benefit or the premiums. In a whole life policy, the cash values are guaranteed, the premiums will never increase, the mortality rates are guaranteed, and the policy earns tax-free dividends. There is tax-deferred growth of the cash accumulations, similar to the case with annuities. Also, you can access your whole life insurance cash values tax-free through withdrawals and loans.

My employer offers "supplemental" group term life insurance at what seems to be attractive rates, with convenient payroll deductions. Is group insurance always better than purchasing additional private insurance?

Not necessarily. Individual term life coverage for persons without significant medical history or other adverse (tobacco use) health factors can often be purchased with guaranteed rates lower than those available under many group insurance plans. In addition to having a guaranteed level cost for 10, 15, or even 20 years, the individual term policy is totally portable and can be continued after your employment terminates. Each situation is unique and needs to be evaluated on the basis of the facts as well as the objectives of the individual. In this regard, a qualified insurance professional or financial planner can be a valuable resource.

LIFE INSURANCE AS AN INVESTMENT

Should I consider life insurance as an investment?

Life insurance, strictly speaking, should be purchased primarily for death protection. Whether the goal is to cover an immediate cash need for an individual, a replacement for a business, or estate protection of assets, the primary reason for purchasing life insurance is to pay the death benefit.

Cash-value life insurance does, however, offer additional substantial benefits to the individual, the business, and the family.

The Internal Revenue Code provides for tax-free accumulation inside an insurance contract that is not a modified endowment contract (MEC). The policy owner can withdraw the accumulated amount tax free up to the total premium paid and borrow the excess cash value of the policy at a very favorable rate. Sometimes, companies have a "net" interest rate (the difference between what you pay in interest and the amount the company credits you) of 0 to 3 percent. In other words, the insurance company may charge you 6 percent to borrow the funds, but it may credit back to your account 5.5 or even 6 percent. The advantage of making loans or withdrawals from a policy is that the owner can access all the cash value including the gain in the cash value without paying any taxes on the gain.

Because of this feature, life insurance compares favorably with other low-risk investments but has the additional advantage of the insurance coverage. Thus cash-value life insurance may be an attractive addition to the portfolio of individuals with high tax rates and a need for insurance.

Are there any pitfalls in borrowing the cash value?

One aspect requires caution: If the amount of the loan exceeds the total premium paid and you do not keep the policy in force, the gain from the policy is taxed at ordinary tax rates in the year the policy lapses or is canceled.

I've heard that one shouldn't mix insurance and investments in the same product. Is this sound advice?

For some people, it is sound advice. If you are investing only for short-term needs, life insurance is not the investment vehicle for you. However, if you need life insurance and you are saving for longer-term needs such as retirement, mixing insurance and investments in the same product may be worth considering.

Until the late 1970s, many people looked at life insurance as a reasonable investment. But then interest rates skyrocketed as inflation soared. Also, in 1979, the Federal Trade Commission announced results of a multiyear study that showed returns on whole life insurance policies held for over 20 years were averaging only 2 to 4.5 percent per year. It also revealed that policies held for shorter periods usually had negative rates of return.

As a result of these factors, consumers were outraged to the point of borrowing large amounts from their policies or even canceling their policies and using the dollars to invest in money markets that were paying over 10 percent. Insurance companies woke up and realized that they had to change and offer a better deal to their policyholders. Ever since, insurance companies have been racing to offer more competitive policies, including investment-oriented policies such as variable life insurance and variable universal life insurance. Over the long term, many of these policies perform better than does the combination of simply buying term insurance and investing in taxable mutual funds.

Is there a way to combine the benefits of tax-free investing with long-term growth?

An overlooked investment alternative that can complement virtually every investment portfolio is variable life insurance. Variable life insurance combines the advantages of investment subaccounts (managed portfolio of equity and debt investments) with term life insurance. The investor pays a premium that covers the cost of the insurance and administration, while any additional money is directed toward a series of investment subaccounts that carry the same investment dynamics as mutual funds. Investment selection can be the responsibility of the contract owner or the financial consultant, but in any event the money over and above the cost of insurance and administration increases without immediate tax liability.

If structured correctly, portfolio earnings can be withdrawn or borrowed through a low-interest or interest-free loan, making the distribution a source of tax-free income. If the cost of insurance and administration is less than the investor's tax bracket, variable life insurance would fit most situations, assuming the health of the investor makes underwriting possible.

Can I create more wealth for my heirs by investing personally or by obtaining a life insurance policy?

Let's assume that you are in the maximum marginal estate tax bracket of 55 percent, which means that, under current tax laws, your taxable estate is greater than $3 million. Any investment that you make, no matter how good the yield, if left in your estate at your passing, will have the first 55 cents of every dollar over $3 million taken away for federal estate taxes. In addition to the estate tax, if your investment is taxable, you will have to pay income tax on your earnings.

Alternatively, you could transfer a sum of money into an irrevocable life insurance trust that acquires a life insurance contract on your life or on your and your spouse's lives. The death benefit would be paid to the beneficiaries of the trust completely tax-free. There would be no income tax, estate tax, capital gain tax, sales tax, or state inheritance tax. (See "Irrevocable Life Insurance Trusts" later in this chapter.)

To match the internal rate of return of the death benefit of most of today's competitive variable universal life insurance contracts, the rate of return for an investment subject to federal estate tax must be substantially higher. If you factor in the income tax rate that you are paying on a taxable investment, you will see that the death benefit at your life expectancy is equivalent to a very substantial taxable yield.

Can life insurance be used as a tax-advantaged way to provide supplemental retirement income?

One of the most advantageous methods of creating supplemental retirement income is through the use of a variable universal life insurance contract. By taking advantage of the tax-deferred growth of the cash value and the tax-free feature of withdrawing or borrowing the cash value, the insured can provide himself or herself with tax-free income. The investment managers now available in quality variable universal life policies are virtually identical in many cases to those available in the mutual fund arena.

If I own a life insurance policy as an investment for retirement, who should own it?

If your intent is to draw upon the policy's cash values, the policy should be owned by you or your living trust. While the death benefit would be part of your taxable estate at your death, maintaining ownership in one of these ways will allow you to access the cash values.

With the stock market going up so dramatically, why would I consider using anything other than a variable life product?

Even though the market has shown tremendous growth, making variable life very attractive, a traditional life insurance product such as whole life or universal life can also make sense, much like bonds and CDs make sense in most investment portfolios. "Fixed-type" life insurance can serve as a "guarantee-type" product to diversify and complement the equity portion of your investment program.

Would variable universal life insurance be appropriate for me?

If you have a need for life insurance and you are already investing in equity investments or are willing to take the risk associated with variable investment subaccounts, you should consider variable universal life. In a sense, you are buying term insurance and investing the difference in a tax-advantaged environment. If you like the premium flexibility of universal life and are also attracted to investing in mutual funds, a variable universal life policy could be for you. However, there is no "best" policy for everyone. The right one for you depends on your specific needs, objectives, and other assets.

LIFE INSURANCE FOR INCOME REPLACEMENT

How can life insurance be used in a two-income family to protect against the loss of one spouse?

A joint first-to-die policy can provide a dual-income family with liquidity when the first of the two insureds dies. The surviving spouse can invest the death proceeds to provide an income stream to replace the lost earnings of the deceased spouse.

In some cases, either spouse's income is sufficient to support the family. However, the simultaneous or premature deaths of the spouses within a short period of each other can create a serious financial problem, particularly if there are minor children or children with special needs. A second-to-die policy can be used to ensure that at the second death resources are available to provide for the family, including educational and special-care needs.

One of the dilemmas in a two-income family is deciding which spouse to insure. Using both a first-to-die policy and a second-to-die policy eliminates the dilemma and make sure that protection is available no matter which spouse dies first.

LIFE INSURANCE IN ESTATE PLANNING

What is the most highly effective estate planning technique or strategy that is most often overlooked by the general public?

Generally, life insurance is the most effective estate planning tool that is overlooked by the general public. A primary reason for this oversight is the stereotypical perception of life insurance as a means of income replacement only. Often, a lack of understanding of both life insurance and estate planning furthers the misconceptions about the significant benefits life insurance can provide in a comprehensive estate planning strategy.

Among the various benefits that life insurance provides are inexpensive dollars to pay costly estate taxes and provide liquid cash to pay expenses and debts of the estate, as well as income replacement and protection benefits for a lifetime.

Ultimately, the benefits received from a life insurance policy, often purchased to fund a well-defined and implemented estate plan, will far exceed the investment. Life insurance benefits both an individual's estate and his or her beneficiaries well into the future. A financial plan without life insurance is not a comprehensive plan but merely a savings, retirement, or investment program.

Life Insurance for Liquidity

Why do I often see life insurance recommended as a solution when it comes to estate tax planning?

Life insurance provides instant liquidity and prevents the executor of your estate or the trustee of your living trust from having to liquidate your investments at a fire sale to pay the settlement costs of your estate.

Is it a good idea to use term insurance in estate planning for the payment of estate taxes and death expenses?

Term insurance can generally be acquired only up to age 65 or 70. If we knew exactly when we were going to die, term insurance might be an appropriate product to provide for the payment of estate taxes and expenses. However, since none of us really knows when we are going to die, we must provide permanent protection rather than temporary coverage in order to have funds available to pay the estate tax liability and other death-related expenses. Therefore, term insurance is generally not appropriate for providing estate liquidity.

Protecting Life Insurance from Estate Taxes

Are the proceeds of a life insurance policy subject to either income tax or estate tax?

Life insurance proceeds are generally not subject to income tax. However, life insurance owned by the insured, or for which the insured has any "incidents of ownership" at death, is included in that person's gross estate.

What are the incidents of ownership that can cause a life insurance policy to be taxed in my estate at death?

The following policy rights, if retained by the insured, have been treated as estate-taxable *incidents of ownership:*

- The ability to change a beneficiary
- The ability to surrender or cancel the policy
- The ability to borrow against the policy
- The ability to assign the policy
- The ability to revoke a policy assignment
- The ability to pledge the policy as collateral for a loan
- The ability to pay premiums with policy loans

Please note that it is the ability to take any of these actions that creates the incident of ownership. The insured does not have to have actually taken any of these actions; having the right to do so is enough.

Any incidents of ownership exercisable by the insured as a trustee could also cause the IRS to include the insurance policy in the insured's estate. This occurs primarily if the insured acts as the trustee of his or her irrevocable life insurance trust.

How are life insurance policies that I own, or have incidents of ownership in, valued for estate tax purposes? On the cash value while I'm living? Or on the cash value at the date of my death?

This question illustrates exactly why life insurance presents an estate tax trap for the unwary.

A life insurance policy may have little or no cash value now or at the date of your death. The estate-taxable value of the life insurance is its full, matured, face amount at the date of your death. In other words, *all* the death benefit proceeds may be taxable in your estate!

For example, if you own a $300,000 life insurance policy, even if it's term insurance with no cash value, the death benefit of $300,000 may be subject to estate taxes at your death. At an assumed marginal estate tax rate of 50 percent, that could mean your family would lose $150,000 to the IRS! The net result is that either you have half the insurance you paid for or you paid premiums for twice the amount of life insurance that your family actually received.

What is the 3-year rule?

Under the Internal Revenue Code, if a person owns or has incidents of ownership in a life insurance policy within 3 years of his or her death, the death proceeds from the policy are included in that person's estate. This *3-year rule* prevents an insured from eliminating the proceeds of a life insurance policy from his or her estate by giving it away within 3 years of his or her death. It does not matter if the insured dies because of an accident or illness or whether the insured knew he or she was going to die. The rule is absolute and is applied regardless of the circumstances.

One way to reduce or eliminate the effect of the 3-year rule is to add an *estate preservation rider* to a life insurance policy. This rider provides for extra coverage, which may be needed to create liquidity, if death occurs within 3 years of the transfer of the policy to someone else.

Generally, an estate preservation rider provides a benefit that is equal to the face value of the policy. For example, a $1 million face-value policy may have an estate preservation rider of an additional $1 million of coverage. If the insured gives the policy away and then dies within 3 years, there will be $2 million of death proceeds included in the insured's estate. Assuming that he or she is in the 50 percent estate tax bracket, there will be $1 million left. This amount, of course, is the original insurance amount, so there is no loss of estate liquidity because of the 3-year rule.

Other options to discuss with your advisors include borrowing from or cashing out the policy and using the funds to purchase a new policy over which you have no incidents of ownership.

Can't my children own the policy if I want the death benefit proceeds to be excluded from my taxable estate?

Yes, they could, but this approach has potential problems:

1. If a child predeceases you, that child's share of the cash value of the policy is included in his or her gross estate and may be subject to death tax.
2. The ownership of the policy and the ultimate benefits from it might fall into the hands of someone other than whom you would desire. If a child's marriage ends in divorce, the child's interest in the policy is an asset subject to property settlement issues. The same is true if your child has creditor problems. Your child's creditor could end up owning life insurance on your life.
3. You cannot be absolutely certain that money you give to a child for premium payments will be sent to the insurance company. The child could divert it for his or her personal use. We have seen instances where this has occurred despite the parents' insistence that it could never happen.
4. If your child owns the policy outright, he or she can change the beneficiary or surrender the policy. There is nothing you could do to prevent this.
5. If only one child owns the policy and the proceeds are payable to other children as well, the child owner may be required to pay gift taxes on your death.

These are just some of the potential drawbacks to having children own a policy directly. Most financial and estate planners try to dissuade parents from making their children owners of a policy, if possible. The loss of control is generally too great a risk to take with an asset as important as a life insurance policy. It may be preferable to have the policy owned by an irrevocable trust.

Why not just make my wife the owner and beneficiary of my life insurance? Wouldn't that eliminate these estate tax problems?

If your wife is the owner of your policy and predeceases you, the cash value of the policy is included in her gross estate and will possibly be subject to federal estate tax.

If your wife owns the policy and you die first, she will receive an outright distribution of the life insurance proceeds free of income tax and federal estate tax. However, on her subsequent death, any unspent proceeds in her estate above and beyond her unused applicable exclusion amount will be subject to federal estate tax. Little is gained by having her own the policy.

If you place the life insurance policy in an irrevocable life insurance trust, the death proceeds can provide for your wife during her lifetime. Upon her death, the remaining trust assets' principal can pass to your children estate tax–free.

What is the best way to exclude life insurance from my estate?

The most common and effective way to remove life insurance from an insured's estate, avoid incidents of ownership, and avoid all the other problems we've discussed in this section is to use an irrevocable life insurance trust (ILIT). The trustee of your ILIT can purchase the life insurance policy on your life directly from the insurer. If the ILIT is properly drafted, implemented, and administered, the life insurance proceeds will not be included in your estate.

Irrevocable life insurance trusts

What is an irrevocable life insurance trust?

An *irrevocable life insurance trust (ILIT)* is used to provide efficient funding for an estate tax liability. As the name suggests, the ILIT is the owner and beneficiary of a life insurance policy insuring the life of the trust maker. The beneficiaries of the ILIT are often the children of the maker, although grandchildren and other heirs can certainly be beneficiaries. To exclude the proceeds of a trust from the maker's estate, the trust must be irrevocable, which means that the maker cannot amend or revoke it and cannot be its trustee.

Upon the maker's death, the insurance proceeds are paid to the ILIT and are not included in the maker's estate. This is because the maker was never the owner of the policy, nor did he or she have any incidents of ownership in it.

How does an ILIT get the money to pay premiums on life insurance?

The trust maker makes gifts of cash to the ILIT. The ILIT's trustee uses these gifts to make the premium payments. One of the unique features of an ILIT is that the gifts the maker makes to the trust to pay the premiums can qualify for the gift tax annual exclusion.

I thought gifts to an irrevocable trust did not qualify for the gift tax annual exclusion. Why do gifts to an ILIT qualify?

Generally, gifts by a trust maker to an irrevocable trust are considered to be gifts of *future interests* rather than gifts of present interests. The gift tax annual exclusion is available only to present-value gifts.

For a gift to an irrevocable trust to qualify as a *present interest,* the trust beneficiaries must be given withdrawal, or demand, rights. These rights (discussed more fully in Chapter 5) allow the trust beneficiaries to withdraw gifts made to the ILIT within a certain period of time. If the beneficiaries do not exercise this power to withdraw, the withdrawal right terminates ("lapse" is the technical term used in the Internal Revenue Code). When the withdrawal right lapses, the trustee can use the gift to pay the life insurance premium. Because the trust beneficiaries had a reasonable opportunity to take their gifts, the gifts are present-interest gifts and thus qualify for the gift tax annual exclusion.

How many annual exclusion gifts do I get in my ILIT?

Each beneficiary of an ILIT is usually given a demand right. An annual exclusion is generally available for each ILIT beneficiary who has a demand right. For example, if your four children are ILIT demand-right beneficiaries, you can use up to four full annual exclusion gifts ($10,000 per person per year) for a total of $40,000 per year. If you and your spouse make gifts, each of you has four annual exclusion gifts available (or you can gift-split) for a total of $80,000 each calendar year.

My tax advisor tells me that an ILIT does not always allow full use of the $10,000 annual exclusion. Is this true?

If drafted properly, an ILIT allows full use of the $10,000 annual exclusion for each beneficiary. However, in some cases, the amount is restricted to the greater of $5000 or 5 percent of the trust assets. This restriction usually occurs in ILITs that have children and grandchildren as beneficiaries.

Your financial and estate planning team should delve into this issue in depth so that you can make a decision that will best meet your planning goals.

I've been told that if I transfer money into an ILIT to buy life insurance, Uncle Sam is virtually paying for part of the premium. How so?

Under current tax laws, if your estate is of a size that exceeds the applicable exclusion amount for estate tax purposes, every dollar above that amount will be taxed beginning at 37 percent and rapidly climbing to 55 percent of every marginal dollar over $3 million. Any amount above the applicable exclusion amount that you remove from your estate through gifts to an ILIT will not be taxed. A portion of the money you use to make gifts to the ILIT would have gone to pay Uncle Sam as taxes had it stayed in your estate; therefore, Uncle Sam is indirectly paying for that portion of the insurance premium.

It sounds as if an ILIT must be set up pretty carefully. What must be done to make sure the ILIT really works?

ILITs must be drafted correctly, set up correctly, and operated correctly. If they are not, the gift tax annual exclusion might be lost or, even worse, the insurance might be included in the maker's estate.

When considering an ILIT, you should seek out expert advisors, including, at a minimum, an attorney, a life insurance professional, and an accountant. The ILIT should be drafted to provide demand-right powers to the beneficiaries and to prevent you, the maker, from having any incidents of ownership. Once you sign the trust, the trustee should purchase the life insurance. As the maker of the trust, you should never be the owner of the policy, not even for just a second.

Beginning with the first premium, you should make a gift of cash to the ILIT so that the trustee can pay the premium. It is imperative that the trustee notify each beneficiary in writing of his or her right to withdraw the gift each and every time you make a gift to the ILIT, including the first gift. Often, when the first gift is made, people forget to make sure that notice is given. Do not allow this to happen.

At your death, the life insurance proceeds will be paid to the trust, and the trust proceeds will be available for distribution to the trust beneficiaries as provided in the ILIT.

What records should we keep for an ILIT to make sure that it qualifies for the annual exclusion and that the death proceeds are not included in my estate?

Here is a list of information that should be available if the Internal Revenue Service examines the operation of an ILIT:

- Copies of all notices to beneficiaries of their right to demand the gifts.
- Your individual and joint checking account records. These records

should show the gifts of the premiums to the ILIT and should be consistent with the demand-right notices.

- The trust's checking account records, which should show receipt of gifts and payment of premiums. A trustee is required by law to keep accounting records.
- All tax returns for the trust. A return is required only if the trust has taxable income or if it has gross income in excess of $600. An ILIT that is funded only with life insurance will usually not meet either of these requirements. However, if the trust has other assets, it may meet these requirements and the ILIT trustee will be required to file a return.

Can my spouse receive any income from my ILIT?

A surviving spouse can be given rights to income from an ILIT, much the same as a surviving spouse can be given rights to income in a family trust created in a living trust or a will.

A spouse can also be given the right to principal from an ILIT. You can direct the trustee, through instructions in the ILIT, to make discretionary distributions of principal and/or to pay the greater of $5000 or 5 percent of the trust assets each year on a noncumulative basis. If you live in a community property state, certain precautions may need to be taken to avoid unintended estate taxation of the trust.

What are the differences between having an ILIT be the beneficiary of life insurance and having an individual be the beneficiary?

An ILIT allows the maker to control how and when life insurance proceeds are distributed to the trust beneficiaries. For example, a maker may want his or her children not to have the death proceeds immediately but, instead, to have one-half on his or her death and the balance in 5 years or some other schedule.

On the other hand, named beneficiaries of the life insurance policy simply receive the death benefit proceeds outright and can use them in whatever manner they wish. There is no control over the use or timing of the proceeds.

Can an ILIT own assets other than life insurance?

Yes, an ILIT can hold virtually any type of assets. Sometimes ILITs are called *wealth replacement trusts* or simply *irrevocable trusts.* Whatever they are called, they have a great deal of versatility and can be applied to many planning situations. As with all sophisticated planning techniques, it is imperative that you seek the assistance of a team of advisors to ensure that the trust is drafted and implemented correctly.

Funding an ILIT

I own substantial amounts of life insurance on my own life to provide income for my surviving spouse and to guarantee liquidity for an otherwise illiquid estate. Can I transfer these existing policies to an ILIT?

If you transfer ownership to another party or to a trust within 3 years of your death, the insurance proceeds will be includable in your taxable estate under the 3-year rule. Obviously, this presents a risk to you and your family if you transfer your policies to an ILIT.

Should this risk be one that you are unwilling to take, and assuming you are insurable, the safest option would be to establish the ILIT and have the trustee purchase new life insurance on your life inside the trust to replace the existing coverage. The cash values, if any, from surrendering your existing life insurance could be given to the ILIT and used to purchase the new coverage.

Alternatively, if replacing existing insurance is not an attractive option due to insurability or economic issues, you may want to create an ILIT and then transfer the existing policies to the trust. If you use an ILIT, it should have a contingent marital deduction clause to ensure that the insurance proceeds are exempt from immediate estate taxation if you do not survive the 3-year transfer period. Any unspent proceeds from the death proceeds will be included in your spouse's estate upon his or her death.

If you are insurable, you may want to transfer your existing policies to an ILIT and then insure against the risk created by the 3-year rule. You can do this by adding an estate preservation rider to the policy or by purchasing term insurance to pay for the estate taxes generated by the life insurance.

Finally, other alternatives to discuss with your professional advisors would be establishing a family limited partnership or creating an intentional grantor trust.

We have a second-to-die policy that we'd like to transfer to an ILIT. Are there tax or other considerations that we need to be aware of?

Yes—and the considerations depend a great deal on who owns the policy before you transfer it to an ILIT. If it is owned by one spouse, the 3-year rule applies if that owner/spouse is the second of you to die within 3 years of transferring the policy to the ILIT.

If both of you own the second-to-die policy that you transfer to an ILIT and either of you dies within 3 years of the transfer, a portion of the cash value of the policy may be included in the decedent's estate. Generally, this included value is a modified cash-value amount called the *interpolated terminal reserve value.* If the surviving spouse subsequently dies, also within 3 years of the transfer, the full value of the death proceeds will be included in his or her estate.

To avoid the risk posed by the 3-year rule, you have the same options with a second-to-die policy as those discussed in the previous question relating to individual policies. However, because the odds of the two of you dying within 3 years are probably very low, depending, of course, on your ages and health, a transfer of your second-to-die policy to the ILIT will not generally be as risky as would be the case if each of you had an individual policy.

Should I wait until my attorney drafts an ILIT before applying for the insurance?

When coordinating your life insurance program with an ILIT, you do not have to wait to apply for the insurance until the trust is drafted. There are several practical reasons for not waiting. You may choose not to purchase the policy, in which case there is no reason to draft the ILIT. You may not be insurable, so you should find that out before you have your attorney prepare the ILIT. And even though you may be in good health today, there is always the risk that your health status may change to your detriment even during the short period of time it takes for the trust to be drafted.

The Internal Revenue Service has ruled that the trust maker can apply for the life insurance that is to go into an ILIT without having an incident of ownership and triggering the 3-year rule. However, once the ILIT is established, the ILIT's trustee should sign a new application and follow all other ILIT formalities to the letter.

If I transfer an existing policy to an ILIT, is that a gift?

Yes. The value of the gift is generally the interpolated terminal reserve, or modified cash-value of a permanent insurance policy. Term insurance generally does not have value when given away except to the extent of any unused premium.

A gift to an ILIT can qualify for the annual exclusion if the ILIT includes demand-right powers. To the extent the gift exceeds the gift tax annual exclusion, the gift is taxable. However, the gift tax can be offset by the applicable exclusion amount.

Before transferring your life insurance to an ILIT or to anyone else, you should see your tax and insurance advisors. A number of complex rules apply to the transfer of life insurance, and not complying with these rules can create potentially devastating tax consequences.

What are the steps in purchasing a life insurance policy in an ILIT to make sure it will not be included in my estate?

As mentioned above, you can initially apply for a policy as the insured but not as the owner while your attorney is drafting the ILIT document.

Once you sign the trust, your trustee must submit a new application. The trustee sets up a checking account for the ILIT. You make a gift of cash to the ILIT sufficient to pay the first premium. The trustee notifies each beneficiary in writing of his or her right to withdraw the gift, as required by the trust. At the end of the demand-right period as stated in the trust document, the trustee writes a check to the insurance company to pay the premium.

Is it reasonable to own second-to die-insurance in an ILIT?

There are four very good reasons to consider using an ILIT in estate planning, and those same reasons apply to funding the IlIT with second-to-die insurance:

1. The premium cost is less for a second-to-die policy than for a comparable single-life policy.
2. Since the estate tax is typically levied at the second spouse's death, your family could use the policy death proceeds to pay the estate settlement costs, including taxes, without having to liquidate your other assets to pay these costs.
3. You could give to a charity some or all of the property in your estate that would be subject to estate taxes. You could then replace the value of this property at *no* estate tax to your family through insurance held in an ILIT.
4. You could spend more of your assets while you are living and be comfortable knowing that your family will always receive the value of the ILIT insurance without any tax liability.

Each of these goals can be accomplished by doing some advance planning and by giving a small percentage of your assets each year to the ILIT to pay the premiums for the ILIT insurance.

After the first insured dies, do the gifts to the ILIT continue so that the ILIT can continue to make premium payments?

Probably. If the premiums being paid by the ILIT are a result of annual exclusion gifts from the makers, the tax-free nature of the gifts may change when one of the makers dies. Here is an example of how that could happen: A married couple with four children are permitted up to $80,000 of annual exclusion gifts (2 × 4 × $10,000). If the premium for the policy is $60,000 each year and one of the makers dies, the surviving spouse has only $40,000 of annual gift exclusions. The additional $20,000 of yearly premium would be a taxable gift, which would require that the surviving spouse pay the gift tax or use part of his or her applicable exclusion amount.

How can we avoid any gift tax complications in our ILIT after the first one of us dies?

One solution is to overfund the policy—that is, pay more than the required premium—while the two of you are alive. After the first death, the surviving spouse could use the extra cash-value buildup to supplement the premium payments. A second solution is to purchase a death waiver option at the time of initial application. A death waiver option eliminates all future premiums after the first death. This option relieves the surviving spouse from having to make ongoing gifts.

Split-dollar life insurance plans

What is split-dollar life insurance?

Split-dollar life insurance is not a type of insurance. It is an agreement between two parties to share the cost of premiums on a life insurance policy and, in some fashion, to split its proceeds even though only one party owns the policy. Split-dollar agreements are often entered into between an employer and an employee (or an ILIT established by the employee) as a way of deferring income or increasing benefits to the employee.

What are the advantages of split-dollar planning?

Split-dollar plans can provide favorable estate and income tax benefits and other advantages for both an employer and an employee.

Some of the advantages to an employer include:

- The employer can offer a split-dollar program to selected employees since there are no government-imposed participation or discrimination requirements.
- The employer recovers the entire investment in the plan, so the only "cost" is the use-of-money factor.

Some of the advantages to an employee include:

- The portion of the premium that is taxable as income to the employee is a small portion of the premiums actually paid.
- The employee can leverage the contribution of a small amount of premium payment into a much more valuable, potentially tax-free gift to his or her beneficiaries.
- The employee controls his or her share of the death benefit.
- The employee can keep the insurance in force if the employer decides to no longer participate in the plan.

How can split-dollar insurance reduce my federal estate taxes?

A typical estate planning strategy is to establish an ILIT to own a life insurance policy on your life and to pay the insurance premiums, with the trust proceeds ultimately passing to your trust beneficiaries free of income tax and estate tax. You make annual gifts to the trust to cover the premiums. Because the amount you contribute to the trust is considered a gift to the trust beneficiaries, any contributions of more than $10,000 per beneficiary (the annual exclusion amount) will be subject to gift tax. If the total premium required on a large insurance policy is greater than your combined annual exclusion amount for all beneficiaries or if you have already exceeded the $10,000 annual exclusion amount for some or all of the trust beneficiaries, you will be making a taxable gift. This is where a split-dollar agreement can come to the rescue.

Under the terms of a split-dollar agreement, the trust typically pays only a small part of the premium (often less than 5 percent). The trust's share of the premium is usually an amount equal to the "economic benefit" (the current actuarial value of the death benefit based on a 1-year term policy) or the government's Table PS-58 rate or Table US-38 rate for second-to-die policies. The other party to the split-dollar agreement, typically an employer, a family business, or a family partnership, pays the remainder of the premium. Through this arrangement, you contribute a relatively small amount (considered a gift to the beneficiaries) to the trust to cover its portion of the premium. The split-dollar arrangement therefore allows you to give beneficiaries a potentially tax-free gift that's worth much more in future benefit than the amount you contribute for the premium.

Is there any disadvantage to using a split-dollar insurance plan in conjunction with an ILIT?

One disadvantage of removing life insurance proceeds from your estate is that you can lose access to the policy's cash value. If this is a concern in your situation, a properly structured private split-dollar arrangement can provide access to cash value for your spouse or other beneficiary. We discuss private split-dollar arrangements later in this chapter.

What is meant by "imputed economic benefit" in split-dollar planning?

The *imputed economic benefit* in split-dollar planning is also know as the PS-58 cost (for individual policies) or the PS- or US-38 cost (for second-to-die policies). Imputed economic benefit is a concept that was established when split-dollar plans were first allowed. Since the 1960s, the Internal Revenue Service has held that when an employer pays the entire premium, the employee receives an "imputed economic benefit" because a certain amount of that premium is, in reality, a benefit to the employee for the pure term costs of the policy. The employee has to recognize this economic benefit as income even though the employee does not actually receive any cash. The IRS ruled that the imputed economic benefit is equal to the cost of a 1-year renewable term life insurance and published a table of the term rates called Table PS-58.

Luckily for taxpayers, when the IRS established Table PS-58, it stated that the employer could report as income to the employee either the imputed economic benefit equal to the rate found in the table or the rate that the insurance company published for a 1-year renewable term contract if this rate is lower than the PS-58 rate. The term rates insurance companies now charge are invariably lower than the rates in Tables PS-58 and PS-38.

Today, advisors typically accomplish split-dollar planning in conjunction with an ILIT, and the imputed economic benefit is used to determine the amount of the premium that is paid by the ILIT. To eliminate some complications in split-dollar planning, advisors routinely require that their clients make a gift of the economic benefit each year to the ILIT. The trustee then uses this amount to pay the trust's part of the full premium. In this way, advisors and clients always know the amount of the gift, when it is to be paid, and how much premium the corporation and the trust must each pay. More importantly, because the employee pays (through his or her gift to the ILIT) the imputed economic benefit, he or she does not pay income taxes on this amount.

The corporation or other employer that is paying the remainder of the premium generally pays its share directly to the insurance company. Since this portion of the payment is merely the payment by the corporation for its interest in the insurance policy, it does not have to pay the premiums to the ILIT.

What are the different types of split-dollar plans?

There are three types, which include endorsement, collateral assignment, and reverse split-dollar plans.

What is an endorsement split-dollar plan?

With an *endorsement split-dollar plan,* the employer owns the policy, including all the cash value. The employer then endorses the death benefit in excess of the cash value over to the insured or the insured's ILIT. When the agreement is terminated, the employer retains ownership of the policy. This form of split-dollar can create some adverse tax consequences, especially if the insured owns a majority interest in the employer.

What is a collateral assignment split-dollar plan?

A *collateral assignment plan* is the most widely used form of split-dollar arrangement. Typically the insured or the insured's ILIT owns the policy and the employer pays a majority of the premium. When the plan terminates, the owner of the policy must reimburse the employer for the premiums paid. If the insured dies before the plan terminates, the employer is reimbursed for its premiums from the death proceeds.

All the parties to the plan sign an agreement outlining the responsibilities for paying premiums. The agreement sets out how cash values and death benefits will be allocated upon termination of the plan or the insured's death, whichever occurs first.

Here are the typical steps for a collateral assignment split-dollar life insurance plan:

- The individual insured creates an ILIT and makes annual gifts of the economic benefit to the ILIT. These gifts qualify for the gift tax annual exclusion.

- The trustee of the ILIT, as owner of the permanent life insurance policy, pays the economic benefit portion of each premium from the gift proceeds and assigns the policy to an employer (corporation, partnership, or limited liability company) as collateral for the split-dollar advances.
- The employer pays all the premium (the split-dollar advances), except for the imputed economic benefit portion of the premium.
- Each year, the economic benefit portion of the premium increases as the insured gets older, so the gifts from the insured to the ILIT must increase each year.
- The split-dollar agreement remains in effect until the corporation is repaid, either during the insured's life from the cash value (or other assets in the ILIT) or at the insured's death from the tax-free insurance proceeds.
- The insurance policy is designed so that the accumulated cash value in the policy will create a "paid-up" policy.

What is a reverse split-dollar plan?

The *reverse split-dollar plan* is used primarily in a business setting. Reverse split dollar is similar to a collateral assignment split dollar except it reverses the premium payments. The insured/employee, or an ILIT created by the insured/employee, owns the policy and assigns the term insurance portion of the policy to the corporation to be used as key personal life insurance. Each year, the corporation either pays a greater portion of the premium as the term insurance costs increase or pays the same premium and purchases less insurance as the insured gets older. Because the corporation is paying only for term life insurance, there is no repayment to the corporation when the reverse split-dollar plan is terminated. The ILIT pays the balance of the premium and is entitled to the policy's cash value when the agreement terminates or the insured dies.

In general, reverse split-dollar plans are more aggressive than regular plans because there are no specific revenue rulings or court cases dealing with the various income and estate tax issues associated with reverse split dollar.

Can second-to-die life insurance be used in a split-dollar plan?

While there is little legal authority to do so, most tax advisors agree that second-to-die life insurance can be used in a split-dollar plan. In fact, with the growing popularity of second-to-die insurance, many professionals are using second-to-die split dollar because of the favorable premiums and because the economic benefit is much lower than that on single-life insurance.

With a second-to-die split-dollar plan, how is the economic benefit calculated after one of the insureds dies?

The economic benefit for survivorship policies changes from the PS-38 rate to the government's PS-58 rate after the first spouse's death. This single-life rate is dramatically higher than the survivorship term insurance rate used when both spouses are alive and can cause problems for the split-dollar plan. It can result in significant imputed taxable income and imputed taxable gifts each year if the split-dollar agreement is continued. In addition, only one spouse's annual exclusion is available, so the amount used for annual tax-free gifts is usually cut in half.

Because of the higher economic benefit costs and the loss of annual exclusion gifts, it is important to plan your life insurance program in such a way that it takes into account these contingencies. One solution to these problems is to purchase a death waiver option with the policy to ensure that the premiums will be fully paid when a spouse dies. Another solution is to attempt to overfund the policy in its early years so that the cash value will continue the policy upon the death of a spouse. Some advisors create plans that allow the ILIT to be funded with other assets that will be available for premium payments when the first spouse dies.

Why would I want to give more to the ILIT than the minimum required by the split-dollar rules?

By giving the maximum amounts allowed under the annual exclusion, you can significantly lower the split-dollar repayment obligation. Then, you may either reduce the planned annual premium or reduce the number of years the split-dollar agreement must remain in effect.

Should the split-dollar agreement terminate before I die?

Your advisors must carefully design a split-dollar arrangement to maintain flexibility. To determine when the agreement should terminate, you and your advisors must consider the cost of the economic benefit. Eventually, the economic benefit is likely to exceed your available annual exclusion amounts and the annual premium, creating gift and income tax issues.

In addition, if the employer pays the entire premium, the insured/employee must report as income the imputed economic benefit. This amount of income can get to be quite high. It is not a good situation for an individual to have to pay both income taxes on income not received *and* gift taxes on the premium payments to the ILIT.

If my split-dollar policy is paid up, do I still have an imputed economic benefit?

Yes. The imputed economic benefit does not expire until the split-dollar agreement terminates and the corporation or other business is paid.

So how do I determine when to terminate a split-dollar plan?

The split-dollar plan should terminate when the policy is paid up or when you die, whichever occurs first. The parties to the plan should develop an "exit strategy" to terminate the split-dollar plan at some future date. Most split-dollar plans will eventually become an economic burden as the insured ages unless there is an effective exit strategy to repay the split-dollar advances or to pay the taxes if repayment is forgiven.

The exit strategy should be developed at the very beginning. If the split-dollar plan does not have an effective exit strategy, adverse consequences can result during the insured's lifetime.

What happens to the life insurance policy if the split-dollar agreement is not properly terminated?

Without careful planning, the policy either may come back into the client's taxable estate or may lapse if the cash values are stripped out of the policy to repay the split-dollar advances. Under endorsement split-dollar plans, all policy benefits revert to the corporation and are no longer payable to the ILIT. With collateral assignment plans, there may not be sufficient cash value available in the policy to repay the split-dollar advances and continue the policy on a paid-up basis (paying the premiums from the cash value).

The typical goal of split-dollar planning is to create income tax–free life insurance in an estate tax–free ILIT. The challenge for the planner is to devise a method for repaying the split-dollar advances or for paying the income tax and gift tax if repayment is forgiven.

What are some split-dollar exit strategies to consider?

There are four primary exit strategies:

- *Policy rollout:* The split-dollar plan is terminated by a lump-sum repayment of the split-dollar advances either from the insured or from the policy values (after the fifteenth year).
- *Policy crawlout:* The split-dollar advances are gradually repaid over time. The split-dollar plan is terminated after the last payment.
- *Bonus method:* In lieu of repayment, the split-dollar advances are treated as a taxable bonus to the employee, for which he or she must pay income taxes. The corporation receives a deduction equal to the value reported as income by the employee.
- *Note repayment:* The split-dollar agreement is terminated and is replaced with a promissory note with repayment terms.

With a rollout exit strategy, how can I use the cash values to repay the split-dollar advances?

In most circumstances, an ILIT has only the life insurance policy as an asset. Consequently, to terminate the split-dollar agreement, policy cash values must be used. For the policy to continue as a paid-up policy after the rollout, the ILIT should contribute higher-than-normal premiums from the outset of the plan. The higher premiums will create more cash value in the policy.

The tax-deferred accumulation of the extra cash value creates excellent tax leverage within the insurance policy. The cost-basis portion of the cash value is used to repay the split-dollar advances without triggering any income tax. The earnings can then remain in the policy to continue it on a paid-up basis.

What can go wrong with a rollout exit strategy when the cash values will be used to repay the split-dollar advances?

If the split-dollar rollout plan is underfunded, one of two undesirable results may occur. If cash values are surrendered to repay the advances, premium payments may have to resume because there is no longer enough cash value to continue the policy on a paid-up basis. Alternatively, if a policy loan is used to pay the split-dollar advances, a loan repayment plan must be established to keep the loan interest charges from consuming the cash value. Both these results require a resumption of annual gifts to the trust so that the trustee can continue to make premium payments. In addition, any withdrawal of cash value during the first 15 years of the policy might trigger income under the MEC rules.

A split-dollar plan that is not well designed can add unexpected costs in order to preserve the policy or else the policy may lapse without value because the trust will not be receiving any additional gifts to pay the premiums.

When the exit strategy calls for cash values to be used to repay the split-dollar advances, should the policy have a level or an increasing death benefit?

Unless it is part of the insured's overall estate plan to decrease the ILIT's death benefit, the policy should be structured to have an increasing death benefit while the split-dollar agreement is in effect. While premiums are being paid, an increasing death benefit allows the ILIT's portion of the death benefit to remain level whereas the company's portion of the death benefit increases annually to ensure recovery of its total split-dollar advances.

If a level death benefit approach were used and the insured later wanted to increase the ILIT death benefit back to the original amount, the insured would have to go through the insurance underwriting process again.

Can a crawlout exit strategy work if the policy is paid up but the cash values are insufficient to repay the split-dollar advances?

Although cash premium payments may stop when a policy is paid up, the economic benefit will continue to be taxed as imputed income each year to the employee and as an imputed gift to the ILIT as long as the split-dollar agreement remains in effect. Also, the economic benefit cost increases each year. The crawlout strategy allows the ILIT to use the annual gifts from the insured to repay a portion of the split-dollar advances.

With a typical corporate collateral assignment split-dollar plan, the crawlout strategy may be used, as follows, when the policy is paid up:

- The corporation stops making split-dollar premium advances.
- The insured/employee continues to give to the ILIT an amount at least equal to the economic benefit each year.
- The ILIT uses the gifts to pay partial premiums at least equal to the economic benefit.
- The ILIT trustee takes annual partial surrenders or withdrawals of cash value to fund annual repayments to the corporation.

- The ILIT trustee determines the annual repayment amount by monitoring the cash value needed to continue the policy on paid-up status.
- The split-dollar agreement is terminated after the corporation is fully repaid.

With a crawlout split-dollar exit strategy, what formalities should be observed?

An annual crawlout repayment strategy should be chosen only if the ILIT pays an annual premium at least equal to the year's imputed economic benefit. The premium may have to be funded by a gift from the insured. By paying this premium, there will be no risk that the insured will have imputed income and gifts.

Also, the trustee of the ILIT should consider waiting until the end of the calendar year to make the repayment. Deferring the payment for as long as possible allows greater tax-deferred cash value accumulation.

How does the bonus exit strategy work?

Sometimes the employer may decide to reward the employee with a bonus and terminate the split-dollar plan. This is the bonus method. The employer that advanced the premiums gives up the right to receive repayment and elects to terminate the split-dollar agreement at the same time.

Before adopting the bonus method, the policy should be paid up. If the employer gives up the right to repayment and terminates the split-dollar agreement before the policy is paid up, the total amount forgiven will be taxable in full as income to the insured/employee and will be considered a gift to the ILIT. The bonus exit strategy significantly reduces the amount of cash value needed in the policy.

When no ILIT is involved, the insured/employee owns the policy and simply removes enough cash value to pay the income tax. With a collateral assignment split-dollar plan, many tax advisors believe that the employee's reportable income will be limited to the corporation's split-dollar advances. The additional cash values that have compounded on a tax-deferred basis should not be taxable unless the employee terminates the policy. However, there is no clear-cut law in this area, so some risk is involved.

When an ILIT owns the policy, the insured/employee must have other assets available to pay the income tax because the cash value belongs to the ILIT. In addition, the employee will be deemed to have made a gift of the forgiven premium advances to the ILIT.

How does the note repayment method work as a split-dollar exit strategy?

The note repayment method may be intended from the beginning or used as a default approach if the tax rules change before any other exit strategy can be implemented. At a predetermined time, the corporation cancels the split-dollar agreement and is repaid with an unsecured note from the policy owner, which is usually an ILIT. In some situations, the interest paid on the note may be less than the split-dollar plan's economic benefit amount. It is not clear whether the IRS will treat this as a form of undocumented split dollar rather than a legal note separate from the insurance policy.

How can I plan for a split-dollar exit strategy before the first premium is paid?

The split-dollar plan should terminate when the policy is paid up, that is, when there is sufficient cash value to maintain the premiums. When you are originally designing the plan, you and your advisors should know how much cash value will be needed to maintain the policy at the time of the anticipated termination of the split-dollar agreement. You and your advisors should also know the amount of the total split-dollar advances that will have to be made. Be conservative when estimating the cash value needed to have a paid-up policy. With whole life and universal life policies, assume that actual results will be worse than the insurance company's current, nonguaranteed assumptions for interest, mortality costs, and expenses. With variable life policies, assume an annual gross crediting rate at least 150 basis points below the expected return for the next 20 years to account for the potentially adverse impact of investment volatility.

Avoid unexpected surprises. If your exit strategy involves the withdrawal of cash values, get written confirmation at the time of the policy's issuance by the insurance company that your policy will not be a MEC—that is, that the cash-value/death benefit ratio will not exceed minimum testing levels during the first 7 years of the policy.

With the rollout technique, you should plan on building up to twice the cash value normally needed to have a permanent policy. With most life policies using the rollout technique, the end of year 15 is the magic year for action. Fifteen years is approximately the time needed for the tax-deferred compounding of most life policies to produce sufficient cash value, based on reasonable assumptions, to repay the advances and have a paid-up policy.

After the split-dollar agreement is terminated, how should a paid-up universal life policy be managed?

When the split-dollar agreement terminates and the policy is paid up, the increasing death benefit on universal life policies should be changed to a level death benefit. This is intended to avoid a potential loss of insurance from increased cost-of-insurance charges. Remember, all permanent life insurance policies (whole life, universal life, and variable life) consist of two elements, a term insurance element and a cash-value element. Each year, the insurance company calculates the difference between the cash value and the death benefit payable if you die. It treats this "net" death benefit as the amount at risk and subject to its annual cost of insurance. The cost of insurance is a term insurance rate that increases annually as you get older.

If the policy has reached paid-up status, the level death benefit allows the net amount of insurance subject to insurance charges to decrease. When the policy is placed on zero premium status, part of the cash-value earnings pays the annual cost-of-insurance charges. The remainder of the cash-value earnings can increase the total cash value each year and ensure the policy will continue for a lifetime.

By comparison, if the policy is left with an increasing death benefit option, the net amount at risk remains level, causing the internal cost-of-insurance charges to increase annually as you age. This may eventually consume all the cash values and cause the policy to lapse with zero value while you are alive. This is certainly an undesired result.

After the split-dollar agreement is terminated, how should a projected paid-up whole life policy be managed?

With whole life policies, when cash payments stop, the annual premium does not vanish or change to zero. The premium is simply paid from other sources. Normally, the dividend option is changed to provide that future dividends will be applied to reduce the net premium due. The net premium is then paid with the surrender of cash values from paid-up additions that were purchased with previous years' dividends. Because the future dividends are not guaranteed, the policy is not guaranteed paid up.

When cash premium payments stop, what steps should be taken to ensure the policy remains paid up?

For all policies, order new in-force illustrations both when the split-dollar agreement is terminated and every few years thereafter to confirm that the policy continues to be paid up on the basis of reasonable assumptions. Review the illustration to make certain the cash values increase every year to policy maturity. Confirm that your policy has an extended maturity option to continue the death benefit beyond age 100 without any further premium payments or insurance charges. You should want the policy to continue until the tax-free death benefit is paid. People are living to age 100 with increasing frequency, and it would be unfortunate to have a paid-up policy terminate at age 95 or 100 with a large taxable gain.

What is the likelihood that the tax rules regarding split dollar will change to my detriment?

Although split-dollar plans have been utilized in various forms for over 40 years, the results are not guaranteed. The current generation of split-dollar plans bears little resemblance to the corporate split-dollar plans of the 1950s and 1960s. The most creative plans use a third party's funds on a tax-favored basis to build up the policy's cash values and provide a tax-free permanent death benefit. You should assume that the Internal Revenue Service may eventually focus on the tax benefits of split-dollar insurance plans and find a way to rewrite the rules.

The significant gift tax leverage available through split-dollar plans will continue to make them desirable planning tools. Split-dollar plans should be considered whenever annual premiums would normally trigger a taxable gift. At a minimum, the split-dollar plan can delay the recognition of the gift until the plan is terminated.

Family Split-Dollar Insurance Plans

I've heard about a type of life insurance policy called family split dollar. What is it?

Family split dollar, also called *private split dollar,* is not a type of life insurance; it is an alternative method of split-dollar planning. Like traditional split-dollar planning, family split dollar separates the life insurance policy into two components, the death benefit and the cash value. The death benefit is typically owned by an ILIT, and the cash value is owned by another person, usually the trust maker's spouse or the spouse's revocable trust. The premium is split between the ILIT and the noninsured spouse.

How does a family split-dollar plan differ from a corporate split-dollar plan?

A family split-dollar plan uses the collateral assignment approach but is simpler because no corporation is involved. It is typically an agreement between the insured's spouse and an ILIT that owns and is the beneficiary of the insurance policy. The insured makes gifts to the ILIT, and the ILIT pays part of the premium equal to the economic benefit (i.e., the term cost or Table PS-58 rate). The insured's spouse pays the remainder of the premium. Because the spouse is entitled to be repaid this amount, the premium payments do not constitute a gift. During the insured's life, his or her spouse may have access to policy cash values through loans or partial surrenders of the policy. When the insured dies, his or her spouse will receive an amount equal to the premiums he or she paid or the cash value of the policy. The ILIT will receive the remainder of the death benefit. The ILIT's interest in the death benefit is usually substantially greater than the noninsured spouse's cash-value interest in the policy.

What are the benefits of family split dollar?

First, by placing the death benefit of a life insurance contract into an ILIT, the proceeds are removed from the insured trust maker's estate—a valuable consideration. Second, family split dollar provides easy access to the policy's cash value. While the death benefit is owned in an ILIT, the cash value is owned by the insured's spouse. The insured's spouse, therefore, has access to the cash value, which is often used to enhance retirement income. Also, there are no adverse income tax consequences for the insured with family split dollar.

What rights does the noninsured spouse have?

The noninsured spouse has the following rights to the policy:

- The right to borrow the cash value from the policy
- The right to recover the premiums paid or cash surrender value of the policy, whichever is greater, when the insured dies
- The right to receive the cash surrender value, if the policy is surrendered before the insured's death

Family split dollar sounds too good to be true. What does the government say about it?

The tax consequences of family split dollar are not fully settled, but in two private letter rulings, the Internal Revenue Service offered some insight into its thinking.

In a 1996 ruling, the insured's spouse entered into a collateral assignment split-dollar arrangement with an ILIT that the insured spouse had established. The insured spouse transferred cash to the trust, which then used the cash to acquire an insurance policy on the insured spouse's life. The insured spouse did not retain any rights, powers, or interests in the ILIT or the life insurance policy. Under the split-dollar agreement, the ILIT trustee owned the policy and was to pay that portion of the premium equal to the lesser of the insurance company's pertinent 1-year term rate for a standard risk or the government's Table PS-58 rate. The spouse was to pay the balance of each premium.

The arrangement gave the spouse the right to receive from the death proceeds the greater of either the cash value in the policy just before death or the premiums advanced (without interest). In addition, the spouse had the sole right to borrow from the policy and the right to receive the cash value if the trustee surrendered the policy or if the split-dollar arrangement was terminated.

The IRS concluded that the noninsured spouse would not be treated as making taxable gifts to the ILIT beneficiaries by virtue of premium payments, since the noninsured spouse was to eventually be reimbursed.

Further, the IRS held that the death proceeds would not be includable in the insured spouse's gross estate at his or her death since the insured spouse did not hold any incidents of ownership in the policy. The IRS declined to rule on whether the interest forgone by the spouse on premium advances would be treated as "imputed" interest income to the ILIT or its beneficiaries under the Internal Revenue Code.

A 1997 ruling involved a second-to-die policy on the lives of a husband and wife who set up an ILIT to own the policy. The couple entered into a split-dollar agreement with the ILIT and agreed to pay the lion's share of the premium directly to the insurance company. The ILIT paid the economic benefit (the government Table US-38 cost). In this case, the couple's access to policy cash values was restricted to receiving their split-dollar premiums at the termination of the plan. Thus, the IRS ruled that the payments made directly to the insurance company by the couple would not be treated as taxable gifts. Nor would the death proceeds, payable to the ILIT, be includable in the couple's net taxable estate.

Besides the situation above, where the noninsured spouse participates in the split-dollar arrangement, what other circumstances warrant family split-dollar consideration?

Family split dollar is applicable to a number of planning situations. For example, a parent could fund a policy for a child or the child's spouse. Grandparents have provided funding for a policy for their grandchildren. Private split-dollar can also be used where there is a need to fund a buy-sell agreement.

In any situation where there is a person who is willing to pay life insurance premiums on another and have access to the cash value, private or family split dollar should be examined. If the parties are related or have economic interests in common, this type of planning may be applicable.

I've heard that family split dollar can be used for funding a generation-skipping trust. Why is that beneficial?

The government imposes a GST tax on gifts or bequests made by an individual to his or her grandchildren. Every person has a $1,030,000 exemption (indexed annually for inflation) for which no GST tax is assessed. Combining the exemption amount with a family split-dollar program can dramatically leverage the exemption because the amount of the gift subject to the GST tax is not the full premium but only the economic benefit amount. Combining generation-skipping planning with family split-dollar planning allows a multiple of the $1,030,000 exemption to be passed free of any GST taxes to grandchildren and future generations.

Life Insurance in a Family Trust

Is life insurance a good way to invest all or a portion of the money in a family (bypass) trust?

A family trust is a trust that is created in a will or a trust after a spouse dies. The primary purpose of a family trust is to "soak up" the deceased spouse's applicable exclusion amount. The trust is created so that the surviving spouse can access the income and principal of the family trust.

The extent of a spouse's ability to take income and principal out of a family trust depends entirely on how it is drafted.

A family trust is a separate tax entity. Any taxable income that it retains is subject to income tax. Since the tax brackets for trusts are compressed, any trust income over $8350 (this amount is adjusted for inflation each year) is taxed in the maximum income tax bracket of 39.6 percent. Therefore, it makes tax sense to invest some or all of the family trust's assets in tax-free or tax-favored investments.

Life insurance is a tax-deferred investment that should be considered. The cash value of the life insurance grows income tax–free. Upon the death of the insured (usually the surviving spouse), the proceeds are income tax–free. If the trust is structured properly, the family trust's life insurance proceeds will not be included in the surviving spouse's estate.

How can I structure my family trust to buy life insurance on my surviving spouse's life?

First, either state law or the trust document itself must allow the trust to hold life insurance policies. If neither the trust document nor the applicable state law allows such an investment, it is unlikely that the trustee can invest in life insurance.

Assuming that a trust can hold life insurance, there may be a problem if the surviving spouse is a trustee of the family trust and also the insured. If the surviving spouse, as trustee, has any incidents of ownership in the life insurance policy, the death proceeds will be included in his or her estate, effectively defeating the estate planning reason for buying the life insurance policy.

For a family trust to purchase life insurance on the surviving spouse, the trust should contain a provision that allows for the appointment of a special independent trustee. This trustee should then be granted the power to apply for and purchase life insurance on the life of the surviving spouse as an investment of the trust. The trust should further state that if the surviving spouse is serving as the trustee, he or she is prohibited from exercising any control over or having any incidents of ownership in any life insurance policy insuring his or her life. The more conservative approach is to not name the surviving spouse as a trustee and to allow others to serve.

Properly drafted and implemented, a family trust can act as an irrevocable life insurance trust holding life insurance on the life of the surviving spouse. The income and estate tax benefits of this type of planning can be substantial.

Life Insurance for Wealth Replacement

What is a wealth replacement trust, and when might it be used?

A *wealth replacement trust* is often used to replace the value of assets given to charity. When assets are placed into a charitable remainder trust (CRT), the donor receives an annuity, or unitrust payment, annually for his or her lifetime and significant tax benefits are achieved. However, the ultimate disposition of the CRT assets is to charitable entities rather than to the trust maker's heirs.

To replace the assets given to charity, the CRT donor creates a wealth replacement trust, also called an *irrevocable life insurance trust,* which purchases, often with part of the saving achieved by the CRT, a life insurance policy on the life of the donor(s). Because the policy is owned by an ILIT, it escapes estate taxation. At the death of the donor(s), the proceeds of the ILIT are distributed to the beneficiaries to replace the value of the assets that go to the charity.

Since assets owned by the decedent would be taxable in his or her estate were they not in the CRT, those assets can be replaced by an amount of life insurance that is substantially less than the value of the assets. For example, if an estate is in the 50 percent estate tax bracket, $1 million of assets owned by the decedent will yield only $500,000 to the heirs. Thus, to achieve the same result when $1 million is given to charity through a CRT, only $500,000 of life insurance is required. Usually the tax savings achieved by the CRT more than cover the cost of the wealth replacement insurance. In most cases, the donor prefers to leave the entire $1 million to heirs, so the ILIT purchases a $1 million policy. Since the policy is owned by the ILIT, the entire death benefit will accrue to the beneficiaries.

Can a charitable remainder trust and a wealth replacement trust be used by a husband and wife as well as by just one person?

Absolutely. It is very common for a husband and wife to create a joint CRT for their lifetimes and replace all or part of the assets with a joint ILIT that holds a second-to-die policy.

What are the advantages of a wealth replacement trust?

A wealth replacement trust has the following advantages:

- The assets in the trust are exempt from estate tax.

- It provides asset protection against divorce concerns for beneficiaries.
- It provides asset protection against creditor and liability issues of beneficiaries.
- The trust assets can be distributed to the beneficiaries the way the maker wants.
- Assets of the trust can be used for beneficiaries' maintenance, support, health, and education needs.
- Assets of the trust can be transferred to future generations.
- The trust can hold certain types of assets in addition to life insurance.
- The trust can last through the lifetime of the youngest beneficiary plus 21 years, in some instances lasting between 80 and 100 years from the date of death of the maker.
- Cash in the wealth replacement trust can be used to purchase assets from an estate, providing liquidity to pay estate taxes.
- The trust can be created by just one trust maker, making it possible for the other spouse to be a beneficiary.

What are the typical funding options for a wealth replacement trust?

There are few restrictions on the types of assets that can be given to or owned by a wealth replacement trust. Some of the options include mutual funds, stocks and bonds, real estate, life insurance, and business interests.

A wealth replacement trust is an irrevocable trust that is funded by gifts. The gifts can be annual exclusion gifts as long as the trust contains demand-right powers. The gifts can also be taxable gifts. In fact, a wealth replacement trust is no more than an ILIT, enjoying all of its versatility and advantages.

Alternative Life Insurance Planning

Are there methods that allow a wealthy individual to use life insurance in estate planning without making substantial gifts?

One means that is sometimes used to fund the purchase of insurance is an *intentional grantor trust (IGT).* The technique involves the sale of assets by the maker to a specific type of irrevocable trust in which the maker is responsible for the income tax on income earned by the trust.

The trustee manages the assets held by the trust to provide the highest rate of return possible, subject to his or her risk parameters.

Initially, the maker makes a small gift to the IGT, and the IGT buys other assets from the maker. The sale is evidenced by a promissory note from the IGT to the maker. The trustee pays interest back to the grantor who sold the assets for the note. The interest rate is the appropriate applicable federal rate required for the loan. All income tax on trust earnings is the responsibility of the grantor, who uses the interest paid from the trust to pay the taxes. Because of the special nature of the IGT, the maker does not have to pay any capital gain tax on the sale of the assets to the IGT, nor does he or she have to pay income taxes on the interest paid from the IGT to the maker pursuant to the note.

The investment earnings in the IGT in excess of the interest paid are retained in the trust to pay life insurance premiums. In this way, the trust can hold life insurance on the maker's life without the need for regular gifts from the maker.

Consult with your financial and estate planning team. They can help you develop a plan using this important technique.

chapter 8

Disability and Health Needs

DISABILITY INSURANCE

What is disability insurance?

Disability insurance is insurance that provides an income to an individual if he or she becomes disabled. The disability income paid is based on the amount of premium that the insured wishes to pay and the amount of income the insurance company will provide for that premium amount on the basis of the insured's age, occupation, and health status. Disability income policies replace only a portion of an individual's current income.

What are the basic purposes of disability income insurance?

The purpose of disability income insurance is to replace a percentage or portion of lost income that is considered "earned income." If a proposed insured is independently wealthy or has substantial unearned income, the insurance company will typically not be able to offer disability coverage.

How important is disability income insurance?

Most financial experts agree that disability coverage is not only important but essential. Typically, an individual's ability to create income is his or her most valuable asset. Without the ability to create income, a person could lose everything he or she worked to build.

During a person's working years, the odds of becoming disabled are significantly higher than the odds of dying prematurely. Statistics show that a 35-year-old male has a greater than 50 percent chance of being disabled for at least 90 days before age 65. Of those disabled, some will remain so for years, if not for life. Most people are ill-prepared to financially survive a short-term disability of even 6 months.

When shopping for disability insurance, what are the key points I should look for to make sure I have complete protection?

Some of the key points in a disability insurance contract are:

- Dollar amount of benefits
- Premium guarantees
- Length of time benefits will be paid
- Waiting period before benefits will be paid
- Definition of disability
- Policy exclusions

Types of Disability Coverage

What are the differences between group and individual disability insurance policies?

Group disability insurance policies are purchased and owned by an employer. *Private* disability insurance is individually owned. Group disability is typically inflexible, providing all employees with the same type of coverage. Benefit amounts are often too low relative to the actual income the employees earn. Any benefits received from a group disability plan are subject to income tax and may be reduced by any benefits received from other sources, such as Social Security or workers compensation.

Individual disability insurance can be tailored to better fit the needs of the insured. Benefits received from an individual disability policy are tax-free.

What premium guarantees are available?

There are two major categories of premium guarantees:

- *Guaranteed-renewable policy:* Premiums can be increased, but the policy can never be terminated, except for nonpayment of premiums. Premiums may be changed by class only and may be subject to approval by the appropriate regulatory agency. "Class-only changes" means that everyone in a particular coverage class will receive a premium increase, not just select policyholders.

- *Noncancelable policy:* Premiums are guaranteed never to increase.

Why is the definition of "disability" important in a disability insurance policy?

It is extremely important because the definition of "disability" is the standard that an insurance company uses to determine whether or not the insured is eligible for benefits. Over the past few years, disability policies have become much more stringent in their definitions. Some policies will pay a benefit only if the insured is unable to work at all. Others will pay a benefit if the insured is unable to work in his or her occupation, even if the insured is able to work in another occupation. This definition, called "own occupation," is seen in fewer policies today.

Is it difficult to buy an own-occupation disability income policy?

If you are unable to work at your specific job or career, total disability benefits are payable under the *own-occupation* definition of disability even if you are able to work—or actually are employed—in another occupation. In the last few years, the claims for own-occupation policies have skyrocketed. In response, the premiums for this type of policy have also gone up dramatically, and many insurance carriers have stopped offering own-occupation policies altogether. Own-occupation policies are still available but at relatively high costs.

Is there an alternative to the own-occupation definition of disability?

A disability insurance policy with a *modified own-occupation* definition will pay benefits if the insured is unable to perform the duties of his or her occupation and does not wish to work in another occupation. However, if the insured chooses to work in another occupation, the insured's benefits are reduced by the amount of income he or she earns.

If I own a business, is there some type of coverage for business expenses?

A disabled business owner or professional may face continued business expenses but have inadequate business income to pay them. *Business overhead expense (BOE) insurance* is a reimbursement policy designed for just such a situation. The proceeds from a BOE policy can help keep a business or practice in operation by reimbursing normal business expenses until the insured recovers or all the total aggregate benefit amount is paid, whichever comes first.

What is disability buyout insurance?

Disability buyout insurance is designed to provide funds for the purchase of a disabled owner's interest in a corporation or partnership after an extended period of permanent and total disability. It is purchased as part of the funding for a buy-sell agreement.

What is key-person disability insurance?

A *key-person disability insurance* policy provides benefits to an employer should one of its key employees become disabled. The benefits can be used to help hire a replacement employee.

Amount and Duration of Benefits

How much disability coverage may be issued?

Unlike life insurance, where the amount purchased does not have to be closely related to the insured's income, the maximum amount of disability insurance available must be carefully calculated. The purpose of disability insurance is to replace earned income lost because of disability. To provide an incentive for the insured to return to work, full income replacement is not permitted. On the average, insurance companies will allow the insured to replace approximately 60 percent of gross income before tax. The percentage is lower for higher incomes.

How much disability coverage should I have?

A properly structured disability contract should allow you to pay your monthly expenses if you are sick or injured.

What are waiting periods under disability income coverage?

The *waiting period* or *elimination period* is the number of days you must be disabled before you become eligible for benefits under your disability income policy. The insured determines the waiting period when purchasing the policy. The longer the waiting period, the lower the premiums.

Some disability contracts refer to waiting periods, and some refer to beginning dates before the disability benefits are paid. Common waiting periods are 31, 61, 181, 366, and 821 days.

How long should my waiting period be for my individual disability contract?

Your waiting period should be the amount of time that you and your family can live comfortably without your income. If you keep 6 months' worth of emergency funds on hand, you might consider a 6-month waiting period. If you do not have cash reserves on which to live, 30 days may be appropriate.

Another consideration may be the premium. A longer waiting period is like a higher deductible for automobile or house insurance. Just as a higher deductible means a lower insurance premium, a longer waiting period results in a lower disability premium.

How long will the insurance company pay disability income benefits?

The contract may cover the insured's regular occupation for total disability during a certain number of years (e.g., 1 year or 5 years) or up to a certain age (e.g., age 65 or 70), depending on what each insurance company offers.

Payment of Disability Insurance Premiums

If the premium from my policy is paid with tax-deductible dollars, what effect does this have on the benefits I receive?

If the premium for a disability insurance policy is paid with either tax-deductible or pretax dollars (as in, e.g., a cafeteria plan), the benefit received is taxable income. Benefits from group disability insurance plans that are provided free of charge to the employee are always taxable.

How should I pay the premiums for my disability insurance?

If you are the owner of a business, you essentially have three choices:

1. Allow the business to pay the premiums and obtain the income tax deduction for the amounts it pays. Any amounts received by you as disability payments will be taxable to you as income.
2. Pay the premiums personally with after-tax dollars, or have the business pay them and treat the payment as compensation to you.

In either case, if you become disabled and receive disability income payments, they will be exempt from income taxation under current law.

3. Have both corporate-paid and personally paid policies. With this option, any disability income benefits you receive from the business-paid policy will be taxable to you but at a potentially lower tax bracket because your income may be lower as a result of your disability. The disability income benefits from the personally paid policy will not be taxable. Done correctly, you can have the best of both worlds.

Which method is best for you depends upon your individual circumstances. Some factors to consider include the amount and cost of your coverage, the tax deductions available to you now, and those that would be available to you in the event of your disability.

Many business owners feel that the likelihood of a disability is low and therefore prefer to take the income tax deduction for premiums paid. This is not an unreasonable viewpoint. However, such a decision is best made after a thoughtful analysis of the potential effects on your tax and financial situation.

Can I deduct the premiums I pay for business overhead expense coverage?

Yes. Premiums you pay for business overhead expense coverage are a tax-deductible business expense.

SOCIAL SECURITY DISABILITY BENEFITS

How much can I expect from Social Security if I become disabled?

According to government tables, the maximum disability benefit payable by Social Security is approximately $1600 per month. This amount is payable only if the recipient paid Social Security tax at the maximum level for at least 40 quarters, which is 10 years.

What is the definition of "disability" for purposes of Social Security benefits?

According to the Social Security Administration, an eligible worker must be unable to engage in any substantial gainful work that exists in the national economy. The disability must result from a medically determinable physical or mental impairment that is expected to result in death or at least 12 continuous months of disability. There is a 5-month waiting period for benefits.

How will Social Security benefits affect my individual disability insurance benefits?

Individual disability insurance benefits are payable regardless of what other benefits an insured may receive. Some individual policies have riders that guarantee to pay a set amount if Social Security denies benefits.

LONG-TERM-CARE INSURANCE

Long-Term Health Care

What is the greatest financial risk in my retirement years?

As you plan for retirement, remember that your doctor and hospital bills are not your largest financial risk. The high cost of long-term convalescent health care presents the greatest financial risk for retirees. Unfortunately, most people do not recognize this problem. According to a survey conducted by AARP, 79 percent of those expecting to need nursing home care believed incorrectly that Medicare would pay the bill. Medicare pays less than 2 percent of the nursing home costs in the country.

What is long-term care?

Long-term care is care or assistance provided to individuals who are functionally impaired. *Functional impairment* means that a person is unable to perform at least two of the six activities of daily living (ADLs) without assistance and/or needs care because of cognitive or other impairment. These activities are bathing, dressing, toileting, eating, medicating, and transferring from a chair to a bed.

According to the U.S. Congressional Report on Aging, long-term-care expenses are the number-one cause of impoverishment among retirees today.

Are there different levels of long-term care?

There are four levels of long-term care defined and provided by nursing-care providers:

- *Skilled nursing care:* Skilled nursing care demands the greatest expertise and requires that care be provided on a 24-hour basis by a physician and an RN or an LPN. Typically, skilled care is a half-step away from full hospitalization.
- *Intermediate nursing care:* Intermediate nursing care is similar to skilled nursing care except that medical attention is not required on a 24-hour basis. It is essentially nursing care with some skilled services.
- *Custodial care:* Custodial care is the most basic level of nursing care provided and the care category within which most benefit recipients fall. It is care in which the patient receives assistance in "activities of daily living." Typically providers in the custodial-care area are not necessarily licensed professionals.
- *Home care:* When medical care or therapy is required, home care is provided at the patient's home. Home care can include such personal services as preparing meals, cleaning the house, and helping the patient bathe and dress. Other home-care services include transportation, assistance with nutritional meals and the securing of goods and services, and certain psychological support systems to raise patients' spirits.

Depending on the severity of an individual's functional impairment, the first three levels of care can be made available and be appropriate at home or in an assisted-living or skilled-care facility.

What is the cost of long-term care?

The cost of long-term care varies from city to city, but the national average cost for custodial care is $125 per day. Intermediate care and skilled care are more expensive. The average cost is $38,000 per year, with an average stay of 2½ years. This makes the cost of an average stay approximately $95,000 in today's dollars.

I've heard that long-term care is something that only those over age 65 need to worry about. Is that true?

No. In fact, 40 percent of the people receiving long-term-care services are under the age of 65. Christopher Reeves is probably the most famous example. However, as people age, their chances of needing long-term-care increase: among persons 65 to 69 years old, 10 percent are receiving long-term care; among those 75 to 79, 20 percent; and among those 85 to 89, 40 percent.

If I need long-term health care, how will the costs be paid?

There are three ways that long-term-care expenses are normally paid:

1. The vast majority of costs are paid by the patient. Most long-term-care expenses are not paid by group or personal medical insurance.
2. Medicare or Medicaid may pay some of the expenses. *Medicare* has very limited benefits for long-term care, and there are several restrictions on payments. *Medicaid* is the government program that is designed to assist persons who have almost no assets. Medicaid requires that the individual and spouse "spend down" their assets, virtually impoverishing themselves, before benefits will be paid. In addition, after death, Medicaid can and usually does seek reimbursement from the sale of the couple's home and any other remaining assets in their estate.
3. Long-term-care insurance can be purchased to cover the costs up to the limits of the coverage. When all is considered, long-term-care insurance usually is an excellent choice.

Medicare and Medicaid

Will Medicare pay part of my nursing home expense?

Medicare is the federal health insurance program for persons age 65 and older. Medicare could potentially pick up part of the cost of a nursing home stay if you meet the eligibility requirements. To qualify, you have to have been hospitalized for at least 3 days before entering a nursing home, you must require skilled nursing care or rehabilitation services under a doctor's care, and you must have the potential for improvement. You must stay in a Medicare-certified skilled-care nursing facility, and the facility's review committee must approve your admission.

Once you qualify for Medicare, it pays 100 percent of all charges for the first 20 days. For days 21 to 100, you copay $97 per day (indexed annually for inflation) and Medicare pays the balance. After day 100, you must pay all expenses. The 100-day coverage is the lifetime maximum number of days that Medicare will cover.

Does Medicare provide any home health care assistance?

Medicare does cover some home health care but only for skilled nursing care. In order to qualify for home health care, the patient must meet Medicare's definition of "homebound." The care must be provided by a Medicare-certified home health agency. In addition, Medicare covers only intermittent visits, and the total number of visits is limited. The number of visits allowed varies by the patient's condition, but the average is twenty-eight visits.

How do I qualify for Medicaid so that it pays my long-term-care expenses?

In order to qualify for Medicaid, you must first use up almost all your savings and assets. This can obviously have a major financial impact on a person, especially if anyone else is financially dependent on the Medicaid recipient.

In the past, people have "spent down" their assets or transferred them to family members in order to qualify. However, Medicaid has instituted a 36-month *look-back period* to determine how the assets have been spent. The look-back period is increased to 60 months if trusts were used to transfer assets, and many states are lobbying for longer periods. Furthermore, one must be destitute for many months after all the assets have been spent down before benefits begin.

The qualifications for Medicaid eligibility and planning for Medicaid are very complex subjects and the eligibility rules vary considerably among the states. If you believe that you may need Medicaid in the future, you should consult with an attorney who specializes in elder law planning.

What does the phrase "estate recovery" generally mean when referring to long-term care?

If a patient who has received Medicaid benefits dies, Medicaid may institute the *estate recovery* process, in which it seeks to recover from the patient's estate money that Medicaid paid for the patient's long-term care. This can even apply to assets in the patient's living trust.

Long-Term-Care Insurance Policies

What is long-term-care insurance?

Long-term-care insurance protects an individual if he or she enters a nursing home or needs special services at home. The key points you should look for in a long-term-care policy are:

- *Daily benefit amount:* Most long-term-care policies provide a daily benefit amount, which the applicant selects at the time he or she makes the application. Daily benefit amounts can be from $50 to

$500 per day, in $10 increments. Most policies pay 100 percent of long-term-care needs up to the daily benefit amount. In addition, most policies also allow benefits not used on one day to be carried forward to future days.

- *Benefit period:* At the time of application, the insured also selects a benefit period, which determines the total value of the policy. Benefit periods can be a specific number of years, such as 2, 3, or 5 years, or unlimited periods.
- *Elimination period:* The elimination period is the number of days of long-term-care services that the patient agrees to pay for before the policy begins paying. The applicant usually can choose elimination periods from 20 to 100 days. As the elimination period increases in length, the premiums for the policy decrease.

Where can I get good, unbiased information about long-term-care insurance?

Some of the best information for evaluating long-term-care insurance is in "A Shopper's Guide to Long-Term-Care Insurance," published by the National Association of Insurance Commissioners (NAIC). This booklet can be obtained from a long-term-care professional advisor, or it can be ordered directly from the NAIC (120 W. 12th Street, Suite 1100, Kansas City, MO 64105-1925).

Insurance professionals are required to provide this booklet to individuals before they purchase long-term-care insurance. It includes several worksheets, as well as the names and addresses of each state's Insurance Department and Agency on Aging.

What are some good reasons for purchasing long-term-care insurance?

Long-term care insurance has the following advantages:

- It preserves the assets you may need later in life.
- It permits you to be covered for expenses during the 36-month look-back period when qualifying for Medicaid.
- It helps you or you and your spouse preserve your independence.
- It reduces the financial and emotional burdens on your family.
- It is easier to budget premiums than it is to budget nursing home bills.
- It allows you to choose where you want to stay rather than have the government choose for you. (Only about 12 percent of the

nursing homes accept Medicaid, and they are not necessarily the best available.)
- It provides peace of mind and eases worry regarding future health needs.

These advantages sound good, yet some people do not purchase long-term-care insurance. What are their reasons?

The most common reasons for not purchasing long-term-care insurance are the following:

- The person is uninsurable.
- The premium cost may be unaffordable.
- There are few assets to protect.
- The person is convinced that his or her family will be physically and financially able to provide care.
- The person does not mind becoming, in effect, a ward of the state.
- The person feels that the premiums paid will be "lost" if he or she never has to use the policy to pay for nursing care.

What basic factors should I consider when thinking about the purchase of long-term-care insurance?

When applying for long-term-care insurance, you should understand that it is designed to provide funds to help you pay long-term-care expenses, thereby protecting your assets. You need to know your financial situation. Generally, long-term-care insurance is not for the very poor or the very wealthy, because the very poor will qualify for Medicaid and the very wealthy can self-insure without invading principal in investments.

Features of long-term-care policies

What are some of the features of the better long-term-care policies?

The better long-term-care policies include:

- Guaranteed renewability.
- Home health care, as well as nursing home care.
- Payment triggered by the policy owner's inability to perform at least two of the six basic activities of daily living.
- Coverage for Alzheimer's disease.
- Coverage throughout the United States.

In a long-term-care insurance policy, what is meant by the term "guaranteed renewable"?

When a policy is *guaranteed renewable,* as long as the premiums are paid on time, the policy cannot be canceled by the insurance company regardless of the insured's health.

For most policies, the premium is fixed at the time the policy is issued unless the policy has a consumer price index inflation rider, which causes the premium to increase each year. The insurance company cannot otherwise increase the premium on the policy unless the premiums for everyone of the same insurance class in the state are increased. Be aware, however, that because long-term care is an emerging area of insurance, companies may experience losses greater than expected, and this may very well cause all rates to be increased.

What is home health care?

Only 15 percent of long-term care occurs in a nursing home. The vast majority of services are provided either in the patient's home or in settings such as assisted-living facilities or adult day-care centers. *Assisted-living facilities* are group apartments where the tenants are provided with an array of services, such as cleaning, cooking, and health services. They are a midpoint between staying at home and entering a nursing home. *Adult day-care facilities* provide daytime activities and are useful for people who may live at home with a spouse or other relative.

With *home health care,* the individual can remain in his or her home as all the necessary services are rendered there. It is anticipated that within the next 20 years, most individuals who have the choice will choose to stay at home and receive home health care rather than go to a nursing home for care.

Should we consider adding home health care coverage to our long-term-care policies?

Absolutely. With a home health care provision, the cost of all long-term-care services rendered at your home by therapists, doctors, and other individuals (skilled or nonskilled) will be paid up to the maximum benefit amount set forth in your policy.

Many of the earlier long-term-care policies were written to cover only in-patient care, usually in a nursing home. As our population ages and our medical technology continues to improve, we are likely to have increased demands for long-term health care. More and more services are available at home, and most patients would prefer to stay in their own surroundings. It is therefore much more likely that you will utilize coverage for home health care than for in-patient care.

If you have an existing long-term policy that does not cover home health care, you should investigate adding this coverage to your policy or buying a new policy that includes home health care.

What are the six basic activities of daily living that determine whether payments are triggered under long-term-care insurance?

The six basic *activities of daily living (ADLs)* are bathing, dressing, toileting, eating, medicating, and transferring from a chair to a bed. The inability to perform at least two of these generally will trigger long-term-care payments.

Is Alzheimer's disease covered under most long-term-care policies?

Alzheimer's disease is considered a "cognitive impairment," and the better long-term-care policies cover cognitive impairment.

Amount and costs of coverage

How should my husband and I determine the proper amount and duration of coverage when purchasing long-term care insurance?

A sampling of the costs for long-term care in your particular geographic area will help determine the amount of daily benefit necessary to cover current costs. Your comfort level and family history should determine the benefit period (duration).

Statistically, most long-term-care patients will have care needs for fewer than 3 years. While it would be prudent to buy coverage to at least take care of the average need, you may want to compare the cost of having benefits for a duration of 5 years or even unlimited lifetime coverage. You should also consider a policy that will pay for benefits for home and community-based care that does not require you to be an in-patient in a nursing home facility.

Some states require that insurance carriers offer an inflation option that will increase benefits regularly to keep coverage in line with rising costs of care. Typically it is a 5 percent simple inflation adjustment, and an individual must sign a waiver if he or she does not want it. A compounding inflation adjustment rider is also available but is considerably more expensive.

What determines the annual price of a long-term-care policy?

As you get older, the premiums for long-term-care insurance become more expensive. The cost of a policy is also based on your health when you apply for the policy.

Health care insurance companies have detailed actuarial information that allows them to calculate with a high degree of accuracy the percentage of people who will need some sort of care and at what ages they will need it. This information is an important element in determining premiums.

The methods that insurance companies use to determine their premiums are not complicated. If the average age of persons entering a nursing home is 72 and an individual wants to purchase coverage when he or she is 69, there is potentially only a 3-year period for the insurance company to collect its money. Therefore, the company will charge a higher rate.

The benefit amount selected, the benefit period, the elimination period, and any inflation-offset option also affect the premium amount.

When looking at the premium for long-term-care coverage, you need to plan ahead: the annual fixed-premium cost at age 45 is approximately 20 percent of the cost for the same policy bought at age 65, and the cost at age 65 is about 35 percent of that for the same policy bought at age 75. Therefore, the earlier coverage is obtained, the fewer dollars it will cost over a lifetime and the longer the coverage will be in force. Also, it is easier to qualify for coverage at younger ages.

What is an inflation rider? Are there any alternatives to the rider?

Perhaps the most important rider available for long-term-care is the inflation rider. Most applicants do not expect to need long-term-care immediately; thus the daily benefit amount they select may not be enough in the future if long-term-care costs increase. While a daily benefit amount of $100 per day may be sufficient today, it may not cover the costs tomorrow.

As an applicant for long-term-care coverage, you have choices. You can accept the loss of benefit due to inflation, you can purchase a higher daily benefit amount at the time of application and hope it will remain adequate, or you can request an inflation rider for the policy.

Taxation of long-term-care policies

Can I deduct the premiums I pay for my long-term-care insurance?

As of January 1, 1997, there are two types of long-term-care policies, tax-qualified and non-tax-qualified. The premiums for qualified long-term-care policies are tax-deductible if they, combined with any other deductible medical expenses, exceed 7.5 percent of the insured's adjusted gross income up to a maximum amount in any one year. The maximum amount is based on the insured's age for a taxable year and is indexed annually for inflation. Currently, the maximum ranges from $220 for people age 40 or younger to $2750 for those age 71 and older.

Are proceeds from a tax-qualified long-term-care policy subject to income tax?

If it were not for an exception in the Internal Revenue Code, the payments received by an insured from a long-term-care insurance contract would be taxable income. For tax-qualified long-term-care policies, the Internal Revenue Code exempts $190 per day (indexed annually for inflation) from being included in an insured's gross income. Your long-term-care advisor can tell you what the current exempt amount is.

What does it take for a long-term policy to be tax-qualified?

To become tax-qualified, a long-term-care policy must meet the following requirements:

- The policy must insure only qualified long-term-care services.
- The policy cannot pay or reimburse expenses that are reimbursable from Social Security programs.
- The policy must be guaranteed renewable.
- The policy cannot provide for a cash surrender value or other value that can be paid, assigned, or pledged as collateral.
- All premiums, refunds, or dividends on the policy must be used to reduce premiums or increase benefits.
- The policy must meet certain consumer protection standards.

In addition, the policy can cover only qualified long-term-care services needed by chronically ill individuals. A *chronically ill individual* is defined as someone who has been diagnosed by a licensed health practitioner as unable to perform two of the six activities of daily living without assistance from other individuals for at least 90 days and who requires substantial supervision to protect his or her health and safety.

Other options for long-term-care coverage

Are there any other ways of paying for long-term-care costs?

In addition to traditional long-term-care insurance policies, there are a number of products that can be used to pay the costs of long-term care. Two options are multibenefit policies and special long-term-care annuities.

Can you explain the differences between these products?

Traditional long-term-care policies are similar to health care policies. The policyholder pays a premium and, if needed, receives a benefit that is spelled out in the contract.

Multibenefit policies are specially designed life insurance contracts that provide additional benefits. Like life insurance, they pay a death benefit to a named beneficiary and have a cash value that can be accessed. But, as an additional feature, the policyholder can receive a percentage of the death benefit (usually 2 to 4 percent per month) for payment of long-term-care services through a nursing home, assisted-living facility, home health care, or adult day care. Specific policy provisions differ, but most policies will pay long-term-care benefits for approximately 4 years.

This type of policy may be preferred over traditional long-term-care insurance if you want your family to receive something (the remaining death benefit) after you die. Amounts received under the long-term-care portion of a multibenefit policy are exempt from taxes, as is the case with traditional long-term-care policies.

A *long-term-care annuity* is a tax-deferred fixed-investment vehicle issued by a life insurance company. This type of annuity has two separate accounts, one that provides a higher-than-market return and another that provides a lower-than-market return. The account with the higher return can be accessed only for specific long-term-care uses; the account with the lower return can be accessed for any other reason. Upon the annuity holder's death, his or her beneficiary receives the lower-valued account. This investment vehicle is most appropriate for funds earmarked specifically for long-term care.

What other alternatives are available to cover long-term-care expenses?

Other types of plans have emerged to help provide funds for long-term care. Among these plans is a *modified universal life insurance policy* with a long-term-care multiplier. This product allows the prepayment of life insurance proceeds for long-term-care needs. Often, the premium is paid in one lump sum providing both a guaranteed death benefit and cash for long-term-care expenses.

For example, assume an individual makes a lump-sum payment of $50,000 into such a modified universal life policy. The policy might provide a $125,000 death benefit, but have $250,000 available to pay long-term-care costs. The amount left to the heirs will be reduced by how much the insured uses for long-term care.

The advantage of this type of plan is the immediate multiplier that provides the insured with more money to cover long-term-care costs. Furthermore, if the insured never uses the money, he ore she has peace of mind knowing that the heirs will receive the death benefit.

There are two disadvantages of the modified life insurance program. While the modified life insurance immediately increases the dollars available for long-term care, only a finite number of dollars are available. If costs exceed that amount, there is no provision to allow a greater amount of funds. Furthermore, even though the insured's heirs will receive death proceeds at his or her death (assuming cash remains inside the policy), if the insured lives to full life expectancy or beyond, the heirs would probably receive more if the money were invested at a higher rate of return.

In spite of these small disadvantages, a modified universal life policy with a long-term-care multiplier is certainly a viable alternative for individuals who want to have access to cash value for other than nursing care and want to pass any remaining death benefits to their families.

HEALTH INSURANCE

What are catastrophic and maintenance plans for health insurance?

Catastrophic health insurance typically is a large-annual-deductible type of plan in which the insured pays a large portion of the initial costs related to an illness or an accident. The plan pays part, and eventually all, of the remaining costs up to a maximum amount.

Because of the growing costs of health care, most professionals suggest that the maximum amount payable by health plans be at least $2 million. In addition, the policy chosen should not have numerous exclusions. As always, it is wise to seek expert advice.

Maintenance plans are growing in popularity because of the escalating health care costs. Unlike catastrophic plans, maintenance plans cover routine care, such as physicals and immunizations.

Maintenance plans can take the form of a health maintenance organization (HMO). An HMO typically covers all medical costs as long as the insured uses his or her primary-care physician. A plan is not likely to cover the use of another physician, other than one seen in an emergency or one referred by your primary physician.

Point-of-service plans are similar to HMOs except that the insured can see a physician other than his or her primary physician without a referral or an emergency. Visiting another physician will trigger some deductible, and the insured will be responsible for some part of the expense as a percentage of the actual costs.

A preferred-plan organization (PPO) is another type of plan that provides for maintenance benefits. A PPO requires that the insured use physicians in a specified network. Part of the physician's office charge is then borne by the insured, as well as some portion of other expenses. If the insured goes to a physician or any other provider outside the network, the plan pays substantially less benefits than it does if the insured stays in the network.

What is the right deductible for me?

Which deductible to choose varies on your general health and your ability to pay for a lower deductible amount. Also, your deductible may need to be adjusted on the basis of what the plan covers. The plan may require that you pay a large part of incurred expenses in spite of the deductible.

It is wise to shop for the plan that best fits the budget and needs of you and your family. A financial advisor can help you determine what is best for your particular situation.

How can I find out how financially stable a health insurance company is?

A number of rating companies and some nonprofit organizations evaluate the financial strength of health insurance companies. You should look for ratings from A. M. Best, Standard and Poor's, and Duff and Phelps. You can call your state insurance commissioner's office and request information regarding health insurance companies that are licensed in your state. Finally, most insurance agents will gladly furnish you with information about various health insurance companies.

How can I self-insure my medical needs?

Self-insuring for any type of risk, including health, is a matter of preference and the ability to tolerate the potential expense. Such a decision should not be entered into lightly. You should always maintain an emergency fund when self-insuring.

At a minimum, you should consider some type of catastrophic coverage with a high deductible. The cost would be far less than that of a maintenance plan, and the coverage would be available if a totally unexpected and expensive health issue arose.

If you do self-insure, you should have a total financial plan and review it annually. In this way, you and your professional advisors can evaluate any changes in your financial status or personal life that may necessitate a change in your self-insurance strategy.

Should I self-insure my company's health insurance?

The benefits of self-insuring come from the ability to design a plan specifically tailored to your needs and objectives. In addition, state premium taxes, which are payable on all premiums, are not payable on claims paid directly.

Stop-loss insurance can be obtained which protects your company from large claims or total claims above a certain point. The claims level, beyond which you purchase stop-loss insurance, would typically depend upon your company size and its capacity to withstand higher-than-expected claims.

When evaluating a self-insured medical plan, take into account that the expected claims for the first year of operation will not be truly representative of an actual year. This is because claims are not actually paid out until some time after they are incurred. It could easily be 2 to 3 months before a normal monthly flow of claims begins, and the delay gives a potentially false sense of savings.

If you should decide to change from a self-insured plan, you will have continued-claim expenses after termination of the plan. Thus, you must be prepared to pay full premiums on the new plan as well as ongoing claims from the previous plan. If you decide to opt out of a partially self-insured plan because of higher-than-expected costs, you might have difficulty finding a stop-loss insurance company that is willing to accept your group at favorable rates.

Generally, a group of 250 employees is the starting point in considering a self-insured plan, although in recent years groups as small as 50 employees have taken this route.

PART FOUR

Retirement and Education Planning

Retirement planning today is more important than ever before. People are living longer and enjoying healthier lives. The fastest-growing segment of the U.S. population is people over 85. Many retirees will spend more time in retirement than they did in their working years. The critical question for many is, "Will I outlive my income?" Therefore, it is essential to forecast income and investments in financial planning. In the past, approximately 70 percent of one's earned income was sufficient for retirement income planning. Not today. Most financial planners suggest planning for 80 to 85 percent of current income for retirement income.

For the most part, Social Security is viewed as a possibility, not a probability. Even if Social Security will be available, it is likely that full benefits will begin at a later age and be a smaller part of the income necessary for a comfortable retirement. Other government programs may or may not be effective in the future. There is no consensus in Congress as to the direction of Medicaid and Medicare. No one knows what funding either of these programs will receive. There is a great deal of complexity in the area of retirement planning. Congress has created a tangled knot of qualified plans, IRAs, and other special plans. They are fraught with confusing rules as to their creation, operation, and disposition.

The clients of our contributing authors are obviously experiencing this retirement uncertainty and the necessity to understand accumulating and investing for retirement, because the bulk of the questions we received from our contributing authors pertain to retirement issues. The topics range from setting retirement goals to the proper disposition of retirement plan proceeds after death. The answers provided by our contributors will give you the broad scope necessary to begin to understand how to untangle the retirement plan knot. Part Four discusses and analyzes the complex rules governing contributions to and withdrawals from IRAs, qualified plans, and nonqualified plans, as well as presenting some very sophisticated planning strategies. All of us are faced with these important issues whether we are young or old, in the planning stage or already retired, or have a great deal of money or a modest estate.

Chapter 9 discusses setting retirement goals and determining how much retirement income you will need and where it can come from. This chapter also explains the effects of inflation and taxes on retirement income.

Chapter 10 presents all the ways to accumulate retirement planning funds in tax-deferred IRAs and employer-sponsored plans.

Perhaps the most complex rules pertain to distributions, or withdrawals, from IRAs and employer-sponsored retirement plans. Our contributors have done an excellent job, in Chapter 11, of explaining these rules in a way we can all understand. They have also included some very sophisticated strategies for "stretching out" IRA accumulations and distributions to later generations.

The final aspect of saving for retirement is how to integrate estate tax planning with retirement planning. For most people, retirement funds will constitute the largest asset in their estates, so it is critical that individuals plan for the disposition of those funds after their deaths to their loved ones in the most tax-efficient method possible. The last part of Chapter 11 provides relevant estate planning considerations for readers.

Of particular interest to parents, grandparents, and others who support the education of those for whom they care are the questions and answers about paying for education expenses. Given the cost of higher education and the growing interest in private schools for lower, middle, and high school students, finding money for education and retirement is often difficult. We included planning for education in Chapter 12 in recognition of its importance in fully planning for retirement. Neither saving for retirement nor saving for education has to be sacrificed one for the other if proper planning is implemented.

Because of the complex nature of retirement planning and the myriad of rules governing the variety of plans available, we have repeated some of the rules in a number of different ways. We find that even if the same rules apply to different kinds of plans, they are easier to fathom when put in context with a particular kind of planning.

We encourage you to read the questions and answers that are relevant to you. You will find that for virtually every area of retirement and education planning, Part Four has vital information that will help you better plan for your retirement.

chapter 9

Setting Retirement Goals

IMPORTANCE OF RETIREMENT PLANNING

What do the facts tell us about the reality of retirement?

According to the Social Security Administration, 38 percent of people over age 65 are kept out of poverty by their Social Security benefits. Overall, 14 percent of those over 65 live below the poverty line even with their Social Security benefits. Without Social Security, some 52 percent of people age 65 and older would now be living below the poverty line.

Why is retirement planning important?

Most Americans identify retirement as a high-priority goal. With few exceptions, they look forward to the day when they can put aside the demands of the workplace and pursue the leisure, travel, and personal interests they now cram into weekends and short vacations. As they grow older, most speak clearly of their wish to maintain financial independence and of their desire to avoid becoming a burden to relatives or to society.

Why do I need to plan for retirement?

According to most financial experts, less than 5 percent of all Americans retire at age 65 with sufficient assets to provide them with a comfortable retirement. Upon retirement, most retirees are forced to reduce their standard of living and live "check to check." Proper planning for retirement can solve these problems.

Will I ever be able to retire?

Although a secure retirement is a dream of almost every American, most fear that they will not have enough money to live a comfortable retirement.

The best time to start planning your retirement is now, no matter what your age. Your choice is to spend today and not worry about tomorrow or to save today to take care of tomorrow. No one will plan your retirement for you; you must take the lead. Every year you put off planning is a year closer to your retirement and the consequences that will result from not planning.

Why should I start planning for my retirement now?

You should start immediately for two reasons:

1. The younger you are, the more time you have to save for retirement and the more time your money has to compound.
2. By starting early, you develop a habit of saving regularly, which most Americans do poorly.

Can you give me an example of how saving early for retirement will affect my savings?

If at age 20 you start investing $2000 at the beginning of every year for 10 years ($20,000 total investment) and assume a 10 percent rate of return, your account will be worth $35,062 at the end of the 10 years. If you never make another investment after the 10 years, 35 years later, when you are 65, your account will be worth $985,337. On the other hand, if you are a typical procrastinator and wait until age 30 to begin saving and then save $2000 at 10 percent for 35 years ($70,000 total investment), at which time you turn 65, you will have only $596,254. This is nearly $400,000 less in your portfolio even though you invested more than three times as much.

With life expectancies continually increasing, if you retire at age 62 and live to 98, the same numbers will apply, so retirees should be reinvesting in their portfolios to combat inflation. In other words, a 62-year-old who saves $2000 per year for 10 years, as in our example, will have nearly $400,000 more than a procrastinator who starts saving at age 72.

How can I effectively plan for the future when I've done a relatively lousy job planning up to now?

Earnest Hemingway said: "Now is no time to think of what you do not have, but rather think of what you can do with what there is." Many people tend to dwell on the past and what they didn't do.

Statistics show that the greatest regret of senior citizens is that they did not plan earlier for retirement. Regardless of whether you are already retired or not yet retired, don't dwell on the past; instead, focus on what you can do now with what you have to improve your financial future.

I hear many financial advisors comment on the tax advantages of retirement plans, yet I hear other practitioners refer to such plans as the worst assets one can own. Who is right?

Retirement plans are great investment vehicles that offer significant tax advantages for accumulating assets. Funds are set aside on a tax-deductible basis and accumulate tax-deferred.

From an estate planning perspective, IRA and retirement plan assets are some of the most difficult assets for which to plan. At death, the beneficiaries have to pay income taxes and may have to pay estate taxes; sometimes they may be left with just 20 to 25 percent of the original value of a plan account. If retirement proceeds are subject to the 55 percent generation-skipping penalty tax, the result is even worse.

Despite the adverse income and estate results, it is important to keep retirement plans in perspective. Original contributions to traditional IRAs and qualified retirement plans are tax-deductible. All the investment growth takes place on a tax-deferred basis. These two features make retirement plans great investment vehicles, even though without effective planning as much as 75 percent (or more) of the assets could be gobbled up by taxes. Setting aside money in a retirement plan is clearly advisable, although some additional strategies should be incorporated into the overall plan.

FACTORS TO CONSIDER IN RETIREMENT PLANNING

I know retirement planning is important. What are some of the things I should keep in mind?

Here are nine ways to help prepare for retirement:

1. Know your retirement needs.
2. Get periodic reports of your Social Security earnings.
3. Learn about your employer's retirement plan and contribute the maximum.
4. Put dollars away in other plans, such as IRAs.
5. Don't touch your retirement assets; the longer your time horizon, the greater the effects of compounding.
6. Set financial goals and stick with them; write them down and look at them every day.
7. Pay only your fair share in taxes.
8. Never spend beyond your means.
9. Never have credit card debt or any debt on which the interest is not deductible.

What factors should I consider when establishing my plans for retirement?

You should consider the following seven factors as you are preparing your retirement plans:

1. Your current income, and how much you can save
2. Your estimated income needs for retirement
3. Your sources of income during retirement
4. Your options for accumulating retirement funds using traditional, non-tax-deferred methods
5. Your options for accumulating retirement funds using tax-deferred arrangements
6. Your options for plan distributions from your existing retirement plans
7. Investment planning strategies after you are retired

I've already gone through the retirement planning process. What should I do to make sure my plan stays current?

You should review your plan at least annually with your advisors. If you have not done this, ask yourself the questions listed below. If you answer no to any of them, you need to see a financial advisor who can help you turn "no" answers into "yes" answers.

- Do I know how much I need, for how long, and how inflation and taxes will affect my planning?
- Has anyone advised me in the past 2 years as to how I can cut my taxes?

- Have I had a personalized report prepared to show my long-term-care insurance options and costs?
- Do I know what my portfolio's annualized rate of return has been for the past few years?
- Have I had an asset allocation strategy analysis completed on my portfolio to be certain I am maximizing my potential returns and reducing risk?
- Do I know if the fund managers in my portfolio have been above-average or below-average?
- Have I had an independent advisor give me a second opinion on my portfolio recently?
- Have I reduced estate taxes to a minimum and provided appropriately for my family and charities?
- Do I fully understand the minimum distribution rules for distributions from my qualified plan or IRA?

I'm already retired. What issues should I be looking at?

Retirement planning does not stop after you retire. There are a number of issues that you should periodically review to ensure a comfortable retirement experience:

- *Retirement period time horizon:* Because your retirement time horizon could be lengthy, you should consider whether taking a greater risk for greater return is necessary to keep pace with inflation.
- *Pattern of using investments:* Ongoing investment advice and planning for the availability of funds when needed are critical during retirement. Invested assets continue to grow in the earlier years, and the initial capital is typically not invaded until the end of the projected retirement period.
- *Mix of taxable and tax-deferred investments:* The interplay of investments inside and outside tax-deferred settings poses complex investment planning issues. Investments within tax-deferred vehicles are eventually taxed at ordinary rates, even if some of the gain is from appreciation. Investments outside tax-deferred vehicles give rise to currently taxable income, both ordinary and capital gain. There is little deferred taxation. Retirees live on spendable after-tax dollars, so the timing of sales and distributions is crucial for maximizing tax efficiencies.
- *Real-life results versus assumptions:* Using "what-if" scenarios is fine, but they may obscure the fact that projections of what might be rarely match the reality of what really happens. Monitoring the

plan at least annually remains important so that you can make adjustments.

- *Uncertainty of date of death:* The retiree who plans for a lengthy retirement period may die prematurely. Thus, every retirement plan needs to take into account projected changes in estate size over time and the effect of unexpected death.

Current Income: How Much Can You Save?

What are some strategies for accumulating investment funds for retirement?

There are some relatively simple ways to accumulate retirement funds. Here are four basic strategies that will help you launch your retirement savings:

1. Begin investing early so that the effect of compounding adds to the size of the funds you accumulate for retirement.
2. Invest regularly in smaller increments over the years to accumulate a larger sum to reach substantial goals.
3. Reduce taxes and other expenses on the accumulating investments because they reduce the net amount that is left to compound and thus decrease returns.
4. Allocate assets appropriately during both preretirement and retirement for the appropriate risk-return balance.

Are there ways to increase the amount of money I can save for retirement?

That depends. If you are an employee and on a relatively fixed income, it is difficult to save more without affecting your lifestyle. However, if your employer has a retirement plan, you should take full advantage of whatever plan is available.

If you are a business owner or a high-level executive, you should consider restructuring your qualified retirement plan to increase contributions and establishing some form of nonqualified plan.

The advantage of a qualified retirement plan is that, in effect, you get an interest-free loan from the federal government amounting to the income taxes you would have paid on the contribution. For example, if you have $1000 of additional income and pay $400 in income tax, you have $600 to invest. When you invest the $600, the earnings on the investment will be taxed as ordinary income or long-term capital gain. If you take the same $1000 and contribute it to a qualified retirement plan, you have a full $1000 to invest and the money grows tax-free until you take it out.

If you are a business owner and are considering a qualified plan, it may be that the cost of employee contributions and annual administrative costs do not make the plan attractive for you personally. If that is the case, a nonqualified retirement plan could prove to be more effective.

Effects of compounding

What is the most important factor in accumulating a retirement nest egg?

Compound interest on your regular savings is the most important factor in accumulating a retirement nest egg. This is because compound interest literally works every day, 7 days a week, 365 days a year.

Unfortunately, too many of us do not allow compound interest to work for us because we save money for the purpose of spending it, typically on depreciating assets, such as cars, boats, and toys. If we leave investments in place over time, the principal earns interest, the interest earns interest, and, for tax-deferred investments, the tax savings earn interest. This is called *triple compounding.*

Can you give me an example of compound interest at work?

Who was the most famous American to use compound interest over many generations? One of our founding fathers—Benjamin Franklin. While many Americans seem to have a difficult time planning for even 5 years in the future, Mr. Franklin did not. He invested $2000 in two trusts in 1790, the year he died. Ben specified that the trusts were to mature 200 years later, in 1990. Who do you think the beneficiaries of these trusts were? At maturity, the trust funds were given to the cities of Boston and Philadelphia for the purpose of funding apprenticeships in the printing business!

If Ben's trusts earned only *simple* interest, let's say 7 percent, less 30 percent income tax, there would have been only $21,600 after 200 years. If his beneficiaries spent the 7 percent interest each year, today they would still have Ben's original trust of only $2000.

If Ben's $2000 trust had grown at 7 percent with *compound* interest, less 30 percent for income tax, his beneficiaries would have over $28 million! That's the huge difference that compound interest makes. If

Ben's $2000 trust fund had not only compounded but also grew tax-deferred, his beneficiaries would have had over $1.5 billion to spend!

What's the moral of this story? Not that you can make your great-great-great-great-grandchildren financially independent by investing $2000 and specifying that no one touch it for 200 years, although that is a possibility. The primary lessons are twofold. First, seek quality investments that not only utilize compound interest but also defer or eliminate income taxes. Second, do not spend all the income and gains on your investments, as many retirees do, but keep investing at least 10 percent of your gains back into the portfolio. Otherwise, you may slowly go broke and lose your purchasing power over time because of inflation.

Reducing taxes

As I'm planning for my retirement, how can I minimize my income taxes?

Planning your investment portfolio to reduce taxes is very important in retirement planning. You should position your investments in three different bundles:

1. *After-tax dollars:* Examples of investments with after-tax dollars are stocks, mutual funds, annuities, bonds, real estate, cash, and CDs. You purchase these investments with after-tax dollars, but the interest, dividends, and capital gains will be taxed in the year that they are realized. This pot of money will give you liquidity that you may need.
2. *Before-tax dollars with tax-deferred returns:* Examples of tax-deferred, before-tax investments are 401(k) plans, IRAs, SEP plans, 403(b) tax-sheltered annuity plans, 457 plans, and employer-sponsored qualified retirement plans. Contributions are tax-deductible and grow tax-deferred. When you take distributions of these funds, they are subject to income tax at ordinary rates. If you take distributions before you reach 59½ years of age, they may be subject to a 10 percent penalty.
3. *After-tax dollars with tax-free returns:* Examples of investments purchased with after-tax dollars that generally provide tax-free returns are municipal bonds, some limited partnerships, Roth IRAs, life insurance proceeds, and the cash value of life insurance. Although you do not get a tax deduction when investing in these vehicles, the income and distributions may be tax-exempt or tax-free. In the case of municipal bonds, the income received is tax-exempt from

federal income taxes and, in some cases, is free from state and local income taxes, although capital gains on municipal bonds are fully taxable.

By investing in all three of these bundles, you may be in a position to control how much tax you pay on investment income and when you pay it. You may even be able to achieve a real income higher than your taxable income. For example, assume you are retired and want an income of $50,000. You should look at pulling income from all three sources. You may want to take $10,000 from your after-tax mutual fund, $30,000 from your deductible IRA, and $10,000 from your Roth IRA. In this situation, you will have total income of $50,000 but taxable income of only $40,000 (if certain requirements are met, income from the Roth IRA is income tax–free).

How can I lower my income taxes?

Start by reviewing your most recent federal income tax return. On page 2 of Form 1040, locate the section entitled "Other Taxes." In this section, there is a line that shows total tax. This is the amount you paid last year in federal income taxes. Also look at your state income tax return and find the amount you paid in state tax. Now, add the two amounts and divide by 12. The answer is what you paid, on average, each month last year in taxes. For most Americans, that figure is the single largest expense of the family monthly budget.

The majority of people pay more taxes than are necessary because they simply have their taxes *prepared.* Taxpayers who pay only their "fair share" have their taxes *planned.* They find professional advisors who can assist them in planning *now* for next April 15. Tax planning does not end on the fifteenth of April; it just starts over again.

It is often said that there are two systems of taxation in the United States: one for the informed and the other for the uninformed. Don't let your dollars become the IRS's dollars. Remember, taxes aren't just taxes; they are real money.

What are some of the most effective methods for reducing my income taxes?

Many people are still unaware of the many ways they can legally reduce their taxes because of recent changes in the tax laws. There are ten main changes, five of which have the greatest impact on retired persons and those retiring soon. These significant changes will help many Americans reduce their income taxes and estate taxes. Here is a summary of the ten changes:

1. Spousal IRA deductions for nonworking spouses have increased from $250 to $2000, regardless of whether the working spouse is an active participant in a company retirement plan, as long as the joint income of the spouses is under $150,000. The deductible amount is phased out between $150,000 and $160,000.
2. The new Roth IRA allows you to sacrifice all or part of the normal $2000 IRA tax deduction in order to receive all the growth tax-free later on. The maximum you can contribute to both a regular IRA and a Roth IRA is $2000 per year. Annual contributions to a Roth IRA are not deductible, but qualified distributions of principal and earnings can be made tax-free after 5 years from the first contribution *and* after the individual reaches age 59½.
3. You can convert your traditional IRA to a Roth IRA if your adjusted gross income is under $100,000 in the year of conversion and you pay the taxes on the rollover amount. The result is that all future gains grow income tax–free and, after certain criteria are met, can be withdrawn income tax–free.
4. If you are a first-time home buyer, there is no 10 percent penalty on a withdrawal up to $10,000 from Roth IRAs or traditional IRAs even if you are under age 59½. First-time home buyers are defined as those who have not owned a home for the previous 2 years.
5. More participants in company retirement plans will be eligible for IRA deductions because the income limits for deductibility are increasing. By year 2005, the phase-out limits are $50,000 to $60,000 if you are single and $70,000 to $80,000 if married.
6. New education IRAs allow you to contribute $500 maximum per child per year, with no gift tax cost to the donor. However, when the child reaches age 30, there are mandatory distributions if the funds have not been used for college costs. A 10 percent federal penalty is imposed and income taxes are due on whatever was not used. Contributions are not tax-deductible, and distributions are tax- and penalty-free only if used for educational purposes or rolled over (or transferred) to another education IRA for the benefit of a family member.
7. The "success tax" has been repealed. In the past, if you were successful enough to save over $750,000 in qualified pensions

and IRAs, there was an extra 15 percent excise tax on that amount. There is no longer any excise, or "success," tax.

8. The amount of your estate that is allowed to escape estate taxes will increase from $600,000 to $1 million between 1997 and 2006. For qualifying business owners and farmers, it increases to $1.3 million. The $10,000 annual gift you are allowed to make each year to any number of people began increasing for inflation in 1999, as did the $1 million generation-skipping transfer tax exemption.
9. The long-term capital gain tax was cut from 28 to 20 percent. However, if you are in the 15 percent tax bracket, the new effective capital gain tax rate is only 10 percent. After year 2000, for assets held at least 5 years, the respective rates decrease to 18 and 8 percent.
10. If you are living in a home you have lived in for 2 out of the past 5 years, you can shelter from taxes up to $250,000 of capital gain if you are single and up to $500,000 of capital gain if you are married.

How can I find out if I'm paying too much income tax?

A qualified tax planner can review your last few years' tax returns to suggest areas in which you can reduce taxable income. The planner can also recommend tax strategies to reduce future taxes. You should find a *tax strategist,* not a tax preparer.

Retirement Needs: How Much Is Enough?

How much will I need to retire comfortably?

A common misconception is that people will need substantially less income in retirement than they did during their working years. Certainly, some expenses lessen or disappear after retirement. However, they are often replaced by others. For example, while clothing costs, education for children, and house payments may decrease, costs of medical care, helping children with housing, education for grandchildren, and travel and other leisure activities are likely to increase.

There are various rules of thumb for determining retirement income. The range that most often appears is 70 to 80 percent of preretirement income, although some planners feel that even this may be low. Very few people ever complain about having too much income, but many are concerned about having too little.

Effects of inflation

What impact does inflation have on retirement needs?

Inflation has a significant impact on retirement needs. Even with very benign inflation, such as we have enjoyed over the past few years, a dollar buys less with the passage of time. In fact, according to the U.S. Bureau of Labor Statistics, the purchasing power of $1 was $0.21 in 1998 compared to $1 in 1967. With increasing life expectancies, it is reasonable to assume that retirement could last 25 to 30 years and possibly even longer. Social Security should not be counted on to provide meaningful income, even if the system is revised.

It is important that each of us save and wisely invest enough to enjoy our golden years. If we presume a well-balanced portfolio that can yield sufficient income and growth to allow us to take an income of 6 percent from principal each year, while leaving enough in the portfolio to grow and accommodate future inflation, we can calculate how much we must have in the retirement fund to provide the income we will require.

For example, assume that your current income is $50,000 per year and that you are 45 years old, expect your income to increase at the rate of 5 percent per year until you retire at age 65, and have no savings. Twenty years from now, when you are 65, 80 percent of that income will be approximately $106,132 per year. In order for that to represent 6 percent of capital, you will need approximately $1,768,867 at age 65. Since you have no savings now, to achieve that goal you will have to invest approximately $31,720 at the beginning of each year, assuming a 9 percent annual rate of return on your invested assets. In this example, we did not adjust the $106,132 for inflation, so this calculation understates the need to plan for the effect that inflation will have on your savings when you retire.

Needless to say, this is a large savings requirement, and the amount is a surprise to most people. It is too easy to underestimate the amount of money that you need in the future, so it is vitally important that you begin a savings and investment program as early as possible.

How do some economists view the effect of inflation on a retired person's income needs, especially for housing and medical care?

Some economists believe that inflation's impact is less severe on the senior population than on the younger population. They reason that the cost of housing, which is a major component of inflation, is largely paid for before retirement and that older people tend to sell their homes at higher prices rather than purchase homes at higher prices. These economists also note that Medicare benefits, like Social Security old-age benefits, are adjusted with cost-of-living increases. However, this analysis overlooks the fact that Medicare deductibles and copayment amounts increase for the Medicare participant and that there are many coverage gaps in Medicare. Thus, attention to inflation is critical in retirement planning to ensure that there are adequate funds available for all a retiree's needs.

Effects of life expectancy

What life expectancy should I assume in my retirement planning?

According to government statistics and life insurance company actuarial information, the average American retires at 63 years of age and lives almost 20 years after retirement. Unfortunately, most people tend to concern themselves with just the first 10 years of their retirement. Dr. Ken Dychtwald, author of *Population Agewave,* stated in a June 1998 speech that with advances in modern medicine, the ability to replace organs and other body parts, and the speed with which modern technology is moving, the average life expectancy in America could very well be age 99 by the year 2015.

A great fear of retirees is that they will run out of money. That is a legitimate fear. If a person retires at age 63 and lives to age 99, that's nearly 40 years of retirement, almost as long as the number of years the person worked for a living. People must plan not only for 10 years of retirement but for their second, third, or fourth decade of retirement, net of taxes and inflation. To do less is to risk running out of money and having to live on the generosity of the government and family members.

How do I calculate my income needs to address both inflation and life expectancy?

To get a ballpark figure of your nest-egg needs assuming you retired today, start with the expectation that you will need 85 percent of your current annual income. Multiply that figure by 1.03 to factor in a 3 percent inflation rate, and multiply the result by the number of years that you expect to live. The answer is an estimate of how much you will need for your anticipated number of years of retirement.

This is a very simple example and does not take into consideration the multitude of variables such as the number of years you actually have until retirement, anticipated salary increases, the effects of taxes, how much you have to invest to achieve this amount, and so on. Financial planners have sophisticated software programs that allow them to enter these and every other required variable to calculate the amount you will need to achieve your goals for retirement no matter how far in the future and how much you need to invest to achieve that amount.

Effects of taxes

Should I plan on being in a higher or lower tax bracket throughout retirement?

Income taxes were permanently instituted in 1913—only after the Supreme Court decided twice that income taxes were unconstitutional. It took the Sixteenth Amendment to the Constitution to make income taxes legal. Income tax began as a flat tax that applied only to the very wealthy. Since its inception, income tax has risen to as much as 90 percent and applies to many, if not most, of the income earners in our country. The conclusion of this short history is that there is no way to predict what the future holds in regard to income tax. As the economy and our elected representatives change, so will tax rates.

When you are planning for the future, it is always wise to use conservative assumptions. A conservative planner would assume a tax bracket that is at least as high as the individual's current tax bracket, and possibly higher, when making assumptions regarding his or her future income.

My friend says that some of his income is taxed at 51.8 percent now that he is retired. Will I be in the same bracket when I retire and collect Social Security?

You may indeed be subject to the 51.8 percent marginal tax bracket during retirement if you're collecting Social Security. Thanks to the Omnibus Budget Reconciliation Act of 1993, better known as the Clinton deficit reduction program, the top marginal tax bracket for some retirees is now 51.8 percent. Those affected are Social Security recipients who have the good fortune (or misfortune, as the tax computation that follows shows) to be subject to both the 28 percent income tax bracket and the new 85 percent inclusion rate for Social Security benefits.

Before we show how it works, you must first understand how Social Security benefits are taxed. The formula begins, as it did before the Omnibus Act, with the calculation of your modified adjusted gross income, which is your adjusted gross income plus any tax-exempt interest income you received or accrued during the taxable year. To that

TABLE 9-1 Taxation of Social Security Benefits

Combined income*	Taxable amount of Social Security benefits
	Married couple
Less than $32,000	None
$32,000 to $44,000	*Lesser* of ½ of Social Security benefit **or** ½ the difference between combined income and $32,000
$44,001 and above	*Lesser* of 85% of Social Security benefit **or** 85% of ($44,000 – combined income) + lesser of $6000 or amount taxable under old rules
	Single individual
Less than $25,000	None
$25,000 to $34,000	*Lesser* of ½ of Social Security benefit **or** ½ the difference between combined income and $25,000
$34,001 and above	*Lesser* of 85% of Social Security benefit **or** 85% of ($34,000 – combined income) + lesser of $4500 or amount taxable under old rules

*Combined income = modified adjusted income + ½ Social Security benefits; modified adjusted income = adjusted gross income + tax-exempt interest received or accrued during taxable year

sum, we add one-half of the Social Security benefits received for the year to calculate your *readjusted modified adjusted income* (referred to below as"combined income").

If the combined income of a married couple is under $32,000 (or $25,000 if single), Social Security benefits are not taxable. If combined income is between $32,000 and $44,000 (or $25,000 and $34,000 for a single person), the taxable amount of Social Security equals the lesser of one-half of Social Security benefits or one-half of the difference between combined income and $32,000 ($25,000 if single). Up until now, the new law and the old law are the same.

Here's where the fun begins. Under the new law, if the combined income of married taxpayers is over $44,000 ($34,000 if single), the taxable amount of Social Security equals the lesser of 85 percent of the Social Security benefits or the sum of 85 percent of combined income over $44,000 ($34,000 if single), plus the lesser of $6000 ($4500 if single) or the amount of Social Security taxable under the old rules. Nobody ever said the new law created tax simplification. (See Table 9-1 for a clarification of these concepts.)

Here's how we come up with the 51.8 percent bracket. In order to illustrate an increase in the marginal tax, you have to compute taxable income. Taxable income, as we all know, is net of allowable deductions and exemptions. The standard deduction, personal exemptions, and tax brackets are all adjusted annually for inflation.

Assume that in 1999 Hank and Winifred are both over 65, file jointly, use the standard deduction, have total adjusted gross income (exclusive of Social Security benefits) of $45,000, and receive $18,000 in Social Security benefits. Thus their combined income is $54,000 [45,000 + (18,000 × .5)]. This exceeds the new $44,000 threshold, so taxable Social Security equals the lesser of $15,300 (85 percent of $18,000) or the sum of $8500 [($54,000 – $44,000) × 85%] and $6000. Since $14,500 is less than $15,300, the taxable amount of their Social Security benefits equals $14,500.

That makes their final adjusted gross income $59,500 ($45,000 + $14,500). After deducting $8900 in standard deductions and $5500 in personal exemptions, their taxable income is $45,100, which puts them in the 28 percent marginal tax bracket. If Hank and Winifred's income goes up by $10 of taxable income, they will pay $2.80 in taxes on the $10 plus $2.38 in tax on the additional $8.50 of Social Security benefits that will become taxable. Combine $2.80 and $2.38 and you get $5.18, or a 51.8 percent tax on a $10 swing in taxable income. Bingo . . . a 51.8 percent marginal bracket, up to an additional $941 of other income, in this example. The tax on additional income is based on the standard tax incremental rates (28 percent, 31 percent, etc.) for each additional dollar of income.

By making changes in your investments and income, you can lower your marginal tax bracket and the resulting taxes that you pay.

It looks as if my municipal bond interest, which I thought was tax-exempt, is being taxed because of this modified adjusted income rule. Can that be?

Modified adjusted income is not the same as the adjusted gross income at the bottom of your 1040 tax return. *Modified adjusted income* is defined as adjusted gross income (not including Social Security benefits) plus 100 percent of tax-free income. You may be thinking tax-free-bond interest and Roth IRA distributions are tax-free, but they can actually cause your Social Security benefits to be taxed under the modified adjusted income rule.

How can I avoid this Social Security income tax trap?

You need to keep your combined income (modified adjusted gross income plus one-half of your Social Security benefits) under $25,000 or at least no higher than $34,000. (If you're married, filing jointly, keep it under $32,000 or at least not higher than $44,000.) If your combined income is below $25,000 ($32,000 for joint-return filers), none of your Social Security benefits are taxable. If your combined income is between $25,000 and $34,000 ($32,000 and $44,000 for joint-return filers), up to 50 percent of your Social Security benefits are taxed. If your combined income is over $34,000 ($44,000 for joint-return filers), up to 85 percent of your Social Security benefits are taxed.

If you have investment income or municipal bond income that is forcing you to pay income tax on your Social Security, you should consider tax-deferred investments. Talk to your financial planner to see if you can reposition your assets to avoid paying income tax on Social Security benefits.

I may decide to work during my retirement. Will every state tax my retirement earned income and investment income the same?

With state and local taxes on the rise, retirees should look closely at tax matters when deciding which state to live in during retirement. Specific taxation issues include:

- *Postretirement income:* Retirees who plan to work should know that state taxation of postretirement earned income varies widely. Some states treat retired seniors like everyone else, some states give retirees favored treatment on earned income, and some impose no tax at all on earned income.
- *Investment income:* Taxation of investment income shows nearly as much variation between states. Retirees in a new domicile must also watch out for unexpected municipal income taxes.
- *Retirement plan income:* Income from government, military, private pension, and other retirement plans is growing increasingly important to the survival of retired individuals. Some states exempt all such pension income from taxation, while others exempt certain types or place limits on nontaxable pension income. Some states even tax former residents on retirement plan withdrawals, creating the possibility of paying income tax in two states. Some states follow federal tax formulas for taxation of Social Security benefits,

others have their own formulas, and some do not tax benefits at all.

- *Sales and property taxes:* Retirees must also consider sales and property taxes. Again, some states offer property tax advantages to retired seniors, while others provide homestead exemptions. Retirees should consider sales taxes when estimating their retirement budget for such items as clothing, household goods, food, and drugs.
- *Estate taxes:* It is important not to overlook the effect of estate taxes upon the surviving spouse. Some states do not provide an unlimited marital deduction. Property ownership laws must also be examined in this area when considering the distribution of possessions upon death.

Changes in these laws must be monitored, as many states will attempt to make their financial environment more appealing to retirees.

What counts as earned income during retirement?

Wages earned as an employee, including bonuses, commissions, fees, vacation pay, and tips that exceed $20 or more per month, are earned income. Also, net earnings from self-employment are considered to be earned income.

Items that are not "earned" include:

- Income from investments, such as dividends on stock
- Interest from savings accounts
- Income from annuities
- Income from limited partnerships
- Rental income from real estate unless earned as a real estate dealer
- Income from Social Security, pensions, and other retirement payments
- Veterans Administration benefits
- Gifts and inheritances
- Royalties received after age 65 from patents or copyrights obtained before reaching age 65

Retirement Income: Where Will the Funds Come From?

Where will my retirement money come from?

There are three major sources of retirement income for most individuals: Social Security, retirement plans, and individual investments. These sources are commonly referred to as the "three-legged stool" because without any one of them, the retirement plan stool is likely to topple.

What is the average percentage that each source makes up of retirement income?

Social Security provides a smaller portion of most people's retirement income than one might expect. Only 27 percent of the average retiree's income comes from Social Security. Company pension plans account for another 25 percent. A major portion of retirement income, 48 percent, comes from part-time jobs, personal savings, and investments.

Social Security

What does the "social" in Social Security mean?

Social Security was established in 1936 to achieve large social goals for society—in addition to ensuring that individual workers receive a fair return on the monies they pay to it over their working years. The social goals include providing a financial supplement for lower-income workers and maintaining a guaranteed check for a lifetime. Also, Social Security was to provide an income stream to families following the death of a breadwinner.

Before Social Security, over half the elderly in the United States lived below the poverty level. Today, the rate is less than 14 percent.

Can I count on Social Security when I retire?

Probably so, but don't count on it for any great portion of your retirement income. If you are in or nearing retirement, odds are you will receive retirement benefits earlier than those who are younger than you are. When Social Security was established in 1936, most eligible retirees reaching age 62 did not have a long life span. In fact, many Americans died before ever collecting retirement benefits. Today, we are living longer, enjoying better health, and becoming a financial burden on the Social Security system.

Currently, three workers support each retiree. By the time the baby-boom generation retires, the ratio will be 2 to 1. Under current projections, the system will continue to take in more than it pays out until 2013, after which it will pay out more money in benefits than it will receive in taxes. Reforms to avoid this dangerous situation are likely, one of which is that the retirement age will be extended to take into account that we are living longer.

The wealthiest 20 percent of people age 65 and older receive a lower proportion of their income from Social Security and a higher proportion from earnings and income from a well-planned retirement investment program.

How much can I expect to receive from Social Security at my retirement?

Social Security retirement benefits are based on the amount you paid into the program via Social Security taxes during your working years. To be eligible to receive benefits, a person must have worked a minimum of 40 quarters, or 10 years, during which Social Security taxes were withheld. The maximum monthly retirement benefit in year 2000 is approximately $1500. You should request a benefits estimate from Social Security at least every 3 years.

How are my Social Security increases determined?

Social Security increases are based on average inflation rates. Inflation is calculated using the consumer price index (CPI). The CPI does not always accurately reflect the living expenses of the average retiree, so do not count on Social Security increases to stay current with your living expenses.

Is it better to take a reduced Social Security check at 62 or wait until normal retirement age and receive full benefits?

There are a number of factors to consider regarding when to take Social Security benefits. A retired worker who has met the minimum requirements can choose to receive benefits at any time between age 62 and 65 (or even later). If benefits start at age 62 (age 60 for an eligible widow or widower), they are permanently reduced by 20 percent. The early bird who decides to get the worm first gets 3 years' worth of checks—thirty-six payments—that the sleeping bird will never see. Thus, it will take some time for the total benefits of the person who waits until age 65 to catch up to those of the early collector.

For those born after 1937, normal retirement age is being extended. Normal retirement age is currently 65, but starting in 2003, the full-benefit age will gradually increase, eventually reaching 67 in 2027. Thus, the early bird will receive even more checks than the retiree who bides his or her time for full benefits.

If the early bird does not need the benefit income and chooses to invest instead of spending the checks, the investment income would partially offset the reduced yearly benefit as well as extend the catch-up period for the age-65 collector. Sounds like most people would opt to be an early bird.

There are other factors to consider, however. Working an extra 3 years will probably increase the patient retiree's benefits. This is so because more earnings will be credited toward the Social Security account. Chances are that old, low-earning years will be replaced in the benefit equation with a current high-earning year. The higher benefits will then shrink the catch-up period.

Delaying retirement benefits until age 70 will also increase the size of the benefit because of a credit provided by the Social Security Administration for such patience. Further, for those born after 1937 who choose to begin receiving benefits at age 62, the reduction-in-benefits penalty is being stiffened from 20 percent to an eventual 30 percent in 2022. The early bird is considering sleeping later.

Taxation of benefits may also enter the picture. Poor timing of Social Security and other income may result in a good portion of early benefits being subject to inclusion in income and painfully taxed. On the other hand, a smaller age-62 benefit may mean that the taxpayer will not meet the combined-income threshold for benefits inclusion.

Empirical studies generally arrive at the same conclusion: Early-bird collectors are ahead of the game for about 12 to 15 years and then are left behind by the late-bird higher-benefit collector.

It might make more sense to begin taking benefits as soon as possible regardless of the net economic benefit in the future. Who knows at 62 what your health will be like in 12 to 15 years. And, at age 62, will you enjoy the Social Security benefits more than at age 75?

I think I might have to work after retirement. What effect will this have on my Social Security benefits?

The effect depends on a number of factors, not the least of which is your age. If you are under age 65, you lose one dollar of benefit for every two dollars you earn over the exempt amount. If you are between 65 and 69, you lose one dollar of benefit for every three dollars you earn over the exempt amount. If you are 70 or over, there is no loss of benefits.

For retired workers under age 65, the exempt amount is adjusted for inflation. The exempt amount for 1999 was $9600.

For workers age 65 to 69, there is a fixed schedule of exempt amounts through the year 2002, as follows: $15,500 for 1999; $17,000 for 2000; $25,000 for 2001; and $30,000 for 2002.

Non-tax-deferred investments and savings

Are there any advantages to selling my home and using the funds to invest?

If you live in a home that has appreciated significantly over time, the 1997 Taxpayer's Relief Act could be a blessing to you. You are now allowed to sell your home and receive up to $250,000 of your gain tax-free ($500,000 for married taxpayers). Many retirees downsize their homes and use the tax-free gain to increase their investment portfolio and, as a consequence, their retirement income.

To qualify for this special law, you must have lived in your primary residence 2 of the last 5 years. There is no age limit and no requirement to purchase another home. In fact, you can shelter the gain an unlimited number of times in your lifetime, as long as you wait at least 2 years between sales.

If you own rental real estate, consider the following strategy: Sell your current home and take out your tax-free gain. Move into one of your rental homes for 2 years and then sell it, locking in the gain on this home.

If you are philanthropically inclined, another strategy is to give your rental property to a charitable remainder trust, which can sell the property to save on capital gain taxes and reinvest the proceeds to provide an additional income stream for life. You will also receive immediate tax deductions based on your age, life expectancy, and payout rate.

Upon my retirement, should I pay off my home mortgage or invest the funds in the markets?

To answer this question you must conduct two tests. The first is the "pillow test." If paying off the mortgage leaves you feeling more comfortable when your head hits the pillow at night, pay it off!

The second test is the financial test. If you believe you can earn more by investing the money, consider borrowing money, especially if you receive a tax deduction, as in the case of a home mortgage. If the investment is not earning more than the interest expenses on the mortgage, pay off the mortgage. Obviously, you must be very careful not to make risky investments and possibly lose the money.

Are there other considerations in deciding whether I should pay off my home mortgage?

While not having a mortgage is the dream of most Americans, paying it off may not be a tax-wise idea. We have all been taught to defer taxes through retirement plans and to save and invest for the future, but the biggest monthly financial obligation for most retirees is income taxes. The interest deduction on a home mortgage is the last remaining tax shelter. Maintaining a mortgage while remaining invested makes sense for people who understand the risks and rewards of such a strategy.

I'm retired and want to diversify my portfolio to create more income. However, most of my assets are in appreciated real estate and stocks and selling would create a tax problem. Any suggestions?

Yes. Let's first discuss your options. If you sell outright, you will pay capital gain tax on your profit. Depending on the asset, a tax may be assessed by both the federal and state governments. After paying the taxes and reinvesting the difference, you may find that selling an asset outright is not always the best solution.

With real estate, a tax-deferred exchange results in immediate tax relief; no capital gain tax is due. However, you remain in the real estate business, with all its attendant risk and headaches, and you have not cashed out.

Another potential problem with a tax-deferred exchange is the federal estate tax. While you may have deferred income taxes, the full value of the property will be included in your estate or that of your spouse. You may lose up to 55 percent of its value to federal estate taxes.

One way to increase income, avoid all capital gain taxes, lower income taxes, and reduce or eliminate estate taxes is to set up a charitable remainder trust (CRT). A CRT is, in a way, a partnership with one or more charities. In essence, a CRT involves a gift to a qualified charity that results in an immediate income tax deduction. For larger gifts, the deduction can be spread over the year of the gift plus 5 additional years.

Appreciated property that is given to a CRT can be subsequently sold inside the CRT without capital gain taxes. The net proceeds can then be professionally invested to produce income tailored to the donor's requirements, on the basis of a selected percentage of the value of the underlying investment portfolio. Specific investment selection is customized to the donor's asset allocation.

A CRT can be created by one donor or by husband and wife as joint donors. In a single-donor CRT, the donor receives an income for life or for a term of years. In a joint CRT, the spouses receive income for their joint lives. At the death of the last spouse, the investment portfolio passes to the charitable partner or partners.

If there are children or other heirs, a companion wealth replacement trust is generally created. It is funded with either a single-life insurance policy or a second-to-die policy. The cost of the insurance is paid, in whole or in part, from the additional cash flow and tax savings created by the CRT.

Establishing a CRT with a wealth replacement trust can create a win, win, win for the donors, the children or heirs, and the charity or charities of choice, rather than having the assets "default" to the world's largest charity, the U.S. government!

If you do nothing with your appreciated assets, your heirs will inherit them, pay the estate taxes, and be able to sell the assets with their new "stepped-up basis." If your heirs sell the property soon after your death, they will pay little, if any, capital gain tax on the sale. You may save the capital gain tax of 20 percent, but if the estate is taxable, the federal estate tax may be as high as 55 or even 60 percent.

Which non-tax-deferred investments are most appropriate to hold outside my tax-deferred retirement plan?

It is generally advantageous to hold growth assets outside a retirement plan. Growth assets do not typically create a great deal of taxable ordinary income, and the growth itself is tax-deferred until the assets are sold. Upon the sale of these assets, the long-term capital gain rates (for assets held 12 months or longer) would be no more than 20 percent and possibly as low as 10 percent. Ordinary-income tax rates are as high as 39.6 percent at the federal level, so the lower capital gain rate is very attractive.

If you should die owning growth assets in your name or as community property, your heirs would receive a stepped-up cost basis, allowing them to sell the appreciated investments without incurring any of the built-in capital gain that you had.

The income from fixed-income-type investments held outside your retirement plan is usually taxed at ordinary-income tax levels, which can be as high as 39.6 percent. Similarly, distributions from a retirement plan, no matter what type of investment was inside the plan, will eventually be taxed to you, your spouse, or your heirs at the higher ordinary-income tax levels. Municipal bonds that create tax-free income avoid ordinary-income taxation of the interest paid, but generally have little growth potential. Because the income is tax-free, municipal bonds should not be held in a retirement plan. When the interest is eventually paid out of the plan, it will be taxed as ordinary income to you.

If you are comfortable with the concept that most of your assets should be growth-type assets, it doesn't make sense to accept potentially (historically) lower yields from fixed-income-type investments just because they are inside a retirement plan. The potentially higher yields of growth assets may well go a long way in making up for the ordinary-income taxation that will occur at a later time, after you are retired. Also, if the retirement plan growth investments are actively managed (as with a stock portfolio, e.g.) or you are using a money manager who turns over the portfolio on a fairly regular basis, the tax shelter and deferrals within the retirement plan would have some advantages.

Don't worry if you are confused about all these tax ramifications. Even investment and tax professionals have reservations about giving specific recommendations in this area. To get the best answer for you, work with a financial planner who can analyze your specific information and pursue results that take into consideration all the relevant assumptions, including your asset allocation preferences.

What rate of return should I target in my portfolio for retirement planning?

You should view your portfolio rate of return just as the major financial institutions view the rate of return of their portfolios. Banks, insurance companies, and mutual funds typically make their money from the spread between what they pay out to investors and what the return is on their portfolios. For example, if a bank is paying 5 percent interest on a CD, it may be charging at least 7 percent for loans, thus making a 2 percent real return. Likewise, you should be targeting a net rate of return of at least 2 percent after taxes and inflation.

For example, the 20-year average inflation rate from 1978 through 1997 was approximately 5 percent. If you invested $100,000 at 5 percent net interest, after fees and charges, you would make $5000 in a year. However, if you were in the 28 percent tax bracket and withheld $1400 for taxes, you would net $3600. With a 5 percent inflation factor, you would have a negative rate of return of $1400.

In this example, if you are planning on meeting your retirement goals by keeping all your money at 5 percent interest, you are planning on "going broke safely." If you are not planning for inflation and taxes and are not saving consistently, you may have to work to earn money for the rest of your life.

Tax-deferred investments

Does tax deferral help everyone decrease current taxes?

No. Whether it helps depends on an individual's time horizon. There are times when tax deferral doesn't work. For instance, if you need all your investment income to maintain your standard of living, tax deferral may not be for you. For tax deferral to work in your favor, you typically need to reinvest the income from your investments, not spend it.

What are the benefits of tax-deferred investments?

Tax-deferred investing means that you invest in assets that defer income and capital gain taxes into the future. Some examples of tax-deferred investments are annuities and the cash value of life insurance. In addition, investing in municipal bonds allows tax-free investing because the interest income is not subject to federal income tax and may not be subject to state income tax either.

Tax-deferred investments are almost like interest-free loans from the government. When you do not have to pay income taxes immediately, you can invest the money that otherwise would have gone to taxes. The compounding effect of having earnings on money that the government has "lent" to you can be very powerful. That is why it is important to defer taxes as much, and as long, as possible.

What are the most popular tax-deferred investments today?

There are three tax-deferred investments that you should consider: individual stocks, life insurance, and annuities.

The appreciation of individual stocks grows tax-deferred until you sell. In the meantime, you may collect some dividend income, which is a bonus. There is generally greater risk in owning just a few individual stocks compared to investing in numerous stocks through a mutual fund. Although many mutual funds are not considered tax-efficient, some have low turnover ratios and can be largely tax-deferred as a result.

Life insurance is tax-deferred, and there are benefits to owning life insurance in retirement. Typically one would not purchase life insurance just for the tax-deferred benefits; there must be a need for the insurance itself. If there is a need, life insurance products offer some very attractive tax-deferral features, including the opportunity to access the cash value without generating any taxable income.

Annuities are a popular tax-deferral alternative. Offered by insurance companies, they are "mini retirement plans" that allow your investments to grow tax-deferred. In addition, many annuities guarantee the return of your money.

I bought a life insurance policy on my life to save money for retirement. Was that a good idea?

It wasn't a bad idea if you had a need for life insurance in the first place. In fact, variable universal life insurance can be an excellent retirement plan investment for many people for the same reasons that it is used to fund nonqualified plans (discussed in Chapter 10).

Are tax-deferred annuities a good type of investment for retirement?

Annuities have become very popular investments in recent years. The biggest advantage of an annuity is the tax-deferred buildup, since there are no immediate income taxes as interest and growth are accumulating within the annuity. Over a period of time, this can become a rather substantial benefit.

Another advantage is that an annuity can be liquidated over a long, continuous period of time and can be guaranteed for a lifetime. In addition, at death, the annuity policy passes directly to a beneficiary, outside the probate process.

Am I required to take minimum distributions after age 70½ from an annuity?

No. There is no mandatory withdrawal rule for annuities. However, there is a penalty tax of 10 percent if you take distributions from a deferred annuity before reaching age 59½. There are some exceptions to this penalty, such as taking withdrawals if you become disabled before reaching the age of 59½.

I have an annuity I don't need for retirement income, so I plan to let it grow and pass it to my children at my death. Is this a good idea?

Annuities are excellent vehicles for accumulating retirement income on a tax-deferred basis. The federal government allows tax-deferred free growth in annuities to encourage people to fund their own retirement so that they won't ultimately be a burden on society. However, if one attempts to use the additional wealth in an annuity as a bequest to the next generation, the results can be unattractive. Annuities are generally poor wealth transfer vehicles.

As with IRAs and qualified plans, annuities can be double-taxed at death. Annuities paid as death benefits are income-taxable to the beneficiaries to the extent of the gain over basis. They are also included in the decedent's estate for estate tax purposes. Therefore, in some cases, affluent people who have annuities and plan to pass them on to their children will find that after 20-plus years of growth, the net amount passing to their children is less than the annuity is worth today!

Consideration should be given to annuitizing the annuity or setting up systematic withdrawals and buying life insurance in an irrevocable life insurance trust with the cash flow thus generated. In most cases, the results of this strategy can be very favorable.

What is the best retirement planning investment?

Since every individual is unique, it is impossible to point to one retirement planning investment as the best for everyone. However, there is one strategy that offers several benefits that rank it high on the list of successful plans. It involves the direct ownership of a variable life insurance policy on the lives of one's parents.

The insurance, owned by you, could be placed on one parent (single-life) or on both your parents (second-to-die). The policy would provide for a buildup of value in a separate subaccount consisting of stocks, bonds, and money market funds. The benefits of this strategy include:

- The death proceeds will be paid to you completely free of income or estate taxes.
- The cash values in the policy grow tax-free and can be accessed on a tax-free basis at any time through withdrawals and policy loans.
- In a properly designed plan, the insurance contract has a zero-net-interest loan feature. While the insurance contract charges interest on loans from policy values, it also credits an equal amount of interest to the contract, creating a net effective rate of zero. Also, no tax will be due on either withdrawals (up to basis) or policy loans as long as the policy is in force.
- Policy cash values can be invested in various subaccounts, which you, as the policy owner, can choose to suit your risk tolerance and goals.
- Because policy cash values are tied to the market and grow inside the contract on a tax-free basis, you have an excellent hedge against

inflation and the potential for significant growth of the premium dollars.

Here is the bottom line: If your insured parents die during or before your planned retirement, the death benefit will represent a significant return on the premium dollars invested. If you are fortunate and your parents continue to live beyond the date of your planned retirement, you can access the cash buildup, including all the growth in the cash values, on a tax-advantaged basis.

A comparison between this strategy and a qualified retirement plan or IRA can be a real eye opener. Both strategies have the potential to allow your funds to grow tax-free in the securities market, but only the insurance strategy allows you to access funds on a tax-free basis—a decided advantage! Furthermore, with the insurance strategy there is no tax penalty for early withdrawal (before age 59½), and the plan becomes fully funded in the event of the premature death of your insured parent or parents.

CONSIDERATIONS FOR EARLY RETIREMENT

My employer has asked me to consider early retirement. What factors should I be concerned with?

When evaluating an early retirement offer, often referred to as an "offer you can't refuse," there are two issues you should address.

First, you must consider the emotional aspects of an early retirement decision. It is possible, in fact, probable, that you never considered retiring today. For many people, especially those in their forties and early fifties, retirement is still a hazy goal, far off in the future. They may not have given any thought to what they will do during retirement—whether they will seek other employment or any of a myriad of other questions.

The offer of early retirement can affect the emotions of those who choose to stay with the company as well. Will they have a positive attitude toward their employer and supervisor? Early retirement programs are often instituted by companies undergoing stressful and uncertain times. Staying around may seem almost as difficult as leaving. You may be unable or unwilling to make financial decisions until you confront these emotional and psychological issues.

The second issue is financial. Obviously, you have two choices: "Do

I stay, or do I go?" Under the do-I-stay question, you need to ask further: What is the financial health of the company? Should I take the money and run? What are the prospects for career promotions and pay increases? Will staying merely postpone an inevitable career change, perhaps under less advantageous circumstances when it eventually happens?

Of course, leaving is also fraught with uncertainty. If you intend to pursue another position, the job search, according to many experts, will last about 1 month for every $10,000 in compensation paid by the former employer. Many early retirees become entrepreneurs, so the prospects for a new business and the need for start-up capital must be considered.

What are some of the common benefits that employers offer in an early retirement package?

Various benefits are offered in early retirement packages, and each company differs in what it offers. You should be aware of some of the possibilities and pitfalls of an early retirement offer.

Health insurance is a major concern for many, so find out whether you will continue to be covered and for how long. Determine the nature of the continuing coverage and how much it will cost you.

Employers with defined benefit plans may be granting additional years of service or assuming early retirees are older than their actual age for purposes of computing their benefit. This is an important consideration in evaluating your offer.

Your employer may offer some additional benefits to tide you over until age 62, when you can begin to collect Social Security. You should understand the financial impact of these benefits. You should also evaluate taking Social Security at age 62 rather than deferring it.

Tax issues also come into play. Numerous special rules may apply. For example, individuals who were at least 50 on January 1, 1986, may use either 5- or 10-year forward averaging if they don't roll over their qualified plan distribution to an IRA. Those who are 55 or older when they receive their retirement plan distribution are not subject to the 10 percent penalty. If you elect to pursue the substantially equal payment exception to the 10 percent penalty, the payments must continue for 5 years or until you turn 59½, whichever is longer.

chapter 10

Saving through Retirement Plans

TAX-DEFERRED INDIVIDUAL RETIREMENT ACCOUNTS

What is an individual retirement account?

An *individual retirement account,* known as an *IRA,* is a savings plan that receives favorable tax treatment under the Internal Revenue Code. All types of IRAs allow interest, dividends, and capital gains on the assets within the IRA to grow tax-deferred during the accumulation period. There are two basic types of IRAs, the traditional IRA and the Roth IRA. The traditional IRA allows tax-deductible contributions; the Roth IRA does not.

Traditional IRAs

What are the basics of the traditional IRA?

In 1974, Congress created the individual retirement account. The IRA allowed taxpayers to place funds into a tax-deferred account that would help supplement their income after retirement. All taxpayers were allowed to have one, and all taxpayers could deduct the contributions made to these accounts. At retirement, the funds distributed were fully taxable. These accounts were simple to understand and to administer.

TABLE 10-1 Traditional IRA
AGI Limits for Deductible Contributions

Year	Single individuals	Married couples
2000	$32,000	$52,000
2001	33,000	53,000
2002	34,000	54,000
2003	40,000	60,000
2004	45,000	65,000
2005	50,000	70,000
2006	50,000	75,000
2007 & beyond	50,000	80,000

Times have changed. The original IRA has evolved into two different types: the traditional contributory IRA and the rollover IRA. Today, even the simple contributory IRA concept spans a confusing plethora of IRA accounts.

What is a traditional contributory IRA?

A *traditional contributory IRA* is an individual retirement account in which an individual can invest funds for retirement on a tax-deferred basis. Both contributions and earnings accumulate on a tax-deferred basis until withdrawn, and the withdrawals are taxed at the individual's then-current tax rate. Contributions to traditional IRAs are tax-deductible for the year the contributions are made. Nondeductible contributions are also allowed.

Contributions to traditional IRAs

How much of a tax-deductible contribution can I make each year to a traditional IRA?

If you meet the adjusted gross income (AGI) requirements shown in Table 10-1 and you are not covered by an employer-sponsored retirement plan, the maximum deductible contribution you can make each year is $2000 or 100 percent of compensation per year, whichever is less.

If I can't make a deductible contribution to a traditional IRA, can I make a nondeductible contribution?

Yes. Individuals whose AGI is above the limits are still permitted to make contributions to an IRA of up to $2000 ($4000 for a regular and a spousal IRA combined) or 100 percent of compensation, whichever is less. Although these contributions are not tax-deductible, as long as they are within the allowed contributory limits, the earnings in the account will be tax-deferred until withdrawn.

If I earn $2000 or less, how much can I contribute to an IRA?

If you earn $2000 or less in a year, you can contribute up to 100 percent of your earned income.

Once I establish a traditional IRA, do I have to contribute to it each and every year?

No. One of the advantages of an IRA is its flexibility. Individuals may contribute whenever they choose and in whatever amounts they choose during the year, or they can contribute different amounts each year, as long as the total contribution in a single year does not exceed the limit of $2000 or 100 percent of earned income.

Is it still a good idea to contribute to a traditional IRA?

In spite of some substantial changes to the traditional IRA deductibility rules over the years, IRA contributions continue to be a viable financial and retirement planning tool.

Remember, one of the greatest benefits of the traditional IRA is the tax-deferred growth your investments will enjoy inside the account. Your earnings will grow much faster when not dragged down by the weight of a current tax bill.

Can I contribute to an IRA on a tax-deductible basis if I'm covered by a plan at work?

Yes, you can, but there are limitations. If an individual's, or a jointly filing married person's, adjusted gross income is within certain ranges, he or she may contribute to a traditional IRA even if covered by a plan at work. Contributions are fully or partially deductible on the basis of AGI. Table 10-2 shows the AGI ranges for the appropriate years.

The AGI ranges for determining the deductibility of a contribution to an IRA for a person who is covered by a plan at work vary depending on the year in which the contribution is made. If a person's AGI equals or is less than the lower range, a contribution that does not exceed $2000 is fully deductible. If a person's AGI exceeds the upper range, a deductible contribution to an IRA cannot be made. Contributions are

TABLE 10-2 Traditional IRA
AGI Limits for Deductible Contributions for Participants in Employer-Sponsored Plans

	Range of AGI	
	Lower	**Upper**
	Married taxpayer filing jointly	
2000	$52,000	$ 62,000
2001	53,000	63,000
2002	54,000	64,000
2003	60,000	70,000
2004	65,000	75,000
2005	70,000	80,000
2006	75,000	85,000
2007 and after	80,000	100,000
	Single or head of household	
2000	32,000	42,000
2001	33,000	43,000
2002	34,000	44,000
2003	40,000	50,000
2004	45,000	55,000
2005 and after	50,000	60,000

*When AGI is below the lower dollar amount for the year, a full deduction is available. When AGI is above the upper dollar amount, no deduction is available.

partially deductible if a person's AGI falls within the lower and upper ranges.

How do I know if I'm covered by a retirement plan at work that would affect my IRA contribution?

Employers are required to check a box on every employee's W-2 stating whether he or she is covered by a plan. Whether you are covered by a plan that would affect your IRA contribution depends on the type of plan your employer has in place. If you are not sure, your employer can tell you.

I've heard that my contribution is "phased out" if I'm covered by an employer-sponsored plan and my AGI exceeds the lower range. What does that mean?

If your AGI exceeds the lower end of the year's range, the deduction for a contribution is phased out on a proportional basis. The lowest amount that can be deducted is $200.

For example, assume that a single person who is covered by an employer's plan has an AGI (excluding any IRA deduction) of $38,000 in the year 2000. Since $38,000 is 60 percent of the way from $32,000 to $42,000, he or she can deduct only $800 of the $2000 contribution and $1200 ($2000 × 60%) is nondeductible.

Can a spouse have a traditional IRA if that spouse doesn't work, doesn't earn any income, and isn't participating in another plan?

Yes. Even though he or she does not earn any income, a nonworking spouse can contribute up to $2000 in his or her own *spousal IRA.* The total contribution made by a working and nonworking spouse is the lesser of $4000 or the couple's combined compensation for the year, and the spouses can divide the contribution any way they choose, as long as neither account receives more than $2000.

Can my spouse deduct the contribution from a traditional IRA if I am covered by an employer-sponsored plan?

If you are covered by a plan but your spouse is not, your spouse's contribution to a traditional IRA is fully deductible up to new phase-out limits of $150,000 to $160,000 of joint income. If both of you are covered by a plan, the deductible limits are the same as shown in Table 10-2.

Is there a minimum age for establishing a traditional IRA?

No. There is no minimum age for making a traditional IRA contribution for tax purposes.

Will I still be able to contribute money to a traditional IRA if I'm working past age 70½?

No. Contributions must end at age 70½.

When do I have to make a contribution to my IRA?

You have until April 15 of the year following the year in which the contribution is deductible. As a matter of fact, you can even open an IRA as late as the April 15 tax deadline that following year.

Distribution rules for traditional IRAs

What are the general rules regarding taking distributions from my traditional IRA?

Although you may withdraw funds from your traditional IRA at any time, there are a number of rules pertaining to withdrawals:

- You have to be 59½ years of age before you can start taking money out without incurring a 10 percent penalty (there are some exceptions).
- You must start taking distributions before April 1 following the year in which you turn 70½.
- If all your contributions were deductible, you will pay income tax at ordinary rates on all your distributions no matter when you take them. If you made nondeductible contributions to your IRA, a portion of your distributions will be tax-free.

Multiple traditional IRAs

I have several IRAs. Should I keep them separate or consolidate them?

In most cases, it is better to consolidate multiple IRAs into a single, self-directed IRA. A *self-directed IRA* allows you to invest in practically anything you would like, such as stocks, bonds, mutual funds, and other types of investments.

A self-directed IRA also reduces unnecessary paperwork and keeps your financial affairs simple because you have one consolidated statement. Upon retirement, you will have to file only one minimum distribution election for this IRA, rather than several for multiple IRAs.

It is very easy to make a mistake when the number of IRAs increases. For example, when you are over the age of 70½, multiple IRAs increase the possibility of incurring the 50 percent penalty because of a failure to start taking out minimum required distributions. Also, should you pass away, your heirs will need a separate death certificate for each of your different IRAs if they are kept separate.

Are there any advantages to maintaining multiple IRAs?

In cases where the IRA owner wishes to name a nonspouse beneficiary of some or all of the IRA balance, additional control and flexibility may be realized by dividing a large IRA account into several smaller accounts. In this circumstance, separate IRAs may reduce potential tax problems and eliminate after-death confusion for distributions.

If you would like to name a charity as one of the beneficiaries of your IRA, you will want to establish a separate IRA for this purpose. If a charity is a partial beneficiary, both you and your heirs will face accelerated minimum distribution requirements.

Roth IRAs

What is a Roth IRA?

Roth IRAs have many of the same guidelines that traditional IRAs have. Earnings grow inside the Roth IRA tax-free, and you can contribute up to $2000 annually.

However, unlike the case with traditional IRAs, contributions to Roth IRAs are not tax-deductible, you are not required to take a mandatory distribution at age 70½, and anything left at your death is distributed to your heirs as tax-free income.

Another major difference between traditional and Roth IRAs is that when you withdraw money from your Roth IRA, assuming you've met all the requirements for withdrawal, you not only do not pay income tax on the contributions (you already paid tax on those) but do not pay income tax on the earnings.

Is there a penalty for early withdrawals from a Roth IRA?

A little-known fact about the Roth IRA is that it does allow for penalty-free withdrawals before age 59½. The IRS taxes withdrawals from Roth IRAs on a "first-in, first-out" basis. The first money that comes out of a Roth IRA is considered your original contribution, and after the contributions have been fully withdrawn, withdrawals are considered earnings. So you can withdraw the total amount of your contributions before you reach age 59½ without incurring an early withdrawal penalty. If you convert a traditional IRA to a Roth IRA, withdrawals of rollover contributions within 5 years will accelerate the tax liability and may cause a 10 percent penalty on the withdrawal.

I am 73. Am I too old to make Roth IRA contributions?

Not at all. You can make contributions after you reach 70½ years of age as long as you meet the other requirements for a Roth IRA.

I'm covered by a plan at work. Can I make contributions to a Roth IRA?

Yes. Provided that you are within certain income guidelines, you can make Roth IRA contributions even if you participate in an employer-sponsored retirement plan.

Contributions to Roth IRAs

How much can I contribute each year to a Roth IRA?

You may contribute up to $2000 a year to a Roth IRA (minus any contributions made to a traditional IRA for that year). Contributions to Roth IRAs are not deductible and must be in cash when made. Table 10-3 shows the AGI limits for annual contributions to a Roth IRA.

The AGI threshold for contributing to a Roth IRA is $95,000 for single individuals and $150,000 for married individuals filing a joint return. For single filers, the allowed contribution is phased out for AGI between $95,000 and $110,000. For married individuals, the allowed contribution is reduced proportionately if AGI is between $150,000 and $160,000. If married taxpayers file separately, the allowable contribution is phased out for AGI between $1 and $10,000.

My company retirement plan and level of income make my contributions to a traditional IRA nondeductible. Can I contribute to a Roth IRA?

Yes; as long as you meet the income guidelines you can contribute to a Roth IRA. In fact, the Roth IRA is a great option for individuals who have maxed-out their retirement plans at work and are unable to make deductible traditional IRA contributions.

Can both my husband and I contribute to a Roth IRA if we are both in retirement plans at work?

Yes. Both of you can contribute to a Roth IRA even though one or both of you participate in a retirement plan at work. Remember, however, that if you and your husband file a joint return and your combined AGI (adjusted gross income) is greater than $160,000, you are not allowed to contribute to a Roth IRA. You will be entitled to only a partial contribution if your combined AGI is between $150,000 and $160,000.

Each of you must establish your own Roth IRA. There is no such thing as a joint Roth IRA.

TABLE 10-3 Roth IRA
AGI Limits for Annual Contributions

AGI	Contribution
Individual	
Less than $95,000	$2000*
$95,000 to $110,000	(AGI – $95,000) ÷ 5†
Over $110,000	None
Married filing jointly	
Less than $150,000	$2000*
$150,000 to $160,000	(AGI – $150,000) ÷ 5†
Over $160,000	None

*Less any contributions you made to other IRAs that year.
†Round to nearest $200.

Are there age limits regarding who can contribute to a Roth IRA?

There are no age limits. Eligibility is based solely on the level of adjusted gross income.

How long can I continue making contributions to my Roth IRA?

You can make contributions for as long as you have earned income.

My wife and I are taking full advantage of our 401(k) plans. Should we consider using a Roth IRA for additional savings?

The Roth IRA is a good choice for additional savings above a 401(k). The tax advantages of a Roth IRA, combined with your 401(k) plans, can work to your advantage, particularly if you have a few years to go until retirement.

Unlike 401(k) contributions, which are pretax now and fully taxed at withdrawal, contributions to a Roth IRA are not currently deductible but do accumulate free of tax and are generally available without income tax at withdrawal. A Roth IRA allows you to pay tax now on a small dollar amount ($2000) and shelter the larger accumulated amount from tax later, thus providing a pocketbook from which you can tax engineer your income.

Make sure that your income levels allow you to establish a Roth IRA. If so, implement a Roth IRA for each of you.

Can I contribute to both a traditional IRA and a Roth IRA?

Yes, but the total annual IRA contribution to both cannot exceed $2000 per person.

Can I have both a Roth IRA and an education IRA?

Assuming the income limits are not exceeded, a husband and wife can each have a Roth IRA and can also contribute to an education IRA. If the child also has a Roth IRA, it is conceivable that the family could be saving $6500 a year, tax-free.

Where do I report my Roth IRA contributions?

You must report your Roth IRA contributions on Form 1040, line 19A, of your annual income tax return. Form 8606, "Nondeductible IRAs," also requires the reporting of your Roth IRA contributions. If you are not taking a distribution from the account, you are not required to file part III of Form 8606.

Distribution rules for Roth IRAs

When can I take my money out of my Roth IRA?

You may withdraw your contributions from your Roth IRA at any time, tax-free. The earnings on your Roth IRA contributions can be withdrawn tax-free and penalty-free provided that the IRA has been in effect for at least 5 years *and* one of the following applies:

- You are age 59½.
- You are deceased, and your beneficiary takes the earnings out.
- You become disabled.
- You are a "qualified first-time home buyer" using the distribution in the purchase of a primary residence.

Distributions of earnings from a Roth IRA that has been in effect for at least 5 years and are taken for any of the above reasons are known as *qualified distributions.* Qualified distributions are not includable in taxable income.

Distributions of earnings that are taken from Roth IRAs before any of the events specified above are met are deemed *nonqualified distributions.* Nonqualified distributions are taxable and potentially exposed to the 10 percent penalty.

Unlike the case with traditional IRAs, there are no requirements to begin distributions from a Roth IRA at age 70½. An individual can continue to defer tax on Roth IRA earnings for his or her entire lifetime.

Multiple Roth IRAs

How many Roth IRAs can I have?

You can have numerous IRAs, no matter what kind they are. Multiple Roth IRAs are often set up to make distributions more effective for the beneficiaries. However, remember that multiple traditional IRAs can create complexity when you must begin taking distributions, so make sure you discuss multiple traditional and/or Roth IRAs with your advisors in the overall context of your financial and estate plans.

I have a large sum of money in my Roth IRA and it's invested in one mutual fund. Can I take this money and put it into another Roth IRA and change some of the investments?

You can transfer funds directly from one Roth IRA to another without any tax consequences and change investments in the new account to meet your needs. Or you may be able to change investments within your existing Roth IRA.

Traditional IRA versus Roth IRA

Which is better: a traditional IRA or a Roth IRA?

The answer to almost all "which is better" questions is, "It depends on your particular circumstances." In deciding whether to make contributions to a traditional IRA or a Roth IRA, a taxpayer should take into account a number of factors, including:

- Eligibility to make contributions
- The number of years remaining to accumulate earnings
- The time projected to begin distributions
- Current versus future tax brackets (A taxpayer must consider whether the current deduction of contributions to a traditional IRA is more valuable than the future recovery of earnings tax-free.)
- Your estate planning goals and your heirs

I'm not married, and my AGI is just over $80,000. Which is better: a traditional IRA or a Roth IRA?

If your AGI is over $75,000 a year, a Roth IRA would probably work out better than a traditional IRA. Because your AGI exceeds the limits for a deductible contribution to a traditional IRA, you would be making a nondeductible contribution. The earnings would accumulate tax-free. When you turn 59½, you can withdraw funds but the earnings will be taxed. And you will be required to take minimum distributions at the age of 70½.

You also would be making a nondeductible contribution to a Roth IRA and the earnings also accumulate on a tax-deferred basis. However, when you turn 59½, you can withdraw not only your original contributions tax-free but also the earnings. And you would not be required to take distributions at age 70½.

You must decide how important an IRA is for investment purposes. The questions you must consider are "Do I want money to accumulate on a tax-deferred basis?" and "Is it worthwhile to have money taken out of an investment in the future tax-free?" In most cases, the answer to both questions is a resounding yes. Even though investors are told that as they get older, their tax brackets go down, there is still the need for cash. The more cash for retirement, the better. Taxes, even lower ones, reduce income, so they should be avoided if possible.

In many instances, the Roth also may offer considerable advantages over a traditional IRA in planning your estate.

Do my heirs inherit my Roth IRA investments tax-free?

When you pass away, even in the first 5 years, your beneficiaries will receive the proceeds income tax–free. The value of the Roth IRA will be part of your estate and therefore may be subject to death taxes.

Converting Traditional IRAs to Roth IRAs

What is a Roth conversion?

A *Roth conversion* is made when an individual transfers an existing traditional IRA to a Roth IRA. There is a tax consequence on the transfer. Taxes are paid according to the individual's tax bracket for the year in which the transfer was made. The IRA conversion money must be left in the Roth IRA for at least 5 years to avoid additional taxes. Thereafter, withdrawals are governed by the standard Roth IRA rules.

Must I meet AGI limitations to qualify for a Roth conversion?

All or part of a traditional IRA's assets may be converted to a Roth IRA if the owner's AGI is not greater than $100,000 in the year of the conversion. The $100,000 AGI limit is determined without regard to any amount included as a result of the conversion and is applicable to single and joint taxpayers.

The funds transferred from a traditional IRA to a Roth IRA are not subject to the 10 percent penalty tax. However, the full amount of the conversion may be subject to income taxation.

Are partial Roth conversions allowed?

Yes. You can convert any portion of your traditional IRA to a Roth IRA.

Can I convert my traditional IRA to a Roth IRA after age 70½?

Yes. You may convert to a Roth at any age. Even if withdrawals have been started, a traditional IRA can be converted as long as the owner's adjusted gross income is below $100,000. In the year of the conversion, the minimum distribution must still be taken from the traditional IRA, even if the conversion takes place before the time that the minimum distribution is made.

Are there any benefits to converting my traditional IRA to a Roth IRA?

If you convert a traditional IRA to a Roth IRA, you have to pay the tax on the amount you transfer during the year of the transfer. This may not be problematic, especially if you pay the taxes out of non-IRA assets. By paying the tax at the time of the conversion, you are effectively making a gift to your beneficiaries of the amount you are paying as income tax without owing any gift tax or using up the estate tax exemption.

There are continued benefits after your death. The beneficiaries may owe estate tax (depending on the size of the estate) but will owe no income tax on withdrawals from the Roth IRA account because you "prepaid" them.

When does it make sense to convert from a traditional IRA to a Roth IRA?

There are a number of factors to take into consideration before making the conversion decision.

First, you must determine if you have non-IRA money to pay for the taxes due on the Roth rollover. The case for conversion is much stronger if you do. If you use IRA proceeds to pay the taxes due on the conversion, it will take a long period of tax-free compounding to make up the loss.

However, if your traditional IRA is mostly made up of nondeductible contributions, without significant accumulated growth, the initial tax bite upon conversion to a Roth IRA will be minimal. In this case, it may not be as important to have other assets to pay the minimal amount of taxes due.

Roth IRA conversion may also make sense if your income tax bracket in future years will likely rise or remain the same. Many retirees do not want or need money from their traditional IRAs after age 70½, but they are forced to begin taking distributions. Since the Roth IRA does not force you to take minimum distributions after 70½, it can be more beneficial in this regard.

Also, because Roth conversion income taxes are paid up front, it will take a number of years of accumulation (depending, of course, on the rate of return of the invested assets in your Roth IRA) to reach the break-even point. Therefore, in deciding whether "to Roth or not to Roth," use the conservative approach and consider that it may be roughly 10 years (returns and time being equal on both sides) before you break even. Generally people who are many years from retirement and who are below the age of 55 will find the Roth conversion decision easier to make. However, there can be significant estate planning benefits in converting for older individuals who meet eligibility requirements.

A traditional IRA is included in your estate when you die, and the proceeds are income-taxable to the beneficiary. The value of a Roth IRA is included in your estate but is not subject to income taxation for your beneficiaries.

Finally, do the math for your particular situation. Deciding on a Roth conversion is often based on complicated issues, with many serious considerations. Most financial advisors have sophisticated software programs that allow them to factor in your particular age, tax bracket, and other variables to show you the results of a conversion. Take the time necessary to do a thorough comparison and evaluation.

I was going to convert my traditional IRA into a Roth IRA but don't have any money to pay the taxes. Should I borrow the money from the bank?

No. Do not borrow any money to pay the taxes. In fact, if you don't have the money to pay the taxes from other funds, you probably should not convert the regular IRA to a Roth.

Who is responsible for Roth conversion "tax tracking" and documentation?

Responsibility for keeping good records, not only for conversions but for traditional IRA and Roth IRA transactions, generally falls on the taxpayer.

EMPLOYER-SPONSORED QUALIFIED RETIREMENT PLANS

What is a qualified plan?

A *qualified plan* is an employer-sponsored retirement plan that allows a participant to contribute or defer current income into an appropriate retirement vehicle. A qualified plan must meet the strict guidelines of the Employee Retirement Income Security Act of 1974 (ERISA), the law that governs these types of retirement plans. To be qualified, these plans must be available, with certain minimum eligibility requirements, to all employees without discrimination.

Contributions to a qualified plan are deductible for the employer and the employee. All growth on contributions (assuming the investment selection appreciates in value) is on a tax-deferred basis.

Generally, distributions must occur after the participant reaches the age of 59½, but no later than April 15 of the year after the participant turns 70½, and distributions are taxable. Plan distributions may be made before the participant reaches the age of 59½, but they are subject to a 10 percent early-withdrawal penalty. The penalty may not be applied to early withdrawals if they are hardship-based or if the annual distributions are based on the participant's life expectancy. If the withdrawals are based on the participant's life expectancy, they must continue for at least 5 years or until the participant is 59½, whichever is longer.

Are there different types of qualified plans?

There are two major categories of qualified plans, defined contribution and defined benefit.

Defined-Contribution Plans

What is a defined-contribution plan?

In a *defined-contribution plan,* the employer contributes to a retirement plan for employees but has no obligation to provide a fixed amount when an employee retires. The amount of an employee's benefit is determined by the amounts contributed and how they grow. Although there are different formulas for determining the amount of the annual contribution that an employer can make for its employees, the amount cannot exceed $30,000 (indexed annually for inflation) per employee without triggering income tax for the employee. The Internal Revenue Code also imposes limits on the amount of the tax deduction that an employer can take for contributions to the plan.

Generally speaking, portability is a major attraction of defined-contribution plans. When an employee switches jobs, he or she has the choice of transferring his or her vested interest in the plan to the new employer's plan or starting a rollover IRA. In this manner, an employee is not starting at ground zero each time.

There are numerous versions of defined-contribution plans, including:

- Profit-sharing plans
- 401(k) cash-or-deferred arrangements
- Savings incentive match plan for employees (SIMPLE)
- Simplified employee pension (SEP) plans
- Target benefit plans
- Money purchase pension plans
- Employee stock ownership plans (ESOPs)

Profit-sharing plans

What is a profit-sharing plan?

A *profit-sharing plan* is an employer-sponsored plan to which the employer can choose to make or not make contributions each year. If the company does not make a contribution, usually because it has not had a good year, the plan will not be disqualified for failure to make a contribution.

Employer contributions are tax-deductible for the employer and are not currently taxed to the employee. Earnings accumulate on a tax-deferred basis. The employer's tax deductions are limited to 15 percent of covered payroll. Employer contributions are limited to 25 percent of an employee's compensation, not to exceed $30,000 (indexed annually for inflation) per year. Distributions are generally fully taxable to the employee.

401(k) cash-or-deferred arrangements

What is a 401(k) plan?

A *401(k) plan* is an employer-sponsored salary reduction plan that is sanctioned under Section 401(k) of the Internal Revenue Code. There are other salary reduction plans under the Internal Revenue Code, including Section 403(b) plans for employees of nonprofit organizations such as schools and hospitals and Section 457 plans for government and municipal employees, but the best-known plan is the 401(k).

Under a 401(k) plan, the employer arranges for participants to invest their own money, which represents a reduction of the salary normally paid to the participant, in different equity, fixed-income, or money market accounts. Sometimes, the employer's own stock is offered as an investment choice.

Generally speaking, a salary reduction plan lets the participant allocate money into as many investment options as he or she wants. In addition, the participant is allowed to move money from one option to another. Today, a good plan allows a participant to switch these options monthly at worst and daily at best. The participant chooses among the investment options and pays the costs of investing.

The participant does not have to pay any income taxes on salary deferred into the plan or on the earnings until he or she withdraws money from the account. When the participant withdraws funds from the account, they are treated as regular income and taxed at the participant's income tax rate.

Many corporate employers will match all or part of the employee's contribution, but the employer's contribution is often subject to a vesting period. For example, a typical formula is to match up to 6 percent of the employee's salary, with the matching amount being fully vested over a 5-year period.

Anyone who does not contribute to a 401(k) plan with a company match is turning down free money and wasting the best retirement savings opportunity available.

How much can an employee contribute to a 401(k) plan?

A 401(k) plan allows eligible employees to defer compensation or bonuses into the plan. The maximum annual amount an employee can defer to the plan is 15 percent of his or her compensation or $10,500 (indexed for inflation), whichever is less.

Can I take a loan out on my 401(k) account?

You can, but unless doing do is unavoidable, it is usually best not to. When you borrow from your 401(k) account, you are mortgaging your retirement. The typical argument for using a 401(k) loan is that the participant is paying himself or herself back the interest, but there is an opportunity cost for this. If the plan's investments are earning 11 percent and if the participant is paying back 7 percent, the participant is losing the opportunity to earn 4 percent. That may not seem like a lot, but over time the real cost of the loan can have a huge impact on retirement savings.

To understand the real impact of borrowing from your 401(k) account, let's look at a very simple example. Assume that you take a loan out for $25,000 for 5 years and you pay yourself back at a rate of 7 percent. You then allow those dollars to grow in the mutual fund (assuming an 11 percent rate of return) for the next 20 years. Your total investment time frame would be 25 years. Under these assumptions, after 25 years, the $25,000 will grow to $282,688. If you did not borrow the funds in the first 5 years and the full amount grew for 25 years at 11 percent, the value would be $339,636. This is a difference of $56,948—a whopping 25 percent more money at retirement.

Savings incentive match plans for employees

What is a savings incentive match plan for employees?

The Small Business Job Protection Act of 1996 created the *savings incentive match plan for employees,* known as the *SIMPLE.* The SIMPLE is available for any business that has 100 or fewer employees and does not maintain another qualified retirement plan. The business can be either incorporated or unincorporated.

There are two versions of the SIMPLE, a SIMPLE IRA and a SIMPLE 401(k). The general provisions of a SIMPLE IRA include:

- The employee elects to take part of his or her compensation in cash or have it contributed, or deferred, to his or her IRA.
- Mandatory employer contributions are tax-deductible to the business.
- Employer contributions are not taxable to plan participants.
- Earnings accumulate income tax–deferred.

What are the eligibility requirements of a SIMPLE?

A SIMPLE must include any employee who has earned $5000 annually in any 2 previous years, any employee expected to earn at least $5000 in the current year, employees covered by collective bargaining agreements, and any nonresident alien employees.

Contributions to SIMPLE IRAs

What are the contribution limits of a SIMPLE IRA?

The current maximum deferral allowed is up to 100 percent of income or $6000 (indexed annually for inflation), whichever is less, per participant per year.

Can I defer $6000 even if other employees do not contribute to the plan?

Yes. There are no minimum participation requirements in a SIMPLE IRA.

Do employers have to make mandatory contributions?

Yes. The employer must satisfy one of two contribution formulas. In the *elective,* or *matching, method,* the employer matches the employee's elective deferral, dollar for dollar, up to 3 percent of compensation. This method applies only if employees are also contributing to the plan. In *the nonelective method,* the employer contributes a mandatory 2 percent of compensation to all eligible employees, whether they defer or not.

Can the employer adjust the matching contributions?

Yes. The matching contributions can be reduced from 3 percent to as low as 1 percent in 2 out of 5 years. The nonelective method requires the full 2 percent contribution without exception.

What are the compensation limits for matching contributions and for the nonelective contribution?

The matching contribution is based on an employee's total compensation but is limited to a $6000 annual match. The 2 percent nonelective contribution is limited to $170,000 in compensation (indexed for inflation) or a maximum of $3400.

Can the employer contribute more than the 3 percent match or 2 percent nonelective mandatory contribution?

No. The matching contribution can be reduced in 2 out of 5 years but it cannot be increased above 3 percent. The nonelective contribution cannot be reduced or increased.

Can an employer that sponsors a SIMPLE IRA change the 3 percent matching contribution to a 2 percent nonelective contribution?

Yes. The employer can make such an election 60 days before the next calendar year, and the election will apply for the full year. The election must be made in writing, and employees must be notified of the election.

Can I have a SIMPLE IRA and a regular IRA?

Yes. A SIMPLE IRA is a qualified plan and does not affect the amount you can contribute to your personal IRA. The SIMPLE IRA *will* affect the amount of the contribution to your traditional IRA that is deductible.

Can I combine my SIMPLE IRA contributions with my regular IRA?

No. SIMPLE IRA contributions must be placed in a SIMPLE IRA account only.

Do I still have to pay Social Security tax on the amount I defer in a SIMPLE IRA?

Yes. Social Security tax is required on any salary deferral plan.

Distributions from SIMPLE IRAs

When can I begin taking distributions from my SIMPLE IRA account?

You can remove funds from your SIMPLE IRA at any time and pay the income tax, but if you take your funds before reaching age 59½, an additional 10 percent penalty may apply. If the distribution is within the first 2 years of your participation in the SIMPLE IRA, the 10 percent penalty is increased to 25 percent.

What is the maximum that can be contributed to a SIMPLE IRA?

Under the matching method, the maximum contribution that can be made in any year to a SIMPLE IRA is $12,000, including the employee's maximum salary reduction ($6000) and the employer's maximum contribution ($6000). Under the nonelective method, the maximum contribution is $9400, including the employee's maximum salary reduction of $6000 (indexed annually for inflation) and the employer's maximum contribution of $3400 (indexed annually for inflation).

Simplified employee pension plans

What is a simplified employee pension plan?

A *simplified employee pension (SEP) plan* is a qualified retirement plan often used by small-business owners because of its low administrative costs. Although a SEP is technically a type of IRA, it is really more like a cross between an IRA and a profit-sharing plan.

As with a profit-sharing plan, the employer's tax-deduction limit for a SEP is the lesser of $30,000 or 15 percent of compensation. Also, as in the case of a profit-sharing plan, the employer's contribution is limited to 25 percent of compensation, not to exceed $30,000 for each employee.

What are some of the limitations of a SEP-IRA?

The employee cannot forward-average a lump-sum distribution, cannot roll a SEP into a new employer's plan, and cannot invest in insurance.

Who sets up a SEP-IRA?

Since SEPs are actually specialized IRAs, they are always set up and controlled by the person who benefits from them, even though they are funded by the employer. There is no vesting period; the funds belong to the employees on whose behalf the employer made the contribution.

When does a SEP-IRA contribution have to be made?

The contribution is due by April 15 of each year for the preceding tax year.

I'm just a small-business owner, so how can I afford the cost of a retirement plan?

The simplest plan for business owners is a SEP-IRA. Employees set up their own IRAs and receive employer contributions. The employees choose their own investments, limiting the liability of the business owner. A SEP-IRA plan does not usually require a Form 5500 tax report.

The form for establishing a SEP is very simple and should be retained by the employer. A SEP may be "integrated with Social Security," which has the effect of skewing contributions toward higher-paid people (who are usually the employers). Be careful, though: The standard IRS form does *not* allow for integration. You must find a prototype that does.

One of the reasons SEPs are so simple is that they offer very few choices for employers. All SEP contributions are always 100 percent vested in the employees. For example, suppose an employer makes $50,000 per year and has two employees who make $10,000 each. If the employer puts in 10 percent for herself, she must put in 10 percent each for the two employees. If one of the employees quits tomorrow, that employee takes the $10,000 with him.

What kind of business can establish a SEP?

A SEP may be established by an S or a C corporation, a partnership, or a sole proprietorship. The plan must be in writing, but there is no complicated adoption agreement to complete or file with the IRS.

What is the deadline for establishing a SEP?

A SEP plan must be established and funded by the business's tax-filing deadline, plus extensions.

Employee eligibility requirements

Are there any employee eligibility rules for a SEP?

Yes, and the rules are fairly strict. An employer must include all employees over 21 years of age who have earned a minimum of $450 (indexed annually for inflation) during the year and have worked for the employer in 3 out of the last 5 years.

Contributions to SEPs

Do I have to contribute the same percentage to all eligible employees?

Yes, unless the plan is integrated with Social Security.

How much compensation can I use to calculate my contribution?

In 2000, you can use $170,000. This amount is indexed annually for inflation.

Can I have a SEP and an IRA?

Yes, but a SEP is a qualified plan and will affect the deductibility of your IRA. However, you can also contribute to a Roth IRA if you meet its requirements.

Can I have a SEP and a SIMPLE IRA?

No. The SIMPLE IRA cannot operate with any other qualified plan in the same year.

Salary reduction simplified employee pension plans

What is a salary reduction simplified employee pension plan?

A *salary reduction simplified employee pension (SAR-SEP) plan* is the equivalent of a 401(k) for businesses with twenty-five or fewer employees. SAR-SEPs still exist but employers may no longer establish them; the SIMPLE replaced the SAR-SEP in 1997.

Target benefit plans

What is a target benefit plan?

A *target benefit plan* is a special type of defined-contribution plan in which the plan contributions are calculated, as in a defined-benefit plan, as the amounts needed to fund a specific target benefit for every plan participant at retirement. The actual benefit received by a participant at retirement is based on his or her individual account balance.

Each participant's target benefit is initially calculated on the basis of the participant's compensation and years of experience. The target benefit, along with interest- and annuity-rate assumptions prescribed by the IRS, is then used to determine a fixed annual contribution.

When the contribution necessary to fund a specific benefit has been determined, it is fixed at that level and generally will not change regardless of the plan's actual investment return. The required contribution must be made regardless of fluctuations in business revenues and cash flows.

Money purchase pension plans

What is a money purchase pension plan?

A *money purchase pension plan* is a type of defined-contribution plan. It operates like a profit-sharing plan except that contributions must be made to a money purchase plan even if the company has marginal revenues—or no revenues at all. The obligation to fund the plan means that a company's failure to make a contribution can result in the imposition of a penalty tax.

Good candidates for this type of plan include companies with a mature, steady, and continuing cash flow sufficient to fund the plan in the future; young owners and key employees; and companies for which simplicity is important.

Bad candidates are companies that want to make only small and irregular plan contributions, companies with erratic cash flow, and companies with one or two highly profitable years that want a deduction now but are unsure about future cash flows.

Employee stock ownership plans

What is an employee stock ownership plan?

An *employee stock ownership plan (ESOP)* is essentially a profit-sharing plan in which employer stock is used for contributions. The maximum annual deduction is 15 percent of covered payroll or 25 percent for a leveraged ESOP. The main distinction between a profit-sharing plan and an ESOP is that all an ESOP's assets must be invested in employer stock except for the cash required to buy out employees who are nearing their retirement.

Like profit-sharing plans, most ESOPs are defined-contribution plans that are discretionary as to the amount the employer contributes. If there are profits, the employer is expected to make substantial recurring contributions. Failure to make contributions can result in disqualification of the plan by the Internal Revenue Service. Generally, contributions during 3 out of 5 years or 5 out of 10 years will avoid disqualification.

Participants are eligible on the basis of months of service or age, and employees who are covered in a union-required retirement plan do not have to be covered. Also, ESOP assets may be used to purchase life insurance under certain conditions.

Vesting is allowed in an ESOP. If participants leave the company and are not 100 percent vested, the nonvested portions are allocated to the remaining participants on a pro rata basis. Typically, ESOPs favor younger participants, as they have a longer time for their funds to grow.

What is the greatest risk with an ESOP?

The greatest risk with an ESOP is that, since the plan is closely tied to the employer's stock, there is a lack of diversification. Anytime a large number of eggs are in one basket (employer stock in the retirement plan), the risk is greater than it would be with several baskets.

On the other side of the coin, it is this risk that many times is the incentive for employees to perform at their highest levels. Since their retirement is based on the performance of the company, it is always in the employees' best interest to work hard, eliminate waste and expense, and create innovative ways to increase productivity.

Defined-Benefit Pension Plans

What is a defined-benefit plan?

Up to this point, we have discussed qualified plans that have minimum and maximum contribution requirements but no guaranteed or specific distributions of benefits. Under a *defined-benefit plan,* the employer contributes money into a plan that pays retired employees, and sometimes their survivors, a regular amount for the rest of their lives. The amount is usually based on the employee's compensation, length of service, and age.

An employer that has adopted a defined-benefit plan must make required contributions into the plan on behalf of the employees every year, regardless of the company's profitability, in order to meet the guaranteed benefit. If a contribution is not made, the plan may be disqualified by the IRS.

Recently there has been a shift from defined-benefit plans to defined-contribution plans because of liability. In a defined-benefit plan the company is essentially liable for the pension deficit. Because of this liability, as well as the complexity of administering defined-benefit plans, most companies have switched to defined-contribution plans. Some small businesses still adopt defined-benefit plans to increase the amount of contributions that may be deducted.

How are the employer's contributions to a defined-benefit plan determined?

A defined-benefit pension plan defines what a participant's retirement benefit will be. The employer then makes an annual contribution to the plan based on actuarial assumptions. Since the contribution is based on assumed, future benefits, the total annual contribution to a defined-benefit plan can be significantly higher than that permitted with a defined-contribution plan.

Assume that a retirement benefit is defined as $100,000 per year for 10 years. An actuary, who is a highly trained mathematician, determines that $1 million of assets are needed by the time the participant is 65 in order to provide this benefit. The individual is 55 years old today, and therefore has 10 years until retirement. If we eliminate interest for purposes of simplicity, the individual would have to contribute $100,000 per year for the 10 years to accumulate $1 million at age 65.

As you can see, we "defined" the benefit and then determined how much the annual contribution had to be. The contribution is limited to the amount that can be proved actuarially to be necessary to provide the future benefit.

RETIREMENT PLANS FOR NONPROFIT INSTITUTIONS

Tax-Sheltered Annuities [403(b) Plans]

What is a 403(b) plan?

Section 403(b) of the Internal Revenue Code provides for salary reduction retirement plans for colleges, universities, school systems, and certain other nonprofit groups. These *403(b) plans* are also known as *tax-sheltered annuities (TSAs).*

An employee may elect to have a salary reduction of 20 percent of includable compensation, not to exceed $10,500 per year. All dollars contributed are before-tax and accumulate tax-deferred. Withdrawals in the future are taxable.

Technically, 403(b) plans are not qualified plans as defined in ERISA, but generally all the qualified plan rules apply to them, with one primary exception. A 403(b) plan has a catch-up option. Eligible employees who did not contribute the maximum amount to the plan and employees who just become eligible have an option to catch up on the contributions they missed. They do so by increasing the percentage of salary they defer and exceeding the maximum contribution limit for as long as 5 years. By catching up, the employee lowers his or her taxes because the extra contribution is not included in the employee's income for each of those 5 years.

What can TSA funds be invested in?

There are three allowable choices for TSA contributions. These include fixed or variable annuities, custodial accounts invested in mutual funds, and endowment life insurance contracts subject to certain limitations.

When is a distribution from a TSA required?

There is a 10 percent penalty for withdrawals before age 59½ unless the participant becomes totally disabled, separates from service after age 55, or dies. Also, the salary reduction amount, but not the earnings, is available for financial hardship, that is, an immediate and heavy financial need that cannot be met with other assets.

In order to avoid penalties, withdrawals attributed to post-1986 contributions and earnings must begin by April 1 of the year following the calendar year in which the participant reaches age 70½. Withdrawals of pre-1986 contributions and earnings may be postponed until the participant reaches age 75.

All TSA withdrawals are taxed as ordinary income unless the distribution is rolled over or transferred to another TSA.

457 Plans

What is a 457 plan, and who is eligible to participate is such a plan?

A *457 plan* is a deferred-compensation plan that is governed by Section 457 of the Internal Revenue Code, which applies to employees and independent contractors of state and local governments and tax-exempt organizations. Actually, 457 plans are hybrids of employer-sponsored plans and nonqualified deferred-compensation plans. As such, 457 plans are generally not subject to the strict rules of ERISA but are governed by their own Internal Revenue Code section, which is tied into some qualified plan provisions.

The primary reason 457 plans are used is that eligible employees can elect to defer income and thereby reduce current taxes. There is no tax benefit to the employer, which is a tax-exempt entity that does not need any income tax deductions.

The assets of a 457 plan created by a tax-exempt organization are held in trust by the employer and are subject to the claims of the employer's creditors. A special type of trust, colloquially named a "rabbi trust," discussed later in this chapter, is often used as part of a 457 plan to protect assets of the trust from being used to satisfy any other corporate purpose. A 457 plan must prohibit employees from taking distributions from the trust before separation from service or attainment of age 70½. The only exception is that employees may take distributions for unforeseen emergencies.

An employee must coordinate his or her contributions to a 457 plan with any other salary reduction plans in which the employee is a participant. Coverage by a 401(k) plan, 403(b) plan, SEP-IRA, and other salary reduction plans is subject to an aggregate limit of $8000 (indexed annually for inflation).

Some 457 plans use life insurance policies as funding vehicles. As with any 457 trust asset, the policies must be owned and the premiums paid by the employer. The employer must also be the beneficiary of each policy; there can be no requirement that the policy be transferred to the employee at any time.

No 10 percent early-distribution (before-age-59½) penalty is applied to 457 plan assets. At the time of distribution, the income payable to the employee or his or her heirs is considered ordinary income when received.

NONQUALIFIED RETIREMENT PLANS

What is a nonqualified retirement plan?

A *nonqualified retirement plan* is a written contract between an employer and an employee that covers employment and compensation that will be provided in the future. The agreement gives to the employee the employer's unsecured promise to pay some future benefit in exchange for services today. Contributions to a nonqualified plan are made on an after-tax basis. A nonqualified plan does not have to adhere to the provisions of ERISA. Such a plan can be tailored to meet the design objectives of an individual participant.

The most desirable aspect of a nonqualified plan is that it can be flexible; the plan for one employee is not necessarily the same as that for another. In addition, a nonqualified plan may be used for select employees; it does not have to cover all employees.

The promised future benefit may be in one of three general forms:

- *Deferred-compensation plans:* This type of nonqualified deferred-compensation plan resembles a defined-contribution plan. A fixed amount goes into the employee's account each year, sometimes through voluntary salary deferrals, and the employee is entitled to the balance of the account at retirement.
- *Salary continuation plans:* This form resembles a defined-benefit pension plan in that it provides the employee with a fixed dollar amount or fixed percentage of salary for a period of time after retirement.
- *Executive bonus plans:* This type of plan provides a death benefit to the employee's chosen beneficiary.

With these advantages, why would anybody set up a qualified plan?

Tax deductions. In a qualified plan, contributions are tax-deductible to the employer when made and earnings accumulate on a tax-deferred basis for the participant. Distributions are taxable income when received by the plan participant.

In a nonqualified plan, contributions are not immediately tax-deductible to the employer but they can grow tax-deferred, assuming they are invested in the proper vehicles. Distributions from a nonqualified plan are deductible to the employer at the time of distribution and, with some exceptions, are taxable income to the individual at that time.

Nonqualified plans typically supplement qualified plans to benefit executives, professionals, officers, and directors.

Are there any disadvantages to the employee under a nonqualified plan?

To obtain the flexibility of being able to pick and choose the employees under a nonqualified plan and the unlimited contributions, both the employer and the employee must give up something. The employer loses the up-front tax deduction for the contribution to the plan. The employee loses some security. The nonqualified deferred-compensation agreement is merely a promise to pay. The promise cannot be secured in any way that would guarantee payment in the future. Therefore, the employee has a number of concerns:

- *Corporate cash flow:* The corporation may not have the ability to meet its obligations when it is time to pay out the scheduled benefits, so the employee may lose his or her benefits. If the corporation is insolvent at the time benefits are scheduled to begin, the employee would be a general creditor of the corporation with no special rights or security.
- *Corporate policy changes:* If the corporation's future board of directors does not agree with the plan, the corporation may simply not honor the agreement.

Deferred-Compensation Plans

What is a deferred-compensation plan?

In a deferred-compensation plan, the employee elects to defer some of his or her current compensation in order to reduce current taxable income. The employer, usually a corporation, simply reduces the employee's current taxable compensation and uses the savings to begin accruing benefits for the ultimate purpose of providing an income payout at the employee's disability, retirement, or death.

The corporation receives no current income tax deduction for the amount of the deferred compensation by the employee. The employee does save on current taxes because his or her current income is less. The corporation will receive an income tax deduction when the benefits are paid to the employee at retirement, and the employee will report those benefits as ordinary taxable income. In the interim, the growth on plan assets is not taxed to the employee, if it is taxed at all.

I'd like to start a nonqualified deferred-compensation plan for myself and a key employee. What more should I know about this type of plan?

The key benefit of a nonqualified deferred-compensation plan is flexibility. The employer can pick and choose which employees participate, including owner/employees. The promised benefit need not follow any of the rules associated with qualified plans. The vesting schedule can be whatever the employer would like it to be.

Most nonqualified deferred-compensation plans cover owners, key employees, officers, or directors. Because the plans cover these types of employees, there is not a great deal of concern about either the tax deduction or the security. It is this ability to tie a flexible plan to key people that makes nonqualified deferred-compensation plans so appealing to many closely held businesses.

I've heard that deferred-compensation benefits can be protected with a "rabbi trust." What is a rabbi trust, and do I have to be a rabbi to use it?

A *rabbi trust* is a common planning technique used in the deferred-compensation marketplace to help alleviate an employee's concerns about the corporation's ability to pay the benefits from its cash flow in the future under a deferred-compensation agreement.

Funds set aside by the corporation in a rabbi trust are not currently taxed to the employee and therefore are not currently tax-deductible to the corporation.

A rabbi trust (so named because the first Internal Revenue Service ruling on this technique involved a rabbi) is often used to provide some security to the employee. An employer establishes a trust for the benefit of an employee who has entered into a nonqualified deferred-compensation agreement. The trust provides that the assets it holds remain accessible by the general creditors of the corporation, but the assets are not available for use by the corporation for any other purpose. The trust prevents the employer from "frittering" away the assets held for the employee's benefit.

However, if the corporation is insolvent or bankrupt, the money is still an asset of the corporation and subject to the claims of the general creditors of the corporation. The lack of security is a risk the employee must be willing to accept.

The Internal Revenue Service has approved a number of these types of trusts. It has even issued a standardized rabbi trust that generally assures the corporation and the employee that the contributions to the trust will not be currently taxable to the employee.

No, you don't have to be a rabbi.

What is a secular trust?

As with the rabbi trust, *secular trusts* can be used in nonqualified deferred-compensation plans when the issue of company creditors' reaching the funds is the paramount concern. To protect the funds, a secular trust can be established to which the employer pays an agreed-upon amount. The trust then invests the funds until the executive's retirement, disability, or death.

Unlike the case with a rabbi trust, the funds in a secular trust are not available to the company's creditors or management, thus ensuring that the funds will be available when needed at retirement. However, because the funds are guaranteed and asset-protected, the contributions to the trust are taxable to the employee during the year they are contributed to the plan.

Salary Continuation Plans

What is a salary continuation plan?

Because of the restrictions on the amount of the annual qualified plan contributions allowed in a given year for highly compensated employees and all the rules governing qualified plans, many companies turn to nonqualified plans, specifically a salary continuation plan, for relief.

In a typical *salary continuation plan,* the employer enters into a written agreement with the executive to pay him or her an annual sum, beginning at retirement or at a specific triggering date or event, such as age 65 or the onset of disability. The payments can be for a period certain (thereby guaranteeing that benefits continue to the executive's named beneficiary in the event of an early death), for the executive's lifetime, or for a combination of both.

To avoid being classified as an ERISA plan and to avoid adverse income tax consequences to the employee, the plan cannot be funded, although informal funding opportunities are available. For example, the employer may purchase a life insurance policy on the executive's life, with the employer naming itself as owner, premium payer, and beneficiary of the policy. The actual policy and the salary continuation agreement are not formally linked, although the policy can provide a source of funds for satisfying the ultimate payout by the employer to the employee.

At retirement, benefit payments made to the executive by the employer are tax-deductible to the employer. These payments are taxed as ordinary income to the executive or his or her named beneficiary. The employer, as the policy owner, can withdraw, surrender, or borrow funds from the policy's cash value to pay the executive's retirement benefit. The employer can also choose to use current cash flow. The employer could recover all its costs in the program at the executive's death through the receipt of the life insurance policy's death proceeds. If the executive dies before retirement, the employer could elect to pay a benefit (usually for a period certain) to the executive's beneficiary.

A salary continuation plan allows the corporation to choose which executives will participate and at what benefit level. The plan requires minimal Internal Revenue Service or Department of Labor reporting. While the costs are not currently deductible, the benefits often outweigh this tax disadvantage, especially in a closely held business.

Executive Bonus Plans

What is an executive bonus plan?

An *executive bonus plan,* also called a *Section 162 bonus program* (named after Section 162 of the Internal Revenue Code), is a means by which the employer helps an executive purchase personal life insurance protection for the benefit of his or her family. The executive often receives a taxable bonus to pay the insurance premium plus the amount of income taxes due on the bonus itself.

Many employees like executive bonus plans because there is no risk of losing the benefits that have already been promised to them by the corporation. However, the corporation could fail to keep its promise of future payments. The corporation, on the other hand, may not like such an arrangement as it does not provide an incentive for the employee to remain with the employer.

Why use an executive bonus program?

The executive bonus program is a nonqualified benefit that allows the employer to freely choose individual executives. These plans don't need any government approval.

The executive now has an additional benefit from the employer. This may allow the executive to use his or her cash flow for other needs instead of using it to purchase personal life insurance.

Funding Nonqualified Retirement Plans

What is an effective funding vehicle for nonqualified plans?

Contributions to nonqualified plans are made with after-tax dollars. To preserve as much ongoing benefit as possible, maximum tax efficiency is of paramount importance so that as the funds grow, as little as possible is lost to taxes.

One of the most effective vehicles for accomplishing this is an individual life insurance policy. Investing the nonqualified plan funds in life insurance offers the chance of growth on a tax-deferred basis. The policy can be either whole life (scheduled premiums) or universal life (flexible premiums). As with any life insurance policy, a portion of the premium is used by the insurance company to cover the policy's mortality charges, sales loads, and internal expense and administration charges.

A life insurance contract that is used as the informal funding vehicle for a nonqualified plan can be designed so that the income benefits are paid from policy equity (cash value), or the employer can choose to have the policy remain in place with retirement benefits paid from cash flow. At the death of the insured, the corporation will recover all or most of the costs associated with the plan through the death proceeds. Neither of these alternatives is better or worse; it is simply a choice of design.

Can a nonqualified plan be funded with a variable universal life policy?

Some employers like the flexibility associated with variable universal life because it enables the employer to contribute excess premiums or to decrease premiums as cash flow allows.

What are some other ways to use life insurance to fund a nonqualified deferred-compensation plan?

A nonqualified deferred-compensation plan defers an employee's current income and provides retirement funds down the line. However, if the employee does not live until retirement, there is a death benefit that is usually paid over a 3- to 7-year period to the beneficiary. The beneficiary can be a spouse, another family member, or the company that is sponsoring the deferred-compensation program.

RETIREMENT PLANS AND ASSET PROTECTION

Individual Retirement Accounts

Will my IRA be safe from creditors?

Your state's laws determine if your IRA account is exempt from creditors. Most states offer creditor protection for IRAs. However, even in a state that exempts IRAs from creditors, funds held in a Roth IRA may not be exempt since most state laws do not expressly protect Roth IRAs.

If creditor protection is important to you, but you live in a state that does not protect IRAs from creditors, rolling or transferring qualified plan funds to an IRA may not be appropriate.

Employer-Sponsored Plans

Are retirement funds protected from bankruptcy?

Federal law, with certain exceptions, exempts benefits held in ERISA-qualified plans from creditors of the participant and his or her beneficiary. Exceptions include tax liabilities due to the federal government and judgments against the participant obtained by the plan itself.

Plans that are not ERISA-qualified may be excluded from a bankruptcy estate through other applicable federal or state laws. These plans include nonqualified deferred-compensation, salary continuation, and executive bonus plans; 457 plans for government or churches; and IRAs. For these plans, you should check your own state's laws. This is particularly important with respect to IRAs, because some states provide an exemption from bankruptcy claims only for IRA rollovers from qualified plans.

INVESTING WITH RETIREMENT PLAN FUNDS

Doesn't it make sense to invest retirement plan assets in conservative investments with lower growth or income? Why take on additional investment risk, with just a chance of earning extra income, if the money's going to be taxed at a very high tax rate?

Although on the surface your reasoning may sound logical, it is not. Your question is a good one: "Wouldn't you pay less tax if you earned $50,000 rather than $100,000?" Of course you would, but you would also net less income, even if the additional income were taxed in a higher marginal tax bracket. Unless the tax was 100 percent, you will always come out ahead.

More is better, unless you would be out of your investment-risk comfort zone if you made more aggressive investments to achieve higher rates of return. Each individual has his or her own comfort zone as to the asset allocation and diversification of investments. Some people are comfortable investing 100 percent in stock equities, while others may prefer 100 percent in fixed-income-type investments. For most, the comfort zone will probably be somewhere in between.

There is no right or wrong percentage of assets that should be allocated to certain investments. The primary consideration is that you invest within your personal comfort zone.

How should I invest my 401(k) money?

Here are some guidelines you should follow to arrive at a good investment decision, whether for a 401(k) or an IRA:

1. *Participate.* Always try to put the maximum into the IRA account or the 401(k) plan, at least up to the amount your company will match. If you are not contributing to an employer-sponsored plan or an IRA, set a date on which you will start.

2. *State investment objectives.* Write a paragraph or two on your investment objectives. The result will be your investment policy statement (IPS). A 401(k) plan is supposed to have an IPS. Ask your employee benefits coordinator for a copy. It should explain the how, why, and what of picking investments for the entire plan, and will give you an idea about your investment alternatives and opportunities.

Your personal investment policy statement should cover:

- The amount you will contribute
- How much risk you will take
- The length of time you will be contributing to the plan or account
- The approximate amount you will allocate to each asset class and to each of the investment vehicles within the asset class, as follows:
  Cash equivalents: savings accounts, CDs, short-term Treasury bills, short-term bonds, and money market accounts
  Fixed-income investments: government bonds, municipal bonds, corporate bonds, and high-yield bonds
  Equity investments: U.S. large-company stocks, U.S. small-company stocks, international stocks, real estate, and international funds
- The criteria for picking the investments

3. *Visualize results.* It helps to visualize the results of your efforts. Project a couple of examples for yourself, just to have a feel for the possibilities of accumulating a nest egg. For instance, take a look at what you can accumulate if you invest $600 on the first of every month for 20 years. If your funds grow at 8 percent, you will have $355,768; at 10 percent, $459,418; and at 12 percent, $599,489—with a total of $144,000 of principal invested. It feels good to think that when you are 55, you might have about $400,000 in your IRA or 401(k) plan.

4. *Obtain information.* Get all the information you can about your investment choices.

How should I invest my qualified retirement plan or IRA funds?

All investment decisions should be based on a predetermined investment strategy. Generally, money inside a qualified plan or IRA is earmarked for the distant future and can be more aggressively invested than money that may be needed in the near future. Stock mutual funds have outperformed fixed-income accounts historically and can make a good choice for long-term dollars.

On the other hand, if your non-retirement-plan taxable accounts are invested in stocks and you want to diversify your portfolio by investing in fixed-income assets, it may be appropriate to "skew" the allocation of assets in your employer's qualified plan or IRA to taxable bonds and other fixed-income assets since the income from these investments is normally taxed at ordinary income rates anyway.

Since assets held outside your IRA or qualified plan at least have the potential for favorable capital gain tax treatment, these accounts should generally be skewed to hold stocks or stock mutual funds. Losses on equities in taxable accounts can be used to reduce taxable gains or carried forward and used to offset ordinary income up to $3000 annually.

Finally, capital gains on assets held in IRA accounts or qualified plans are taxed as ordinary income to beneficiaries; whereas the investments held in taxable accounts generally receive a full step-up in basis at the owner's death, so the beneficiaries pay no capital gain or income taxes.

What types of investments are usually found in IRAs?

All types of investments can be found in IRAs: cash equivalents (CDs, money market funds, and Treasury bills), bonds (Treasury, agency, corporate, and high yield), equities (large, mid, and small cap and international), and mutual funds of all types. Other investments, including preferred stocks, convertibles, REITS, and some approved precious metals and coins, are also used.

Investments that cannot be held in IRAs are those that are considered collectibles (paintings, gemstones, antiques, and baseball cards) and life insurance.

Can I transfer stock to my IRA?

Contributions to an IRA must be in cash only. Stocks, bonds, or other property cannot be used as a contribution to an IRA. If you do not have cash to make a contribution and you sell something to raise the cash, you must pay tax on any capital gain.

There is a strategy that will allow you to have your cake and eat it too. If you sell your stocks after a decline in value, you can fund the IRA and also get a capital loss on the sale. Furthermore, if you desire, your IRA can repurchase the same stocks immediately. The "wash rule" shouldn't apply since you and your IRA are separate legal entities.

Are mutual funds or variable annuities good investment vehicles for my IRA or qualified plan?

First, consider that with a traditional IRA or qualified plan you receive an income tax deduction for money you invest. There is no tax payable on dividends, interest, or capital gains until you withdraw money, at which time the amount you withdraw is subject to tax as ordinary income.

Next, consider that one of the primary purposes of a variable annuity is to defer taxes until the funds are withdrawn. There are other advantages, such as the death benefit, but most advisors would agree that tax deferral is the most important and valuable characteristic of variable annuities. Investors are willing to pay fees to the annuity company because the ability to defer tax payments to a much later time has monetary value, which can be substantial.

If an IRA or qualified plan already provides tax deferral, it would seem that the additional costs associated with a variable annuity are not justified unless the death benefit has particular value and is considered to be worth the cost. Therefore, when a managed and diversified portfolio of investments is desired within an IRA or qualified plan, pure mutual funds are more often than not the appropriate vehicle.

Are municipal bonds good investments for my IRA or 401(k)?

No. Municipal bonds are poor investments for your IRA or qualified plan. Municipal bonds pay tax-free interest, and because they do, their interest rates are lower than those of taxable bonds (government, agency, corporate, and high-yield bonds). So if municipal bonds are invested inside an IRA or qualified plan, the interest income will be less than it would be if taxable bonds were the investments. Also, if the IRA is a traditional IRA (not a Roth IRA), all the distributions are taxable. Thus, if municipal bonds are the investments, you've taken a tax-free income instrument and made it taxable to you at the time of distribution.

Recently, some taxable municipal bonds have come on the market. Naturally, they pay a higher interest rate, are taxable, and are acceptable as IRA or qualified plan investments.

In summary, tax-free municipal bonds are poor investments for IRAs and qualified plans because they are already tax-advantaged (tax-free income). They remain excellent tax-free investments outside of IRAs and other tax-deferred retirement vehicles.

Should I own life insurance inside a qualified plan?

While some planners promote the purchase of life insurance within a qualified plan such as a pension or profit-sharing plan, this approach must be reviewed on a total plan basis. Make sure there is an exit strategy to get the insurance out of the plan at some point. Also, recognize that qualified plan assets are the most difficult to plan for when it comes to estate tax situations.

chapter 11

Distributions from Retirement Plans

What are the penalties I need to be concerned about with regard to retirement plan distributions?

You need to be careful of running into what is sometimes referred to as the "Goldilocks" problem. You remember the story of the three bears, where the porridge was too hot and too cold. With retirement plan assets, the problems to watch out for when taking distributions are too soon, too little, and too late.

- *Too soon:* If distributions are taken before age 59½, there is a 10 percent penalty on top of the income tax due. These are called *early distributions.*
- *Too little:* At age 70½, minimum distributions are required each year. This is the absolute minimum which must be withdrawn, although more can always be withdrawn. If for some reason the withdrawal is less than the minimum required distribution amount, there is a 50 percent penalty on the difference between what should have been withdrawn and what was withdrawn.
- *Too late:* The first minimum distribution is required to be taken by April 1 of the calendar year after the year in which one reaches age 70½. Thereafter, the minimum distributions have to be taken within each calendar year, or there is a 50 percent penalty on the amount not taken that year.

DISTRIBUTION RULES

Traditional IRAs

What are the rules regarding distributions from traditional IRAs?

You can withdraw money from your IRA at any time and pay income tax on the amounts withdrawn. However, because your IRA is intended to be a long-term investment, unless certain exceptions are met, withdrawals before age 59½ are subject to a 10 percent penalty. The 10 percent penalty is *in addition* to the income taxes due on the total amount of the withdrawals.

On the other end of the spectrum, you are required to take distributions from traditional IRAs on your "required beginning date." Failure to do so can result in significant penalties.

What is the required beginning date, and when is it?

The *required beginning date* is April 1 of the calendar year after you turn 70½. However, you are allowed to postpone your first distribution until the following tax year, but doing so sometimes creates an inadvertent income tax problem. This is because the second distribution will be in the same tax year as the first distribution, most likely pushing you into a higher marginal tax bracket than necessary. In most cases, bunching the two distributions into one year would not be prudent, unless you had significant tax write-offs for that year. Thus, even though you can postpone your first required distribution, check with your tax advisor before you do so, or the postponement may cost you additional tax dollars.

With the exception of the postponement rule, for all other years, IRA distributions need to occur by December 31. Failure to make timely distributions is subject to penalties.

Roth IRAs

What are the distribution rules for Roth IRAs?

You can take money out of your Roth IRA at any time, just as with a traditional IRA. Unlike the case with a traditional IRA, however, you will not pay income tax on withdrawals of your contributions. Any amounts you withdraw from a Roth IRA are deemed first to be contributions up to the aggregate total of all contributions to all Roth IRAs. Only after you have taken all contributions are distributions considered to be distributions of your earnings. You also will not pay income tax on the distribution of your accumulated earnings if they are part of a qualified distribution. If the distribution of your accumulated earnings is not a qualified distribution, you will pay income tax and possibly a penalty on the earnings you withdraw.

What is a qualified distribution of earnings from a Roth IRA?

A distribution of accumulated earnings from a Roth IRA is considered *qualified* if you make the withdrawal after a 5-year tax period (beginning generally with the first tax year in which you made the contribution to the IRA) and it meets one of the following five requirements:

- It is made on or after you reach age 59½.
- It is distributed after your death to your beneficiary.
- It is made because you are disabled.
- It is made to pay expenses directly incurred for the purchase of a principal residence and you are a first-time home buyer.
- It is made to pay qualified higher-education expenses.

Does the 10 percent penalty tax apply to my Roth IRA?

Yes. The 10 percent penalty tax on distributions before 59½ generally applies to all IRAs, including Roth IRAs. However, this penalty applies only to certain withdrawals from Roth IRAs, which are discussed in detail later in this chapter.

Does the Roth IRA, like the traditional IRA, require that I take minimum distributions at age 70½?

No. One of the distinct advantages of the Roth IRA for many retirees is that they are never forced to take withdrawals from the account.

How will the distributions from a Roth IRA affect the taxes that I'll have to pay on the money I receive from Social Security?

Qualified distributions from a Roth IRA are not taxable and will not be counted as income on your tax return, so they will not affect the calculation for taxes against Social Security earnings.

Employer-Sponsored Qualified Plans

When may I begin taking distributions from my company's qualified retirement plan?

With some exceptions, you may not take penalty-free distributions from your qualified plan until you reach age 59½.

When do I have to begin taking distributions from my qualified retirement plan?

You must begin taking minimum required distributions from a qualified plan by April 1 of the calendar year following the year in which you turn 70½ unless you qualify for deferring distributions. This rule applies to all qualified plans, including 403(b) and 401(k) plans.

Can I defer distributions beyond the age of 70½?

Yes. If you do not own more than 5 percent of the company sponsoring the plan when you are age 66½, you may defer distributions until April 1 of the year following your retirement even if that is after age 70½.

EARLY-DISTRIBUTION RULES

Traditional and Roth IRAs

Is it possible to take penalty-free distributions from a traditional IRA before turning 59½?

All early distributions from a traditional IRA are subject to a 10 percent penalty unless an exception applies. An *early distribution* is any distribution taken before the owner reaches 59½ years of age. There are eight exceptions to this rule for traditional IRAs:

1. The owner dies before reaching age 59½, and the distribution goes to a beneficiary or the owner's estate.
2. The IRA owner becomes totally and permanently disabled.
3. Distributions are part of a series of substantially equal periodic payments.
4. Distributions are for higher-education expenses for the IRA account owner or his or her spouse, children, or grandchildren.
5. Distributions are for medical expenses that exceed 7.5 percent of the IRA owner's adjusted gross income.
6. Distributions are for health insurance premiums for the account owner or his or her spouse and dependents after the account owner has become unemployed.
7. Distributions are used by first-time home buyers for expenses up to a $10,000 lifetime cap.
8. A qualified rollover to another IRA is made.

How does the 10 percent penalty apply to my Roth IRA?

The penalty tax is assessed on 10 percent of the withdrawals from an IRA that are included in your gross income. Since withdrawals of contributions from a Roth IRA are never included in gross income because you already paid tax on those dollars, the penalty tax does not apply to such withdrawals. However, withdrawals of earnings from a Roth IRA before you reach the age of 59½ are subject to the 10 percent penalty tax unless an exception applies.

Can I take penalty-free distributions from my Roth IRA before turning 59½?

The 10 percent early-distribution penalty applies to Roth IRAs to the extent that earnings are withdrawn and the withdrawal is made before a 5-year tax period elapses (beginning generally with the first tax year in which the contributions were made to the IRA). The same exceptions to the 10 percent penalty for traditional IRAs apply to Roth IRAs.

Employer-Sponsored Qualified Plans

How can I withdraw money from my qualified retirement plan before age 59½ without incurring the early-withdrawal penalty?

There are a number of exceptions to imposition of the early-withdrawal penalty tax for qualified plans. The primary exceptions are:

1. The plan participant dies, and the distribution goes to a beneficiary or the participant's estate.
2. The plan participant becomes totally and permanently disabled.
3. Distributions are part of a series of substantially equal periodic payments that begin after the participant no longer works for the employer.
4. Distributions are made to a participant who separates from the service of an employer after reaching the age of 55.
5. Distributions are for medical expenses that exceed 7.5 percent of the participant's adjusted gross income.
6. Distributions are for health insurance premiums for the account owner or his or her spouse and dependents after the account owner has become unemployed.
7. Payments are made to the participant's former spouse or child under a qualified domestic relations order (QDRO).
8. A qualified rollover to an IRA or another qualified plan is made.

401(k) Plans

Are there different exceptions to the early-withdrawal penalty for 401(k) plans?

The exceptions to the early-withdrawal penalty for 401(k) plans are similar to, but not the same as, those for other qualified plans and IRAs. The 401(k) exceptions are:

1. The plan participant dies, and the distribution goes to a beneficiary or the participant's estate.
2. The plan participant becomes totally and permanently disabled.
3. Distributions are made to a participant who separates from the service of an employer.
4. Distributions are made upon termination of the 401(k) plan by an employer, and the employer does not replace the plan with another defined contribution plan (other than an ESOP).
5. Distributions are for hardship, which is defined as an immediate and heavy financial need.
6. Distributions are made upon the sale of substantially all the company's assets or of the division or subsidiary where the participant worked.
7. A qualified rollover to an IRA or another qualified plan is made.

I need the money in my 401(k) plan to buy a new car, and I don't care about the penalty. Should I cash in my account?

No. After subtracting taxes and penalties, you could lose 40 to 50 percent of the account's value. For example, if your 401(k) is worth $25,000, you might net only $15,000.

The not-so-obvious cost of cashing out of your plan is the opportunity cost that you lose. Let's say you are 28 years old and have worked for a company for several years. Your 401(k) account is worth approximately $25,000. Let's also assume that your 401(k) investments are earning 9 percent. You want to cash in your account and use the net proceeds to purchase a car.

Now, what is the real cost of the car? If we apply the Rule of 72, your money should double every 8 years. That is, the $25,000 you have now, at age 28, will increase to $50,000 by age 36, to $100,000 by age 44, to $200,000 by age 52, to $400,000 by age 60, and so on.

As you can see, by cashing in the 401(k), you will lose the opportunity to let the $25,000 grow until you are 60 (and perhaps even longer). At that time, you could have a total balance of $400,000—

without adding additional contribution dollars to the 401(k). It appears that the car will really cost you $400,000, not $15,000; and even if you still have the car when you are 60, it won't be worth $400,000.

Exceptions to Early-Distribution Penalties

First-time home purchase

I have a Roth IRA and want to use the money to purchase a home. What are the requirements that I must meet to avoid any penalties?

To qualify for the first-time home buyer distribution, whether you are the owner of an IRA or the participant in an employer-sponsored qualified plan, you must meet the following requirements:

- The purchase must be for a principal residence.
- The person for whom it is a principal residence must be the owner/participant or a family member.
- You must be a first-time home buyer, which is defined as someone who has not owned a home in the previous 2 years.
- The purchase must cover "qualified acquisition costs."
- The owner/participant may not treat more than $10,000 in his or her lifetime as qualified first-time home buyer distributions.
- The purchase must be made within 120 days of the distribution date.

Our son wants to buy a home for the first time. Can my husband and I each take a distribution from our separate Roth IRAs and have both approved as qualified distributions?

As long as the distribution is for a qualified relative, which your son is, each of you can take $10,000 from your respective Roth IRAs and give it to your son for his first-time home. Both distributions are qualified (and both gifts are within your annual exclusions). You might also compare the results of these withdrawals with other alternatives such as increasing your current mortgage or taking out a home equity loan on your home.

When taking money from my Roth IRA for a first-time home, how soon do I have to invest the proceeds into the home without penalty?

Your distribution will not qualify if you take out money too far in advance of the closing of your new home purchase. The payment must be used to pay for qualified acquisition costs before the close of the 120th day after the date on which the payment or distribution is made.

Substantially equal period payments

Is the exception for a series of substantially equal periodic payments the same for both IRAs and qualified plans?

The exception works the same for IRAs and for qualified retirement plans that allow this exception, and it is one of the most popular ways to access retirement savings without incurring the 10 percent early-withdrawal penalty. This exception to the 10 percent early-distribution penalty has specific guidelines to which you must adhere. There are three different approved ways to receive substantially equal periodic payments.

How long must the substantially equal periodic payments last?

The substantially equal payments must extend for 5 years or until the taxpayer turns 59½ years old, whichever is longer. Once this requirement has been satisfied, taxpayers can change the amount they are receiving. If the amount withdrawn is altered prematurely, the penalty tax applies retroactively to the first substantially equal withdrawal.

What are the three ways to receive substantially equal periodic payments?

The payments may be calculated under any one of the three approved IRS methods: single or joint life expectancy, amortization, or annuity.

How does the amortization method work?

Amortization of the taxpayer's account balance is accomplished in a three-step process:

1. The distribution must be based on the life expectancy of the individual requesting the distribution or on the joint life expectancy of the individual and his or her designated beneficiary.
2. The payments must be made at least annually for at least 5 years or until the individual has reached the age of 59½, whichever is longer.
3. The interest rate used to compute the payment must be based on

a reasonable rate of interest as defined by the Internal Revenue Code.

Unless the taxpayer becomes disabled or dies, this payment distribution, once started, cannot be changed until the time requirement has been met. Afterward, the amount of the distributions can be amended or stopped altogether.

What reasonable interest rate must be used for amortizing substantially equal periodic payments?

The higher the interest rate used in the amortization method, the more income the taxpayer receives. Because of the way the interest rate affects the computation, determining the right rate is important.

The Internal Revenue Code defines the interest rate to be used, but its definition is subject to interpretation. Many experts agree that the safe position is to use a rate that is no higher than 120 percent of the 2-year Treasury-note or -bill rate in effect at the time that the substantially equal periodic payments begin. However, it appears that the Internal Revenue Service may accept an interest rate that is equal to the expected rate of return of a particular investment.

What are the consequences of making a change to the periodic payments within the 5-year period or before I reach age 59½?

Unless a qualifying event occurs (disability or death), a change in the payment amount of a substantial and equal distribution within the restricted time frame will result in a penalty tax that would have been due, plus interest, if the exception had never been taken.

Qualified rollovers

What is a qualified rollover?

A *rollover* is the process of rolling funds from one type of account to another without paying any income tax. Allowable rollovers include:

- Rollovers from one traditional IRA to another traditional IRA
- Rollovers from an employer-sponsored qualified plan to a traditional IRA

You cannot roll over a traditional IRA to a Roth IRA tax-free, and you cannot roll over from a qualified plan to a Roth IRA at all.

What types of distributions qualify for a tax-free rollover?

The term that is used to describe a plan distribution that qualifies for a tax-free rollover is *eligible rollover distribution.* Generally, any distribution from a qualified plan, IRA, 401(k) plan, or 403(b) plan is an eligible rollover distribution, with these exceptions:

- Any distribution that is part of a series of substantially equal payments made over the life expectancy of the participant or the joint life expectancies of the participant and his or her designated beneficiary.
- Any distribution made for a specified period of 10 years or more.
- Any distribution that is a required minimum distribution.

If I go to work for a different company that has a qualified retirement plan, can I roll my retirement funds over to its plan?

This will depend on your new employer. Some employers will allow you to roll over the proceeds from your qualified plan into their qualified plan. However, it would be wise to determine the investment options the new qualified plan offers before you roll over your money into that plan rather than into an IRA.

For example, if your new employer's plan is 100 percent invested in its own company stock, analyze the stock before deciding whether or not your best option is to place all your retirement funds into one investment. In addition, you usually have more control of your investments in an IRA than in an employer's plan.

In most circumstances, the smartest move is to roll over into your own IRA, rather than into the new company's plan.

How often can I roll one IRA over into another (if I want to invest in something else)?

IRA rollovers may be made tax-free only once per year for each IRA. For example, if you have five different IRA accounts, you may roll over each IRA once into different IRAs or consolidate them into one IRA.

It is certainly easier to open one self-directed IRA, which will allow you to make new investments without always having to do rollovers.

Calculation of the Taxes on Early Distributions

How is the income tax and the 10 percent early-withdrawal tax penalty calculated for early distributions from qualified retire-

ment plans, IRAs, 403(b) accounts, and other tax-deferred retirement vehicles?

First, the taxpayer must determine the taxable portion of the distribution. This amount is then added to any other taxable income received by the taxpayer during the year in which the distribution is made. Income taxes are paid on the total amount. Second, an additional penalty tax of 10 percent is imposed on the taxable portion of the plan distribution.

The amount of the total tax on the distribution can be as high as 49.6 percent *plus* the individual's state tax liability.

If I need to take money out of my Roth IRA during the initial 5-year holding period, what are the tax implications?

Withdrawal of your original after-tax contributions within the first 5 years does not create taxable income. Since you already paid income tax on the contributions before you put them into your Roth IRA, taxes are not due. There is no 10 percent penalty tax on this portion if you are under age 59½. Remember, under the Roth IRA rules, the first distributions are considered to be a return of your contributions.

To the extent that your withdrawals exceed your contributions, there are income tax implications. In the initial 5-year period, this portion is subject to ordinary-income taxation plus a 10 percent penalty if you have not yet reached 59½ or if one of the other exceptions does not apply.

DISTRIBUTION OPTIONS FOR QUALIFIED RETIREMENT PLANS

Assuming I am either 55 and separating from service or have reached 59½, what are the payout options for most qualified plans?

Generally speaking, there are four payout choices:

1. You can take an annuity based on life expectancy.
2. You can take an annuity over a fixed period of time.
3. You can take a lump-sum distribution in cash.
4. You can roll over the lump-sum distribution to a traditional IRA or other qualified plan.

I'm required by my employer to fill out paperwork before my retirement. Are there things I should know before I do so?

If there are annuity options available, it is imperative that you contact your financial and tax advisors to go over your alternatives and determine which one is the best for you. Once you make this election, it is usually irreversible.

In addition, you may be able to take your retirement distribution in a lump sum rather than in an annuity. The plan document, or the summary plan description (SPD), will provide you with the answers you need. It is also important to determine whether an IRA rollover is a viable alternative. Again, you should review all the different options before making this election.

What should I discuss with my financial planner and tax advisor before selecting my payout options from my qualified plan?

A lump-sum distribution calls for updating your investment policy and goals, taking into account the appropriate time horizon and also considering minimum distribution requirements. If a rollover IRA is used, investing in a tax-deferred environment continues. If not, the taxable nature of the total return and your tax situation must be considered.

Investment selection and allocation considerations are similar to those in investing an inheritance for long-term cash flow. If you receive periodic distributions that exceed current needs, investment issues involve reinvesting smaller sums to ensure adequate growth to fund a potentially long retirement.

Annuities

What is meant by annuitizing my pension?

Annuitization is the process of taking a fixed amount of principal and income for a specific period of time. Usually the time period is a set number of years or the remainder of one's life, with payments occurring at least annually.

What are the annuity options that are available under my pension plan?

Not all qualified plans are required to provide an annuity option, but when they do, there are typically three main annuity options:

1. The annuity amount is calculated on both your and your spouse's

life expectancy. It is payable to both of you while you are living and to the survivor after one of you dies.

2. The annuity is calculated on your life expectancy only and stops when you die.
3. The annuity is guaranteed for a fixed period of years. Under some plans, the annuity can be paid to a named beneficiary should you die before the period of years is up.

What are some advantages of annuitizing my pension?

When you annuitize your pension over your life expectancy, you essentially remove it from your estate and reduce your estate taxes. In addition, if the annual income generated from the annuity payout is sufficient for your retirement needs, annuitization may be attractive because your check comes regularly and you do not need to worry about managing the asset.

Are there any disadvantages to annuitization?

Even though the regular income sounds terrific, annuitization has some major drawbacks. Technically, you cannot touch the remainder of the money once it is annuitized. You have given up that right. If you have a major medical emergency, you might have to liquidate another asset to cover expenses. Also, you usually lose the ability to change options, although some pension plans make adjustments to joint-life annuities if the participant's spouse predeceases the participant. In essence, an annuity is an irrevocable choice, so you must fully understand the implications of "locking" your asset up.

What is the life expectancy annuity option?

A *life expectancy annuity* is a regular payment for the employee's life or for the joint lives of the employee and his or her spouse. In a qualified plan, the employer contributes money into a plan that pays retired employees a regular amount for the rest of their lives. The amount is usually based on the employee's compensation, length of service, and age.

The benefits of a life annuity include the security of knowing that payments will come on a regular basis, the payments will last for as long as the employee and his or her spouse live, and the employee cannot outlive the payments.

There are disadvantages to life annuities. Most annuities are not indexed for inflation, which means that the fixed payments from the annuity will likely buy less as time goes by. Taxes are due on all or a portion of the amount received each year, and some tax advantages may be lost.

My plan's annuity option provides a survivor's income for my wife but involves a substantial reduction in benefits during my lifetime. I'd prefer to take the maximum pension income during my lifetime but want to protect my wife if I die first. Is there an alternative to the company-subsidized survivor's benefit?

Possibly. If you are young enough and have sufficient resources for alternative planning, you may find it attractive to take the maximum pension (without survivor benefits) and use a portion of this increase in benefits to purchase an individual life insurance policy on your life in an amount sufficient to fund an appropriate survivorship "pension" for your wife. If your wife survives you, the tax-free insurance proceeds paid on your death can be invested for income or can be used to purchase an annuity for her. If your wife predeceases you, you can continue the policy with other family members as beneficiaries or discontinue it.

What is the periodic payment option?

Periodic payments are installment payments, usually of equal amounts, paid over a specific period, often 5, 10, or 15 years.

The advantages of periodic payments are assurance of regular payments at set intervals, relatively large payments because of the short time frame, and the ability, under some circumstances, to roll some or all of the payments into an IRA.

Disadvantages include the commitment to a payment schedule that limits the ability to receive a lump-sum amount if needed; no assurance of a lifetime income, so the employee may be left without funds after the payments end; potentially higher income taxes; and the erosion of purchasing power over time by inflation.

Lump-Sum Distributions

What is a lump-sum option?

Many plans offer a *lump-sum option,* which allows the employee to take a one-time cash benefit and leave the plan. The employee can either take the benefit in cash and pay income taxes on it or transfer the funds to an IRA and pay taxes on the funds when they are eventually withdrawn.

In many cases an employee can assume the risk and create a larger retirement income benefit by transferring the funds to an IRA and properly investing the proceeds.

What are the tax rules relating to lump-sum distributions of retirement funds?

Lump-sum distributions can be rolled over (in whole or in part) to an IRA on a tax-free basis. Alternatively, employees can take the lump sum in cash and either pay the entire tax due or use 10-year forward averaging, if available, for paying the taxes.

When is the lump-sum option available?

A lump-sum distribution from a qualified plan may be made when the employee dies, reaches age 59½, or separates from service.

Lump-sum cash distribution

What are the advantages and disadvantages of a lump-sum cash distribution?

The primary benefits of taking a lump-sum distribution in cash are the employee's ability to control the funds for investing and making gifts and the ability, under some circumstances, to qualify for forward-averaging to reduce taxes.

The disadvantages of taking a lump-sum cash distribution are that the funds are normally taxed immediately and that the funds might be lost because they were spent too quickly or lost as a result of poor investment decisions. Thus, there is no assurance of a lifetime income.

Lump-sum distribution rollover to IRA

What is an IRA rollover?

An *IRA rollover* is a lump-sum distribution from a qualified plan deposited into a special IRA account. The employee can deposit the distribution himself or herself or the employer can transfer it directly.

Rollovers to IRAs are popular because they offer substantial benefits. The money in the IRA continues to grow tax-deferred in investments that can be controlled by the IRA owner, and there is flexibility in how and when distributions are taken.

Can I roll my lump-sum distribution into a Roth IRA?

No. You may roll funds over directly from a qualified plan only to a traditional IRA. If you are willing to pay the taxes on the entire amount of the rollover, you can roll the traditional IRA over to a Roth IRA in another year.

Can I roll my money over into an existing deductible IRA?

The simple answer is yes, but many advisors suggest keeping your IRA segregated, since not doing so could prevent you from transferring your rollover IRA into a new employer's qualified plan should you wish to do so at a later date. However, if you will not be going back to work for another company, a rollover into an existing IRA should not make a difference. Having one IRA may also simplify your paperwork.

If I want to do an IRA rollover, do I have to roll over everything?

No. You have a number of options. You may request that the retirement plan administrator directly transfer part of your retirement account to an IRA and send the balance to you. The amount that is payable to you, and not directly transferred to an IRA or other qualified plan (with the exception of after-tax contributions), will be subject to the 20 percent federal withholding and possibly to penalties. The non-IRA amount is not eligible for any forward averaging. It is also important to note that a qualified plan is not required to issue more than one check.

Can I roll over or transfer the full amount of my distribution?

Generally, yes. However, there is one common exception that often trips up taxpayers. If after-tax contributions were made to your plan, these amounts are not taxable to you but are merely a return of your principal and are not eligible for IRA rollover. In fact, if you roll over any part of the after-tax contributions, there will be a penalty for rolling over too much! Also, you will be taxed again on these contributions when you withdraw them from the IRA.

If you elect a direct rollover to an IRA, your retirement plan administrator will normally send the taxable portion of the distribution to your IRA or will make the check payable to the IRA custodian and send you the check. Any after-tax contributions will usually be sent to you in a separate check. There is no tax or withholding due on this portion of the distribution, since you have already paid the taxes.

However, not all plan administrators will send two checks. There is a possibility that the entire distribution from a retirement plan will be transferred directly to the IRA. The recipient can remove this excess contribution to the IRA, assuming that the withdrawal is done in a timely manner. This distribution from the IRA will not be taxable to the IRA owner, since it is for after-tax contributions. However, it is best to review the paperwork thoroughly to make sure that no mistakes have been made.

What do I need to know if I want to do a rollover to an IRA from a qualified plan?

If you decide on a direct rollover to an IRA, make sure you have an IRA set up so that the transfer is done correctly. If you do not have an existing IRA, you must open one. Whether it's a new IRA or an old one, you should meet with your financial advisor and fill out the proper forms so that the funds are transferred correctly. Failure to do so can result in many problems, creating an unnecessary tax liability and/or having the plan administrator withhold taxes when what you are trying to accomplish is a tax-free exchange.

Can you summarize the rules and considerations for making a rollover distribution?

Here are some facts to keep in mind when deciding whether or not to do a rollover:

- The rollover must take place within 60 days of the receipt of a lump-sum cash distribution; any amounts not rolled over in this period are taxable.
- All pretax contributions and all earnings from the employer's qualified plan in the future may be rolled over; any after-tax contributions are not taxed and cannot be rolled over without severe penalties.
- Regardless of whether the contribution is deductible, it is still possible to make an annual $2000 IRA contribution to a traditional IRA rollover account. However, mixing traditional IRA contributions with the rollover balance will prohibit rolling the distribution back into another employer's qualified plan in the future.
- If noncash assets (e.g., employer stock) are received as part of the distribution, they can be rolled over directly to a traditional IRA. (Noncash assets cannot be contributed to an IRA under any other circumstances.)
- Distributions may be made from a traditional IRA rollover account at any time after age 59½ free of penalty, just as with a contributory traditional IRA.

- The traditional IRA rollover account provides an opportunity to continue building assets during working years while continuing to defer income tax until beginning to receive distributions. This continued growth can mean the difference between living simply and living well during the retirement years.

What happens if I have the check made out to me and then I decide to roll the funds into an IRA?

If you want the check made payable to you, there will be a mandatory 20 percent withholding on the distribution. If you have any outstanding loans against your account, withholding is due on those amounts as well. You must roll over 100 percent of the taxable distribution from your plan within 60 days to avoid taxes and penalties.

Here is an example of how withholding works: Bill is terminating employment from XYZ corporation and has $100,000 in his company's retirement plan. There are no after-tax contributions. Inadvertently, Bill requests that his lump-sum distribution be made payable to him. A few weeks later, he receives a check for only $80,000. What happened to the other $20,000? The employer did what it is required to do and sent it directly to the IRS. Bill must now pay, out of his own separate funds, an additional $20,000 in order to roll over the full amount of $100,000.

If Bill does not have the additional $20,000 and rolls over only $80,000 to his IRA, the $20,000 that was not rolled over will be subject to income tax. Bill will most likely receive a tax refund the next year, but he has lost the ability to invest the $20,000 on a tax-deferred basis. Please note that the IRS will not give Bill any interest on his refund.

If Bill has not reached the age of 59½, he will likely be subject to the 10 percent penalty tax on the $20,000 that was withheld. This is another, $2000 insult that is added to the injury of failure to fully roll over.

I have two retirement plans at work. I'd like to roll over the proceeds from one of them into an IRA and use forward averaging on the proceeds from the other. Can I do this?

Unfortunately, no. If you roll over even one dollar from one of these plans to an IRA or another qualified plan, any other distributions from the same company during the same year will be treated as ordinary income and not be subject to forward averaging. A much better approach would be to take a lump-sum distribution that qualifies for averaging in one year and then take a distribution from the other plan in another year, rolling over those proceeds into an IRA.

Special Considerations for Distributions of Stock

If I have employer stock in my retirement plan, is there a tax advantage to taking the stock as a distribution when I retire?

Yes. There are tax advantages to receiving employer stock instead of rolling it over at retirement to a traditional IRA.

It is not uncommon for employees to have a significant amount of employer stock in their qualified retirement plans. When it comes time for employees to leave their companies, most are willing to directly roll over all qualified plan assets into a traditional IRA. Such a rollover offers avoidance of an immediate income tax consequence, the retiree remains in control of his or her retirement assets, and the benefits of tax deferral can continue.

However, there may be another option available that should be considered, a type of combination approach. In this option, employer stock is distributed to the retiree, and the remaining balance of the participant's assets is directly rolled over into a traditional IRA. This combination approach, though not for everyone, may have significant advantages.

By not including the employer stock in the traditional IRA rollover, the retiree is exposed to income taxes immediately. This is because he or she is receiving the shares as a taxable distribution. However, the taxes due will be only on the *cost basis* of the stock, not its current value. In most cases, the cost basis of the employer stock will be much lower than its current market value, so exposing the stock to taxes now may be advantageous in the long run. (It is important to know what the actual cost basis of the employer shares is in the retirement plan. The plan administrator should have this information.)

The stock will continue to defer taxes on its appreciation. When the retiree ultimately decides to sell the shares, he or she will pay long-term capital gain rates on the stock's appreciation over the cost basis—currently capped at 20 percent. In addition, there are no minimum distribution requirements starting at age 70½ or other nasty penalty taxes for this block of employer stock, allowing for more planning flexibility.

Lastly, if the stock's value continues to rise during retirement, the retiree's heirs may receive a big tax break. By having the shares held outside the traditional IRA, the heirs may enjoy a step-up in cost basis to the current market value from the market value on the date the shares were distributed from the retirement plan, so they avoid significant capital gain taxes. However, the net unrealized appreciation between the retiree's cost basis and the share's market value on the date of distribution will be subject to capital gain tax—even for the heirs—when the shares are sold.

There are many technical requirements that must be met for the distributed employer stock to qualify as a lump-sum distribution. Of course, diversification considerations and other investment fundamentals may show that rolling over stock to a traditional IRA is the more prudent choice in many cases. Therefore, it is highly recommended that retirees considering such a maneuver obtain professional advice.

What is the cost basis of the employer stock that I receive in a lump-sum distribution, and do I have to pay taxes on the fair market value of that stock?

An employee does not usually have to pay taxes on the fair market value of employer stock received in a lump-sum distribution because of an important concept called *net unrealized appreciation.*

Most stock savings plans allow the employer to make matching contributions in the form of the company's stock. If you take all or part of your distribution in the form of stock, you will pay tax only on the actual cost of the contributions that were made to your account. Let us assume, for example, that the total contribution to the plan in the form of company stock was $50,000 and the fair market value at distribution is $100,000. The difference of $50,000 is the net unrealized appreciation. If you take this stock in your name in the form of stock and do not roll it over into an IRA, you will pay taxes only on the cost value of $50,000.

However, remember that this is your new capital gain tax basis. In the event that you sell the stock later for more than $50,000, you will have to pay income tax only on the difference between what you sell it for and the $50,000 basis, not on the entire selling price. The income tax will be at the favorable capital gain rate rather than the ordinary rates.

Although a stock distribution is certainly good in principle, many times the cost value of the stock is so great that there is a significant amount of immediate income tax to pay. It may then be necessary to take other money from your IRA in order to pay the tax, and this increases your income tax even more. Therefore, it is imperative to review your income tax and your liquidity before you make this election.

I'm getting quite confused about all this paperwork and the complexities of the tax laws. I have a stock savings plan at work, and

I'd like to transfer everything into my IRA at the credit union. Can I do this?

To avoid the mandatory 20 percent withholding, you must have the check made payable to the IRA custodian, and you must also have the stock certificates issued in the custodian's name.

Many IRA custodians do not accept stock certificates. You must make sure that the custodian you choose will accept them. If not, you will have to take the stock directly and end up paying taxes on it.

If you are going to take employer stock as part of your retirement plan distribution, you should consider creating a self-directed IRA rather than setting up an IRA at your credit union. Your self-directed IRA should be able to accept the stock with few problems.

Because of the complexities involved in taking employer stock as part of your retirement plan distribution, you should always see your financial advisor before you fill out any paperwork. By doing so, you will eliminate many of the problems that may occur after you receive your certificate.

Evaluating Distribution Options

After I leave my job, should I leave my 401(k) retirement account at work and take an annuity or roll the account over to an IRA?

Although you could certainly leave your 401(k) proceeds at work, doing so may not be a good idea for various reasons. Like any other retirement plan decision, there are pros and cons.

On the positive side, many of the fees inside a 401(k) plan are less than the fees outside the plan. In addition, you may be able to buy some of your company's stock at a discount or be able to sell the stock within the stock account—assuming that you have one in your 401(k) plan—without incurring significant expenses, such as commissions.

However, the negative consequences of leaving money in a 401(k) plan usually outweigh the positive reasons for keeping it in. The average number of investment alternatives in a 401(k) plan is seven. Should you roll your money out of your 401(k) and into a self-directed IRA, you will have virtually unlimited investment choices—stocks, bonds, mutual funds, stock options, and possibly even real estate, as well as other investments. Also, most 401(k) plans typically have only one or two specific types of investments in each broad investment category. There may be only one large-cap equity fund, for example. If you roll your 401(k) money into an IRA, you will have many alternatives. In addition, many 401(k) plans limit the number of transactions you can make and often do not execute a transaction on the same day you request it. In an IRA, you would be able to move investments around as often as you like, usually with no limitations.

One of the major advantages of a self-directed IRA is that you can invest in investments that may have lower expenses than do the mutual funds or variable subaccounts inside your 401(k) plan. You should, however, compare the specific charges among these investment alternatives to see which is less expensive. Also, look at the total return after expenses and risk-adjusted returns, not just at the expenses, when you are comparing investment alternatives.

Often a significant portion of your 401(k) balance consists of the employer's stock. This may or may not be good, depending on your particular company. However, it is usually not prudent to have more than 10 percent of a portfolio in one particular stock.

In addition, most 401(k) plans require complete distribution of your plan benefits after your death.

Often, it is difficult to discern the differences among investments, so you may be dollars ahead if you retain a financial planner to help you manage your money and recommend investments for an IRA. Typically, an IRA allows you and your advisor to manage your investments more actively than investments in a 401(k) plan.

What options should I consider before taking a lump-sum distribution in cash or as a rollover?

An immediate cash distribution generates taxes for the year in which you receive the distribution. The after-tax balance is available for investment in any manner that you desire.

An IRA rollover ensures that assets will continue to achieve tax deferral and work to provide for your retirement. Under current law, you do not have to begin taking distributions from your traditional IRA until you reach age 70½.

REQUIRED MINIMUM DISTRIBUTIONS

When I was 59½, I chose an annuity option under my employer's qualified plan. I'm now approaching 70½. Do I have to be concerned about the required minimum distribution rules?

No, you do not, as long as you made the proper annuity election. An annuity election that is properly made, by its own terms, meets the required minimum distribution rules.

Must I take all my money out of my traditional IRA when I reach 70½?

You do not have to take all the money out of your IRA when you reach 70½, but you are required to take an annual minimum amount, called the *required minimum distribution.* However, you can still take as much as you want from your IRA at any time as long as you are prepared to pay the taxes on the amounts withdrawn.

What happens if I don't begin taking required minimum distributions after I turn age 70½?

Required minimum distributions must start no later than the *required beginning date.* If you do not take them, you will be assessed a penalty of 50 percent on the difference between what you took and what was required to be taken.

For example, if your minimum distribution is $10,000 and you take only $4000, you are $6000 short. Your penalty will be $3000, in addition to income taxes that may be due. Talk about a mistake!

What is the actual required beginning date?

The required beginning date, as defined in the Internal Revenue Code, is April 1 of the calendar year following the individual's attainment of age 70½. In most instances, an individual participating in a qualified retirement plan who does not own more than 5 percent of the plan's sponsor as of age 66½, directly or by attribution, can defer receiving benefits until April 1 of the calendar year following actual retirement.

What happens if I withdraw more than the required minimum distribution from my IRA?

No surprises. You can withdraw as much as you want over the required minimum distribution amount. Remember, though, that for all funds you withdraw, you will owe federal and state (if applicable) income taxes at your current tax rate.

Payout Options

My husband and I are 70 and 68 years old, respectively. Each of us has a traditional IRA. What will we have to do before we reach 70½ in order to comply with the required minimum distribution rules?

There are three fundamental decisions that each of you must make before reaching 70½. Each of you must choose a payout option, name a beneficiary, and choose a calculation method.

How important are the choices I make regarding minimum distributions?

Extremely important. The payout option and calculation method you choose by age 70½ are usually irrevocable after April 1 of the following year. Even if it is later determined there is a better option for meeting your future planning needs, the only changes the IRS will recognize are those that will increase your required minimum distribution, and this is not what people are usually trying to achieve.

What are the payout options?

Your IRA withdrawal schedule has to be set up in such a way that, if you follow it, you will get all the money out of your account within one of the following periods of time:

- *Your actual lifetime:* This payout option usually takes the form of an annuity for your life.
- *The actual joint lifetime of you and another person you choose:* This payout option usually takes the form of a joint-and-survivor annuity.
- *Your life expectancy:* Your life expectancy is based on actuarial tables for people who are your same age.
- *The joint life expectancy of you and any person you choose:* This time period is based on actuarial tables for people who are your age and the age of the person you choose.
- *Any period that is shorter than any of the above.*

You are allowed to set the length of the shorter period. The life-expectancy time periods are dictated by the life-expectancy tables the IRS provides in Publication 590, "Individual Retirement Arrangements."

The penalty for not taking the required minimum distribution is 50 percent of the difference between what you took out and what you should have taken out. Because IRA investments are tax-deferred, you must report your IRA distributions as income for the year in which you receive them.

How do I decide whether to use single life expectancy or joint life expectancy?

This decision depends upon your goals and your particular situation. The required minimum distribution will be lower if you base it upon a joint life expectancy rather than just on your own life expectancy because the longer the life expectancy, the lower the required minimum distribution. Most individuals choose the joint life expectancy.

What are the calculation methods to choose from?

There are two calculation methods: the recalculation method and the term-certain method (also known as the nonrecalculation method or the 1-year reduction method).

Designated Beneficiary

What is a designated beneficiary?

The *designated beneficiary* is used in determining the life expectancy of the joint-life payout option. For example, if your spouse is the designated beneficiary, your and your spouse's ages are used to calculate joint life expectancy. Any individual may be a designated beneficiary, and a trust may be a designated beneficiary under certain circumstances.

The joint life expectancy factor is based on your age and the age of the designated beneficiary. You cannot name your spouse as the designated beneficiary and then use your children's ages to determine the joint life expectancy factor in order to get a lower required minimum distribution. The factor is based on who you designated as the beneficiary at your required beginning date.

If a proper trust is named as a designated beneficiary, the age of the trust beneficiary who has the shortest life expectancy is used to determine the required minimum distribution.

Is the death beneficiary I named on my IRA a designated beneficiary?

Your death beneficiary can be a designated beneficiary. "Designated beneficiary" is a term defined by the Internal Revenue Code and has a particular meaning for required minimum distributions. The beneficiary you have selected to receive your retirement proceeds at your death may or may not meet the definition of designated beneficiary under the Code.

When the term "designated beneficiary" is used with regard to the payout options of the plan, it refers to the person whose age is being used to calculate the required minimum distribution. Used in the context of death, it refers to the person to whom the death proceeds will be paid.

Don't most people already have beneficiary designations for their tax-favored retirement plans?

Yes, but in many instances those beneficiary designations are improperly prepared. The beneficiary forms are usually preprinted and do not cover all the options available to the participant or IRA owner. In addition, the default beneficiary (the beneficiary who would receive the proceeds if there are no living beneficiaries named) in almost all instances is the estate of the owner.

If the owner's estate is the beneficiary and the owner dies before his or her required beginning date (age 70½), the owner's ultimate heirs will not be able to defer distributions and, therefore, the income tax more than 5 years. This may or may not be good planning. Also, the plan assets are subject to the claims of the owner's creditors because they will go through probate.

It is amazing how many beneficiary designations of retirement plans and IRAs are incorrect. A beneficiary designation is a legal document and should be prepared with special care.

Can I name a beneficiary of my IRA who is not my spouse?

You can calculate your minimum distribution on the basis of your life expectancy and the life expectancy of any person you designate. However, if your designated beneficiary is not your spouse and is more than 10 years younger than you, the designated beneficiary is deemed to be exactly 10 years younger than you regardless of his or her actual age.

What are the implications if I name one of my children, who is obviously more than 10 years younger than I am, as a beneficiary of my retirement plan?

If your child (or grandchild) is more than 10 years younger than you, the measuring period for purposes of a joint-life payout cannot exceed the joint life expectancy of you and a beneficiary 10 years younger than you. For example, let's assume you are 70 years old and you designate your 40-year-old daughter as beneficiary. Instead of using a joint life expectancy based on the actual ages of 70 and 40, you will use an "artificial" joint life expectancy calculated on the ages of a 70-year-old and a 60-year-old. This is known as the *minimum distribution incidental benefit (MDIB)* rule.

Can I have multiple beneficiary designations on the same IRA?

You can have multiple beneficiary designations, but you can have only one of the beneficiaries as a designated beneficiary within one plan. When you specifically name multiple beneficiaries, such as "Tommy Jones, Mary Jones, and Davey Jones," or collectively "my surviving children," the payout period is computed using the joint life expectancy of you and the beneficiary with the shortest life expectancy, that is, the oldest person.

The most dangerous pitfall in naming multiple beneficiaries is that all members of the group must be individuals in order to use the life expectancy of the oldest individual as your measuring period. If even one dollar of the benefits is paid to a nonindividual, such as a charity or a trust that does not qualify as a designated beneficiary, the owner is deemed to have no designated beneficiary.

Since the minimum distribution from a retirement plan with multiple beneficiaries is calculated on the life expectancy of the oldest beneficiary, can I separate my retirement plan into separate retirement accounts?

Certainly, as long as the plan document allows it. In fact, many individuals separate retirement plan assets and IRAs into several accounts to accommodate the ages of each beneficiary. For instance, an individual may want to segregate retirement assets or create separate IRA accounts for several ages or age groups. After the death of the participant/owner, this will allow each group to obtain the longest deferral possible given their ages. Also, owners/participants who have second families commonly use this technique.

If you are contemplating separate accounts, you should consult with your retirement planning advisors to make sure that you do not make mistakes when it comes time to calculate your required minimum distributions from multiple accounts.

Since enormous amounts may be involved in my retirement account, can I name a trust as the designated beneficiary of my retirement plan?

Absolutely. Until recently, the process was complicated and not too clear. Today, trust planning can help you control your retirement assets far beyond your lifetime.

For a trust to qualify as a designated beneficiary, it must comply with five rules:

1. The trust must be valid under state law.
2. All beneficiaries of the trust must be individuals.
3. The beneficiaries must be identifiable from the trust instrument.
4. The trust may be revocable as long as it becomes irrevocable at the participant's death.
5. A copy of the trust (or certain information about the trust) must be sent to the plan custodian either on the required beginning date or 9 months from the date of the owner/participant's death. Be sure to keep a copy of a transmittal letter to your plan custodian for your records, as this appears to be one of the first things the IRS agent asks for in an audit.

If the trust has multiple beneficiaries, the age of the oldest beneficiary will be used for determining the required minimum distribution.

Why might I want to have my living trust as the beneficiary of my IRA and other retirement accounts?

For estate planning, it may make good sense to name your living trust as the beneficiary of your qualified plans and/or IRAs. With a living trust you can ensure proper distribution of the account proceeds, particularly if a named beneficiary should pass away before you. In a trust, you can select a trustee to manage the proceeds for beneficiaries who may need investment help. You can provide creditor protection for your beneficiaries, such as against claims of ex-spouses.

In some cases, it may be best to name your spouse or other persons as the first (primary) beneficiary of your IRAs and retirement accounts and name your living trust as the secondary (contingent) beneficiary. You should consult with your estate planning attorney and financial advisor before making your beneficiary election.

Calculating Required Minimum Distributions

How do I calculate the minimum distribution once I designate a beneficiary and select the payout option?

Publication 590, "Individual Retirement Arrangements," which can be obtained from the Internal Revenue Service, provides a divisor based on the age of an individual or on joint lives. You divide the fair market value of your IRA as of December 31 of the year that you turn age 70½ by the appropriate divisor. The result is your minimum distribution requirement.

For example, a 70- and 65-year-old have a joint life expectancy of 23.1 years. If your IRA is worth $200,000, divide $200,000 by 23.1 to determine your minimum distribution ($8658.01). This is your minimum distribution for the first year. The required minimum distribution for each year thereafter will be determined by the calculation method you choose.

Nonrecalculation method

How is the nonrecalculation, or term-certain, method used to determine my RMD after the first year?

In *nonrecalculation,* the life-expectancy factor, or divisor, is a fixed number of years, which will be reduced 1 full year for each year after the first year. For example, if you are age 70½ and have selected your individual life expectancy as the payout option, your life-expectancy factor, or divisor, is 16 years. The first year's required minimum distribution is a sixteenth of your total plan balance. The life-expectancy factor in the second year for nonrecalculation is 16 minus 1 year, or 15 years. Therefore the minimum required distribution in the second year is a fifteenth of the plan's value. In the third year it is a fourteenth. And so on.

After 13 years there will be 4 years of life expectancy left, so the minimum distribution will be one-quarter of the account balance. In the sixteenth year, 1/1, or 100 percent, will have to be distributed. The minimum required distributions will deplete the entire plan by the end of the sixteenth year.

How is the nonrecalculation method used to determine RMD under the joint life-expectancy payout option?

The only difference between this calculation and the example above is that you and your spouse are using a joint-life-expectancy factor rather than a single life expectancy. For example, a participant who is 70 years old and a spouse who is 65 years old have a joint expectancy of 23.1 years. Each year, the life expectancy is reduced by 1 year.

How does the nonrecalculation method work if I name my husband as the designated beneficiary of my IRA and one of us dies?

Assuming the nonrecalculation method (term certain) based on both of your lives, if your husband dies first, you will continue to use the initial joint-table calculations with which you started; your life expectancy was locked in when you chose a term certain. If you predecease your husband, your husband has the option of staying with the same joint-table calculations or rolling over the balance of your account into his own IRA account (a spousal rollover).

Recalculation method

What is the recalculation method?

With the *recalculation method,* life expectancy, and thus the RMD, is recalculated every year. As one continues to live, life expectancy is pushed out a little further. For example, the life expectancy for a 70-year-old is 16 years. If the expectancy is recalculated 16 years later, at age 86, it will be 6.5 years. By "recalculating" the life expectancy of the owner or the joint life expectancy of the owner and the designated beneficiary, withdrawals are spread over a longer period, producing a lower required minimum distribution than that with the nonrecalculation method.

The recalculation method can be used only when a spouse is the designated beneficiary; it cannot be used when children, nieces, nephews, or a trust are the designated beneficiaries.

How does the recalculation method work if I name my husband as the designated beneficiary of my IRA, and one of us dies?

Assuming you have chosen the recalculation method based on the joint life expectancy of you and your spouse, let's look at the scenarios in the event that one of you predeceases the other.

If your husband dies first, his life expectancy goes to zero years. This leaves you on a recalculation basis, but on your life only, using the single-life-expectancy table. Each year thereafter, you must recalculate the required minimum amount based on your life expectancy.

Let's change the scenario and presume that you die first. Your life expectancy goes to zero, and your husband moves to the single-life-expectancy table on a recalculation basis. When your husband eventually dies, his life expectancy goes to zero, and the entire account balance in the retirement plan must be disbursed.

Is recalculation better than term certain, or vice versa?

The primary advantage of recalculation is that it gives you the smallest possible required minimum distribution. Theoretically, it also has the

TABLE 11-1 RMD Calculation for Married Couples Blended Methods

Option	Participant/owner	Spouse
1. Recalculation	✓	✓
2. Nonrecalculation	✓	✓
3. Recalculation	✓	
Nonrecalculation		✓
4. Recalculation		✓
Nonrecalculation	✓	

advantage of never letting you outlive your retirement benefits. But realistically, the retirement plan balance becomes smaller and smaller in later years while the RMD grows larger and larger.

If the spouse is the designated beneficiary, the participant can select recalculation for both spouses or nonrecalculation for both. He or she can also select nonrecalculation for one and recalculation for the other. Again, the recalculation method cannot be used for a nonspouse beneficiary. Table 11-1 summarizes these combinations.

These options can be confusing. But before dismissing them as too detailed and irrelevant, speak with an expert financial advisor. There are some effective planning strategies that can result from using these options in just the right way.

Can you give an example that compares the recalculation and nonrecalculation methods so that I can see how the results differ?

Yes. Table 11-2 compares the two methods for a married couple.

Hybrid method

In addition to the recalculation and nonrecalculation methods, is there any other method that spouses can use?

While it is not a totally different method, option 3 in Table 11-1 has been given a specific name because of its planning flexibility. It is sometimes referred to as the *hybrid method.* The participant's life expectancy is recalculated annually, but the spouse's is not. This option hedges the "order-of-death bet." If the participant's spouse dies first, the recalculation method is locked in for the life of the participant. If the participant

TABLE 11-2 Comparison of Recalculation and Nonrecalculation Methods

The husband is age 71 and the plan owner; his wife is age 69. Husband's retirement plan balance today is $100,000. The husband dies first at age 77, and his wife dies later at age 85. For illustration purposes, figures assume 0 percent growth on the IRA assets.

			Distribution			
	Age		Recalculation		Nonrecalculation	
Year	Husband	Wife	Fraction	Amount	Fraction	Amount
1	71	69	1/20.7	$ 4,831	1/20.7	$4831
2	72	70	1/19.8	4,807	1/19.7	4831
3	73	71	1/19.0	4,756	1/18.7	4831
4	74	72	1/18.2	4,704	1/17.7	4831
5	75	73	1/17.3	4,676	1/16.7	4831
6	76	74	1/16.5	4,620	1/15.7	4831
7	77	75	1/15.8	4,532	1/14.7	4831
8	dec.	76	1/15.0*	4,780	1/13.7†	4831
9		77	1/11.2	5,975	1/12.7	4831
10		78	1/10.6	5,749	1/11.7	4831
11		79	1/10	5,519	1/10.7	4831
12		80	1/9.5	5,229	1/9.7	4831
13		81	1/8.9	4,994	1/8.7	4831
14		82	1/8.4	4,696	1/7.7	4831
15		83	1/7.9	5,031	1/6.7	4831
16		84	1/7.4	4,691	1/5.7	4831
17		85	1/6.9	4,351	1/4.7	4831
18		dec.	1/1‡	25,673	1/3.7§	4831
19					1/2.7	4831
20					1/1.7	4831
21					1/1	3380

*Wife continues taking her required minimum distributions based on her single life expectancy and recalculation method.

†Wife continues taking her required minimum distributions under husband's original fixed term.

‡Under the recalculation method, at wife's subsequent death, her life expectancy goes to zero, and entire balance must be distributed to beneficiaries by December 31 of the year following the year of her death.

§Under nonrecalculation method, at wife's subsequent death, beneficiaries can continue taking their required minimum distributions under the husband's original fixed term.

passes away first, the surviving spouse continues distributions over his or her term-certain—nonrecalculated—life expectancy and is allowed to roll over the proceeds into his or her own IRA. The result is a guaranteed minimum payout period without the risk of a sudden acceleration and 100 percent distribution of benefits if both spouses die prematurely.

If the surviving spouse rolls the money over into his or her IRA, that spouse can start the process all over again by naming a new designated beneficiary and choosing a payout period based on the joint life expectancy of his or her age and that of the new designated beneficiary.

Are there any drawbacks with the hybrid method?

There are a few. After the first year, the minimum distribution is always a little larger than it would be had both spouses chosen the nonrecalculation method. But most practitioners feel this minor disadvantage is offset by the potentially greater planning flexibility the hybrid method provides.

The biggest apparent drawback is that a surprisingly large number of IRA custodians do not offer the hybrid option. Other custodians allow the option but are unable to provide the calculations. In those cases, calculation factors can be easily obtained from an advisor who specializes in IRA distribution planning. Another possibility is to move the account to a custodian that does offer the hybrid option.

Changing RMD Choices

Once withdrawals begin, can the plan owner change from the annual recalculation method to a different method of determining the distribution period?

Generally, no. The method cannot be changed after April 1 of the calendar year following the year in which the plan owner reaches 70½ or, for a person who owns 5 percent or less of the company sponsoring the plan since age 66½ and is participating in a qualified plan, April 1 of the calendar year following the year the participant retires. For this reason, unless there are no other family members, it is best not to use the annual recalculation method if the primary goal of the minimum distribution planning is deferral of income tax and maximization of the family's wealth.

There are a few exceptions to the general rule. The Internal Revenue Service will allow a change in the minimum distribution factor as long as it places the plan owner in a worse tax position, with a higher minimum distribution required. A change will also be allowed if a surviving spouse does a spousal rollover and, therefore, restarts the process. The final exception is conversion of a traditional IRA to a Roth IRA, assuming the IRA owner qualifies.

If my spouse, as my primary beneficiary, survives me, can she change the method of distribution?

Yes. Your spouse can roll the benefits to her own IRA and begin a new measuring period for distributions. When your spouse dies, the ultimate beneficiaries, who are usually children, grandchildren, or trusts for their benefit, have a measuring period of approximately their own life expectancies over which to withdraw the funds.

Income Tax Effects of RMD Choices

For the owner/participant

How will I be taxed on my pension benefit?

Benefits received from a qualified retirement plan are subject to income tax for the year in which they are received.

When I begin to take withdrawals from my traditional IRA, how will I be taxed?

The answer depends on whether your IRA contributions were fully deductible, partially deductible, or nondeductible. If the contributions were totally deductible, withdrawals will be 100 percent taxable. If the contributions were partially deductible, the deductible portion and any growth will be taxable and the nondeductible segment can be taken tax-free. Finally, in the case of the totally nondeductible contribution, again, the growth portion of the withdrawal proceeds will be taxed and the original contributions will not.

I was told that if I don't need money from my IRA, I should leave it in as long as possible and let it grow tax-deferred. Is this always the best idea?

Not necessarily! It depends on your income tax bracket and other important issues. For example, some individuals have significant amounts in their IRAs but are in low income tax brackets, and many of them have a negative taxable income. They are living off the principal of investments outside their IRAs. For these individuals, it may be best to take money from their IRAs to at least bring them up to the top of the 15 or 28 percent income tax bracket.

If you have a large IRA and your required minimum distribution will be sizable and push you into a higher income tax bracket, it might be best to take withdrawals before 70½ but after 59½ and take advantage of the lower income tax bracket while you still can. Current withdrawals may also permit you to make lifetime gifts and eventually reduce the estate tax on your IRA. This is an excellent reason to look at your overall income and estate tax planning before making any decisions on your IRA.

For beneficiaries

How will my spouse be taxed on my pension benefits or IRA distributions after my death?

Benefits received by your spouse from your qualified retirement plan or IRA are subject to income tax for the year in which they are received. In some cases, a surviving spouse can roll over your retirement plan to an IRA without current taxation and delay taking distributions from the account until his or her required beginning date.

When the owner of a traditional IRA or qualified retirement plan dies and the proceeds pass to a nonspouse beneficiary, how are they taxed?

Distributions paid to a beneficiary at the death of the plan owner are taxed as income in respect of a decedent (IRD). The distribution received is added to the recipient's other taxable income for that tax year. With larger distributions, beneficiaries can face federal income tax rates up to 39.6 percent.

What are the required minimum distribution rules in the event of my death when I'm the retirement plan participant?

The rules differ depending on whether the plan participant dies before or after age 70½, and there are various exceptions to these rules.

Participant/owner dies before required beginning date

What are the RMD rules if the plan participant dies before his or her required beginning date?

The general rule is that the entire amount in the plan must be distributed to the beneficiaries by December 31 of the fifth calendar year following the death of the owner/participant. There are exceptions:

Spouse as designated beneficiary

- The distributions can be based on the spouse's life expectancy. The first minimum required distribution needs to take place by December 31 of the calendar year following the participant/owner's death or December 31 of the year in which the plan participant would have been 70½, whichever is later.
- The surviving spouse has the option of a spousal IRA rollover and thus of naming a new designated beneficiary and selecting a new calculation method.

Nonspouse as designated beneficiary

- The beneficiary can take the entire account balance and pay the taxes in the same year.
- The nonspouse beneficiary can elect to spread the distributions over his or her single life expectancy. The first distribution must begin no later than December 31 of the calendar year following the owner/participant's death.

If there are several nonspouse beneficiaries listed, such as "children," the life-expectancy factors for all the beneficiaries are based on the oldest, thereby requiring the fastest distribution. If the plan assets were divided into separate accounts, with each child named as the designated beneficiary of a separate account, then each beneficiary uses his or her own life-expectancy factor.

What if I die and my son is the sole beneficiary of my plan?

First, your son as your sole beneficiary will be considered your designated beneficiary. When the designated beneficiary is an individual other than your spouse and you die before your required beginning date (RBD), payments to your son can be made over your son's life expectancy, as long as the first payment is made in the year after your death.

Participant/owner dies after required beginning date

What are the RMD rules if the plan participant dies after he or she has begun receiving distributions?

If a plan participant dies after reaching his or her required beginning date, the remaining portion of his or her plan assets must be distributed at least as rapidly as they would be under the method of distribution in effect at the time of the participant's death.

What are the distribution options if my brother—5 years my junior—is my designated beneficiary and I die after my required beginning date?

Because you had already begun taking required minimum distributions, the payout to your beneficiary is determined by the payout option and calculation method you selected at your RBD. Since you named a designated beneficiary, more than likely you chose a joint-life payout option. Since the designated beneficiary is not your spouse, you had to choose the nonrecalculation method for your brother at your RBD.

If you selected the *recalculation* method for yourself, then upon your death, your life expectancy goes to zero. At that point, your brother's RMD will be based upon his *original* life expectancy as of your RBD reduced by the number of years of distributions already made between your RBD and the date of your death.

Still assuming that you used a joint life expectancy with your brother, if you selected the *nonrecalculation* method to calculate your RMD during your life, you received a joint fixed number of years within which to take your distributions. Your death has no impact on this calculation method. Your brother's RMD will be based upon the original joint life expectancy as of your RBD reduced by the number of years of distributions between your RBD and the date of your death.

Does the same hold true if my daughter is my designated beneficiary and I die before her?

No. Because your daughter is more than 10 years younger than you, naming her as the designated beneficiary meant you had to use the minimum distribution incidental benefit (MDIB) rule and an "artificial" joint life expectancy to calculate your RMD. Upon your death, the MDIB rule goes away; your daughter will go back to the *actual* single life or joint life expectancy at the time of your RBD and use those factors to determine her RMD. Even if you used the recalculation method, your daughter can use only nonrecalculation, so she will calculate a term certain based on her *actual* single life expectancy at the time of your RBD minus the number of years in which you took distributions. If you used nonrecalculation, your daughter will calculate her RMD using your *actual* joint life expectancy at the time of your RBD minus the number of years in which you received distributions.

Income Tax Planning for Spouses

How does the spousal IRA rollover work?

After the plan participant's death, the surviving spouse has the option to roll the assets of each retirement plan over to an IRA. Although the spouse could roll over the retirement plan assets into his or her own existing IRA, it is usually best to establish a new, separate spousal roll-over account.

How quickly should a spouse do a rollover?

In most cases, it is probably advantageous for the spouse to do an immediate IRA rollover, but there are a few exceptions. For example, if the spouse is under age 59½ and needs the income, a rollover may not be appropriate. A beneficiary, including a spouse, under the age of 59½ can continue to receive the required minimum distributions after the death of the plan owner with no 10 percent early-distribution penalty. However, if a surviving spouse rolls over the plan assets into his or her IRA and withdraws money before he or she turns 59½, the penalty will be assessed.

Are spousal rollovers a good idea in second marriages?

A spousal rollover can be a problem in a second marriage. Usually the participant wants the surviving spouse to receive income during the spouse's lifetime but also wants his or her children from a prior marriage to ultimately inherit the retirement plan assets. Once the retirement plan assets are placed in the spousal IRA rollover, they become the spouse's assets and he or she has control over them.

What are the advantages of a spousal rollover?

A spousal rollover enables the surviving spouse to establish new distribution options, such as naming children as designated beneficiaries and using the MDIB table to create stretch-out possibilities.

My husband just passed away, and I'm the beneficiary of his IRA. Should I roll his IRA over into mine?

A rollover may be advisable if you are over the age of 59½.

If you are under age 59½ and do not believe you will need the money from your husband's IRA, it may be advisable for you to roll his IRA over into your own IRA. On the other hand, if you are under age 59½, as the beneficiary of your deceased husband's IRA, you can take money from his account without paying penalties. You cannot avoid the early-distribution penalty if you roll over the proceeds into your own IRA.

Keep in mind that if you take money from your deceased husband's IRA, you may not be able to later roll over the balance of the IRA into your IRA tax-free and start over with new RMD choices. However, if you think you might want to do a spousal IRA in the future but you need some immediate funds from your deceased husband's IRA, there is a potential solution: Estimate how much you have to take from your husband's IRA to cover your needs until you are 59½; retain this amount in his IRA, and roll over the remainder to a spousal IRA. You should take this planning approach only after consulting with a qualified tax advisor.

Income Tax Planning for Nonspouse Beneficiaries

If an IRA owner's spouse predeceases the owner after his or her required beginning date (age 70½), can the account owner still provide tax deferral for nonspouse beneficiaries?

Generally, no. Since the IRA owner has to decide on the payout and the required minimum distribution calculation method, the payout to the beneficiary is determined by the method that was elected by the IRA owner.

Is it possible to designate a trust as beneficiary of an IRA or other tax-deferred retirement account without losing the advantages of lifetime tax deferral for a nonspouse beneficiary?

Yes. With careful planning and coordination of trust provisions and beneficiary designations, a trust can qualify as a designated beneficiary receiving plan distributions for the trust beneficiaries and continuing tax deferral on amounts not paid out from the plan. If multiple beneficiaries are named in the trust, the life expectancy of the oldest trust beneficiary is used for calculating required minimum distributions to the trust. The trust must meet the designated-beneficiary rules for trusts, as described above.

Should I transfer the title or ownership of my IRAs into my living trust now?

Absolutely not! Transferring title or ownership of IRAs or other retirement accounts to a living trust creates an immediate income-taxable event on the entire balances. You only change the beneficiary designation of your IRAs and other retirement plans to the name of your living trust. You should seek proper professional advice before naming your living trust as a beneficiary of these accounts.

Also, be sure you have a durable general power of attorney as part of your estate plan. Thus, if you become disabled, the person you name as your attorney-in-fact under this power can access these accounts even though they are not titled in the trust's name. This may be important in order to avoid unnecessary taxes and penalties for failure to make minimum required distributions.

I've heard that I can stretch out the payout from my IRA over my and then my children's life expectancies. Why would I want to do this?

Flipping or *stretching out* an IRA is a planning strategy that enables your beneficiaries to keep money in your IRA for as long as possible after your death. The longer the plan assets remain in the tax-deferred account, the greater the tax-free accumulation. Tax-free accumulation and income-tax deferral combine to greatly increase the value of the account for children or grandchildren.

How does this strategy work?

This strategy essentially creates an exception to the rule that once a participant dies, payments must continue to be paid to the beneficiary as fast as they were being paid to the participant.

The key to using this strategy is to name a child (or children) who is more than 10 years younger than you as the designated beneficiary. By doing so, the minimum distribution incidental benefit rule applies. This rule states that no more than 10 years' age differential may be used between the participant and the beneficiary.

With the flip strategy, if the participant dies before all benefits have been paid from a plan, there is a life-expectancy "flip" to the remaining *actual* joint life expectancy of the much younger beneficiary minus the number of years payments were made to the participant before death. This new time period is used as the divisor to determine the length of payout rather than the artificial MDIB divisor. This causes the payments to shrink because the new divisor is larger than the artificial divisor. Thus, the payout period is stretched out.

Are there any drawbacks to the flip/stretch-out strategy?

Although this strategy stretches out the income taxes for a period of time, its most significant drawback is that it fails to address the estate tax exposure of the retirement plan assets.

Where does the designated beneficiary get the necessary funds to pay the estate tax on a large retirement plan balance? Unfortunately, lack of sufficient planning in this area often forces the beneficiary to take a total distribution of the remaining plan balance in order to have the cash needed to pay the estate tax. Without planning for the estate tax liability, the flip, or stretch-out, strategy will often not succeed.

Can you give me an example of how the flip/stretch-out strategy works?

Let's assume that Dad, a widower, is the participant at age 70½ and his only daughter is age 45. Their real joint life expectancy is 38.3 years, but the overriding MDIB rule places their joint life expectancy at 26.2. (No more than a 10-year age spread is allowed.)

Let's further assume that Dad dies 12 years later, at age 82. His life expectancy goes to zero, but his daughter's life expectancy "flips" to her original-age life expectancy at 45, which is 37.7 years. Since 12 years have already passed, the daughter has the option of using the remaining 25.7 years (37.7 minus 12 years) to calculate her required minimum distribution.

The daughter stretches out her future required minimum distributions, and the income taxes on those distributions, over the balance of 25.7 years rather than being forced to pay all the income taxes on the entire retirement plan value by the tax year following Dad's death.

In your example, must the daughter stretch the payments out, or can she take more if she wants to?

These calculations apply only to the required minimum annual distribution. The daughter may withdraw as much as she wants, up to 100 percent. Even if the daughter is not age 59½ at the time of Dad's death, there is no 10 percent penalty for making a pre-59½ distribution, as the plan is technically still in the plan participant's (her dad's) name.

The daughter, however, cannot roll over the account into her own IRA without paying income taxes on the entire amount. Only spouses are permitted to do a spousal tax-free rollover.

Is it really worth trying to figure out all the various options to take advantage of stretching out the income taxes?

The answer to this depends on a couple of things. Certainly, the size of the retirement plan assets is a factor. If the IRA account is small, it might not be practical to go through the process.

Another consideration is one's tolerance level for dealing with the complexity of the process. Even an individual who enjoys researching all the angles may reach a level beyond his or her complexity tolerance. Seeking qualified professional advice generally minimizes this concern.

Most individuals who devote time to planning in this area find the process is very worthwhile. The longer taxation can be deferred on plan distributions, the better. The potential benefits for a plan owner, his or her spouse, and eventually his or her heirs can be substantial.

I see the income tax benefits of a flip/stretch-out strategy. Can you give me another example of the actual financial benefits?

A widow, age 75, rolled over her husband's IRA into her name. This allowed her to reestablish the required minimum distribution choices, even though she was past age 70½. At the time of the rollover, the total plan was worth $650,000. She wanted her two sons to share the money equally at her death, so she created two $325,000 IRA accounts and named each son as the designated beneficiary of one of the accounts. Splitting the original plan into two accounts and naming each son as a beneficiary permitted her to use each son's life expectancy to calculate her RMD from each account rather than using just the older son's age on one account. The widow continued to take her minimum required distributions but withdrew the money in such a way that the accounts were kept equal.

To fully illustrate the financial benefits of this strategy, we would use the "best-case" scenario, that of the younger son, as an example. But to avoid overstating the benefits, we'll use the older son's "worst-case" example. The older son is age 50, with an actual life expectancy of 33.1 years. Because he is more than 10 years younger than his mother, the MDIB rule results in an artificial joint life expectancy of 21.8 years during the widow's lifetime. She chooses the recalculation method for herself and the nonrecalculation method for her older son (required because he is a nonspouse beneficiary).

If we assume that she dies 13 years later and that each account has grown at 8 percent, each account is worth approximately $400,000 at her death. As you can see, at an 8 percent growth rate, the accounts continued to increase even while the widow was taking her required minimum distributions.

After the widow's death, each son's future required minimum distribution is based on each one's actual life expectancy. The older son's original life expectancy was 33.1 years. Deducting from that the 13 years that his mother took distributions leaves him with 20.1 years as the required minimum distribution factor. This new factor requires approximately 5 percent of the account balance (1 divided by 20.1 percent) as the minimum distribution. The following year his factor will be 19.1 years (20.1 minus 1) on the basis of the term-certain (nonrecalculation) method; it will be 18.1 years the year after that; and so on. He is effectively able to stretch out the income taxes over 20 years rather than having to pay the income tax bill within one year of his mom's death. Assuming that growth continues at 8 percent and that the son takes out the money on the same percentage basis, the stretch-out IRA will provide an extra $125,000 of income (after taxes) compared to what he would have if he had been forced to pay all the income taxes up front.

Can you give an example involving a younger beneficiary, such as a grandchild?

Let's change the scenario, and assume that the widow wants her grandchildren named as the designated beneficiaries. Depending on the number of grandchildren, she will likely establish separate accounts, designating each grandchild as a beneficiary of an account. Assuming the oldest grandchild is age 38 at the time of the grandmother's death, this grandchild will be able to stretch out the distributions and income taxes over 44 years. The stretch-out will be longer for the younger grandchildren.

If all the grandchildren choose to stretch out the IRA income over the 44-year period at an assumed 8 percent growth rate, an additional $2 million in income will be generated in their IRAs from this planning. The impact of compound interest can be staggering.

ESTATE AND TAX CONSIDERATIONS FOR RETIREMENT PLAN ASSETS

Estate Planning Considerations

Preserving IRA funds for future generations

Can I leverage an IRA tax deferral into multigenerational wealth?

If there is a sufficient amount of other assets to fully fund a husband's and wife's applicable exclusion amounts, the spouses should consider using the husband's IRA to create a multigenerational tax shelter. The husband should name his wife as the beneficiary of his IRA so that if she survives him, she can make a spousal IRA rollover. She could then apply the flip/stretch-out strategy to designate children, grandchildren, or trusts for the children and grandchildren as beneficiaries. This approach allows the husband's IRA money to retain its tax-deferred status for a substantial period of time after both the husband and wife are deceased.

Another alternative is to convert the traditional IRA to a Roth IRA and name the grandchildren as the beneficiaries. This assumes, of course, that the funds are available to pay the income taxes in the year of the conversion.

What is an eternal IRA?

An *eternal IRA,* also referred to as a *dynasty IRA* or *stretch IRA,* is an IRA for which the account owner names grandchildren as beneficiaries to stretch the payout period as long as possible and maintain the retirement assets for the ultimate use of the grandchildren—and perhaps even great-grandchildren. If grandchildren are to be the beneficiaries and one or more of them are minors, be sure to name a guardian or custodian in the beneficiary designation and not the grandchild directly.

Generation-skipping transfer (GST) tax issues also come into play. The IRA transfer cannot convey more than $1 million to grandchildren or lower generations without incurring a GST penalty tax.

With careful planning, an irrevocable trust for the benefit of grandchildren may be named as the beneficiary, thereby providing additional asset protection benefits.

Is the eternal IRA a planning technique that my IRA custodian would know about?

The eternal IRA is a sophisticated planning idea. Many, if not most, IRA custodians are not in the business of planning; they are in the business of managing assets. So it is not likely that your custodian will inform you of this technique or help you to make the proper elections.

If your custodian does not know about this technique, you should insist that he or she find out about it. You should also be working with a financial advisor who is well versed in this technique. If it is a technique that fits your planning goals, you and your advisor can then work with your custodian to ensure that the proper elections are made and the plan is put in place.

Can a trust act as a named beneficiary in an eternal IRA plan?

Yes. The Internal Revenue Service has ruled that the beneficiaries of a properly drawn trust may make the necessary elections to facilitate the eternal IRA.

Can a participant create an eternal Roth IRA?

Yes. Roth IRAs are especially popular because distributions are income tax–free to the participant and the beneficiaries. Further, a Roth IRA beneficiary can receive distributions over his or her life expectancy exactly like a beneficiary of a traditional IRA.

The Roth IRA can provide tax-free compounding rather than the tax-deferred compounding of a traditional IRA, with far more dramatic results.

Second-marriage considerations

Does an IRA owner's remarriage create any special planning issues regarding the ultimate distribution of the IRA or other tax-deferred account?

Yes. Quite often a remarried individual who has children from a previous marriage has to deal with a conflict between providing financial security for his or her surviving spouse and leaving an inheritance for children of both marriages or just those of the previous marriage. This situation is most often handled by creating a special trust for the income needs of the surviving spouse and making the trust the primary beneficiary of the IRA or qualified plan. After the death of both spouses, the trust typically provides for the account owner's children and not the family of the deceased spouse of the second marriage.

When a trust is the beneficiary of an IRA, the income tax may be higher than it would be if the spouse is the beneficiary, because some of the tax-deferral options are lost. If properly structured, the trust will qualify for the marital deduction, allowing the estate taxes to be postponed until the second death. But the payout period cannot be extended beyond the spouse's lifetime, and this results in the loss of the potential stretch-out of the taxes over the children's or grandchildren's life expectancies.

Special-needs considerations

Can a handicapped adult—a child or other family member—be

the beneficiary of an IRA account without risking the loss of Medicaid, SSI or Social Security disability benefits?

Yes, by designating a *special-needs* or *Medicaid* trust as the beneficiary of an IRA, it may be possible to avoid losing government benefits and continue satisfying the IRA required minimum distribution rules for tax-deferred accounts. Care must be taken to ensure that trust disbursements are for "supplemental" needs of the income beneficiary only.

Controlling the assets for heirs

What are the estate planning advantages of naming a trust as the designated beneficiary of my retirement plan?

It is not unusual to use a trust to better manage the distribution of retirement plan assets for the benefit of the beneficiaries. Perhaps the plan participant feels his or her spouse does not have the necessary investment expertise, or perhaps his or her spouse does not wish to manage the portfolio. Perhaps it is a second marriage, and the plan participant wants to be sure that the account assets are eventually passed on to his or her children but, until that time, wants the spouse to have all the income for the spouse's lifetime. If the beneficiaries are children or grandchildren, a trust might be used to alleviate some of the "value" concerns regarding how much money and when money is to be distributed. A trust may also provide additional protection against the claims of spouses or creditors of beneficiaries.

Estate Taxation of IRAs and Qualified Retirement Plans

How are IRAs, qualified plans, and annuities taxed at death?

If assets are owned in an IRA, qualified plan, or annuity at the time of the owner's death, there will be more than one tax on their value. Distributions from these plans trigger taxable income to the recipients. Such distributions are referred to as *income in respect of a decedent,* or *IRD.* Since these assets are also included in their owners' taxable estates, the assets are also subject to federal estate tax.

How will our children be taxed on my pension benefit after both my spouse and I are deceased?

Depending upon the value of your estate, your IRA or employer-sponsored qualified plan is subject to federal estate taxes ranging from 37 to 55 percent. In addition, distributions from traditional IRAs (not Roth IRAs) and qualified plans are subject to federal income tax. However, the beneficiary will receive an income tax deduction for the estate taxes paid as a result of the IRA or qualified plan, so a portion of the tax burden will be alleviated. Even with the income tax deduction, the total tax can be as high as 75 percent of the value of the plan's assets.

I thought my IRAs and other retirement plans pass to my named beneficiaries on my death outside of my estate. Isn't that right?

Although the balances in your IRAs and other retirement plans may pass directly to your named beneficiaries outside of your probate estate, these balances are still considered assets owned by you and are part of your federal taxable estate.

The full value of these accounts at the date of your death, without deduction for any income taxes that may have been deferred, can be taxed at up to 55 percent, and even 60 percent for estates over $10 million!

Will stretch-out or eternal IRA income tax planning help with estate tax planning as well?

A stretch-out or eternal IRA stretches out income and any taxes associated with it. The value of the IRA is still subject to federal estate tax, and the heirs will have to pay the estate tax within 9 months after the IRA owner's death.

To be able to take full income tax advantage of the stretch-out option, there needs to be sufficient liquidity from other assets that the heirs can use to pay the estate tax. If heirs are forced to withdraw money from the retirement plan in order to pay the estate tax, they will trigger income tax upon the withdrawal, thereby defeating the purpose of the stretch-out strategy. In effect, the heirs are being taxed on the money they had to take out of the plan in order to pay the estate tax.

Purchasing life insurance is one way of minimizing this problem. Whether to purchase life insurance to cover any estate tax due is a matter of determining the cost efficiency of the insurance. Sometimes, families jump to preconceived conclusions about the cost of life insurance. It is imperative to have a qualified practitioner perform an economic analysis of the potential taxes due and the cost of the insurance to pay taxes. It is often a pleasant surprise to families how effective life insurance is in preserving an estate.

If I'm married and my total estate, including IRAs and other retirement plans, does not exceed the applicable exclusion amount at my death, won't my retirement plans pass estate tax–free to my beneficiaries?

Not necessarily! Most married couples assume they are protected from federal estate tax if they have done proper estate planning using a will or living trust with provisions designed to fully use each of their applicable exclusion amounts. However, well-done estate planning assumes that all of a decedent's assets will pass through the plan, thus triggering the full use of each spouse's applicable exclusion amount, but this may not be the case.

If the primary beneficiary of IRAs and other retirement accounts is the surviving spouse, which is usually the case for income tax reasons, a married couple may not get the full use of their combined applicable exclusion amount. This is because when a spouse is named as a beneficiary of an IRA or other retirement plan, the assets *bypass* the estate plan and go directly to the surviving spouse. If the deceased spouse does not own enough assets outside the IRA and/or other retirement plan, the parts of the estate plan that are designed to "soak up" the applicable exclusion amount may not be fully utilized. The result may be heavy estate taxes, depending, of course, on the size of the IRAs and other retirement plans and the value of the other assets in the estate. This problem may be minimized if the spouse is named the primary beneficiary and the revocable living trust is the secondary, or contingent, beneficiary. The spouse then uses a technique called a *disclaimer* to disclaim any rights to the proceeds from the retirement plans so that they pass instead to the revocable living trust.

Also, many people do not factor in the future growth of the retirement accounts. It is the value of these accounts on the date of death that determines estate taxes, not the value when they are created.

If you have sizable IRAs or other retirement plans and expect to live for a few years, these accounts may create an estate tax problem. You should consult a competent advisor to determine the extent, if any, of this potential problem and how you can plan to overcome it.

Strategies for Reducing Estate Taxes on Retirement Plans

Early distributions to purchase life insurance

I have a large IRA, and my wife and I have substantial other assets. Are there any planning techniques I can use to minimize the estate and income taxes after we both die?

Yes, there are. One of the best ways to reduce the overall tax is to "prepay" the tax by taking partial distributions from the IRA before you reach 70½ years of age, paying taxes on the distributions, and purchasing a second-to-die life insurance policy to cover the double tax when the surviving spouse dies. Generally, no income tax or estate tax is payable when the first spouse passes away, assuming that the IRA beneficiary is the surviving spouse. An estate tax will, however, be due and payable when the second spouse passes away.

By using annual exclusion gifts to purchase second-to-die life insurance in an irrevocable life insurance trust, you effectively pay the overall tax at a very significant discount. Obviously, the result will depend on your and your spouse's health and ages. See your advisor to "run the numbers" to make sure this strategy makes sense in your situation.

Using the living trust as beneficiary

I want to name my trust as the beneficiary of my retirement plan proceeds for estate planning purposes. How would this work after my death?

A revocable living trust can be, and often is, the beneficiary of a retirement plan or IRA. Naming your trust as the beneficiary of your retirement benefits can accomplish a number of estate tax planning objectives. However, by doing so, you may limit or forgo the possibility of stretch-out income tax planning, as described earlier.

At your death, the plan benefits will pass to your revocable trust. Depending on the size of your estate and the nature of your other assets, the plan benefits will pass either to your family trust or to the marital trust or they may be divided between the two trusts, with a portion of each required minimum distribution going to one trust and the balance going to the other. If the trust has been properly drafted, the beneficiaries of the trust will be considered the beneficiaries of the retirement plan or IRA account for purposes of the designated-beneficiary rules. Assuming your spouse is a beneficiary of your living trust, distributions from the plan to the trust will occur under the same minimum distribution rules that would apply if you had named your spouse as designated beneficiary of the plan or account.

To the extent that plan benefits pass to the marital trust, they will escape federal estate tax under the marital deduction. Your spouse will receive at least all the income generated annually from the retirement plan. Depending on the terms of the trust, your spouse may be able to roll over the plan benefits out of the marital trust and into a spousal IRA to facilitate stretch-out or other planning.

It is also possible that all or part of the retirement plan or IRA proceeds may be used to "soak up" your applicable exclusion amount and pass to your family trust. This usually occurs because the decedent does not have sufficient assets outside the retirement plan to fully fund the family trust.

For example, let's say a married couple's $1.5 million estate consists of jointly owned assets totaling $900,000 (home, $300,000; nonretirement investments, $500,000; miscellaneous assets, $100,000) and the husband's IRA of $600,000. With the assets owned in this manner, part of the IRA may have to be used to fund the family trust.

Let's assume that it is 2006, when the applicable exclusion amount will be $1 million per person. The husband dies. His estate, in a non-community property state, will likely consist of his IRA and one-half the value of all the other assets: a total of $1,050,000. Proper estate planning would call for $1 million to be allocated to a family trust in order to fully utilize the husband's $1 million applicable exclusion amount. To accomplish this goal, all the IRA proceeds need to be placed into the family trust.

This is all well and good for estate tax purposes, except that the family trust is not really worth the full $1 million. The $600,000 IRA will be subject to income tax as required minimum distributions are taken by the beneficiaries. If the proceeds are taxed at the highest income tax bracket, which is a distinct possibility, about $240,000 of the $600,000 IRA will be gone. The result is an underfunded family trust; the full $1 million applicable exclusion amount will not pass to heirs at the surviving spouse's death.

In a community property state, the tax result would be virtually the same. Assuming all the couple's property is community property, the husband's estate will be $750,000 (one-half of the total $1.5 million estate). Half will pass to the bypass trust, also leaving it underfunded. However, the value of the IRA in the family trust will be $300,000, meaning the loss in the applicable exclusion amount because of taxes would be about $120,000.

As is readily apparent, using IRA or other retirement plan proceeds to fund a family trust is often not very tax-efficient.

Gifts to heirs

A large part of our estate is invested in a rollover IRA. How can we minimize the double hit of income and estate taxes?

Retirement plans are subject to federal income tax and federal estate tax. By comparison, non-retirement plan assets are subject only to estate taxation at death, not income tax. Non-retirement plan assets receive a step-up in tax basis to the fair market value as of the date of death. Furthermore, they are generally taxed at capital gain tax rates, not ordinary-income tax rates. This is not true of retirement plan assets.

In some cases, it may be wiser to take more than is needed out of your retirement plan today, pay the income taxes today, and make gifts to your heirs now rather than leaving them a large retirement plan subject to both estate and income taxation.

Gifts to charities

Testamentary gifts to charities

Why can't I just leave my retirement plan assets to charity?

This is an excellent option, especially in light of the significant income and estate taxes that retirement plans can generate. Heirs may net as little as 25 percent of the retirement plan assets, while a charity will end up getting 100 percent.

Of course, if you name a charity as the ultimate beneficiary of your retirement plans, your family will not inherit the assets. But if you are considering leaving a portion of your estate to charity in any event, retirement plan proceeds make excellent charitable gifts.

Can I give my IRA directly to a charity while I'm living?

No. Your only option is to make a withdrawal from the IRA and give that to charity. Income taxes are due when you make the withdrawal, but you will receive a charitable deduction that you can take against your income. Due to the limitation on charitable deductions, the deduction may not totally offset the income tax on the amount you withdraw.

I'm considering naming a charity as a beneficiary of part of my IRA. Is there any problem with this?

Naming an IRA beneficiary that is not an individual or a qualified trust could be a critical mistake. The law is clear that when a charity is named as a beneficiary of an IRA, the plan has no designated beneficiary. The seemingly innocent charitable beneficiary designation not only will require that you take higher minimum distributions than you would otherwise have chosen but also will subsequently require that the plan assets be paid to the other beneficiaries either within 5 years of your death if it takes place before you are 70½ or by December 31 of the year following your death if it takes place after age 70½. The possibility of stretching out payments for any longer period of time is lost.

If you want to make a postdeath gift to charity from your IRA, consider setting up a separate account for the amount of proceeds you want to pass to charity. In this way, the other IRA account assets can be stretched out while still meeting your charitable objective.

Charitable remainder trusts

I want my spouse to receive lifetime income from my IRA account and want the remaining account balance to go to charity after my spouse's death. How can I accomplish this?

One method involves establishing a charitable remainder trust (CRT) either during your lifetime or at your death and making it the primary beneficiary of your IRA account. The lifetime beneficiary of the charitable remainder trust would be your spouse, and after your spouse's death, the remainder would be paid without income or estate taxes to the charitable beneficiaries designated in your trust. With this approach, the required minimum distribution rules no longer apply to your beneficiary, and your spouse pays tax on trust income only as he or she receives it.

Can you tell me more about using a charitable remainder trust as the beneficiary of my IRA?

Naming a charitable remainder trust as the beneficiary of your IRA may have merit if you are charitably inclined. Your spouse can be named as the CRT's beneficiary, with the children as contingent beneficiaries. For that matter, anyone can be the beneficiary of the CRT.

On your death, when the IRA proceeds flow into your CRT, the assets do not belong to your heirs. The beneficiaries have a right to only a stated percentage of the IRA assets held in the CRT each year. When the IRA proceeds are paid into the CRT, there are no immediate income taxes. However, the amounts paid to the CRT beneficiaries are subject to income tax as they are paid out, just as income paid to them directly from an IRA would be.

When individuals other than a surviving spouse, such as children, are named as beneficiaries of the CRT, there will be estate tax due. The estate tax is calculated on the present value of the future income stream the nonspouse beneficiaries will receive. Thus, the estate must have other assets from which to pay the estate taxes, as the estate cannot invade the principal of the CRT to pay the taxes.

This strategy takes a great deal of planning. As with any sophisticated retirement planning device, it should be implemented only when it is appropriate to a particular situation and has been thoroughly analyzed by knowledgeable professionals.

chapter 12

Planning for Children's Education

Why is planning for my children's college education such an important part of the financial planning process?

Setting aside dollars towards college education expenses is a critical part of the financial planning process. Most parents understand that the value of an education from a school of their choosing significantly surpasses the cost of that education. To meet that cost and not deny the child a quality education, one must often take advantage of the compounding effect of a growth investment. This requires both time and a higher rate of return than can be found in guaranteed investment vehicles.

Saving for college expenses should be an integral part of financial planning so that you can also achieve other goals, such as financial independence or retirement. Unless you plan for college expenses, you may be forced to use retirement funds to meet education costs.

Why is planning for children's education so important?

Raising a child and putting him or her through college is one of the largest expenses parents face today. The cost of tuition, room, board, and other related expenses can sometimes reach $250,000 for a 4-year private school. The cost of college is so intimidating that parents might not even try to save, particularly when there is more than one child to consider.

Most parents, regardless of income, do not start saving for college until their children are in their teens, when reality sets in. If they would start the saving process early, there is a good chance they could accumulate a large portion of the cost. When people have children later in life, saving can become a balancing act between retirement and college expense needs, highlighting the importance of comprehensive planning. Starting early is a key to success in both areas of planning.

Another area of concern in planning for minor children is the possibility that the parents will not be available to take care of their minors' needs, due to illness, disability, or premature death. This issue also must be addressed when planning for the education of children.

How can I pay for college expenses?

Basically, there are five ways to pay for a college education. They are:

- Use current income
- Use savings and investments
- Borrow
- Use gifts from third parties
- Obtain financial aid

SAVING AND INVESTING

Should I save first for college and then for retirement?

The best approach is to save for both at the same time. Parents simply cannot afford to delay starting the retirement process until after the last child has graduated from school. The 10 to 15 years of lost tax-sheltered accumulations would be virtually impossible to make up at a later age. Fortunately, tax laws have made it easier to use tax-sheltered plans, such as Roth and traditional IRAs, to save for college.

Should I save in my child's name?

There are advantages and disadvantages to saving in your child's name. However, whose name is on the savings account may not be the most important element of the planning process. For purposes of college funding, the real key is to invest as much as you can, as early as you can. Start with a systematic monthly investment plan and then add lump sums when you get bonuses, tax refunds, or gifts. When you get a raise, increase the monthly savings amount.

If it is unlikely that your child will qualify for any financial aid, saving in the child's name can make tax sense. For example, once a child turns age 14, the child's income is taxed in his or her income tax bracket. Under the new tax rules, a child would most likely pay only 10 percent capital gain tax on gains from a stock investment sold to pay for college.

A major disadvantage of putting investments in a child's name is that when he or she reaches the age of majority, the money is the child's to do with as he or she pleases. You need to weigh tax advantages versus control of assets when deciding whether to title the savings or investment vehicle in your child's name.

Another possible benefit of having investments in the child's name is asset protection. In the event of your own divorce, bankruptcy, or creditor problems, your child's money will be protected for its intended purpose, out of the reach of creditors or an ex-spouse.

What options are available for saving for college?

In addition to savings and investment accounts, there are custodial accounts through the Uniform Transfers to Minors Act (UTMA) and the Uniform Gifts to Minors Act (UGMA) and trusts, such as irrevocable life insurance trusts and minor's trusts.

Congress has enacted educational programs such as education IRAs, the Hope Scholarship Credit, and the Lifetime Learning Credit. It is also possible to make penalty-free withdrawals (subject to certain restrictions) from traditional and Roth IRAs to pay college expenses.

Each of these choices has advantages and disadvantages, depending on your particular situation, but often the best approach is to use more than one strategy to achieve your financial goals. You should work with your financial and legal advisors to determine which strategies best fit your particular needs.

What types of investments should I consider for college funding?

For the most part, the age of your child determines the type of investment vehicle that you should use. Assuming you have more than 10 years before your child starts college, individual stocks and stock mutual funds are the best choice for college savings, whether in a regular, non-tax-deferred account or in an IRA.

Stock and stock funds have provided the greatest returns over time. This greater return has come with greater volatility, which may not be a comforting feeling as you get closer to paying the bills. Therefore, as your child nears the college start date, you may prefer to modify your asset mix by including fixed-income assets.

If you are saving in a regular account, tax-efficient investment vehicles such as municipal bonds or tax-deferred savings bonds are beneficial. There are stock funds that have relatively little portfolio turnover and, therefore, little capital gain. When it comes time to sell either a stock or shares in a stock fund to pay tuition, the tax will be at the lower capital gain rate.

Another investment choice is a variable life insurance policy. The policy can be on the life of a parent, a grandparent, or even the child. With a properly structured variable universal life insurance policy, you can accumulate funds tax-deferred inside the professionally managed subaccounts and have access to a significant portion of your money on a tax-free basis, through withdrawals and low-cost policy loans, to pay for the education. If you have a need for life insurance, the cost of the death benefit will likely be minor compared to the flexibility and tax savings that this alternative can provide.

If we decide to make investments in the names of our minor children, what investments should we consider?

There are several investment opportunities that will help minors develop an intermediate and long-term investment program. As time goes by, you should inform your children that they have an investment program that will enable them to pay for a college education, meet emergencies, help with a future marriage, and even provide for their future children after they marry.

An education IRA is a simple, easy, and inexpensive means of creating an investment program for a child. Five hundred dollars per year per child under the age of 18 can accumulate tax-deferred and be withdrawn tax-free for college education purposes. The money can be invested in any prudent investment. Mutual funds, stocks, CDs, Treasury bills, Treasury bonds, and savings bonds, such as E bonds and I bonds, are just a few of the different types of investments that are available.

Gifts are another means of helping children develop their own investment portfolio. Each individual can give $10,000 a year, indexed for inflation, gift tax–free to anyone. Thus parents and grandparents can each place in the child's name up to $10,000 per year ($20,000 if gift splitting between spouses is used). There are generally no forms to fill out. There are no tax consequences. The money can be placed in any prudent investment.

Giving life insurance or an investment to my grandchildren seems so impersonal. Is there any way that I can personalize such a gift?

Of course. You can write a letter to your grandchild in which you express your love and explain the reason that you made the gift, whether it be for college, emergencies, or another worthwhile purpose. After signing the letter, keep it in a safe place and be sure to tell someone else, such as the executor of your will, where it is. This way, if you should die before the time comes to give the letter to your grandchild, the other person could deliver the letter at the appropriate time.

Traditional IRAs & Roth IRAs

What is the best way for my working son to save for college?

As long as your son has at least $2000 a year in earnings, he can contribute it to a traditional IRA. The contribution is tax-deductible and grows tax-free, and when your son withdraws the money to pay for college, it will be taxed at his income tax rate, typically 15 percent. There is no 10 percent IRS penalty for early withdrawals, before age 59½, provided the money is used for college.

Alternatively, your son can contribute as much as $2000 per year to a Roth IRA. The contribution is not tax-deductible, but the money will grow tax-free. Your son either can withdraw his contributions (not the earnings) tax- and penalty-free to pay for college or can take advantage of the penalty-free exception for higher-education expenses and withdraw both contributions and earnings. The income tax on the earnings will still be at the lower, 15 percent rate.

Can my wife and I use a Roth IRA or a traditional IRA to put away money for our children's college expenses?

Because it offers easy access to the funds for preretirement needs, the Roth IRA is a good choice for parents or grandparents who want to save for children's or grandchildren's college expenses. With a Roth IRA, you can withdraw your contributions at any time, tax- and penalty-free. You can also withdraw the earnings from the account without penalty to pay college expenses, but you must pay income tax on early withdrawals.

Parents and grandparents can also use traditional IRAs to provide for college. The proceeds of the account will be taxed upon distribution, but there is no penalty for withdrawal before age 59½ if the funds are used for college.

Because a married couple can contribute as much as $4000 into Roth or traditional IRA accounts each year, it is recommended that each parent save in an IRA to maximize the availability of funds at college time. It would be wise to also fund your 401(k) or other retirement plans at the same time to ensure that you will have a nest egg at retirement.

Can employing a minor in a family business be used to help fund the costs of the child's college education?

Employing children in a family business is often a good way to reduce the overall family tax bill, as it shifts income to individuals in a lower tax bracket. Employment in a family business can also provide the $2000 earnings a child needs to establish either a Roth or a traditional IRA.

Let's examine these advantages in detail. The family business can take a deduction for a reasonable salary paid to the child. Payments to the child can reduce your self-employment income and tax by shifting to the child income that otherwise would have gone to you.

Since any salary the child receives is considered earned income, it is not subject to the kiddie tax rule for children under age 14. As long as the child's wages and other income are equal to or less than the standard deduction, no income tax will be due. Also, children under age 18 who are working for an unincorporated business are not subject to Social Security tax.

If the child is making less than the standard deduction and would not be paying taxes anyway, a Roth IRA might be more suitable than a deductible IRA. However, you and your child may want to consider a traditional IRA, as the deductible contributions can offset earned and unearned income. This would allow the family business to pay the child an additional $2000 above the standard deduction without the child's having to pay income tax.

An important point to remember is that the family business must make certain that the wages are reasonable for the work performed and that the services performed were necessary to the business.

Education IRAs

What is an education IRA?

An *education individual retirement account (education IRA)* is an account that is created for the purpose of paying certain expenses of higher education for the IRA's beneficiary. The contributor must create a separate education IRA for each child, and contributions are *not* deductible.

Are there any downsides to an education IRA?

Even though earnings on investments in an education IRA grow tax-free (as long as they are used for qualified higher-education expenses), the $500 annual investment will grow to only around $22,800 over 18 years assuming 10 percent growth. That barely pays for 1 year of private college at today's prices. Also, you cannot contribute to a prepaid tuition or state savings plan and an education IRA in the same year, and you cannot receive a Hope Scholarship or Lifetime Learning Credit in years when education IRA funds are withdrawn. Since the money is in your child's name, his or her eligibility for financial aid might be affected.

Are there any additional restrictions on an education IRA?

Yes. The money in an education IRA must be used for education expenses by the beneficiary's thirtieth birthday. If not used, the money may be rolled over to an education IRA for a younger family member. Otherwise, the IRA must be distributed within 30 days of the beneficiary's thirtieth birthday, and the earnings are fully taxable and might be subject to a 10 percent penalty.

Who can establish an education IRA?

Anyone—parents, grandparents, and even friends—can transfer funds to an education IRA if his or her adjustable gross income is less than $95,000 on an individual return ($150,000 on a joint return). But the total contribution for each child cannot exceed $500 per year, making the account very restrictive.

Can I establish an education IRA for more than one child under the age of 18?

As long as your AGI meets the contribution requirements, you can establish separate education IRAs for any number of children under the age of 18.

Can several people get together and create several education IRAs for the same child so that we can exceed the $500 limit?

No. No more than $500 can be contributed for each child each taxable year whether by one individual or by many individuals. Also, only one rollover per education IRA to a younger family member is allowed during a 12-month period ending on the date of distribution.

Does the person who establishes the account decide which funds the initial deposit will be invested in?

At the time of establishing the account, the person can decide between several investments choices. However, final authority falls to the parent or guardian designated to manage the account. He or she has the authority to redirect investments or to direct any additional contributions. All assets may be invested in mutual funds but not in life insurance contracts.

Who can manage an education IRA account?

The law requires that one of the child's parents or guardians must be responsible for managing the account. If someone other than the child's parent or guardian establishes the account, the establishing depositor must then designate a parent or guardian to manage the account. In addition, the establishing depositor may choose to have the account turned over to the child when the child reaches the age of majority.

Is an education IRA account opened in the child's name or the parent/guardian's name?

The account is opened in the name of the child, but the names of the person who establishes the account and of the parent or guardian who will be responsible for managing it are also included on the account.

What are the qualified education expenses that an education IRA can cover?

Qualified higher-education expenses include tuition and fees and the costs of books, supplies, equipment required for enrollment or attendance, and room and board for students enrolled at least on a half-time basis. Institutions eligible are those offering credit toward a bachelor's degree, an associate's degree, a graduate-level or professional degree, or another recognized higher-education credential.

Does establishing an education IRA guarantee that higher-education expenses will be met?

No. The contribution amount is limited to $500 per year, and the amount available at the time the child begins college is dependent on several factors. These factors include the number of years before college that the IRA is established, the number of years in which contributions are made, and how the money is invested. In addition, the cost of college depends on the school selected, the inflation rates of tuition costs, and the number of years of study.

Other Investments

Is a tax-deferred annuity an appropriate investment for saving for my child's college education?

A tax-deferred annuity offers the advantage of investment growth on a tax-deferred basis, and annuities receive preferred treatment under financial-aid rules. However, to avoid the 10 percent early-withdrawal penalty, this strategy should be used only by a parent or grandparent who will turn 59½ before the first withdrawal. In addition, the owner should keep the annuity in the accumulation phase for 10 years or more to offset the differential between long-term capital gain taxation and ordinary-income taxation. Withdrawals of gain from annuities are subject to ordinary-income tax, whereas stocks and stock mutual funds may be subject to the lower capital gain tax rates.

Are U.S. savings bonds appropriate for college funding?

If deferring income until a time when you are in a lower tax bracket is important and if a guarantee of principal and interest is more important than potential growth, U.S. savings bonds may be an appropriate investment choice. You purchase these bonds at a discount and do not have to recognize income until you cash them. If you have 5 years or less before college expenses arise, you might also consider using savings bonds for the fixed-income portion of your portfolio.

If your adjusted gross income is less than $54,100, or $81,100 for joint filers (figures indexed annually for inflation), income from a U.S. Series EE savings bond used for qualified higher-education expenses is totally tax-free. The tax-free amount decreases and is completely eliminated at an AGI of $69,100 for single filers and $111,100 for joint taxpayers (figures indexed annually for inflation).

If you do not expect to receive the earnings tax-free because you will be over the threshold, other investment options might make more sense, especially if there is a longer investment time horizon.

When does it make sense to use fixed-income vehicles to fund a college education?

Asset allocation modeling favors fixed-income vehicles when the child is close to entering college, perhaps within 3 to 5 years. At that point, it might be wise to shift a portion of the assets, if this has not already been done, into fixed-income vehicles with staggered maturities. By doing this, you will reduce the risk of market volatility or a drop in the market as the tuition bills come due. Otherwise, consider the use of short-term bond funds, which can also provide the necessary liquidity.

Owning stock is important—especially since a college education takes 4 or more years, perhaps as many as 8 to 10—so that you can slowly liquidate the stocks as needed. Since the typical business cycle lasts 3 to 5 years, having a portion of assets in fixed-income or cash equivalents will help eliminate some of the market risk.

GIFT PROGRAMS

Gifts to Minor Children

Can I give money or other property to a minor?

Of course. Anyone can make gifts of money or other property to a minor. In fact, one of the most attractive opportunities for current income tax savings is the use of annual gifts to transfer income-producing property to family members in lower tax brackets.

Are gifts of money for college expenses considered taxable gifts?

Although in most states it is not considered a legal obligation, the payment of college expenses normally falls within a parent's responsibility to support a child. Therefore, when a parent pays a college tuition bill, the payment amount is not subject to the gift tax rules. In addition, tax-free gifts in excess of the $10,000 annual gift tax exclusion are permissible for certain types of educational and medical expenses as long as the expenses are paid directly to the institution.

What special tax rules apply for children under age 14?

Minors are taxpayers for any income they earn, whether through employment or investment. However, when a child is under the age of 14, a special *kiddie tax* rule applies to the taxation of his or her investment income. If such a child has investment income that exceeds $700 (indexed annually for inflation), the excess income is taxed at the highest marginal bracket of the child's parents. *Investment income* is defined as any income other than earned income and may consist of interest, dividends, royalties, rents, and profits from the sale of assets. Only investment income is subject to tax at the parents' top rate.

Once a child reaches the age of 14, he or she is considered a separate taxpayer and is taxed at rates that may be significantly lower than the rates of his or her parents.

How can I give property to minor children?

In many states, minors cannot legally hold title to or manage property, so a guardian, custodian, or trustee must hold the property for the benefit of the child:

- A *guardian* is an institution or individual named in a will or appointed by a court.
- A *custodian* is an institution or individual that holds property on behalf of a minor under a state's statute that governs gifts to minors. Most states have adopted either the Uniform Transfers to Minors Act (UTMA) or the Uniform Gifts to Minors Act (UGMA).
- A *trustee* is an institution or person named in a trust that holds assets for the benefit of the minor.

What type of assets should be given to a minor?

While a child can be given virtually any type of asset, a potential donor should consider giving appreciated property, such as common stock, to a child. For example, a parent can hold the stock until his or her child is ready to enter college. At that point, the parent can give the appreciated stock to the child, using the gift tax annual exclusion. The child can liquidate the stock and pay the capital gain tax either at the child's lower income tax rate or at no more than a 20 percent rate if the stock is held long-term. A gift of appreciated stock can be ideal for either short-range or longer-range educational financing needs.

What are the Uniform Gifts to Minors Act and the Uniform Transfers to Minors Act?

To provide a means for giving gifts to minors efficiently, all states have enacted either the Uniform Gifts to Minors Act (UGMA) or the Uniform Transfers to Minors Act (UTMA). Any gifts made under these statutes are treated as complete for purposes of property, income, and gift tax laws.

Under either law, it is easy to establish a custodial account for a minor. To do so, a donor appoints a custodian to hold and invest assets for the benefit of the minor beneficiary. This custodian maintains control of the assets on behalf of the minor until he or she reaches the age of 21 (18 in some states).

What is the difference between UTMA and UGMA?

The Uniform Gifts to Minors Act was passed by many states so that gifts of stocks and other common investments could easily be made to minors. The law was "uniform" in that the various states adopted laws that were similar.

As time passed, it became apparent to the legislators of many states that UGMA was too restrictive in the types of assets that custodians could hold for the benefit of minors. A newer version of UGMA, the Uniform Transfers to Minors Act, was introduced by the legal commission that drafts uniform laws for the states. UTMA is far less restrictive than UGMA as to the extent of assets that can be held in a custodial account. Now, UTMA has been enacted by many states.

Your attorney can tell you which law is applicable in your state. You can then look into the possibility of establishing a custodial account under that law for a child or grandchild.

Is a gift or transfer made to an UGMA or UTMA account irrevocable?

A transfer to either type of account is irrevocable. The minor's Social Security number must be used for tax-reporting purposes. The custodial property must be held and used for the benefit of the minor beneficiary until he or she reaches an age specified in the state's UGMA/UTMA, typically either 18 or 21. At that point, the remaining assets must be turned over to the beneficiary to do with as he or she pleases.

Who may be custodian of an UTMA or UGMA account, and what are the custodian's responsibilities?

The custodian may be the person who made the gift or transfer, another adult, a bank trust department, or a trust company. If the person who made the gift appoints himself or herself as custodian and subsequently dies before the funds are distributed to the minor, the custodial property is included in that donor's estate for estate tax purposes. Therefore, if grandparents, for example, give money to a grandchild in an UTMA or UGMA account, you may want to have a third party act as custodian.

A custodian is obligated to use prudent management in dealing with the property belonging to the minor. A custodian may use the assets as he or she considers advisable for the use and benefit of the minor. The custodian may not use the funds for his or her own benefit, other than reimbursement for reasonable expenses incurred during the performance of his or her custodial duties.

Is establishing an UGMA or UTMA account a good way to save for a minor's education?

Maybe, but there are drawbacks. Having a child own assets in an UGMA or UTMA can present a problem if a scholarship or grant is at stake, and the account will count against the child for purposes of qualifying for financial aid.

With an UTMA or UGMA account, the donor loses control over the account assets when the minor reaches majority, which is either 18 or 21 depending on state law. Also, if the donor is the custodian, the full amount of the account is included in the donor's estate if the donor dies before the account is distributed to the child.

Consider accumulating the education funds in your name. This will not remove the assets from your estate, but it will enable you to maintain control of them. Alternatively, consider creating a trust that allows the assets to remain in the trust after the child reaches majority or any later age you determine. This enables you to maintain control of the assets and removes them from your estate for estate tax purposes.

Gifts in Trust

Is there a way to give money to minors so that I can control when my child receives the assets?

Any gift given to a minor under an UTMA or UGMA account must be released to him or her at majority (18 or 21, depending on the state in which the child is domiciled).

A better strategy is to make gifts to a Crummey demand trust (discussed more fully in Chapter 5). A Crummey trust can contain detailed instructions on exactly when and how the trust property is to be distributed. This gives the donor, through the language of the trust, more control over who gets what, when they get it, and how they get it.

Does an ILIT have to own life insurance?

ILITs are commonly used because of the demand-right powers that are found in them. With these powers, a gift to the trust can qualify for the gift tax annual exclusion. In addition, an ILIT can contain instructions that control the distribution of assets to the children.

ILITs do not have to hold life insurance policies. An ILIT that does not hold life insurance is merely an irrevocable trust with demand-right powers. (Irrevocable trusts and demand rights are discussed in detail in Chapter 5.) This type of ILIT can hold virtually any type of asset and is often used as a means of financing a child's college education.

What other advantages are there of making gifts in trust to minors, or even adult, children?

Making gifts to a child through a trust enables the maker to delay the child's receipt of the trust property until a specified age or event. In the meantime, the trustee can be given broad investment powers and the ability to use trust assets for the benefit of the child.

Are there trusts other than ILITs that can be used for making gifts to children?

Many types of irrevocable trusts can be used for the benefit of children. One of the most common is a *2503(c) minor's trust.* This type of trust is named after the Internal Revenue Code section that allows gifts made to a special trust to qualify for the annual gift tax exclusion.

Because of a special provision passed by Congress many years ago, all gifts to a minor's trust qualify for the gift tax annual exclusion even though they may not otherwise qualify for the exclusion.

The trustee of a 2503(c) has wide discretion in investments and in distributions to the minor beneficiary. However, when the minor reaches the age of 21, he or she has the right to the trust assets, much like the case with an UTMA or UGMA account.

Many attorneys, when drafting a 2503(c) minor's trust, require that upon the child's twenty-first birthday, the trustee must give notice to the child that he or she has 30 days to take the trust assets out. If the child does not exercise this demand right, the assets stay in the trust for as long as the trust requires under its terms. This "delayed" demand right allows the trust to continue without any gift or estate tax penalty. Usually, the child does not exercise the demand right. If he or she does, there is nothing the trust can do. That is the weakness of using a 2503(c) minor's trust.

OTHER EDUCATION PAYMENT OPTIONS

What is a college prepayment plan?

Traditional *prepaid tuition plans* allow parents to pay, either in installments or as a lump sum, for future college bills at today's prices. The appeal is that when the child is ready for freshman year, the account will cover tuition no matter how much it has risen. The plans guarantee a return of principal equal to the rate of tuition inflation at state universities.

What is a state college savings plan?

Many professionals feel that traditional prepaid tuition plans are too conservative and inflexible, especially considering the long time horizon before a child may be attending college. *State college savings plans* are becoming more attractive and are best suited for long-term savers with children because they provide market returns on the savers' investment.

State savings plans generally allow a child to attend any state-accredited institution. If one child does not attend a state college, the account can often be used by another family member. These savings plans are an improvement over both the prepaid plans and the education IRA. Generally, state savings plans are set up as trusts and are managed by an independent trustee.

Not all states have these plans, but those that do have a specified asset allocation that becomes increasingly more conservative as the child gets closer to the college entry date. The earnings from the plans grow unencumbered by federal taxes, and, depending on the state, the money can be used for any college, even if it is not in the same state.

An example of one of these plans is New York State's College Savings Program. It allows a contribution up to $100,000 per child and invests in a blend of stocks, bonds, and money market funds, depending on the child's age. Residents of any state can open an account under the New York program, but only residents of New York State can deduct up to $5000 in contributions on their state income tax returns each year.

A state college savings plan can be a good way to impose discipline on your savings effort and get a tax break as well. Investors at all income levels are eligible. To find out more, check the Internet at www.collegesavings.org. Look at plans that offer flexibility, invest according to the age of the child, allow use of the money at any college, and do not have a low cap on annual contributions.

I've paid into the state tuition program for college education. Should I use an education IRA as a supplement?

If you made a contribution to any qualified prepaid tuition program for a child, you cannot add money to an education IRA during the same year.

Can you give me an overview of how a person qualifies for financial aid for higher education?

To determine who qualifies for financial aid, the federal government provides a formula that subtracts the expected family contribution from the cost of schooling. The formula takes into account the combined assets and income of the parents and the child, giving greater weight to any assets or income in the child's name. Therefore, it is not a good strategy to give assets to children if you are going to request financial aid.

Certain assets that are tax-advantageous to the parents also have preferred status under financial aid laws. Tax-deferred cash-value accumulations and favorable loan provisions make permanent life insurance very attractive for funding a college education. However, there should be a valid need for the insurance; otherwise, the funds might better be invested in vehicles that do not carry charges for a death benefit. Having the parent as the insured makes the most sense, because he or she is generally the source of the funds for college. In the event of the parent's death, educational goals, if properly planned for, can still be met.

Employer-sponsored plans, such as 401(k), defined-benefit, and defined-contribution, as well as individual annuities also have preferred status under financial aid laws. Many retirement plans allow borrowing to pay for education expenses. Typically, a maximum loan of $50,000 can be borrowed, to be paid back within 5 years.

Are there ways to increase eligibility for financial aid?

If it looks like your child has a good chance of qualifying for financial aid, you might try to lower your taxable income by increasing your 401(k) contributions. Increasing your contributions will not only improve your eligibility for getting aid but provide a potential source of funds from which to borrow later.

When you borrow 401(k) money, you need to pay it back at a moderate interest rate, typically prime rate plus 1 point, over a 5-year period. The loan will not be taxed as a distribution from your plan as long as you repay it. However, if you leave your company or miss scheduled payments before the loan is repaid, you may be subject to income tax and an early-withdrawal penalty if you are not 59½.

Is there a way of paying for my grandchildren's education if I've already exceeded the $10,000 annual gift?

Yes. If you make a payment directly to an educational organization as tuition for your grandchildren, the payment will not be considered a gift.

appendix A

Finding and Working with a Financial Advisor

What advisors do I need on my team?

With the aid of an accountant, a financial planner, an investment advisor, an insurance agent, and an attorney, you can design a plan that accomplishes your financial and estate planning objectives.

INSURANCE AGENTS

Why should I work with a life insurance agent when I can buy life insurance through the Internet?

Today people can purchase almost any investment without ever talking to anyone. To make an informed purchase of life insurance, the buyer must learn a tremendous amount of information about the types of life insurance policies available. An individual looking for the cheapest price may not get what he or she needs in a life insurance policy.

How much and what type life insurance should you buy? A life insurance agent can learn what your goals and requirements are and present the best policy for your needs. As time goes by, the insurance agent can modify your insurance policies by fine-tuning, updating, and making small changes that will keep your policies in line with your goals for the future.

How do I select a life insurance agent who can best meet my needs?

Life insurance agents offer a valuable service, especially considering the benefit life insurance provides in managing risk, providing protection, and offsetting estate tax costs. To the consumer, insurance seems simple enough: you pay a premium, and, upon your death, the insurance company provides a death benefit to your beneficiaries. The truth is there is a great deal more to insurance than most people realize. Depending upon the type and design of the policy your agent presents, there can be large differences in the premiums you pay, the amount of cash value that builds in your policy, and the amount of the death benefit paid to your beneficiaries. Consequently, you should seek the best life insurance advice available.

This advice can be yours if you rely upon the sound judgment and skill of a professional life insurance agent who has demonstrated his or her commitment to the industry and to serving your needs on an ongoing basis. In selecting such an agent, consider these factors:

- *Education:* To obtain the best advice and give you confidence in the advice, find out if the agent has any professional education credentials or advanced insurance designations. Also ask the agent how many hours of continuing education he or she is required to take and how many he or she actually takes.
- *Knowledge:* The agent you are interviewing should be able to answer your questions and help guide you through the planning process. He or she should provide you with up-to-date information on the latest insurance policies. Most of all, you should look for an agent who can clearly explain all your alternatives.
- *References:* Do not hesitate to ask an agent for references from clients whose age, income, and net worth are similar to yours. Call the references and ask questions such as, "How well did the agent explain everything to you?" and "How well did the agent perform in following through with implementation?"
- *Referability:* Your choice of agent should be someone you would not hesitate to recommend to others. This means you want an agent who finishes what he or she starts and always does what he or she says is going to be done.
- *Trustworthiness:* Above all, the life insurance agent you choose to work with must be someone with whom you feel free to share your feelings, thoughts, and goals without hesitation. Evaluating trustworthiness is subjective. However, the above factors will give you

a basis upon which to make your judgment. When it comes to your financial well-being, to use less than the best is to invite disaster.

Our estate plan requires additional life insurance, but we're not sure how to choose the best policy for us. What should we know about working with a life insurance agent?

Trust and objectivity are two prerequisites in working with life insurance agents. Since you already know that you need more insurance, you may want to have your financial professional secure a number of quotations on your behalf. A qualified life insurance agent will be able to give you comparative information on several companies' policies, as well as a variety of possible solutions to your insurance needs. You should confirm several things at the beginning of the process, namely, that the life insurance agent is:

1. Licensed to sell variable insurance products if they are appropriate
2. Experienced in working with the technical estate planning tools you are putting in place
3. Willing to spend time to confirm that the recommended insurance is consistent with your overall goals

INVESTMENT COUNSELORS/MONEY MANAGERS

How do I choose an investment advisor?

In today's world there are over 11,000 different mutual funds and over 2000 money managers. How do you choose one? If you want an investment advisor to assist you, the following questions will help you select one:

- How many dollars of assets does the advisor have under management?
- How many accounts does he or she have (if applicable)?
- How many years has the advisor been assisting clients in investing?
- Who owns the company?
- How many investment professionals are in the company?
- What is the minimum account size?
- Who are some representative clients?
- How long have the key personnel been there, and what qualifications do they have?

- What is the process they use to choose the investments?
- Do they have in-house research, or do they rely upon the "street"?

What standards should an investment professional be held to?

The Uniform Code of Fiduciary Conduct stipulates that investment professionals:

- Prepare written investment policies, and document the process used to derive investment decisions.
- Diversify portfolio assets with regard to the specific risk/return objectives of the participants/beneficiaries.
- Use professional money managers (prudent experts) to make investment decisions.
- Control and account for all investment expenses.
- Monitor the activities of all money managers and service providers.
- Avoid conflicts of interest.

FINANCIAL ADVISORS

What do financial planners do?

Financial planners look at all aspects of your financial life—including making and spending money, debt, taxes, investments, estate planning, and insurance needs. A financial planner helps you put together a plan to reach your financial goals (e.g., funding your children's education, investing for retirement, buying your first home). To help you with your financial plan, a good planner should:

- Ask questions to identify your financial goals and determine how much risk you're willing to take to reach those goals.
- Review your monthly income and expenses, total assets and debts, taxes, retirement plans, insurance coverage, wills, investments and other financial information.
- Recommend a realistic course of action based on your goals and financial resources.
- Monitor and review results.
- Adjust your financial plan, if necessary, to account for changes in your job, your family, your goals, or the economy.

No one can predict the future economy, tax changes, or family problems. Why should I bother having someone else try to help me do a financial plan when so much of the future is beyond my control and theirs too?

Many people have put off creating a financial plan because the long-term goals may seem too difficult to attain or be too far in the future to conceptualize. Yet steadily moving toward those ideals will result in far better results than leaving things to chance.

Before a pilot leaves the runway and before a ship's captain pulls out of port, they have already chosen a route to ensure they'll arrive at the desired destination on schedule. They've accounted for other vessels traveling about them and may have to plan and adjust for weather conditions as the journey progresses.

Like these helmsmen, you can control your own family's financial destiny. Despite the many unknown factors that lie waiting for you in your financial future, a well-designed and monitored financial plan will help you achieve your family's goals with far more efficiency and fewer surprises than would be possible without such planning.

In what ways can I benefit from consulting a financial planner?

Meeting with a financial advisor offers significant benefits:

- *Integrate all aspects of financial planning.* He or she will help you compile a complete financial statement and analyze your current and future financial picture. Often, individuals simply implement investments, tax strategies, or insurance without regard to the complete picture. You hear people ask, "What's the hottest investment for this year? Shouldn't I put my money there?" A financial advisor cannot answer that question without first knowing your tax bracket, your income needs, your current portfolio situation, your estate tax situation, your risk tolerance level, and your insurance needs.
- *Pinpoint weaknesses and recommend improvements.* You don't meet with a financial advisor just to hear that everything looks great. You want to find out if there are weaknesses and potential problems and learn ways to solve those problems.
- *Coordinate the implementation of your plan.* The advisor will focus not just on planning but also on keeping you accountable in implementing your plans.
- *Monitor your progress.* Because it is important to monitor your progress, you and your financial advisor will review your portfolio and your progress toward your goals at least annually or, for larger portfolios, quarterly.
- *Ensure continuity of management.* A financial planner can provide

continuity of management if you are ill, disabled, or die and your spouse, children, or others must step in to handle your financial and legal affairs.

What is the best way to find a financial planner?

There are a number of ways to find a financial planner. Talking with friends about who handles their money and asking your attorney, CPA, and other professionals for recommendations are just two ways you can find out about good financial planners.

Perhaps the easiest way to get the names of several advisors in your area is to contact a financial planning association. Well-known professional associations that provide referral services for consumers are listed in Appendix B, Table B-1.

What credentials should I look for when choosing a financial planner?

In the increasingly complex world of finance, it is more important than ever that consumers be knowledgeable about a financial professional's training, licenses, and history. Therefore, you should be aware of the licensing and registration requirements of financial advisors:

1. Professionals who sell investment securities (stocks, bonds, mutual funds, variable life insurance, etc.) for a commission in the United States must be licensed by and registered with the Securities and Exchange Commission (SEC) and the securities divisions of the state(s) in which they practice. These professionals are known as *broker/dealers* or *registered representatives of broker/dealers.* The SEC has delegated the regulation and supervision of broker/dealers to the National Association of Securities Dealers (NASD). The NASD requires that the management and representatives of broker/dealers pass certain tests to ensure that they understand SEC and NASD rules and are competent to perform their duties.
2. Professionals who manage clients' investments in the United States must be registered with the SEC (if they have $25 million or more under management) as *registered investment advisors* or with the state(s) in which they practice (if less than $25 million under management) as *registered investment advisors, investment advisor representatives,* or such other designation as the state requires or allows.

Many individuals and companies are both broker/dealers and registered investment advisors. This allows them to provide investment advice, manage investments, and sell securities. Being a broker/dealer *or* a registered investment advisor does not guarantee competency other than the minimal regulatory requirements.

Is there a way I can check to see if my financial advisor is licensed with these regulatory agencies?

Appendix B, Table B-2, lists the telephone numbers, street addresses, and web-site addresses of the regulatory agencies. You can check with these agencies to determine the "standing" of your investment manager or financial advisor.

What are all the acronyms that I see after my financial advisor's name?

Many training organizations and schools within the financial services industry offer education programs for financial advisors to improve their competency. Other organizations are formed by financial planning practitioners to promote advanced study. These organizations limit their membership to professionals who have a certain number of years' experience, have earned specific designations, and follow specific standards of conduct.

All these organizations allow their graduates or members to use particular professional designations as long as they maintain required standards. In Appendix B, Table B-3 lists most of the designations available and the requirements for attaining them; Table B-4 is a comprehensive list of the organizations that award the designations. Some of the most renowned designations are:

1. *Certified financial planner:* To have a CFP license, practitioners must pass five 3-hour exams and one 10-hour exam, have strict ethics, and complete 30 hours of continuing education every 2 years. The CFP Board of Standards regulates CFPs.
2. *Chartered financial consultant:* To earn the ChFC designation, practitioners must passs 10 examinations covering a wide area of financial planning expertise. ChFCs are also required to complete at least 60 hours of approved continuing education every 2 years and to adhere to a strict code of ethics.
3. *Registered financial consultant:* The RFC designation is awarded only to full-time practitioners who have a minimum of 4 years' experience in financial planning and have already earned one of the other designations(CFP, ChFC, etc.). RFCs must complete 40 hours of

continuing education annually. The International Association of Registered Financial Consultants awards this designation.

Besides the licensing and professional designations, are there any other things I should look for in an advisor?

Many professional organizations provide support and education to their members in the financial services industry. You should ask your advisor which ones he or she belongs to and what benefits he or she derives from those organizations.

What is a registered investment advisor?

A *registered investment advisor* (RIA) must be registered with the SEC or with his or her state's equivalent of the SEC. RIAs manage clients' investments in addition to providing financial planning services. Some RIAs are fee-based only, while others charge a fee to the client and receive a commission for placing assets with a financial institution.

Who is responsible for regulating RIAs?

The regulatory body depends on the size of the assets managed by the RIA. If the assets under management are $25 million or more, the RIA must be registered with and is regulated by the SEC. RIAs that manage lesser sums are regulated by the individual states.

Once I find several advisors, how do I choose the one I want to work with?

Meeting with several financial planners will give you a good idea of which one you feel most comfortable with. Although all the financial planners you meet with may be excellent, one personality may fit best with yours. One advisor may seem to have more in common with you; another advisor may be more specialized in a field that is more important to your financial success; still another might be surrounded by other professionals who will help you not only now but in the future.

The best financial planner for you is the financial planner who makes you feel most comfortable and wants to form a lasting relationship with you. Your financial planner will be someone who is interested in helping you establish your goals, design the plan for achieving those goals, and find the solutions that will best fit your plan today and in the future. The relationship and the security that your financial planner will provide do not come on day 1. What comes on day 1 is a feeling of comfort and a feeling that a relationship can form that will enhance your investment plans.

What sorts of questions should I ask?

You should ask the following:

- What areas do you specialize in (i.e., estate planning, retirement planning, insurance)?
- How will you analyze my particular situation?
- How do you go about preparing a plan? How detailed is it?
- Do you research all products you recommend, or do you rely on someone else?
- How often will I meet you to review my goals and investments? (This should be at least once a year.)
- Do you charge fees, commissions, or both? (Find out how fees are set.)
- If I cannot afford a full plan, can you work with me on some limited planning?
- Are there any potential conflicts of interest I should know about?
- May I call two or three of your other clients who have situations similar to mine?

Some of the guidelines and questions we presented in regard to insurance agents and investment counselors may also be applicable.

What questions should a financial planner ask of me?

A financial planner will ask you:

- What are your goals for the future?
- What are your assets and liabilities (what do you own, and what do you owe)?
- How much is your monthly cash flow?
- Where do you invest your money?
- Do you have a retirement plan?
- What kind of insurance coverage do you have?
- What is your current tax situation?
- Do you have an up-to-date will? Do you have an estate plan?

We've decided to get a divorce, but we want to keep the same advisors. Can they continue to advise both of us?

Attorneys, accountants, and financial planners are obligated to maintain client confidentiality. However, care should be taken not to put them in a position where this obligation may conflict with another client's well-being. Don't confuse a sympathetic ear with an agreement to take your side in a dispute with your spouse. When it is not possible for professionals to maintain impartiality, they should remove themselves from advising either party or should align with one person while properly notifying the other.

Frequently, spouses may decide to separate in a more civil fashion, without placing their advisors in the middle. In deciding whether either spouse or both will continue working with the same accountant, attorney, financial planner, or other advisors, each spouse should discuss his or her intentions with the professionals involved, as these advisors may have reservations or ethical concerns. If all parties are agreeable to the arrangements, each spouse should expect his or her advisors to treat future confidentiality issues without prejudice—as would any client.

I'm confused by the papers my advisor recently sent me. Should I just sign them and send them back as requested?

If you need greater clarification, you should definitely not sign anything until you've spoken with your advisor and resolved your confusion. A true professional will welcome the opportunity to make sure you understand what he or she is helping you with. If your advisor does not show an interest in verifying that the two of you are in agreement, you should consider seeking a second opinion.

What should I do if my advisor's getting ready to retire?

A sound strategy would be to speak with your advisor about this and see what he or she suggests as a proper course of action for you. Your advisor may have colleagues whom he or she will recommend to you and who may readily welcome the opportunity to serve you.

The new advisor should meet all your personal criteria for working with him or her. Peer recognition among professionals is a compliment that most value highly. When referred by a colleague, the majority of advisors strive hard to live up to the confidence placed in them.

How often should I review my financial and estate plan?

Depending on the structure, your asset mix, and what you are trying to accomplish, quarterly or semiannual conferences work best after the first year. While you may be paying a retainer or two after the initial planning fee, professionals will keep you on track and may save you additional money through tax analysis in future years. You will also want to be kept up to date on changes in the income tax and estate tax laws.

appendix B

Consumer Information

TABLE B-1 Information and Referral Organizations

Organization	Services
American Association of Individual Investors (AAII) 625 North Michigan Ave. Chicago, IL 60611 312-280-0170 800-428-2244 www.aaii.com	Provides publications, seminars, home-study texts, educational videos, and software on asset management; local chapters focus on investing and investment techniques; offers the booklet "The Individual Investor's Guide to Investment Information."
Certified Financial Planner Board of Standards 1700 Broadway, Ste. 2100 Denver CO 80290-2101 303-830-7500	Makes CFP referrals to the public; verifies whether an individual is a licensed CFP.
Esperti Peterson Institute 410 17th St., Ste. 1260 Denver, CO 80202 303-446-6100, ext. 119 www.epinstitute.org	Makes Fellows of the Institute referrals to the public.
Investor Protection Trust (IPT) 703-276-1116 www.investorprotection.org	Serves as an independent source of noncommercial investor education materials and assists in the prosecution of securities fraud; operates programs under its own auspices and uses grants to underwrite initiatives carried out by other organizations.
Institute of Business & Finance (IBF) 7911 Herschel Ave., Ste. 201 La Jolla, CA 92037-4413 800-848-2029 www.millenianet.com/icfs	Makes CFS referrals to the public referral. (formerly Institute of Certified Fund Specialists)

TABLE B-1 Information and Referral, *Cont'd.*

Organization	Services
Institute of Certified Financial Planners (ICFP) 3801 East Florida Ave., Ste. 708 Denver, CO 80210 800-282-PLAN www.icfp.org	Consumers can contact the ICFP for a listing of 3 CFP Practitioners in their area or for free brochures about financial planning.
International Association for Financial Planning (IAFP) 5775 Glenridge Drive NE, Ste. B-300 Atlanta, GA 30328 888-806-PLAN www.iafp.org	Provides brochures on financial planning and disclosure forms on up to 5 local financial advisors.
International Association of Registered Financial Consultants, Inc. P.O. Box 42506 Middletown, OH 45042-0506 800-532-9060 www.iarfc.org	Makes member referrals to the public.
Life & Health Insurance Foundation for Education (LIFE) 1922 F St. NW Washington, DC 20006-4387 202-331-2170 www.life-line.org	Offers information and education on life, health, and disability insurance.
National Association of Investors Corporation (NAIC) 711 West 13 Mile Rd. Madison Heights, MI 48071 877-275-6242 www.better-investing.org	Provides investment information, education, and support; membership consists of investment clubs and individual investors.
National Association of Personal Financial Advisors (NAPFA) 355 West Dundee Rd., Ste. 200 Buffalo Grove, IL 60089 888-FEE-ONLY www.napfa.org	Offers lists of fee-only financial planners by area; provides information on comprehensive, fee-only financial planning.
National Association of Securities Dealers Regulators 1735 K St. NW Washington, DC 20006 800-289-9999 www.nasd.com; www.nasdr.com	Provides, in writing or on its web site, information on the disciplinary history of financial planners and financial services professionals.

TABLE B-1 Information and Referral, *Cont'd.*

Organization	Services
National Center for Financial Education (NCFE) P.O. Box 34070 San Diego, CA 92163-4070 619-232-8811 www.ncfe.org	Offers help on spending, saving, investing, insuring, and planning for the financial future.
National Committee on Planned Giving (NCPG) 233 McCrea St., Ste. 400 Indianapolis, IN 46225 317-269-6274 www.ncpg.org	Facilitates the education and training of the planned giving community; members of its planned giving councils develop, market, and administer charitable planned gifts.
National Endowment for Financial Education (NEFE) 5299 DTC Blvd., Ste. 1300 Englewood, CO 80111-3334 303-741-6333 www.nefe.org	Partners with other organizations to provide financial education to the public—in particular, to underserved individuals whose financial education needs are not being addressed by others.
National Fraud Exchange (NAFEX) 800-822-0416	Provides, for a fee, information on the disciplinary history of financial planners and financial services professionals.
National Investor Relations Institute (NIRI) 8045 Leesburg Pike, Ste. 600 Vienna, VA 22182 703-506-3570 www.niri.org	Facilitates communication among corporate management, the investing public, and the financial community; members are corporate officers and investor relations consultants.
North American Securities Administrators Association (NASAA) 888-846-2722 www.nasaa.org	Provides phone numbers of state securities commissioners who monitor the records of securities-licensed financial planners.
Securities Investor Protection Corporation (SIPC) 805 Fifteenth St. NW, Ste. 800 Washington, DC 20005-2215 202-371-8300 www.sipc.org	Protects customers of SEC-registered broker/dealers against losses caused by the financial failure of a broker/dealer (but not against a change in the market value of securities); funded by its member securities broker/dealers.
Society of Financial Service Professionals (SFSP) 270 S. Bryn Mawr Ave. Bryn Mawr, PA 19010-2195 888-243-2258 www.financialpro.org/sfsp	Makes financial planner referrals to the public. (formerly Society of CLU & ChFC)

TABLE B-1 Information and Referral, *Cont'd.*

Organization	Services
State insurance commissions	Often have toll-free numbers for lodging complaints against individuals providing insurance products or advice.
U.S. Securities and Exchange Commission (SEC) 450 5th St. Washington, DC 20549 202-942-8088 800-732-0330 www.sec.gov	Verifies registration of broker/dealers, representatives, and investment advisors/advisory firms; provides (usually through the NASD) information on the disciplinary history of financial planners and financial services professionals.

TABLE B-2 Licensing and Regulatory Agencies

Agency	Functions	Area regulated
Federal Trade Commission (FTC) 600 Pennsylvania Ave. NW Washington, DC 20580 (202) 326-2222 www.ftc.gov	Enforces federal antitrust and consumer protection laws; ensures that the nation's markets function competitively, efficiently, and free of undue restrictions; eliminates practices that are unfair or deceptive; conducts activities such as consumer education.	U.S. marketplace
Financial Accounting Standards Board 401 Merritt 7 PO Box 5116 Norwalk, CT 06856-5116 (203) 847-0700 www.rutgers.edu/ Accounting/raw/ fasb	9-member board sets the accounting rules of the U.S. under the auspices of the SEC; also establishes the standards of financial accounting and reporting for the private sector. (The SEC has statutory authority to establish these standards for publicly held companies but has relied on the private sector for this function to the extent that the private sector does so in the public interest.)	Financial accounting & reporting standards
Internal Revenue Service (IRS) 1111 Constitution Ave. NW Washington, DC 20224 (800) 829-1040 www.irs.gov	"Enrolled" means licensed by the federal government; "agent" means authorized to appear in place of the taxpayer at the IRS. (Only EAs, attorneys, and CPAs may represent taxpayers before the IRS.)	Enrolled agents

TABLE B-2 Licensing and Regulatory, *Cont'd.*

Agency	Functions	Area regulated
National Association of Securities Dealers (NASD) Regulators 1735 K St. NW Washington, DC 20006 (800) 289-9999 www.nasd.com; www.nasdr.com	Self-regulates the securities industry and the Nasdaq stock market through registration, education, and examination of member firms and their employees, creation and enforcement of rules designed for the protection of investors, surveillance of markets operated by Nasdaq, and cooperative programs with government agencies and industry organizations.	Registered broker/dealers, investment advisors/advisory firms, representatives; various series licenses
National Association of State Boards of Accountancy (NASBA) 150 Fourth Ave. North, Ste. 700 Nashville, TN 37219 (615) 880-4200 www.nasba.org	Serves as forum the nation's state boards of accountancy, which administer the Uniform CPA Examination, license CPAs, and regulate the practice of public accountancy in the U.S.; sponsors committee meetings, conferences, programs and services designed to enhance the effectiveness of its member boards.	CPAs
National Futures Association 200 West Madison St., Ste. 1600 Chicago, IL 60606 (800) 676-4NFA www.nfa.futures.org	Self-regulatory organization ensures high standards of business conduct by its members. Any person or firm engaged in business that involves buying or selling futures contracts for the public must be a member.	Those engaged in buying or selling futures
North American Securities Administrators Association (NASAA) (888) 846-2722 www.nasaa.org	Is responsible for investor protection and regulatory oversight of the securities industry; recommends national policies and provides model legislation for state agencies. Its state securities commissioners serve as coregulators of the industry with the SEC.	Securities industry
State insurance commissions	Administer and enforce the state's insurance laws.	Insurance sales
U.S. Securities and Exchange Commission (SEC) 450 5th St. Washington, DC 20549 (800) 732-0330 www.sec.gov	Independent, quasijudicial regulatory agency helps establish and administer federal securities laws; regulates firms engaged in the purchase or sale of securities, people who provide investment advice, and investment companies.	Registered investment advisors/ advisory firms, broker/dealers, representatives

TABLE B-3 Professional Licenses and Designations

Designation	Accrediting institution & requirements
AAMS: Accredited Asset Management Specialist (awarded to investment professionals)	College for Financial Planning: complete program, pass exam, commit to code of ethics, pursue continuing ed.
AAPA: Associate in Annuity Products and Administration (for those who work with annuities)	LOMA: complete 6-course program, pass exams.
AEP: Accredited Estate Planner (available to estate planning practitioners who have completed certain graduate estate planning courses	NAEPC & American College: pass exam in trust banking, insurance, accounting, law; meet NAEPC's continuing ed requirements.
ATA: Accredited Tax Advisor —one who handles tax needs of highly compensated clients & owners of closely held businesses	ACAT: complete 6 courses & pass exams; fulfill experience, ethics, and continuing ed requirements; pay annual registration fee.
ATP: Accredited Tax Preparer —one who prepares tax returns for individuals	ACAT: have 1 year's experience in preparing income tax forms and returns for compensation, complete course, register with ATP council, meet continuing ed requirements.
BCE: Board Certified in Estate Planning	IBF: complete 5 modules, pass test or CFS exam, take 15 hours continuing ed per year.
BCF: Board Certified in Financial Planning	IBF: complete Insurance, Estate Planning, and Securities (or Mutual Funds) certification programs; have 5 years' experience in financial services industry; pass test or CFS exam; meet continuing ed requirements.
BCI: Board Certified in Insurance	IBF: complete 5 modules, pass test or CFS exam, take 15 hours continuing ed per year.
BCM: Board Certified in Mutual Funds	IBF: complete Certified Fund Specialist program and Board Certified Requirements, pass test or CFS exam, take 15 hours continuing ed per year.
BCS: Board Certified in Securities	IBF: complete 5 modules, pass test or CFS exam, take 15 hours continuing ed per year.

TABLE B-3 Licenses and Designations, *Cont'd.*

Designation	Accrediting institution & requirements
Broker/dealer —one that is licensed to buy and sell investment products for or to clients; "dealers" sell securities they own, "brokers" buy & sell securities on behalf of investors	SEC
CCIM: Certified Commercial Investment Member —one who handles commercial real estate brokerage, leasing, asset management, valuation, and investment analysis	Commercial Investment Real Estate Institute: complete 240 hours of graduate-level curriculum, prepare résumé of qualifying experience, pass exam.
CEBS: Certified Employee Benefit Specialist	International Foundation of Employee Benefit Plans: complete study program, pass exams, abide by CEBS principles of conduct.
CFA: Chartered Financial Analyst (available to experienced financial analysts) —one who is a securities analyst, money manager, & investment advisor focusing on analysis of investments & securities of company or industry groups	Association for Investment Management and Research: complete course, pass 3 annual exams, fulfill AIMR ethics requirements, submit to regulatory authority of AIMR.
CFM: Certified in Financial Management (available to management accountants who are members of IMA)	ICMA: meet educational & work requirements, pass exam, comply with ICMA ethical standards.
CFP: Certified Financial Planner (available to those with bachelor's degree who have completed financial planning curriculum at U.S.-accredited college or university & have 3 years' financial planning experience, or 5 years without degree)	CFP Board of Standards: pass exam, adhere to CFP Board code of ethics, periodically disclose investigations or legal proceedings related to professional or business conduct, take 30 hours continuing ed. every 2 years, complete biennial licensing requirement with CFP Board, submit to regulatory authority of the CFP Board.
CFS: Certified Fund Specialist (available to financial services professionals)	IBF: complete course, pass exam, adhere to IBF code of ethics, take 15 hours continuing ed per year, register annually.

TABLE B-3 Licenses and Designations, *Cont'd.*

Designation	Accrediting institution & requirements
ChFC: Chartered Financial Consultant (for accountants, attorneys, bankers, insurance agents, brokers, & securities representatives with 3 years' business experience)	American College: complete 10-course curriculum, pass exams, adhere to the college code of ethics, take 60 hours of continuing ed every 2 years.
CIC: Chartered Investment Counselor (available to those employed by an ICAA member firm who have 5 years' experience in an eligible occupation)	ICAA: complete the CFA exam before the CIC is awarded, provide work and character references, endorse ICAA Standards of Practice, complete an ethical conduct questionnaire.
CIMA: Certified Investment Management Analyst (the only advanced designation specifically for investment consultants; must have 3 years' experience in investment management consulting)	IMCA: complete program, pass exam, adhere to code of ethics, recertify every 2 years by taking 40 hours of continuing ed.
CIMC: Certified Investment Management Consultant (for financial consultants)	Institute for Investment Management Consultants: meet ethical, experience, and continuing ed requirements, pass 2 levels of NASD-administered exams.
CLU: Chartered Life Underwriter (for insurance and financial services professionals with 3 years' business experience)	American College: pass 10 college-level courses, abide by the college's code of ethics.
CMFC: Chartered Mutual Fund Counselor (for investment practitioners)	College for Financial Planning & Investment Company Institute: complete program, pass exam, commit to code of ethics, pursue continuing education.
CPA: Certified Public Accountant	AICPA: pass Uniform CPA exam, satisfy work experience and statutory & licensing requirements of the state(s) in which one practices.
CRPC: Chartered Retirement Planning Counselor	College for Financial Planning: complete program, pass exam, sign code of ethics commitment form.
CRPS: Chartered Retirement Plans Specialist (for those who design, install, and maintain retirement plans for the business community)	College for Financial Planning: complete program, pass exam, sign code of ethics commitment form.

TABLE B-3 Licenses and Designations, *Cont'd.*

Designation	Accrediting institution & requirements
CSA: Certified Senior Advisor	Society of CSAs: attend 3-day program or complete correspondence course & testing, take home-study exams to maintain certification.
DS: IRA Distribution Specialist (for financial advisors)	IRA Distribution Council: pass exam & meet other requirements.
EA: Enrolled Agent (for those who want to represent taxpayers before the IRS at all levels of examination, appeal, and collection)	IRS: pass exam (or have 5 years' qualifying employment with IRS), have application approved by IRS, pass background check, take 72 hours' continuing ed every 3 years.
Fellow of the Institute (for financial advisors and accountants who have technical knowledge of financial, estate, insurance, and investment tools)	Esperti Peterson Institute: complete program, attend classes annually, participate in monthly conference calls, prepare a case design book for a hypothetical client.
FLMI: Fellow, Life Management Institute (a university-level program in insurance)	LOMA: complete 10 courses, pass exams.
FRM: Fellow in Risk Management (an advanced designation in risk management)	The Insurance Institute of America: pass courses & exam, adhere to code of ethics, complete continuing ed requirements.
JD: Juris Doctor, or Doctor of Jurisprudence (the basic law degree; replaced the LL.B. in the late 1960s)	Accredited law schools: complete required studies, pass exams.
LL.D.: Doctor of Laws (an advanced law degree)	
LL.M.: Master of Laws (an advanced law degree)	
MS: Master of Science (in taxation) (graduate-level study in financial planning, wealth management, tax planning, retirement planning, and estate planning)	College for Financial Planning: complete 12 courses with 3.00 (B) grade-point average.
MSEP: Master of Science (emphasis in estate planning)	College for Financial Planning: See MS above.
MSFS: Master of Science in Financial Services	American College: complete 36 course credits, including 2 residency sessions.

TABLE B-3 Licenses and Designations, *Cont'd.*

Designation	Accrediting institution & requirements
MSRM: Master of Science in Risk Management (for insurance underwriters, brokers, financial analysts, and risk managers)	College of Insurance: complete curriculum, prepare a thesis or pass exam.
REBC: Registered Employee Benefits Consultant (for those involved in the sale and service of employee benefits plans)	American College: complete 5-course curriculum; meet experience, ethics, and continuing ed requirements.
Registered Investment Advisor —one who recommends stocks, bonds, mutual funds, partnerships, or other SEC-registered investments for clients	SEC and/or state securities agencies: file an ADV (Advisor) form detailing educational and professional experience, file a U-4 Form disclosing any disciplinary action.
Registered Representative (also called stockbroker) —one who is affiliated with a stock exchange member broker/dealer firm, recommends to clients which securities to buy and sell, and earns a commission on all trades	NASD and/or state securities agencies: pass NASD & any exams required by the securities agency of the state(s) in which one practices.
RFC: Registered Financial Consultant (available to those with a securities/insurance license or one of the following: CPA, CFA, CFP, CLU, ChFC, JD, EA, or RHU)	IARFC: meet education, examination, experience, & licensing requirements, take 40 hours per year of continuing ed., abide by IARFC code of ethics.
RFP: Registered Financial Planner (available to members of RFPI)	RFPI: complete study course, have experience in the field.
RHU: Registered Health Underwriter (for those involved in the sale and service of disability income and health insurance)	American College: complete 3-course curriculum, meet experience, ethics, and continuing ed. requirements.
Series 2: NASD Nonmember General Securities	NASD: pass exam.
Series 3: National Commodity Futures	NASD: pass exam.
Series 4: Registered Options Principal	NASD: pass exam.
Series 5: Interest Rate Options	NASD: pass exam.
Series 6: Investment Co./Variable Contract Representative —one who sells investment company products (e.g., mutual funds) and variable contracts (e.g., annuities)	NASD: pass exam.

TABLE B-3 Licenses and Designations, *Cont'd.*

Designation	Accrediting institution & requirements
Series 7: General Securities Representative —one who sells corporate stock, bonds, government and municipal bonds, tax shelters, real estate syndications, real estate investment trusts (REITS), and mutual funds	NASD: pass registered representative exam.
Series 8: General Securities Sales Supervisor	NASD: pass exam.
Series 11: Assistant Rep/Order Taker	NASD: pass exam.
Series 15: Foreign Currency Options	NASD: pass exam.
Series 22: Direct Participation Programs Representative —one who sells tax shelters (not REITS)	NASD: pass exam.
Series 24: General Securities Principal	NASD: pass exam.
Series 26: Investment Co./Variable Contracts Principal	NASD: pass exam.
Series 27: Financial and Operations Principal	NASD: pass exam.
Series 28: Introducing Broker/Dealer Financial Operations Principal	NASD: pass exam.
Series 39: Direct Participation Program Principal	NASD: pass exam.
Series 52: Municipal Securities Representative	NASD: pass exam.
Series 53: Municipal Securities Principal	NASD: pass exam.
Series 62: Corporate Securities Representative —one who sells common & preferred stock, corporate bonds, stock rights, warrants, American depository receipts, shares of closed-ended investment companies, money market funds, privately issued mortgage-backed & other asset-backed securities	NASD: pass exam.
Series 63: Uniform Securities Agent State Law	NASD: pass exam. (Meets requirements of most states & replaces individual state test for licensing professionals to sell securities.)

TABLE B-3 Licenses and Designations, *Cont'd.*

Designation	Accrediting institution & requirements
Series 65: Uniform Investment Advisor Law	NASD: pass exam on legal and regulatory context. (In more than 40 states, a prerequisite to becoming an investment advisor at the state level.)
Series 66: Series 66 Licensee (enables an individual to become a registered representative and become associated with a registered investment advisory firm)	NASD: pass exam.

TABLE B-4 Professional Associations

Organization	Functions
American Bar Association (ABA) 750 North Lake Shore Dr. Chicago, IL 60611 312-988-5000 www.abanet.org	Ensures the continuation of programs promoting quality legal services, equal access to justice, better understanding of the law, & improvements in our justice system; provides members with information & tools; sponsors workshops, seminars, CLE sessions, & publications.
American Institute of Certified Public Accountants (AICPA) 1211 Avenue of the Americas New York, NY 10036 888-999-9256 www.aicpa.org	Represents the accounting profession in public practice, business, government, & education; provides technical support, standard setting (including GAAP), & guidelines in conjunction with FASB; designs the Uniform CPA exam.
Association for Advanced Life Underwriting (AALU) 1922 F St. NW Washington, DC 20006 202-331-6081 www.aalu.org	Proposes & monitors legislation & regulation regarding advanced life underwriting; provides education & leadership in improving the business environment for advanced life insurance professionals.
Estate planning councils	For those who specialize in tax, estate, and business planning, provides opportunity to interact, exchange ideas, and pool knowledge; organized at local level.
Financial Planning Association (FPA) Washington, DC 800-322-4237 www.fpanet.org	Embraces the principles of International Association for Financial Planning (IAFP) & Institute of Certified Financial Planners (ICFP); open to everyone affiliated with the financial planning profession. (formerly IAFP & ICFP)

TABLE B-4 Professional Associations, *Cont'd.*

Organization	Functions
Institute of Management Accountants (IMA) 10 Paragon Drive Montvale, NJ 07645-1759 800-638-4427 www.imanet.org	Keeps members up to date on changes affecting management accounting and financial management professions, provides new insights & ideas, & gives ethical guidance.
IRA Distribution Council www.stretchira.com	Researches tax laws and disseminates information on qualified savings plans.
Million Dollar Round Table 325 West Touhy Ave. Park Ridge, IL 60068-4265 847-692-6378 www.mdrt.org	Provides members with resources for improving technical knowledge, sales skills, & client service while adopting high ethical standards; comprises top 6% of life insurance producers worldwide.
National Association of Enrolled Agents (NAEA) 200 Orchard Ridge Dr., Ste. 302 Gaithersburg, MD 20878 800-424-4339 www.naea.org	Promotes professionalism & interests of its members; acts as advocate of taxpayer rights.
National Association of Family Wealth Counselors (NAFWC) 20 Circle Dr. Franklin, IN 46131 317-736-8750 nafwc.org	Provides members with opportunities for education & networking in family wealth counseling field.
National Association of Insurance and Financial Advisors (formerly National Association of Life Underwriters) 1922 F St. NW Washington, DC 20006 888-515-NALU www.naifa.org	Serves as advocate for insurance agents & consumers; encourages legislation to protect policyholders, develops policy, & advances its position with lawmakers & regulators; enhances professional skills of members, promotes ethical conduct, & offers education; organized at state & local levels.
National Association of Personal Financial Advisors (NAPFA) 355 West Dundee Rd., Ste. 200 Buffalo Grove, IL 60089 888-FEE-ONLY www.napfa.org	Helps fee-only professionals enhance skills, market services, & gain a voice with government & consumers; publishes monthly *NAPFA Advisor* & offers educational opportunities to members.

TABLE B-4 Professional Associations, *Cont'd.*

Organization	Functions
National Association of Tax Practitioners (NATP) 720 Association Dr. Appleton, WI 54914-1483 800-558-3402 www.natptax.com	Serves professionals working in all areas of tax practice, provides assistance on federal & state tax questions, & presents workshops.
National Committee on Planned Giving (NCPG) 233 McCrea St., Ste. 400 Indianapolis, IN 46225 317-269-6274 www.ncpg.org	Facilitates education & training of people who develop, market, & administer charitable planned gifts & enhances communication among them; organized as a federation of planned giving councils.
National Society of Fund Raising Executives (NSFRE) 1101 King St., Ste. 700 Alexandria, VA 22314 703-684-0410 www.nsfre.org	Advances philanthropy through education, training, & advocacy based on research & a code of ethics; certifies fund-raising executives.
Planned giving councils & roundtables	Promote the concept of planned giving; organized at local level, but many are associated with NCPG.
Risk & Insurance Management Society (RIMS), Inc. 655 Third Ave. New York, NY 10017 212-286-9292 www.rims.org	Provides products, services, & information for managing all forms of business risk; offers member publications, education for the ARM designation, & other services.
Societies of CPAs	Promote the accounting profession within government & to the public; provide members with education, information, & opportunities to interact with colleagues & participate in community service projects; organized at local level.
Society of Financial Service Professionals (SFSP) 270 S. Bryn Mawr Ave. Bryn Mawr, PA 19010-2195 888-243-2258 www.financialpro.org/sfsp	Sets & promotes standards of excellence for professionals in financial services; supports members' commitment to advanced education & high ethical standards. (formerly Society of CLU & ChFC)

appendix C

The Contributory Book Series and Protocol for *21st Century Wealth*

Eileen Sacco, Managing Editor

History of the Contributory Book Series

With the publication of *Wealth Enhancement and Preservation* in 1995, the Institute established its Contributory Book Series, in which fifty-two highly regarded professionals from all over the United States participated to create a comprehensive book on financial planning. In 1996, the Institute published a second edition of *Wealth Enhancement and Preservation,* which incorporated more research from ten additional contributing authors. It next invited a select group of eighty-seven members from the National Network of Estate Planning Attorneys to participate in a similar research project, which culminated in 1996 with the publication of *Legacy: Plan, Protect and Preserve Your Estate. Legacy* focused on the most commonly asked questions about estate, business, and tax planning. In January 1998, the Institute published *Generations: Planning Your Legacy,* a reconceptualization of *Legacy*—with forty-nine new contributors, completely up-to-date information, and more comprehensive questions and answers.

One of the most complex and, thus, misunderstood planning areas for most Americans is retirement planning. In January 1998, the Institute published its first cross-discipline text, which brought together the expertise and experience of both the legal and the financial planning professions, to assist the public with understanding how to plan properly for retirement and how to coordinate the results of that effort with their estate planning. *Ways and Means: Maximize the Value of Your Retirement Savings* is the result of that research project.

With the passage of the Taxpayer Relief Act of 1997 and the IRS Restructuring Act of 1998, new rulings issued by the Department of the Treasury and the Internal Revenue Service, and the excitement surrounding the new millennium, the Institute launched *21st Century Wealth: Essential Financial Planning Principles* to present to the public the most current and sophisticated financial planning strategies available. Fifty-one expert financial planning professionals across the nation participated as contributors to this text.

The objectives of each book in the series are:

- To be the most professional research project of its kind, one that will be recognized as unique in both its focus and its scope
- To ascertain the critical planning questions that clients are asking their professional advisors nationwide and the precise answers of those advisors
- To publish meaningful text that will assure readers that they can get immediate assistance from professionals on the basis of the planning concepts and strategies learned from the book
- To heighten the public's understanding of the contributions that highly experienced financial advisors, attorneys, and accountants bring into the planning and investing lives of their clients
- To improve the quality of financial, estate, and business planning services offered by professionals to clients by sharing the ideas and techniques of a number of authorities in a user-friendly form
- To be recognized as a major contribution to the financial, estate, and business planning literature

Protocol

Definition of "Expert"

The Institute defines an *expert* as an outstanding professional who is technically competent, is an effective communicator, and has a proven record of meeting his or her clients' needs over a minimum of 5 years.

Research Protocol

As with all previous contributory books, the first step in following the protocol was to create the "Research Questionnaire" for *21st Century Wealth,* which is an outline of potential topics for the book, organized in a cohesive chapter format. However, every contributing author is encouraged to provide his or her own input outside the parameters of the "Research Questionnaire." On the basis of logistical considerations of time, demanding schedules, and the need to eliminate as much repetition as possible, the Institute established a protocol of a minimum of thirty questions and answers from each contributing author.

Qualifying Financial Planning Professionals: The Application Process

When developing the protocol for the first research project, the Institute submitted its definition of *expert* and the objectives of the research project to financial planning colleagues and asked them to design criteria that would help the Institute not only identify potential contributors but also judge the level of their expertise and credentials. On the basis of the input of these colleagues, the Institute established criteria for an expert and developed an extensive "Application and Profile" for the financial planning professionals. It also established criteria for evaluating each applicant, which were appropriately weighted on the basis of input received from colleagues and were set by Bob Esperti, Renno Peterson, and the Institute staff before the first research project. Before contacting prospective contributors for *21st Century Wealth,* Institute staff asked several of the Institute's Financial Planning Fellows to review and update the criteria, application, and requirements.

Each applicant had to provide a completed "Application and Profile," ADV Part II, and U-4 form. After receipt of this information, a member of the Institute's staff carefully reviewed and graded the person on the established criteria. In addition, a staff member checked the NASD web site or the applicant's state securities division for pending disclosures (arbitrations, claims, lawsuits, etc.) and checked the applicant's state insurance commission for the same information. Before the Institute finally accepted an applicant for *21st Century Wealth*, the editors, Bob Esperti and Renno Peterson, reviewed the "Application and Profile" and conducted a telephone interview with the person if they did not already know the applicant personally.

The telephone interview allowed the editors to determine the applicant's level of financial planning knowledge and to satisfy themselves that the applicant was committed to the project and understood all its parameters. The interview also allowed the applicant to ask questions of the individuals who would be editing the research.

The Institute then mailed a letter of either nonacceptance or acceptance to the applicant. For an acceptance, the Institute also sent the applicant a "Contributing Expert and Authority Agreement," a "Research Questionnaire," and specifications for submitting a photograph, a personalized introduction, and biographical information.

Research Editing Protocol

The Institute staff organized the research from all the contributing authors by "Research Questionnaire" category. The managing editor reorganized and outlined the research, on the basis of its actual content, into a standard book structure and delivered it to the Institute's senior legal editor, who eliminated those questions and answers that were *not* common to a majority of the contributors. The remaining research *and* the eliminated questions and answers were delivered to Bob and Renno. They read the research questions (and confirmed that the eliminated research was not applicable), combined similar material, and edited the remaining questions and answers to provide the cohesive and understandable questions and answers that appear in this text.

The managing editor and senior legal editor reviewed the resulting working manuscript for clarity and technical accuracy. The Institute provided a working manuscript to each contributing author for purposes of review. In this way, the Institute ascertained the validity of the responses and added to the quality of the final text, and contributors were able to increase the level of their participation in the research project. A number of contributing authors provided a series of subsequent edits to the working manuscript.

The logistics of a Contributory Book Series project is daunting, to say the least. To initiate the project; create the materials for the invitees, applicants, and contributing authors; follow up on all the invitations; process the applications and check credentials; collect and track all the necessary information and paperwork, including the questions and answers; and then turn the material into a book calls for an extraordinary level of organization and commitment from the contributors, the editors, the Institute, and its staff. In fact, this brief overview of the process does not do justice to the project simply because the volume of information and the project protocol involved hundreds of pages of material and thousands of hours of effort. The Institute is proud of the degree of professionalism displayed by all participants in the creation and completion of *21st Century Wealth.*

appendix D

Contributing Authors

Thomas H. Bell
Wealth Enhancement & Preservation of South Carolina, L.L.C.
38 Spanish Pointe Drive
Hilton Head Island, SC 29926
843-681-5701 fax: 843-681-7910
tbellleap@aol.com

David M. Boike, CLU, ChFC
Boike-Flenniken Financial Services
3060 South Dye Road
Flint, MI 48532
810-732-5752 fax: 810-732-5767
DMboikechfc@aol.com

William E. Dendy, CLU, CFP, MBA
Addison Securities, Inc.
8144 Walnut Hill Lane, Suite 397
Dallas, TX 75231
214-706-2855 fax: 214-706-2828
wmdendy@aol.com

Paul S. Devore, CLU, CFP
Financial Management Services, Inc.
6345 Balboa Boulevard, Suite 290
Encino, CA 91316
818-609-7575 fax: 818-609-0185
PDevore@FMS3.com

Monroe M. Diefendorf, Jr., ChFC, CLU, CFP
Diefendorf Capital Planning Associates
152 Forest Avenue
Locust Valley, NY 11560
516-759-3900 fax: 516-759-3928
Roey@DiefendorfCapital.com

Robert A. Esperti, J.D.
3561 E. Sunrise Drive, Suite 135
Tucson, AZ 85718
520-529-9060 fax: 520-529-9360

James P. Furrow, CFP
Senior Financial Advisors, Inc.
11911 N.E. 1st Street, Suite 312
Bellevue, WA 98005
425-635-0600 fax: 425-635-0056
FNIC@aol.com

Graydon C. Garner, CFP
Colburn International Inc.
2700 Westchester Avenue, Suite 315
Purchase, NY 10577
800-392-9776 fax: 914-253-8511
Graygarner@aol.com

Tomas B. Gau, CPA, CFP
Oregon Pacific Financial Advisors, Inc.
370 Lithia Way
Ashland, OR 97520
541-482-0138 fax: 541-488-6272

Todd Goedeke, CFP
Raymond James Financial Services
1017 Fond Du Lac Avenue
Sheboygan Falls, WI 53085
920-467-1110 fax: 920-467-0136
tgoedeke@rjfs.com

Robert E. Grace, J.D., CLU, ChFC
3781 Vineyard Woods Drive
Cincinatti, OH 45255
513-947-0442 fax: 513-947-0443
REGRACE@aol.com

Carl P. Grissom, CLU
Carl P. Grissom Organization
8191 College Parkway, Suite 206
Fort Myers, FL 33919
941-437-6800 fax: 941-437-6228
grissomone@aol.com

Robert B. Hardcastle, President
Delta Investment Services, Inc.
16100 Chesterfield Parkway W, Ste. 150
Chesterfield, MO 63017
800-969-6878 fax: 636-532-3981
delta@moneytalk.org

Norman C. Hayden, MSFS, CFP, CLU, ChFC
Raymond James Financial Services
100 Rialto Place, Suite 720
Melbourne, FL 32901
321-984-2639 fax: 321-951-4685
nhayden@rjfs.com

Todd D. Heckman, CFP, CLU, ChFC, MSFS, AEP
Estate Planning Advisors, L.L.C.
4445 North A1A, Suite 245
Vero Beach, FL 32963
800-994-0300 fax: 561-234-0309
EPAtdh@aol.com

N. Douglas Hostetler, CLU, ChFC, CFP
Hostetler, Church & Anderson, L.L.C.
10420 Little Patuxent Parkway, Ste. 490
Columbia, MD 21044
410-740-3303 fax: 410-740-0716
dhostetler@pfinancial.com

John L. Jenkins, CFP, EA
Asset Preservation Strategies
5090 Shoreham Place, Suite 209
San Diego, CA 92122
858-455-1825 fax: 858-455-6211
assetps@aol.com

Reid S. Johnson, MSFS, CIMC, CFP, ChFC
The Planning Group of Scottsdale, L.L.C.
8777 N. Gainey Center Drive, Ste. 265
Scottsdale, AZ 85258
480-596-1580 fax: 480-596-2165
theplanninggroup@uswest.net

R. Marshall Jones, J.D., CLU, ChFC
R. Marshall Jones, Inc.
470 Columbia Drive, Suite G-201
West Palm Beach, FL 33409
561-712-9799 877-600-0029 fax: 561-712-9899
marshall@rmjplan.com

Philip J. Kavesh, J.D., LL.M. (tax), CFP, ChFC
Kavesh, Minor & Otis, Inc.
970 West 190th Street, Suite 690
Torrance, CA 90502
310-324-9403 800-756-5596 fax: 310-324-0517
phil.kavesh@kaveshlaw.com

E. Michael Kilbourn, CLU, ChFC, CCIM, AEP
Kilbourn Associates
3033 Riviera Drive, Suite 202
Naples, FL 34103
941-261-1888 fax: 941-643-7017
Mike@KilbournAssociates.com

Robert G. Kresek, CFP, CIMC
Founders Financial Network
10050 North Wolfe Road, SW1-281
Cupertino, CA 95014
408-366-8920 fax: 408-366-8925
Kresek@FoundersFinancial.Net

Paul R. Lang
Investment Representative
Edward Jones
24 Woodstock Road
Roswell, GA 30075
770-998-0202 800-441-8202 fax: 770-998-3024
prlbroker@mindspring.com

Jerry W. Lawson, CLU, ChFC, MSFS
Lawson & Watson, L.L.C.
823 North Elm Street, Suite 100
Greensboro, NC 27401
336-379-8207 fax: 336-379-8349
jlawson@lawson-watson.com

Robert S. Madden, CLU, ChFC
The Island Financial Group
1000 Woodbury Road, Suite 400
Woodbury, NY 11797
516-364-3333 fax: 516-364-3647

Michael D. Miller, CFP
Capital Planning Corporation
3605 132nd Avenue SE, Suite 403
Bellevue, WA 98006
425-643-1800 fax: 425-586-3678
mmiller@capitalplanningcorp.com

James W. Monteverde, CLU, ChFC, AEP
The Monteverde Group, Ltd.
Three Gateway Center, Suite 2400
Pittsburgh, PA 15222
412-391-0419 fax: 412-391-0338
jmonteverde@dsl.net

W. Aubrey Morrow, CFP
Financial Designs, Ltd.
5075 Shoreham Place, Suite 230
San Diego, CA 92122
858-597-1980 fax: 858-546-1106
morrow@prodigy.net

Frederick E. (Fritz) Mowery
President/Chief Investment Officer
Oxford Advisors Corporation
5999 Summerside Drive, Suite 102
Dallas, TX 75252
972-447-2720
Fritz.Mowery@OxfordGRP.com

Richard E. Mundinger, CFA
Vice President Investment Officer
Dain Rauscher
3430 East Sunrise Drive, Suite 250
Tucson, AZ 85718-3210
520-299-4444 800-766-1512 fax: 520-299-3671
remundinger@dainrauscher.com

Robert J. Myers, President
R.J. Myers & Associates, Inc.
5299 DTC Boulevard, Suite 805
Englewood, CO 80111
303-741-6226 fax: 303-741-1973

Alan G. Orlowsky, J.D., CPA
A.G. Orlowsky, Ltd.
630 Dundee Road, Suite 125
Northbrook, IL 60062
847-291-9771 fax: 847-291-9774
AGOLTD@aol.com

David C. Partheymuller, CFP, CEP
The RGS Normandy Group
410 17th Street, Suite 1240
Denver, CO 80202
303-893-8700 fax: 303-446-6104
David@Normandygrp.com

M. Todd Petersen, CFP, MBA
Financial Network Investment Corporation
2339 Gold Meadow Way, Suite 102
Gold River, CA 95670
800-635-4585 fax: 916-638-7211
todd@theRetirementAdvisor.com

Renno L. Peterson, J.D.
2 North Tamiami Trail, Suite 606
Sarasota, FL 34236
941-365-4819 fax: 941-366-5347

Daniel W. Pinkerton, CFP, RFC
Pinkerton Retirement Specialists, L.L.C.
2201 Ironwood Place, Suite 100
Coeur d'Alene, ID 83814
208-667-8998 fax: 208-667-5868
prs@dmi.net

Darrin G. Plys, ChFC
American Express Financial Advisors, Inc
28601 Chagrin Boulevard, Suite 200
Beachwood, OH 44122
216-464-3220 fax: 216-464-4133

Gary F. Poling, President
President's Trust Company, department of Green Co. Bank; Greeneville, Tenn.
125 Castle Heights North, Suite B
Lebanon, TN 37087
615-449-2904 fax: 615-449-2906

Gregory J. Poulos, CLU, ChFC
Investors Partner Life
4115 Blackhawk Plaza Circle, Suite 100
Danville, CA 94506
925-648-2008 fax: 925-648-2068
gpoulos@jhancock.com

Charles J. Randazzo, CFP, CEO
Financial Network of America
2214 Enterprise Parkway East
Twinsburg, OH 44087
330-425-9199 fax: 330-487-5406

Joseph C. Randazzo, J.D.
Financial Network of America
2214 Enterprise Parkway East
Twinsburg, OH 44087
330-425-9199 fax: 330-487-5406
JCRFNA@aol.com

Jon M. Rogers, Ph.D., CLU, ChFC
Rogers Financial Group
1 Whitsett Street
Greenville, SC 29601
864-250-1376 fax: 864-250-1377
jrogers6@MSN.com

Jeffrey G. Scott, CLU, ChFC, CFP
Sagemark Consulting
2070 Chain Bridge Road, Suite 300
Vienna, VA 22182
703-749-5021 fax: 703-749-5076
jgscott@LNC.com

William V. Scott III, RFC
Asset Planning Solutions, Inc.
17065 Via Del Campo, 1st Floor
San Diego, CA 92127
619-451-0137 fax: 619-485-9036
WilliamScott@home.com

Simon Singer, CFP
1st Global, Inc.
4138 Regal Oak
Encino, CA 91436
800-350-0909 fax: 818-728-8064
simsing@earthlink.net

David B. Stocker, CFP, CLU
Wealth Strategies, Inc.
207 North High Street
Muncie, IN 47305
765-289-3366 800-560-3366 fax: 765-289-3368
DSTOCKER@aol.com

Robert W. Tiller, CFP, CSA, CFS, DS
Tiller Enterprises, Inc.
Angel & Associates, Inc.
6709 Ridge Road, Suite 108
Port Richey, FL 34668
727-844-3232 fax: 727-844-0665

Harry R. Tyler, CFP, CLU, ChFC
Tyler Wealth Counselors, Inc.
1450 East Boot Road, Suite 200C
West Chester, PA 19380
610-344-0900 800-798-9537 fax: 610-344-7656
Info@TylerWealth.com

Byron J. Udell, J.D., CFP, ChFC, CLU
Byron Udell & Associates, Inc.
3180 MacArthur Boulevard
Northbrook, IL 60062
800-442-9899 fax: 847-480-7380
lifeinsure@aol.com

Larry W. Warren, CRPC
Warren, Gilchrist & Ekblad Financial Services
919 South 7th Street, Suite 300
Bismarck, ND 58504
701-222-3268 fax: 701-222-0339
WGFS@btigate.com

John C. Watson III, CLU, ChFC, AEP, RFC
Lawson & Watson, L.L.C.
823 North Elm Street, Suite 100
Greensboro, NC 27401
336-379-8207 fax: 336-379-8349
jcw3@lawson-watson.com

Kirk S. Wimberly, CLU, AEP
Kirk S. Wimberly and Associates
400 Interstate N. Parkway NW, Suite 1700
Atlanta, GA 30339
770-612-4668 fax: 770-953-2578
ksw3@bellsouth.net

Michael G. Zulinski, CLU, ChFC
A-Z Financial Services
3130 Dixie Highway
Waterford, MI 48328
888-637-3131 fax: 248-674-8219
a-zfinancial@sigmarep.com

appendix E

Geographic Listing of Contributing Authors

Arizona
Robert A. Esperti
Reid S. Johnson
Richard E. Mundinger

California
Paul S. Devore
John L. Jenkins
Philip J. Kavesh
Robert G. Kresek
W. Aubrey Morrow
M. Todd Petersen
Gregory J. Poulos
William V. Scott III
Simon Singer

Colorado
Robert J. Myers
David C. Partheymuller

Florida
Carl P. Grissom
Norman C. Hayden
Todd D. Heckman
R. Marshall Jones
E. Michael Kilbourn
Renno L. Peterson
Robert W. Tiller

Georgia
Paul R. Lang
Kirk S. Wimberly

Idaho
Daniel W. Pinkerton

Illinois
Alan G. Orlowsky
Byron J. Udell

Indiana
David B. Stocker

Maryland
N. Douglas Hostetler

Michigan
David M. Boike
Michael G. Zulinski

Missouri
Robert B. Hardcastle

North Carolina
Jerry W. Lawson
John C. Watson III

North Dakota
Larry W. Warren

New York
Monroe M. Diefendorf, Jr.
Graydon C. Garner
Robert S. Madden

Ohio
Robert E. Grace
Darrin G. Plys
Charles J. Randazzo
Joseph C. Randazzo

Oregon
Thomas B. Gau

Pennsylvania
James W. Monteverde
Harry R. Tyler

South Carolina
Thomas H. Bell
Jon M. Rogers

Tennessee
Gary F. Poling

Texas
William E. Dendy
Frederick E. Mowery

Virginia
Jeffrey G. Scott

Washington
James P. Furrow
Michael D. Miller

Wisconsin
Todd Goedeke

index